Jo Grimond
MEMOIRS

Books by Jo Grimond

THE LIBERAL CHALLENGE
THE LIBERAL FUTURE
THE COMMON WELFARE
MEMOIRS

By Jo Grimond and Brian Neve
THE REFERENDUM

Jo Grimond

MEMOIRS

Heinemann : London

William Heinemann Limited
10 Upper Grosvenor Street, London W1X 9PA

LONDON MELBOURNE TORONTO
JOHANNESBURG AUCKLAND

Printed in Scotland by
Morrison and Gibb Ltd, Edinburgh.

For my wife — Laura

Contents

Illustrations

Grizelda and Fiona Corbett dressed in the clothes of the Oakbank Grimonds.

Unloading goods from a flit-boat at Papa Westray, Orkney.

Aerial view of St Andrews, 1929.

Preface

IF THE REMINISCENCES which follow are scrappy—why not? Everyone's life is disjointed, a basket filled with odds and ends, mine in particular. Mark Bonham Carter on first looking into my room in Orkney remarked in his caustic way that he had never seen such a clutter outside Pratt's Club, that eyrie of bric-a-brac. This book indeed might have been less sententious if I had stuck to a simple account of some of the events which interested me however disconnected they may have been. But to make plain meat palatable by itself entails a high standard of cooking. I do not aspire to such a literary tour de force so I have tried to string my life together on a few threads which like a sauce I hope will make it more digestible.

I have followed certain themes. As I have never been at the centre of events, it would be absurd for me to pretend that I could add anything to the inside history of the general or political history of my time. What I have attempted to do is to describe how certain incidents looked from a fairly low vantage point, if not a worm's eye view then a bird's eye view from the lower branches of the undergrowth. I am well aware that this view may have been badly askew, it was nevertheless my view.

I detect a fairly continuous movement in politics marked by milestones registering stages on the way. Among these milestones I see the war, the end of the Attlee Government, Suez, the era of pretence when the Tories pretended all was well while on the centre-left Kennedy and Gaitskell though rejecting conservatism were nevertheless confident that in the right hands the existing western democratic system could enable us to scale new heights: the awakening from this dream followed by disillusion and the rapid growth of bureaucratic attitudes ending inevitably in inflation. Another set of milestones has been the series of economic crises.

Other events I describe have been those affecting the Orkney and Shetland Islands, not only agreeable but interesting places without parallel in Britain.

The third theme has been my family and friends. Neither by temperament, inclination nor ability am I capable of baring my own or other people's souls in the manner, say, of *Father and Son*. I am aware that at times my reminiscences are as flat as Christopher Hollis's celebrated spoof memoirs of Mr. Attlee. 'I was sorry when I had to stop being Prime Minister. I was having tea at Paddington Station when they came and told me that I had lost the Election'. I went to tell the King but he had already heard it on the BBC so I do not think that he was very interested.'

Acknowledgements

I SHOULD LIKE to thank many people for help over this book, particularly my wife, daughter Grizelda and sons Johnny and Magnus for having read and done their best to correct parts of it, and my secretary, Miss Catherine Fisher, for her genius in deciphering my handwriting which has not improved since I was at Oxford when I received a letter from Con O'Neill which began as follows: 'I should give you a First on your handwriting alone, which in its present form conveys almost as little to me as would the finest, oldest and tawniest philosophy.'

I must thank my sister Nancie for several of the anecdotes in this book, one or two of doubtful accuracy. Also I am grateful to that noble man Sir William Walker, the reigning head of one of the last jute families thirled to Dundee, for unearthing the photograph of the Grimond Camel recumbent over our factory gate, averting its sardonic eye from Walker's Caldrum Works across the way. Gibbie Irvine whose photographs and marked proofs adorn the *Shetland Times* took the picture of myself looking rather proprietorial at Lerwick Harbour.

I should also like to thank Faber & Faber Limited for permission to quote from 'Childhood' by Edwin Muir, and Gerald Duckworth & Co. Limited for permission to quote from 'Lines to a Don' by H. Belloc.

CHILDHOOD'S WORLD IS small and seems permanent. St Andrews, where I was born in 1913, was itself a small world—a self-contained little planet revolving peacefully in its own time. To be a child in St Andrews was like being one of those wooden Russian dolls which live inside one another.

Our house was Number 8, Abbotsford Crescent, a plain, grey, stone house in a plain row of houses such as you see in many Scotch towns. St Andrews is a famous and ancient city but the part we lived in was not particularly old having been built in the 19th century to the west of the old town by James Hope. Hope was a successful parliamentary barrister. The *Dictionary of National Biography* remarks that he was much given to charitable and religious work. But it was the growing popularity of golf (the facetious might say that golf had become a religion) that drew him to lay out three streets of 'gentlemen's houses' as a speculation. The streets, one straight, one convex and one concave, were called respectively Hope Street, Howard Place and Abbotsford Crescent. Howard Place got its name from Hope's second wife who was a daughter of the 14th Duke of Norfolk. Abbotsford Crescent was called after Scott's Abbotsford which Hope rented, having married as his first wife Lockhart's daughter, Scott's granddaughter. He later added Scott to his name. Hope had been a friend of Gladstone at school. John Gladstone, W.E.'s father, invested some money in Hope's St Andrews project.

None of this I knew until I read Professor Checkland's excellent book *The Gladstones*. I am glad to think our house had some Liberal ancestry. The Gladstones speculated considerably in commerce, railways and property. Before the Stock Exchange had blossomed, in the days when Government borrowing was smaller, wealthy families turned to direct investment, for better or worse. Often they lost their money but the country on balance surely gained.

The three streets that Hope built were arranged round a roughly triangular garden, those in the Crescent being four stories high with a basement. Over the gutter outside our house was a mounting block. Several houses in the Crescent had such blocks. At the end of the Crescent, across the road which separated us from Hope Street, was a 'crossing', a slightly raised causeway of cobbles laid for the convenience of walkers when the road was muddy, kept clean in its heyday by crossing sweepers. These peculiarities must have been rather out of date even when I was born but they survived through most of my youth. To St Andrews, and therefore to me, they did not seem peculiarities at all. The last sedan chair in St Andrews only gave up, I believe, in 1850. Throughout my boyhood the normal means of passenger transport, if something more than a bicycle was required, was the cab. My memories are redolent with the delicious smell of cosy, well-padded, musty, velvet cabs with the buttercup yellow light of their oil lamps reflected from the rumps of the velvety horses. Up to the second world war travellers were wafted to and from the station in horse-drawn buses. In those days, while there were railway bridges over the Tay and Forth, there were no road bridges below Perth on the Tay nor across the estuary of the Forth. St Andrews was isolated and most journeys outside it were by rail. Never, however, did St Andrews seem to me as a boy out of time or out of step. On the contrary, it was to me the real world. In some ways it still is. Everywhere I have been since then seems at times a little transitory and unreal. Perhaps we all have this feeling that since childhood we have been on a tour, pleasant or unpleasant, interesting certainly, but a tour from which we shall return home one day to the place where we grew up.

My father was a jute manufacturer in Dundee—where he went every day. The Grimond family can trace their connection with textiles back to the start of the last century, in expansive moods they have gone further, asserting that they descend from Huguenot weavers, refugees from France. Whether this is a spurious claim I cannot say but at least the name Grimond used to appear more frequently in French than in British telephone directories.

I was the youngest of my parents' three children: much the youngest, so that I was in some ways brought up as an only child, and spoilt. However, that was pleasant. It also relieved my sisters of responsibilities. Of my children I fear Andrew suffered from being the eldest, partly because parents get mellower as they grow older but also because being the eldest is apt to wear the nerves. Grizelda, who is now the eldest of our three living children, survived very well due to innate characteristics and in spite of being educated at day schools. One of the arguments for a spell at a boarding school (which she did not have) is to allow the eldest children to recuperate from home life.

My two sisters, Gwyn and Nancie, were fourteen and eleven years older than I was. I hardly remember them before they were grown up. They appear, however, in numerous photographs dotted around my house, usually dressed in white smocks looking exceedingly fetching with intent faces and long, thick hair. Sometimes they are with my mother, who must have been beautiful in her young days and remained good looking until her death. She was always what she herself would have called immaculate and is to be seen in the photographs in her well-cut long dresses and high hair style, bolt upright in an upright chair. Throughout her life she was much given to exercise, in her younger days chiefly golf, later long walks. Even in her late sixties I remember her walking one afternoon down the river Eden from Cupar to Guardbridge, a distance of perhaps eight miles, made more tiring by having to splash down the middle of the river for some distance to escape a bull. It was from her that we inherited our feelings about the importance of games. From her, too, my sisters inherited their athletic abilities. None of my family had any pretensions to being intellectual. My mother filled in the time when she was not playing games or walking or bicycling or dealing with household matters by playing bridge or, in later life, doing crossword puzzles. She was, however, a woman of natural intelligence and imagination so that she often guessed obscure literary clues, though never having opened the books in question. My eldest son, Andrew, who was a great favourite of hers was, like most children, very much attached to a trio of moth-eaten toy animals. My mother had them photographed in a group for him so that he could have them, neatly framed, on his table just like grown-ups. She was good company, and became something of a St Andrews character.

She had been a Miss Richardson and came from Birkenhead. Her brother, Foster Richardson, lived close to us in Hope Street. He had joined the family business of J. & A. D. Grimond in Dundee. My mother felt, on the one hand, almost maternal affection and responsibility for him and, on the other, constant irritation. However, he had in her eyes two redeeming features even at times when she would describe him as 'a tiresome wretch': he was a scratch golfer and very fond of my father. Indeed, such was his devotion that though my father's handicap never sank below nine they played together year after year in the foursomes competition known as the Calcutta Cup, once winning it. Uncle Foster was a small man (another rather illogical source of irritation to my mother) who I see now led a reasonably normal life with his wife, May. Their only child died young and their amusements, not unnaturally, took the form of entertaining their friends and contemporaries. My mother, who was keen on good behaviour, and had a rather touching and melodramatic belief in the wickedness of the world had dark suspicions about the goings-on at 10, Hope Street—especially in regard to drink—though her brother was by normal standards an abstemious man.

Her sister, Aunty Jo, was a spinster who was very deaf indeed. When I was young she lived in a semi-detached villa in a Beatrix Potter-like *ménage* consisting of Mary Munro, who was as bright as a button and I am sure an excellent clear starcher, and Miss Cunningham, an enigmatic old lady in a white cap, rather like a female Mr. Jackson the toad. Aunty Jo always came to lunch on Sunday. She and my mother were apt to have a row about ear trumpets, which they both rather enjoyed. Aunty Jo looked on her brother and sister with tolerant amusement. Though she had little money she didn't want any more which put her in a strong position. After Sunday lunch I went for a walk with her, her dog, Waif, a fox terrier and Auntie May's poodles—rather repulsive dogs and a further source of disapproval by my mother.

When I was six my elder sister, Gwyn, married Billy Corbett (why Billy? His Christian names were Thomas Godfrey Polson). He was still recovering from being wounded in the war to which he had gone straight from Eton. My sister had met him through our next door neighbours, the Currans. Mrs. Curran was his aunt. One of my earlier memories is of being driven by Billy with my sister to see a captured German submarine at Dundee. We had no car, for inhabitants of St Andrews seldom left it. The first amateur golf champion, Mr. McFie, having decided that after twenty years he must go on a short jaunt took a ticket to Edinburgh, but on reaching Leuchars Junction found the world so repellant that he returned home.

I lately came across a record of my childhood views on the motor car, suitably tinged by my St Andrews upbringing and my Scots chauvinism.

'I think a motor is very necessary when staying in the country but I do not think that the average town person who does not travel or go away much needs one. I have also noticed that a great many of richer farmers have motors and the Gig is getting more and more out of date: though the farmers are at present contenting themselves with cheap motors. Another thing I think about motors is that if you are Scottish or live in Scotland you should buy a Scotch motor. If you are English an English. If American buy an American motor. If you are French a French. If Italian an Italian.' A sign of the influence of heredity is that my son Magnus holds the same nationalist views, at least about buying British cars.

An expedition to Dundee in Billy Corbett's car was quite an event, especially as it meant catching the Tay ferry. However, in Guardbridge,

18

we unfortunately grazed a woman carrying a can of hot water. She was furious and the G.W.K., which had to be started by working a handle under the running board, refused to fire. I sat on the pavement among hostile paper workers full three miles from home and forlorn. This trip was one of the first of many kindnesses which I received from my brother-in-law. One of the seldom mentioned advantages of having two older sisters is having brothers-in-law—or at least it was to me. So Gwyn passed out of St Andrews but by no means out of my life.

Nancie, however, remained at home until the 1930s. My mother was convinced that she was delicate; her husband, Willie Black, got a particularly bad mark by suggesting that she would outlive him—which she has done by many years. I don't say that she took advantage of this concern for her health but long afternoons before the fire were excused for her, for others golf was expected; and indeed by me enjoyed. St Andrews was, as I have said, a good place for children and number 8, Abbotsford Crescent a comfortable home. Children like stability. No doubt to those who had known the Edwardian world the twenties and thirties were alarming. By today's standards they were tranquil. So steady was the value of money that the price could be printed on every wrapper. Quite long bars of chocolate cost 2d. and continued to do so year in year out. Some sweets could be bought for 1d. (less than the $\frac{1}{2}$p. of today). *The Times* also remained at 2d. delivered, of course, free. When my mother became a crossword addict she ordered two copies of *The Times*, every day because Nancie and I complained about having it cut up. This was considered an inordinate extravagance—particularly by the newsagent. It doesn't seem so outrageous today when *The Times*, if it is published, costs the equivalent of three old shillings. The inhabitants of St Andrews seemed immutable. It did not occur to me that anyone except myself would die (I was rather worried about death and the dark and often persuaded my parents to let me sleep in their room). Indeed, people lived to formidable ages in St Andrews. If you survive the first sixty years of the East of Scotland climate you are probably good for another thirty. Even now when I go back there I see people I could swear died long ago. Our neighbours remained unchanged. There was little or no new building in the centre of the town. University professors were not obsessed with clambering up the career structure as they are today. They remained immovable and behaved like Belloc's dons.

> Good Dons perpetual that remain
> a landmark walling in the plain
> the horizon of my memories
> like large and comfortable trees.

As a whole the University came into my life later. But two professors were figures of my childhood, M'Intosh and D'Arcy Thompson. Both bearded, one white, one brown. Professor M'Intosh was our landlord. In that capacity he was one of the local worthies with whom my mother enjoyed waging war. She was convinced that the ceilings at Abbotsford Crescent were falling down. Professor M'Intosh was convinced that they were not. Only under extreme pressure could he be persuaded to view a crack in the plaster of the spare room. He was the 'bad' professor, a reputation which I doubt if he deserved. He was a far-famed authority on marine biology. The rent of our house remained at £100 per year. Professor M'Intosh lived and professed into his eighties, dying from a chill caught on returning by train from Dundee after a wet day's partridge shooting because some silly young man opened the carriage window—or so I believed. D'Arcy Thompson was the 'good' professor. He had a bevy of charming and musical daughters in one of the tall, old South Street houses. I used to go to tea there when he would appear with his big brown beard, dispensing presents. I got two stuffed birds one day. Outside he wore a wide-brimmed hat like the one Tennyson wears in old photographs. Everyone wore hats or caps. He taught at St Andrews for over 50 years. I am sure it never occurred to him to go anywhere else.

Number 8, Abbotsford Crescent was the still point of this gently turning world. Children get to know rooms intimately. The main room in Abbotsford Crescent was the smoking room which looked out from the ground floor across the 'area' to the square garden. It was a brown and green room with cushions and a footstool which could be used to make the chairs into houses. Here my sister sat and from here my mother ran the house, telephoning for the messages. On picking up the telephone she at once demanded 'are you there?' and continued until answered. (When writing to shops her letters started 'Mrs. Grimond writes to say'.) The drawing room was, according to the Scotch custom, on the first floor and looked north. Its furniture was uncomfortable. It was seldom used except when people came to dinner or sometimes on Sunday afternoons. It had, however, one attraction which was a window seat from which you could watch the people going up and down to the golf course and the Royal and Ancient Club. It even had a mirror fixed to the wall so that you could keep an eye both ways. In the fifties or sixties when I went with a Parliamentary delegation to Holland we passed through a Dutch town where the houses had similar mirrors. I was the only person in the bus who knew what they were for.

Every piece of furniture in 8, Abbotsford Crescent was friendly and familiar. They never moved except when I moved them to make a house: when I woke or went to bed the pictures, the ornaments, the clocks were all exactly in their accustomed places. The odd corner behind the sofa in the smoking-room, for instance, was always the same size. Now in my own house I find the furniture is always moving or being moved around—most disturbing for small children.

The road at the back of 8, Abbotsford Crescent below our drawing room was one of the main streets into the town. Up it came the coal carts clanking their way from the old railway station, the harness of the Clydesdales jingling, swinging and glinting in the sun. There were two farms in St Andrews when I was a boy. Every day a herd of cattle was driven in to be milked. There was also a blacksmith's forge in which the smith in leather apron hammered out red-hot horse-shoes—a glimpse of hell for passing children. The cows came mooing and mooching up the hill, causing a wild ringing of bicycle bells from the message boys and some disapproval of their sanitary habits from the more fastidious old ladies. Golfers for the links and the children for the shore clumped along the pavement and on Sunday morning the cry of the paper seller competed with the church bells *Sunday Post, Post, Post*. Then as now the *Post* went into every house, the best liked of popular newspapers.

It was on this hill that my Aunt Gia once met the Dean of Guild, Mr. Linskill, the historian of St Andrews ghosts, of which there are a great many. Seeing his thumb in plaster she asked after the cause. 'Trod on it going home last night' was the reply. Aunty Gia lived on this street. You could always tell when she was arriving or going by the yelps which her Pomeranian contributed to the general racket. Her proper name was Miss Gordon. She was my father's half-sister. It was she who first interested me in gardens, an interest which has continued all my life. From her I learnt the rudiments of gardening. Eight, Abbotsford Crescent only had a patch at the back shielded from all but the late summer sun. Aunty Gia was also a fount of gossip. Since she died we have never been so well instructed in what goes on in the town.

In the streets behind our house too the golf-club makers plied their trade. One shop looking across the eighteenth hole still bore the fabled name of Tom Morris, greatest of golfers, next to it came Forgans and on the brae itself, where my aunt lived, the two Auchterlonie families and Anderson's with a giant's club in his window. Willie Auchterlonie had been open champion, he and Lawrie were professionals to the Royal and Ancient Club. In those days clubs were made by hand, often to measure. In the local shops a child could watch the planing and turning and polishing, see the curves of the club head teased out from wooden blocks and try the hickory shafts for spring.

My nurseries, day and night, were on the second floor. All the rooms in Number 8 were light and agreeable. My day nursery had two windows overlooking the square, a sofa inhabited by a collection of stuffed animals, a cupboard for my 'collection' (of shells etc.) and a toy cupboard in the wall, a fire and fire guard hung with washing, a rocking chair for Jessie Anderson, my nurse, and the crockery appropriate for a nursery. Poor Jessie, I was beastly to her. When she fell asleep reading to me I would ruthlessly prod her awake. Jessie Anderson was a remarkable woman. She had been my father and sisters' nurse. She can never have been paid very much but out of her savings she provided the money to educate a boy from Monifieth who became a distinguished professor. After a life of devotion I fear she had a rather sad old age for I was a tiresome child. However, sometimes things ran tranquilly and now I like to think of nursery days as in the Child's Garden of Verse.

'For we are very lucky with a lamp before the door,
  And Leerie stops to light it as he lights so many more.'

We had a lamp outside our door and Leerie lit it.

Jessie and I, so long as she was able, also went for walks in convoy with other nurses. Looking back I am amazed at how long these walks took. There is a burn which runs through the edge of St Andrews with a path along it—the Ladebraes. Its total length cannot be more than a mile. But Jessie and I would spend all afternoon meandering along it and hardly ever reached the end. There were seats for Jessie and for me detours down to the water or up the banks. The end was worth reaching for there was a mill, a mill pond with white ducks, a farm and a tree which had marked on it the height of some flood, which I assumed was the flood on which the Ark was launched.

At the end of the Ladebraes lay also Philip Boase's garden at the bottom of which he had made a pond. In the pond swam gigantic trout. A cellar had a window into the pond against which monsters of up to 10lb. belched and ogled, or more exciting still, you could dangle a mussel on a reed over the water and suddenly a fish would erupt and seize it.

Jessie was fond of turnip: every now and then we returned from our walk with a neep in my pram. Every night she brought me a taste of her supper. Macaroni to this day reminds me not of Italy but of the redwood wardrobe opposite my bed and its smell of musk.

Next door to us lived the family of Curran, great friends of us all. The two elder and surviving sons had been friends of my sisters, as had their sister, Lilian. Geoffrey was my friend, the Curran parents were friends of my father and mother. To round off the party Mrs. Curran was my brother-in-law Billy Corbett's aunt and Nanna Curran was an old crony of Jessie's. Nanna was the best tempered of St Andrews nurses and a great favourite with children. Jessie and I were constantly in and out of their house, having delicious nursery teas or playing with Geoffrey's soldiers. Mr. Curran was small and neat. He was said to have eloped with his wife. Elopement to me meant escapes down ladders, running away with your bride in your arms or at least on the pommel of your saddle. I was amazed that such a small man as Mr. Curran could have managed these feats with his wife, who must have been twice his size. Mr. Curran did nothing but sing, play golf in wash-leather gloves and occasionally translate Shakespeare into French for his own amusement. No one in St Andrews thought this a wasted life. Mrs. Curran, dressed in black, was occasionally to be seen sailing along Abbotsford Crescent, an umbrella clutched across her chest, a slight beard on her large, pale face, greeting a friend with a caw; but more often she was stretched out in her drawing room. Many Scotch ladies seemed to suffer from premature exhaustion partly I suspect owing to their mountainous size.

Other steadily revolving stars in the firmament were the maids. The longest surviving were Maggie, the cook, and Alice the housemaid, both of whom were eternally cheerful. I suppose 'domestic service' was often depressing and sometimes degrading, perhaps my memories are distorted by distance, or maids put on a special act for children, but they certainly seem to me to have been far merrier than many shop assistants and typists are today. They lived in that attractive world where work and play are mixed up—which was one of the attractions of old fashioned farming. The kitchen indeed was rather like an Orkney farm yard when I first went to the islands (and like they are still to some extent). Maggie would be inspecting various large iron pots, tea would be dispensed at the table, Alice would come and go with her brooms and visitors—the Currans' maids, message boys, etc. would drop in. At a suitable age Jessie was supplemented by Miss Mathieson, a governess, who came for a few hours every day and sowed the seeds of my interest in history.

My father in the early twenties still worked in Dundee at the firm of J. & A. D. Grimond, founded by his grandfather, J. Grimond, who had taken A.D. his brother into partnership. They spun and wove jute. My father was a gentle man who had been seriously ill as a boy, an illness from which his health never quite recovered. We were greatly attached to one another. When he came home in the summer evenings we would go off to putt. In winter there would be games such as Ludo in the smoking room before he went down to the Club for an hour or so. Fathers and sons commonly disagree: but though I now see that in many of the ways in which human beings irritate one another we were very different, he tidy, I very untidy, he knowing his own mind, I seldom knowing mine, yet I never remember finding anything to criticize in him. At the time I took it for granted that he liked his life. I now doubt if he did. Though he had a few close friends in St Andrews he was not suited to the life of a Dundee businessman. He drank almost nothing, played no card games and took little part in either public life or the more boisterous male social life around him. He would, I think, have liked to have lived at least part of the year in London or the South of France. My great-grandfather had numerous children, but my father was the only child of his eldest son and had no male Grimond cousins in Britain. He therefore took on the business as a matter of course. He managed it as well as possible I imagine —the hey-day of jute was passing—and certainly conscientiously. Having devoted his life to it, perhaps against his inclinations, he was naturally incensed when Hatry proposed to buy it so as to form a combine of the bigger jute firms. We were second only to Cox's, rather bigger than our neighbour, the Walkers. His cousin, Louis McIntyre, however, who was joint managing director with him was anxious to sell. He and my father's aunts, Nellie and Amy, with sundry other relations held a majority of the shares. My father's only allies were a family of Grimonds who lived at Oakbank near Blairgowrie. Their father had been my great-grandfather Joseph's eldest brother. A. D. Grimond who was a bachelor left them most of his shares. But they and my father were outvoted and the business became part of Jute Industries. Perhaps, looked at from a purely selfish point of view, it was no bad thing. Jute did badly in the late twenties and thirties. My father could not have carried on much longer. It enabled him to spend more time in sunnier places and I was too young to take over.

But it was a heavy blow to him. He had the good sense never to have been taken in by the 'bigger is better' school. We never as a nation learn from past experience. Had we studied the amalgamations after the first world war perhaps we might have avoided the follies committed after the second—British Leyland, for instance—not to mention the nationalised industries which might never have been spawned. But the Labour Party is still intent on repeating the pattern. When 19th century capitalists are criticized I think of the concern which my father showed for his work people and for the good name of the Grimond business. He disliked the idea of financial manipulation and neither he nor his Blairgowrie cousin, John, had any illusions about Hatry. Indeed, the story goes that when the deed was done and the old stockholders paid off Cousin John would have none of Hatry's cheques or bills or scrip but brought an attaché case and insisted upon taking his share in bank notes. The story of J. & A. D. Grimond was repeated on a much larger scale all through the industrial areas of Britain.

My great-grandfather was the third son of a large family born in a little house, Lornty, near Blairgowrie where his father farmed and ran a flax mill—about the size of a large English barn. He was sent off to

Lancashire where he learnt the trades of spinning and weaving. Returning to Dundee with little or no capital he built what was then the second or third largest jute mill in the world—Bowbridge—a great Kremlin-like range of buildings magnificently constructed of dressed stone with his trade mark—a camel—life-size in stone, recumbent over the main gate. It remains incomprehensible to me how he—and those who built the much bigger mills and factories in Yorkshire, Lancashire, Glasgow, Paisley and the Midlands of England, erected these huge structures in a few years with none of the aids of the modern building industry and no government grants.

Dundee in the late 19th century was dominated by the jute and flax families, Coxes, Grimonds, Walkers, Sharps, Gilroys, Cairds, Ogilvies, Baxters and so on. Their chimneys or stalks rose above the town as it climbed the hillsides above the Tay. Cox's stalk, a great Renaissance affair, could be seen from St Andrews. They built themselves Scots baronial houses in Broughty Ferry or further afield and vied with each other over their carriages, shrubberies and greenhouses. Now they are gone and so are their chimneys and villas. They were a tough lot. They achieved much. But let no one be taken in by nostalgia when considering Scottish cities. They had confidence and capacity but under their reign Dundee was ridden with slums and poverty. I can remember as a boy the tenements and the cobbled streets around which semi-naked children played. When we are shocked by the violence of our own time I think of Saturday night in Dundee when it was unsafe to walk in many of the streets, women in shawls trudged round to find their husbands who might have been dragged off drunk and handcuffed to a policeman and fights were staged on many common stairs. I know very little about the character of my great-grandfather. One of his more agreeable traits was his liking for his cart-horses. He always kept lumps of sugar in his pockets for them. There is a story that he was standing by the kerb one day in Dundee when a carter's horse came up and began to nuzzle his coat. It was an old J. & A. D. Grimond horse and he insisted on buying it back. I suspect that he treated his work people no better and no worse than did his contemporaries. Many years ago a porter at Dundee station came up to me and said he had worked at Bowbridge or Maxwelltown (Grimonds' other works) and asked if I was a member of the family. Rather nervously I said I was. To my surprise he spoke of the fun they used to have rolling the jute bales down the hill and tilting at each other on the trolleys. But all that had been stopped under Jute Industries when managers from business efficiency schools took over and time and motion studies were introduced. He left and had been happily banging trolleys on the railways ever since.

I have a poem dating no doubt from the woe-begone days of one of the 19th century recessions in the Jute industry when sackings were common and attempts were made to cut wages. No pap about 'Industrial Action' in those days. The heading is 'The Great Strike in Dundee'.

'Our great merchant princes hae turned sae braw
  by screwing down workers, why, they would like to grab a'
  Wi' estates, cash and castles their heids in a creel,
  Put a gold hunter on horseback, he'll ride to the de'il.
  To reduce their good workers by twenty per cent
  Is the most cruel action we ever yet kent,
  For their workers, who made them, they little do feel,
  Put a tyrant on horseback he'll ride to the de'il.'

However, some masters were more kindly, or perhaps more canny, than others.

'Mr. Sharp is also on full-time and keeping very brisk
  He was too sharp to join the clique and run so great a risk.
  Great Grimmond's works are all alive, in happiness and joy
  By taking all the orders from that foolish Castle Roy.'

I like to think that it was high-minded devotion to the principles of enterprise, free competition and good management rather than any sordid taste for gain that over-rode family feelings in my great-grandfather's breast: the Gilroys of Castle Roy were our cousins twice-over.

To return to my childhood, the tradesmen and shop people of St Andrews were a delight to small children. I cannot understand G. K. Chesterton's dislike of grocers. St Andrews had marvellous grocers: Aikman & Terras—reeking of coffee; Haxtons and Robertsons where Miss Robertson was always good for a bar of chocolate. At Robertsons, too, sacks stood open on the floor, full of mysterious grains—the whole place was reminiscent of Ginger and Pickles. Shops I have always considered a major pleasure of life. A liking for shopping is considered peculiar by many males today. In the case of the Grimonds it is hereditary. I take after my father for whom it was a treat to walk down Bond Street looking in the shop windows. I notice that my son John and daughter Grizelda are compulsive shoppers.

Shopping for my mother was an elaborate exercise. A list was made out, partly from a slate kept in the kitchen on which the meals were inscribed after a morning conference between my mother and Maggie. Then, after wrestling with the telephone, my mother would set off whistling, on foot or bicycle, with list and basket. In the shops, particularly in the draper's shop which stretched far, or so it seemed, into back premises past shelves of stuffs and ribbons, chairs would be provided. For shopping was not to be rushed. Even children could spend half a morning in the gramophone shop. Most of the shops retained their old-fashioned wooden fittings. One of my favourites was Wilson the ironmonger, with ordinary house windows, flagged floors and the smell of oil, and where bales of twine, scythes and so on, hung from the ceiling. Plastic is convenient but the departure of wooden counters has ruined shops. There is one shop in Finstown, our village in Orkney, which still has an open fire and a bank of glass-topped wooden containers for biscuits such as Robertson's used to have. I never go into it without being reminded of St Andrews. To round off a morning's shopping or, when older, after golf or tennis, there was the Victoria Café. The Grimonds, who in their time had occupied several houses in St Andrews, had once lived there. It made the best ice cream and ice cream sodas ever created. If cafés had stars, in its hey-day it would have deserved four

It is time I said something about golf. At the back of Abbotsford Crescent lay the Old Course. Not that you could see much of it from the Crescent; but it was perhaps two hundred yards to the Royal and Ancient Club and the first tee. Just as St Andrews was a little out of step with the rest of the world so the Old Course was more than a little out of step with all other golf courses. There are, I now realise, two games; the game played at St Andrews and golf. Of these the former is infinitely superior. The only drawback about having been brought up at St Andrews is that you can never deeply enjoy golf anywhere else. Perhaps the links have changed now, made lush by the imported grass continually sown to cover the divot holes of modern golfers. If so, the change must be for the worse. The point about the old St Andrews game was its freedom and its peculiarities—appropriate to the City.

To begin with the golf itself was free, at least to ratepayers and their children. Half the Old Course was on common land. Not so long before my time people used to dry their washing on the whins. The Town Council, as owners of the common land, had to get an Act of Parliament to protect themselves and the golfers after being taken to court by a woman who was hit by a golf ball and sued them for allowing a nuisance on public property. Carts and family parties crossed the eighteenth and first fairways on the way to the shore. The remainder of the course had belonged to the Cheape family who lived in their house at Strathtyrum and had a hereditary right to play off whenever they chose. I am told that the destruction of the sacred lands were narrowly averted when they, not being golfers, were persuaded not to remove the sand from world famous bunkers to spread upon their farms.

Behind the first tee stood the Royal and Ancient Golf Club. Beside the Club congregated the caddies, ranged in age from eight to eighty, a famous collection of characters said to be descended from fishermen but never putting to sea. Mr. Martin, a one-armed man of independence and charm, used to caddy for my mother. I sometimes recognised pieces of Grimond clothing on his person—or more often on his children's. The claim often made for the Scots that they are a poor, proud and democratic people is exaggerated but it was true to some extent of the world of St Andrews golf. The members of the Royal and Ancient were posh and well-heeled while the tattered caddies earned 5/- or so for a morning's work. I do not remember the boy caddies being barefoot but there were plenty of bare-footed boys at the poorer end of the town. However, bare-footedness at least in summer has never seemed to me as painful as hunger, lack of coal or a leaking roof. But caddies took pride in their work and men and women were judged by their prowess at golf rather than according to their money or standing. Margot Asquith, for instance, who was a lamentable golfer was looked on as an amusing half-wit.

Behind the last green at St Andrews rears a monstrous red building which used to be the Grand Hotel. Some blathering duffer constantly asking his caddy for 'the line' was told with increasing disdain as his score mounted 'Play on the Grand Hotel'. When he set out on another round in the afternoon he remarked to the same caddy 'Now you can't tell me any more to play on the Grand Hotel.' 'No,' the caddy replied, 'Just keep your arse on it.'

Among the caddies was a man with a red beard known as The Lion. He was hit full in the face by a golf ball which broke his nose with a report like a pistol—but he refused to go home. He may have been the caddy in the story about A. J. Balfour, another poorish golfer. As the ex-Prime Minister approached the tee the starter in stentorian tones announced that Mr. MacDonald was carrying for Balfoor. The starter in my time was a one-armed character called Alexander, one of the many grown-ups at St Andrews who made it a delight to be young in the town. Long before school children's rights were pompously proclaimed he protected us from those grown-ups, often worse golfers than we were, who tried to do us out of our turn. He lodged in a sort of mobile sentry box and his word was law. When my sister, Nancie, married Willie Black, he sent them a telegram, 'Black v Black, play away.'

That the caddies were connoisseurs of other things than golf is shown by an experience of my Aunt Gia. She possessed a fine nose, not an aggressive nose, the nose of the toucan rather than the eagle, but well-shaped, none the less. One day when her nose was clearly reflected in a shop window into which she was looking she heard beside her a murmur of admiration. 'It's very fine, it's a very fine nose; it's a Roman nose.' On looking round she found a caddy of her acquaintance gazing into the window.

I played a great deal in my youth with five off-shoots of well-known St Andrews families, Elliott Playfair, Jimmy Blackwell and John Paton, Teddy Lee and Alison Hopwood. The Playfairs are one of those gifted families which without being aggressively Scotch contributed so much to local life in Scotland in the 19th and early 20th century. Alas, many of the descendants of these families were killed in two wars or have flitted South. One Playfair was Minister of the Town Church of St Andrews—a dour figure in frock coat and top hat. He bullied the congregation into paying for an expensive and successful restoration of the building. A restoration which they did not want or indeed as good Presbyterians, approve. At the meeting to celebrate its conclusion it is alleged that he announced that there was £500 still owing. 'A sum,' he went on to say, 'that I could easily pay myself but I would not deprive you of the privilege,' and collected it there and then with relish. Another Playfair was a Jeremy Fisher-like character who lived in Hope Street and was known as Unky Bin. He had been a Colonel in the Indian Army and presented me with a cat o' nine tails. Nigel Playfair was a well-known actor-manager. Elliott, in spite of a stammer, followed in his footsteps. He was an erratic golfer but good on his day. The Hopwoods also lived near us in Howard Place: Al was, with Margaret Paton, my first girl friend.

There were four Blackwell brothers of the previous generation, a constant delight to those who expected Scots to look and behave like Scots. Except for Earnley, who was the only one who sought notoriety outside St Andrews and who achieved an important position in the Home Office, they were large and craggy men. Earnley, apart from being something of a renegade from the family way of life, was the worst golfer, though not bad, about 4 handicap—and a frequent partner of Margot—not even a knighthood would put him on a par with his brothers: Jim, in an old mackintosh, looked after the links and had been a good player; Ted and Walter were still good, Ted with determined stance and shaggy eyebrows drove the ball prodigious distances. He was said to have driven it up the Club steps from the 18th tee—some 350 yards—with a wooden-shafted club of course. He and his brother made a redoubtable combination. But they were not given to emotion or loose talk. All Ted said when his brother Walter, having holed a putt of awkward length to win the Calcutta Cup— a foursome competition—picked the ball out of the hole was 'I think that's my ball, Walter.' Walter told a story of how he was travelling by train in America when the only other occupant of the compartment looked out of the window and remarked, 'Isn't that strange, we have stopped at a station called Blackwell and my name's Blackwell too.' When asked what he said in response to this double coincidence he replied, 'I said nothing.' Jimmy, the son of old Jim, was probably the best golfer of us four.

But my particular friend was John Paton, the son of a local doctor, whose mother came from another family of talent—the Boases. Dr. Paton, Jock, was a favourite of my family and of myself. Many, many happy days I spent in their house or on the rough shoot they took just outside the town. He too was typical of much that was best in the Scotland of the time, a most kindly man who nevertheless would recount with approval how at a class in first aid, which he attended, the old doctor in charge discovered that one of the girl pupils was apt to faint if peculiarly gruesome injuries were described. When the old rogue wanted to give the class some practical work he would indulge in some appropriate gory anecdote and then when the unfortunate girl keeled over would turn to a member of the class saying, 'Weel, weel, Jeannie's awa' again, off we go and revive her.'

John was a natural athlete as well as being clever and very good company. He was killed in the war, as was his brother Neil. So much of the holidays would pass in golf during the day and in the evening, when we were small, rounders in the square garden or later tennis. Few other occupations have ever given me such frequent and sustained pleasure as playing games. Not only the actual playing of the game but the preparations and the aftermath. The particular and general pleasures of golf were ever present. There was the setting off down the back stairs. There was the snap of a well-hit shot and the gurgle of a sunk putt. Then there were the general satisfactions, the thin turf of the Old and Eden courses —as boys we played on the Eden a lot—an excellent course, much under-rated, one of its particular pleasures was the smell of tar on sunny days when you crossed the railway on a wooden bridge, the pungent mustardy smell of whins when the days were warm (this too pursues me to Orkney), lying on one's back waiting to play with the larks singing and the general sensation of sun. East wind, wool stockings and sand. Golf has to be played reasonably well and seriously. I was brought up to play it seriously by my father but never played it well. However, the miraculous thing about St Andrews was that the Old Course catered for duffer as well as pro. You could hit the ball left or right on to wide expanses of turf; you could take two, or three or four shots to reach the green and the Old Course presented you with its little hills and valleys, its blind corners and huge rolling greens to form a landscape which never lost its interest. Not for nothing was part of it known as the Elysian Fields—more subtly

Elysian than the Champs Elysées. Later when I went to Gibbs School in Sloane Street, the only school I ever enjoyed, I remember the ecstasy of playing football. The journey to the Harrodian grounds at Putney was bliss, the feel of the football boots (bars or studs—a matter for discussion) and at the age of eight or so I reached my zenith as an athlete. But golf has an advantage in that you can play by yourself—or practise. I enjoyed practising with mashie and putter, particularly to the 17th hole on the Old Course. In winter the course was turned back to front sometimes as I believe it was originally played and was largely deserted. You could hit balls up to the 17th green from beside the Old Station. I hope Dante has provided a special Hell for the directors of British Railways and the architect who built that monstrosity of a hotel which now disgraces the site of the black sheds. That their names may go down to posterity in shame I record them. The architects were Mathews, Ryan & Partners and, when it opened the Chairman of British Rail was Sir Henry Johnson.

The only satisfaction I get from thinking that golfers on the Old Course plod round in four-hour rounds and that it costs £4 per day to play on it is that such penances are what the appalling denizens of that appalling building deserve but it is hard luck on the decent folk of St Andrews.

However, to return to the more agreeable subject of the Grimonds and their doings. Some pages back we left my sister, Nancie—Gwyn having gone off with her husband—curled up before the fire in the smoking room at Abbotsford Crescent. I have left you with a rather too limpid impression of our life. We had our troubles, troubles which were all taken seriously though in retrospect of varying degrees of importance. There was the General Strike of 1926. As my father had by then ceased to work in Dundee it did not directly affect him but it perturbed him none the less. The only people directly involved in St Andrews were the railwaymen. The railway was, as I have suggested, important to St Andrews. It was our main means of communication. As it was not easy to cross the Tay or Forth by car, as the week-end habit was unknown and the countryside looked upon as a primitive jungle inhabited by uncivilised lairds, the journeys the St Andreans took tended to be by rail. The station staff were for me lumped with 'good' professors, scratch golfers and the more admired shopkeepers. Lees, the guard, had only one arm and sometimes allowed you to travel in his van. But he was no respecter of persons. Long silent is his cry which rang on the windy platforms of Leuchars: 'Leuchars Junction change for St Annerus'. The old porters and guards had voices to rattle the windows. They would have scorned loud-speakers as new-fangled contraptions. A fuss-pot once poked his head out of the carriage and called to Lees, 'My man' (not a term to which Lees would take kindly), 'Where's this? Is this the junction for St Andrews?' 'Pit your heid back,' came the reply, 'I'm just away to cry it.' But my heroes were Haddow and Docherty, the foremen porters. I had once been caught crossing the line to get a starling's egg out of a nest in a crack of the wall opposite the platform. That evening Haddow called at our house and taking off his porter's cap produced two eggs out of it. I have always liked railwaymen. I find the staff at Kew Gardens station and Turnham Green very like the old St Andrews lot—helpful, jolly and uninhibited. How different they are from the deep-frozen stereotypes the Airways would like to breed. On aircraft you might as well have gramophone records but on the railways accents, personality and temper still persist. I suppose there was a 'career structure' on the North British Railway or the LNER but it never seemed to affect Lees, Haddow and Docherty. In pre-inflation days everyone did not always have St Vitus' dance. The Staff at St Andrews station were against the General Strike. They kept the trains running. The General Strike is for the moment in that limbo between current events and history. Winston Churchill's paper reached us but little else in the way of news. I was due to go back to school. As the St Andrews trains were running and to St Andrews the world ended at Leuchars Junction we set off. As we progressed South, losing time all the way, it was apparent that all was not well. At the Waverley Station in Edinburgh we saw a train with all the windows smashed. The level crossings in Northumberland were guarded by troops. Somewhere in Yorkshire we passed a derailed engine with its wheels in the air like a beetle on its back. At York we were told we could go no further. To my relief I spent the night in that splendid station hotel instead of at school.

One of the pleasures of my boyhood was going on trips with my father and mother to France or the South of England—or sometimes for a few days fishing with my father. Fishing, billiards and golf were the sports he enjoyed. He was a good fisherman and a good billiards player. Everything my father did he did carefully. Everything he had he kept in good condition. He never hankered after new equipment. In those days, of course, we had not reached the 'throw away' age. I still have the golf clubs with which he played ever since I can remember, his greenheart rod, his two volumes of Coward's *British Birds*, which he carried on our walks, and indeed his overcoat.

These expeditions were planned well in advance. They were not routine week-end jaunts. The longer ones greatly exercised my mother. As we had no car the bus had to be ordered to take the luggage—usually including a large trunk—to the station. She was always in negotiation with local tradesmen. Around the corner from Howard Place there dwelt Scott, the joiner, and his assistants. They were dressed in long white aprons and moved about what appeared to be an ex-church, designed goodness knows

The 'Camel'. Trade mark of
J. & A. D. Grimond mounted
over the gate of Bowbridge Works
with keeper, alleged by ribald
Dundonians to be an early Grimond.

The entrance to Bowbridge Jute Works.

A Blairgowrie curling team of the last century with my great-great-uncle,
Mr. Grimond of Lornty, seated, as Skip.

Old Rowallan Castle.

for what, full of wood shavings, saws and the smell of glue. Scott himself was an Old Testament character with a beard. His fault was the fault of all carpenters down the ages. He never came. If he removed a chair it was added to the collection in his workshop where reposed numerous bits of furniture long forgotten by their owners. When we were going away my mother would make valiant efforts to get him to finish some jobs before we left. She usually failed. Scott was also the undertaker. I remember him and his assistant looking down from my mother's bedroom at an old neighbour hopelessly twisted and bent by rheumatism (a common St Andrews disease) and Scott saying, 'We'll hae sair trouble wi' him.'

Scotch winters did not suit my father. I went with my parents to Hyères where we spent a month or two: very pleasant, with walls along dusty roads where the warm air was full of new scents and new insects. A child's view is nearer to a dog's than a grown up's. The crumbling walls, the lizards and the feel of reflected sun, these were very different from St Andrews. At other times we went to Dinard, Le Touquet, Lelant, Newburgh on the Ythan, Budleigh Salterton and an inn in Devon beside tumbling waters where I caught a fish on the first evening. Alas, it turned out to be the only evening. My mother lived in terror of damp sheets, which might give my father a chill, or me the fell disease of croup On thrusting a hand mirror into the beds at this delectable inn she detected a slight clouding on the surface. After a night spent more or less fully clothed with numerous hot water bottles we were removed the next day. Our holiday places were chosen for warmth, golf and occasionally trout fishing. On the whole they turned out well though starred by occasional disasters as when at Lelant, after a special dispensation to play on the course where children were frowned upon, I drove a ball through the club-house window. My father enjoyed Hyères particularly, with its golf course where the hazards were hurdles not bunkers. He was much given to expeditions by char-à-banc. Indeed on leaving Hyères we drove the whole way across France in a convoy of char-à-bancs which were going to Dinard—highly enjoyable. At Hyères there was a variation on the char-à-banc—'Le petit sud', a light railway which pottered along the coast. Pure heaven for children, so slow, so near the earth that you could watch the grass spring back between the rails when the train had gone by. Journeys ended in afternoons on the narrow grey Mediterranean beaches, poor things compared with the noble swathe of yellow sand that runs north from St Andrews, with its striped bathing boxes drawn to the sea by horses or in winter with waves flinging themselves upon the shore 'like ocean on a western beach,' the surge and thunder of which Andrew Lang wrote. On one of these trips by the petit sud a friend of my parents, Affie Grant, was with us, also some badly behaved children. Affie saw that in a quarter of a mile or so we should run into a tunnel. Turning a face of thunder on these unruly brats he threatened them with utter darkness if they didn't stop giggling. They didn't. With beautiful timing the train crashed into the tunnel spewing steam into the black carriage. The children were reduced to terror.

Ludo Kennedy who, with his entrancing wife, Moira, was later a friend of Laura's and mine, has the distinction of being Affie Grant's great-nephew Mr Grant has another claim to reflected glory: at a house near St Andrews where the sacriligious played tennis on Sundays (and to which Nancie went to the half-suppressed anxiety of my mother) he was challenged by Lionel Tennyson to a match on the tennis court in which he would play with a racquet and Tennyson would field with his hands—Tennyson won.

The Grants and the Kennedys are indeed Lads and Lassies o' pairts. Ludo once assured me that he was essentially a communicator. I suppose he knows best but I am not sure what 'essentially' in this context means. If he had been invented before television he might well have been an actor in the C. Aubrey Smith mould perhaps. He was nearly a Member of Parliament and would have made a top-hole M.P. As will be seen, I am not wholly uncritical of my countrymen, the Scotch, but they, at their best, are both versatile and exact—professional I suppose it is now called—the point is that they carry their dedication into everything they do. Ask Moira Kennedy to open a garden fete with a five minute speech and you will get a speech with a beginning, middle and end which finishes bang on the sixtieth second of the fifth minute and is as finished and acute as her most exquisite pas seul. If Scotland ever becomes semi-independent Moira and Ludo should be joint Viceroy and Reine.

Back to France where other memories concern food. Since I was greedy from birth there were delicious patisseries, oeufs en cocotte for supper and a few English delicacies which my father managed to secure—marmalade and huge blocks of plain chocolate. We usually did a little bird watching, my father and I; the birds had to be fairly trusting birds—not for us the hide or the crawl. And, especially in the south of England, we visited the local sights, Lands End for instance, by char-à-banc, of course. Apart from the unfortunate affair at Lelant, the visit which caused my parents most anxiety was at Le Touquet. They did not relish fashionable life and even in those days Le Touquet was fairly gay. Nancie, who always had wide ranging tastes in young men with perhaps a passing bias for the undesirable, or at least the dashing, picked up a Spanish count. In my eyes he was an excellent choice. He had a low, red, open car. In this he and Nancie not only disappeared into the pinewoods—to my mother's alarm—but drove round and round the outside of the Golf Hotel, to the fury of the guests. I was not encouraged to join these riotous goings-on but occasionally managed to do so. One day a boyfriend of Nancie's acquaintance fell through the glass roof of the restaurant. He was rich and related to the proprietor so was excused but my mother again felt a pang of uneasiness.

Few boys can have had a more sheltered, indeed pampered, life than I had. I am grateful for it. Indeed, I am grateful to my parents for many things; for the trouble they took in interesting me and in teaching me as well as for the affection they showered on me. But not least am I grateful that they never demanded demonstrations of affection in return. Nor were they ambitious for me. Emotional demands and high aspirations are prolific causes of family trouble. They were delighted if told I had done well but being unintellectual the nature of any success had to be explained.

As we lived in Scotland and none of my family had ever been to an English boarding school, why was I sent to a preparatory school near London and then to Eton? My parents no doubt thought it would be good for me to leave home. If I was to be sent to a boarding school then they perhaps rightly or wrongly felt that some of the English schools gave a better education than their Scottish equivalents which had mostly been set up in imitation of them. Anyway, to England I was sent.

I HAVE NEVER KEPT a diary and remember by people and places rather then by dates. My St Andrews boyhood ran on through the holidays from school. School was a different, parallel, and unpleasant experience. But alongside St Andrews, so to speak, also ran Rowallan. Rowallan was my brother-in-law Billy Corbett's house near Kilmarnock. Billy's mother had been a Miss Polson of the cornflour family. She had inherited a good deal of money before she married Billy's father (Uncle Archie) who himself owned property in and around Glasgow and in London. Billy's grandmother decided to build a country house for her daughter further out from the city than Thornliebank and Rouken Glen (the Corbetts' Glasgow estates). Billy's father, who was a Liberal M.P. for Glasgow (Tradeston) and had no liking for country amusements was complacent but unenthusiastic. After looking at various possible estates she pitched upon Rowallan.

The old castle at Rowallan is one of the most endearing buildings I have come across in Scotland. It stands in a hollow by a burn with grass and woods around it. When I first saw it much of it was ruinous and on one side a huge ash tree grew out of a mound of earth and masonry. The front consisted of a long flight of stone steps tightly flanked by two round towers looking as though it had been transported from some small château of the Loire. Inside on the first floor at the top of the steps the house had been built round a courtyard and just enough of it was habitable to house one ancient retainer. Two sides were completely roofed and comparatively dry. It had been built by the Mures of Rowallan around 1562. From it Elizabeth Mure had eloped with Robert II of Scotland. The last Mure heiress had married a Loudoun and most of the furnishings at the Castle had been removed to their great house nearby. For years it mouldered peacefully. Of course Mrs. Corbett and Lorimer her architect should have restored it. Lorimer would, under supervision, have done it well. Look what a success he made of Earlshall and Hill of Tarvit in Fife. Lorimer's style, like that of Lutyens, has been out of fashion in the recent age for match-box buildings, he was the leading Scottish architect of the early twentieth century developing the Scottish baronial tradition. But Mrs. Corbett no doubt wanted something grander as was customary in Edwardian times and Lorimer was not averse to grandeur either. Then I suspect that it was thought unhealthy—in a hollow, by a burn. My brother-in-law maintained that in any case it could not easily have been enlarged.

So a new Rowallan arose on a hill about half a mile to the north of it. Lorimer at least refrained from pulling down the old castle which might well have been its fate at the hands of many architects. Indeed, he built a nice stone bridge over the burn and laid out the walled garden for the new house beside it. Whatever may be said about the inconvenience of his houses, the extravagance of their fittings and layout, the snobbishness of their bogus baronial trappings, the absurdity of their towers, the uselessness of many of their rooms, Lorimer was a good architect by any standards and a towering genius compared with his successors. Compared, for instance, with Le Corbusier he stands for civilisation against barbarism and as for the desecrators of London—and indeed Edinburgh—one can only hope that in his presence above they show some of the shame they conspicuously lacked on earth. He was almost in the class of Robert Adam. There is something very pleasant about the feel of a Lorimer house. Any reasonably sensitive person must feel it. Unlike the concrete forts of the modern school it has individuality. Lorimer had a great crowd of workmen in his wake and firms such as Whytock & Reid in Edinburgh provided furniture and fittings for his houses. They all, therefore, bear his imprints; the door handles, the plaster ceilings, the green marble tops to the mantelpieces. Lorimer no doubt liked having his own way. He liked a riot of Scots baronial nonsense but he adorned it with a sense of proportion. He could be kept under control and he could be responsive to other styles as at Lympne in Kent. I have mentioned Hill of Tarvit, an estate near Cupar in Fife. Like Rowallan it had belonged to a distinguished family, the Scots of Scotstarvit. Their tower still stands intact. As at Rowallan when Mr. Sharp bought the estate he and Lorimer left the tower as it stood and set about enlarging an 18th century house nearby. Mr. Sharp was a great friend of my father's. The Sharps manufactured jute but also and more profitably ran the Alliance Trust. My father and Fred Sharp were admirably suited to each other. Fred too, apart from a little golf and gentle indulgence in shooting, was averse to violent exertion. Like my father he enjoyed conversation and pottering about collecting oddments of silver and furniture. I have the sideboard he and my father carried off from a joiner in Dundee who used it to stand on when he got down his implements—by which misuse he split the top. Mr. Sharp would have no baronial nonsense. The result is that Hill of Tarvit has some highly agreeable rooms with French windows leading on to a terrace and is also convenient to run.

At Rowallan there was no Mr. Sharp. As you come up the hill and turn into the gravel sweep outside the front door you are confronted by stone massed in fortress blocks and pierced—except in the kitchen—the one room which looks out this way—by singularly few windows. As is often the way in Scottish houses the main rooms were on the first floor and very agreeable they are. The drawing room, originally intended as a connecting gallery, is a lovely room with great windows to the West. The dining room and library were panelled in oak with beasts on the bookshelf ends and furniture designed by Lorimer. The house must have covered over an acre and was three storeys high. Yet when my brother-in-law and sister first went there it had only four main bedrooms and two dressing rooms. The bedrooms were magnificent but the only window in one of the dressing rooms was screwed into a corner about five feet up. The rest of the house consisted of billiard rooms and garden rooms, a nursery passage, a sewing room and a labyrinth of tiled back premises. In the centre of the house was a dungeon containing nothing but the hot water system; one bedroom had a spiral stone stair leading from it to the roof, another spiral stone stair led from the top to the bottom of the building and off these stairs were two or three small rooms quite useless and indeed exceedingly difficult to get at. The main staircase between the first floor and the four bedrooms contained a good portrait by Lockhart of old Mr. Polson, his daughter's portrait also excellently painted by Lockhart, hung over the drawing room mantelpiece and many Patersons were to be found—well suited to the house. Over the fireplace in the library was a small gallery with another useless room behind it; indeed the gallery itself was quite purposeless being perhaps big enough for one mandolin player standing up. It was mainly used as a test of strength. A tallish man could just grip the base of the railing which enclosed it and if suitably athletic haul himself up. I never came near achieving it but my son, John, did it quite easily. I have always marvelled not only at the craftsmanship but the solidarity of Lorimer's work. It has been subjected to every kind of rough usage but hardly a scratch can be detected. In fact, as you can imagine, what the house is really designed for is games such as hide and seek, sardines and kick the bucket: all of which appealed to the energies of my sister. It had, and has, I don't know why I write in the past—it is all there still—an extraordinarily cheerful atmosphere. To wake at Rowallan looking up at the plastered ceilings, each a masterpiece of design and work, was to start the day with a glow. The room my parents and after them my wife and I usually occupied had a ceiling like an inverted fountain surrounded by grapes. To contemplate the wash-stands built into the walls and surrounded by blue tiles (with in the pre-war days copper cans of hot water), to sleep in brass bedsteads and be warmed by wood fires was the height of well-being. Above all, Rowallan was designed for children. However, it is just as well it stopped where it did. It had rambled far enough. When it was about two-thirds finished, old Mrs. Corbett died. Her husband, Uncle Archie, Billy's father, halted all further work, gave the estate to his son and retired to Brooks's Club.

I never saw much of Uncle Archie. He seldom visited Rowallan and I was not often in Brooks's. He had the reputation of being a bore in the class of the Ancient Mariner. It was said that some younger members of Brooks's could occasionally be seen cornered and cowering under the statistics of butter fat—for Uncle Archie, though no lover of country life, was a cornucopia of agricultural and other information. But I was fond of him. This bears out my belief that children like stability. They also like information and contrary to modern beliefs often like being instructed. Uncle Archie was eminently stable and endlessly instructive. He was always dressed in black and when going out wore a black coat with a fur collar. He addressed children in his macaw-like voice in just the same manner he used to his contemporaries or, I have no doubt, to the House of Commons. Once when my sisters had been detailed to look after me in London on my way to Scotland from my private school they told me as a joke that they were staying at the Ritz. As my taxi was proceeding down Albemarle Street I remembered that Uncle Archie slept at Brown's Hotel. I decided I must call on him and there I was found by my sisters (who were staying there and not at the Ritz) listening contentedly to him like the boy in the picture called 'The Boyhood of Raleigh'—though Uncle Archie was very unlike an old salt. It must also be said in his favour that he presented Glasgow with two or three magnificent parks.

Every summer we spent part of August at Rowallan. I rode or went out in a trap most mornings. One of the departed luxuries are traps. They went at the right speed for the right distance so that you could examine the trees and hedges, watch the rabbits, discuss the route. In the evenings I would go shooting with my father or Duncan the groom, who seemed always ready to potter round the corners of the woods where I hoped to catch an unwary rabbit. I never shot one though I once had a triumph by killing a sitting wood pigeon, but then I only had an air gun. Meanwhile Jessie and an old Corbett retainer sat gossiping in the sewing room. At

Christmas we returned as I continued to do during much of my life. I must have spent nearly fifty Christmases at Rowallan; what heaven it was to escape from school into a sleeper and wake up in Scotland.

My sisters were keen on tennis which at Rowallan took the place of golf. The hard court lay behind the castle and there with the Collins brothers, Ian and Billy, they played continuously and became very good. They played together at Wimbledon and Gwyn played for several years with Ian Collins—being at one time the mixed doubles champions of Scotland. Ian Collins figured largely in Rowallan life. He worked in William Collins and Sons, the publishers in Glasgow and for years dropped in on his way to Troon where his family lived. He never, it seems to me, got his due as an athlete. He could have laid claim to being the best all-round amateur performer of his generation. He played cricket for four years for Harrow, he then broke his leg playing soccer for Oxford. In spite of that he represented Britain for many years in the Davis Cup with Colin Gregory and I believe they were never beaten. He was a scratch golfer, a good billiards player and rode in many point to points, being at one time Master of the Eglinton Hounds. One summer he made 50 at cricket for Scotland against the Australians, reached the semi-final of the amateur golf championship and beat Cochet at Wimbledon. Pretty good for someone with one knee more or less at right angles to his leg. He was also an extremely nice man, a shrewd director of Collins and in World War II had an adventurous war record in SAS. When I think of Rowallan, his up-turned nose and his face alternately creased by smiles or by concentration on some matter of moment, such as tennis or what price to ask for a Collins best-seller, are never far away.

I see now that those who give most to life stretch out their hands to seize what they can from living. My sister, Gwyn, was a natural enjoyer, unhagridden by introspection, education, ambition, or the need to make an impression. She was a child of nature but not of the breed idealised by the followers of Rousseau. She was more real than that. Though unpretentious, free from soul-searching and immediate in her responses, she stuck to certain canons of behaviour. She was the adult of her upbringing which she took for granted as having been the best possible. She was spontaneous. She dragged less certain spirits in her wake. She assumed, perhaps selfishly, that everyone was enraptured with life, that to be alive was in itself a feast to be gobbled up. Every minute was a sensation not to be missed. Sometimes she made an effort to put herself in other people's shoes but more often she assumed that they must want what she wanted. She assumed that you would want to eat because you were hungry, play tennis because it was enthralling, ride because it was exciting. That is how she behaved and she wanted everyone to enjoy what she enjoyed. Her certainty was a profound relief—no wearisome to-ing and fro-ing between alternative plans. At dinner parties in her house when she had eaten enough she left the table; as she ate with remarkable speed this was apt to happen when she was a course ahead of the older guests. She was simple and sometimes a little pathetic as are all the nicest people I have known for if rebuffed she never could understand why. Gwyn liked happiness and wanted everyone to be happy too. Though a moderately observing Christian her behaviour was pagan. She rarely questioned the rules under which she had been brought up, she was shockable and occasionally shocked but shocked by the sins of darkness, actions that distressed other people, those that were mean or incomprehensible, not by the Calvinist sins that threatened the personal soul. She was stoic in never complaining. Never once did she by word or gesture indicate to me that she felt ill-used. She had a rather child-like sense of duty but no sense of her own importance. She was a stranger to self-pity. I think she expected to go to heaven—though heaven I suspect was Rowallan, not writ large but repeated all over again, with perhaps my father and sister, Nancie, as perpetual guests.

She was not self-sacrificing. She had no need to be, and she would have squandered her gifts had she been. Immersed in her life and endowed with flashing vitality Rowallan afforded opportunities which she grasped. But if she had been born in the Dundee tenement which might have been her lot had the Grimond fortunes gone differently I am sure that she would have been a cheerful, blowsy mother in a drugget skirt, blowing her children's noses and getting her husband off to work in the same triumphant way that she created a home, or second home, for the Corbetts and her respectable brother. At Rowallan 'She made a golden tumult in the house. Like morning in the hills.'

After a rather happy term at Gibbs to which I have referred I was sent to a 'private' boarding school. I draw a veil over my life there. It eventually surpassed Evelyn Waugh's wildest imaginings. Admittedly it was not like that when I went there. My parents must have known how much I disliked it—at least I constantly told them and it perturbed them a great deal. But they were ignorant—as are most parents—about the iniquities of their children's world. Also to remove a boy from school was unthinkable.

Eton, when I reached it, came as a great relief. To have a room of one's own was in itself a pleasure. Though Eton was quirky beyond belief it was infinitely pleasanter than Evelyn's. I liked being in a town and being able to walk about and eat huge teas.

Tedium set in during the middle reaches at Eton and at no time would I not have leaped at the chance of going home. But it had many advantages and the teaching, though peculiar, I now see was very good. As this book is not a contribution to serious history, but a series of footnotes about things and people as I saw them, I might record my impression of Eton teaching. We were taught in large classes, thirty or so in a class, a number which I believe horrifies educationalists. But then much about Eton would horrify them. The houses and classrooms would cause a strike among modern teachers in the state schools. My house was full of wood, knotted, dusty, riddled with woodworm and had no fire escape. The forty boys shared two baths in cupboards on the landings and a small battery of lavatories in which one was forbidden to shut the doors. The school as far as ability was concerned, was comprehensive, ranging from boys of incurable stupidity up to brilliant scholars. Your place was more or less fixed upon entry. After that it depended on how you did at Trials, the examinations held at the end of each term or half. Unless you failed, which was quite difficult even for the spectacularly idle and stupid or were a genius and got a double remove, you went up one form at a time. Within the forms were classes of different abilities, but even within the classes some boys were much cleverer than others. Once you reached 'the first hundred' (as far as I remember about the beginning of your last year or a little earlier) your place was immutably fixed. You remained between the same two boys however well or badly you or they did. It seems the ideal of some modern schools of educational thought.

All boys did Latin and at least half the school, Greek. I have been taught Greek and Latin for some ten years yet I cannot decipher the dog Latin on a tombstone. We got by with cribs. These were bought in Windsor or from older boys. The custom was to bind them in the covers of other books (I had an invaluable set bound in the covers of Tennyson's 'Dream of Fair Women'). Latin and Greek are supposed to improve the mind and oddly enough I believe they do: indeed, using a crib may be a useful skill in future life. I have always maintained that one of the minor advantages of an Eton education is that it teaches you to cheat acceptably.

But the high quality of Eton education was due to the masters. They were a curious lot, like a flock of exotic birds in an aviary. Mr. Headlam taught history and was also a housemaster. While with other masters cribs were seldom actually brought into class Mr. Headlam's pupils suffered no such deprivation. If you sat well back in the room and kept it covered up it was also possible to spend the time reading an agreeable book. Such 19th century classics as I have read were read in Mr. Headlam's history class. Some of the oddest features of Eton's many-sided education were the customs associated with this particular master. When Headlam arrived in flowing gown, one side of the classroom would chant 'How does the master enter the room' to which the other side would reply 'Like a tall ship in full sail.' Headlam was an able man who suffered from illness and boredom. He was an Etonian cult. Unlike my nurse and Uncle Archie he was not stable; you could never be sure of his mood. It was the custom for housemasters to go round each boy's room after he had gone to bed saying goodnight. If the Master had guests who knew some of the boys, or were interested to go round with him, they would accompany him. Headlam appeared one evening on his rounds in full Guards uniform (he had served with the Brigade) accompanied by the film star Anna May Wong. There were other eccentrics among the masters. Mr. Prior, said to be half French peasant, who went for long walks; if he found a man ploughing he would ask if he might take a turn and would then plough expertly and happily for many hours. There was Dr. Porter, a distinguished scientist, defrocked, so the boys believed, for suggesting that Shadrack, Mishak and Abednego wore asbestos in the burning fiery furnace. Most of the masters, such as my own admirable housemaster, Mr. Howson, were more humdrum but nearly all were conscientious, good scholars and good teachers. The best teaching was done in what would now be called tutorials or seminars. Here as a boy wound his way up the school he was likely to find some corner suited to his talents or some teacher who could arouse his interest.

Then, as now, the boys ran innumerable societies at Eton; one of these was the Political Society. This society never debated politics but invited M.P.s etc. to harangue it from time to time. I invited Mr. Gandhi. He accepted. The school authorities were vexed when I first broke it to them, not surprisingly complaining that I might have told them in advance. However, they soon recovered their poise and fended off the indignant letters fired by blimpish Old Etonians.

I met Gandhi's party on a cold and wet evening at the Great Western railway station in Windsor. The first I saw of Mr. Gandhi was a pair of chocolate coloured matchstick legs dangling out of a third class carriage followed by his bat-like face. He wore only a loin cloth. He was accompanied by a missionary who was continually straying off by himself, and a friend, Miss Slade, who was muffled up in a sari and cloak—much the best dressed of the party. This did not prevent Mrs. Alington, the Headmaster's forthright wife, who had known her father, an Admiral, greeting her with the words 'Your father would turn in his grave if he saw you dressed like this.'

The visit was only a modified success. Mr. Gandhi was long-winded and shuffled round all direct questions. He did not impress the boys. He bristled with curious habits and demands, some to the British verging on the unsavoury.

Henry Marten the Vice-Provost and Robert Birley were teaching at Eton when I was there as a boy. Marten was, with Carter, the author of

43

the best textbook of British history. Once a week or so each class of history specialists used to go to his library where we were allowed to take down and read any book we liked. In the middle of thirty or so boys spread about the chairs and floor, Marten sat with his little red spaniel, carrying on back-chat and asking questions. A spare, white-haired man with a rather pursed-up face he barked away in the friendliest manner, his spectacles glinting, every now and then calling out half the name of some historical event which the class had to finish. 'And then there was the treaty of Hunkiar, and we would all join in completing the name 'Hunkiar, Eskelisi'. Occasionally he offered prizes of threepence or six-pence to anyone who could answer some question he would fire off. He usually then borrowed the money from some other boy. The other master of genius, Robert Birley, a gangling figure with straying hair, could hardly contain his enthusiasm for history even after teaching it for ten or fifteen years, 'much the most exciting thing that ever happened' was his constant introduction to each of a whole string of events. The result of these two and a number of other competent historians was that history was well taught when I was at Eton. We were also made to learn small pieces of poetry which we chose ourselves—an admirable and simple requirement.

Teaching at Eton seems to me a neglected subject. Had Eton been a new experimental school or a showpiece of the state system numerous theses would no doubt have been written about it. Perhaps Doctorates on Etonian teaching methods exist. If so, I have not come across them. The methods and results were surely worth some study. Out of a long history odd customs had been carried on for some forgotten reason—were we not in mourning still for King George III—some of which have now been re-discovered and elevated to the van of new educational thought. Mr. Headlam did not think of himself as a way-out trail blazer—but allowing boys to do what they like has now its upholders. On the other hand, the completion by shouting of historical landmarks would I fear now be frowned upon, yet perhaps five-sevenths of the history that I actually remember was taught to me by Marten and the idea that lessons might be exhilarating I got from Birley. Then there were the queer byways which Eton offered. I can't say that Prior taught me to plough. But for a term or two I did botany with Mr. Weatherall—Botany Bill. I learned little botany —though he was a good botanist—but sitting in a garden and talking to him made botany worth while. Botany Bill had a cockney accent and none of the arrogance expected from Eton. He was at once critical of Eton and more particularly of Etonians and also fond of the school. I have found very few people who could be as loyal yet censorious as Weatherall. It is a virtue we sadly lack. I notice how almost never nowadays do lawyers,

Trades Union officials, civil servants, members of the CBI or any of the other countless bureaucracies which infest the country bring serious criticism to bear on their own organisation. Still rarer is it to find evidence of affection towards such bodies by their members. It would indeed be difficult to feel affection for say the National Union of Public Employees or to take any pride in its activities. Few of these sharks ever suggest that their power or rewards should be reduced. They gobble up everything they can get. It seems to me that there is a lesson to be learnt from the mixture of discipline, personal instruction and eventually the encouragement of going your own way which made up teaching at Eton. It also showed the value and limitations of competition. As I have said, as far as getting up the school faster was concerned, there was not much competitive spirit. But the clever boys, particularly in college, competed vigorously for prizes. And the final lessons of Eton for the modern comprehensive system is that being yoked with the clever will not of itself cure the idle of their idleness nor the stupid of their stupidity. You can, however, provide curious paths down which they may stray. Eton with its happy-go-lucky education no doubt blighted the lives of some who under pressure would have been made scholars. Perhaps boys were left too readily to go to the devil in their own way but if you could take them, Eton offered all sorts of opportunities to all sorts of boys.

If I have written flippantly about some aspects of Eton, I must not leave the impression that Eton education was frivolous: a school which produced Gladstone, the Huxleys and George Orwell could hardly be that. Boys were taught that what they did mattered. They were taught that responsibility rested with them and could not be sloughed off. They were taught to behave as members of a community and to have regard to the wider communities of their country and their fellow men.

The unsolved problem of education is to pick the right moment. When I first learnt to read fluently I would have read almost anything. I should have been plied with those 18th- and 19th-century novels which unless read on the first tide of discovery of the magic world of books you will never read at all. Then about the age of fifteen I was almost unteachable and should have been put out to grass. Other children no doubt grow up differently. But we cannot have a class for each. What is also true of British teaching is that it is abominably wasteful of time. There is no excuse for teaching languages so badly. Once or twice a week a period would be devoted to French. That no boy who had spent hundreds of hours on this jig-saw puzzle arrangement of classes could carry on the simplest conversation in French worried the masters no more than their even more laborious failure to teach Latin. At the end of a lengthy and expensive education no boy of my time could speak a foreign language, read a balance sheet, mend a motor car, cook, type, darn or knit. We were accomplished makers of toast, however, for our elders. I doubt if things are much better today in either state or private schools. The state schools, equally with the private, take about twice as long as is necessary to teach what they do. There are large gaps in the curriculum. And in my experience when they do teach cooking or carpentry they provide tools of an extravagance and profusion that no pupil will see again.

At the top of this strange Eton pyramid of boys and masters sat the Provost. M. R. James was a scholar of such learning that I have heard Roger Mynors—himself perhaps the only man who held the Professorship of Latin at both Cambridge and Oxford—say that when he died a mass of knowledge died with him which cannot be replaced. He was oblivious to hierarchy, prestige or age. When I was thirteen he invited me to dinner for no other reason than that a boy a few years older than me, Bernard Fergusson, had suggested that he should do so. The invitation flustered my tutor. Boys, especially smaller boys, had to be in by seven, and have their lights out by nine. However, no one argued with the Provost. His dining room was a large room, rather like a small college dining hall, with an open fireplace at one end and a screen at the other. Here presided M. R. James, slumped at the head of a polished black table, his stiff shirt bulging, a lock of hair across his broad forehead which topped off a broad face, chatting in a desultory manner to boys, masters, guests, whoever took his fancy. It was his presence and his unspoken encouragement to get others to talk, rather than what he said, that enhanced him. Though an excellent host, he was susceptible to bores. I enjoyed his comments on them—'Just so, as I said before' he would murmur.

I dined, was plied with claret and port, and returned to my house half an hour after midnight, very slightly drunk—the first time I ever was drunk. The panelled 'parlour' where we met before dinner and the drawing room, seldom used in his time, was lined with portraits of 18th-century boys by such artists as Romney and Beechey. It was then the custom for the top boys to present their portraits on leaving. It is a unique collection. Luckily, the custom coincided with one of the best periods of British portrait painting. We have got so used to the raddled or bloated faces surmounted by wigs which look out of the well-known pictures of the time, that these fresh-faced boys come as a delightful surprise. Later when the Provost was ill I used sometimes to visit him in bed, or rather, half falling out of it. On the staircase to the bedroom floor hung some huge oil paintings by Lear.

James was not only a scholar of extraordinary distinction but the most impressive man I have ever met. It is impossible to compare him with Churchill or De Gaulle, wrapt about in the aura of their achievements.

But in force of personality he struck me, perhaps because I was younger when I knew him, and knew him better, as more redoubtable than either. On one occasion when a dinner party was breaking up he asked a rather senior master to dinner on some future date. The master tried to excuse himself as he had a previous engagement. 'Dinner will be at eight' was all that James said. When he walked about the school grounds slowly and heavily everyone was aware of his presence yet he made no effort to be impressive, insisted on no protocol and talked to the smallest boy in exactly the same way as he did to the most distinguished visitor. M. R. James was a highly civilising element at Eton as he would have been anywhere. He stood outside the petty ambitions and jealousies of the Eton world. He curried no favour by playing to the boys or flattering their important parents. Most boys who came across him regularly did so at the Shakespeare Society—reading Shakespeare's plays round the fire in his dining room. James himself was a marvellous, even-toned reader, especially of the Bible, and there was the added interest of wondering if Mr. Tattersall, presumably of the horse-dealing family, who often stayed with James, would fall asleep. When he finally keeled over he would be sent to bed.

Another man I met when I was rather older, who resembled James was Dr. Stewart, a fellow of Eton and dean of the chapel at Trinity College, Cambridge. He also had the gift of treating everyone alike. As he was a great authority on Pascal and Vauvenargues he assumed that I, who could hardly read French, must be interested in Pascal too. When I stayed with him in Trinity he took me to dine in hall. There were very few guests that night but as far as I remember five holders of the Order of Merit. I sat next to Housman, who talked to me about cricket. He was wearing a black skull cap, having fallen on his head out of a taxi in Lyons. I did not then know of the opening to the speech he had made in the hall where we dined. 'In this great hall where Wordsworth was once drunk and Porson was once sober, here stand I, a better scholar than Wordsworth and a better poet than Porson, betwixt and between.'

A boy's life at Eton, however, was made by the boys. The custom was to have tea every day with one or two other boys—high teas they would be called in Scotland: toast, sausages, eggs and a loaf of bread. I 'Messed' with Colum Gore-Booth, a Gore-Booth of Lissadell, 'the light of evening Lissadell, great windows open to the South.' His socks were sometimes darned by the Countess Markiewicz's daughter, or so he claimed. My sisters had a friend, Rowley Scovell, who came from Ireland. One day, naively, I said to Rowley that I had a friend from Ireland. On hearing who this was, Rowley replied, 'Oh yes, I know his family, his aunt shot my father.' Apparently old Scovell had been sitting in the window of his club in Dublin in Kildare Street, perhaps (where decades later my wife and I were to spend a weekend of comfort, rest, and nostalgia owing to the generosity of Terence de Vere White). The Countess Markiewicz fired through the window, hitting him in the shoulder. Flinging *The Times* to the ground he staggered to the telephone and rang up Colum's father; 'Look here, Gore-Booth, I want an apology, your sister has just shot me, and in our club.'

Of the boys at my house the one of whom I have seen a good deal during the rest of my life is William Douglas-Home. He looked like an intelligent mouse, inherited from his father an excellent character shared with all his family and from his mother the eccentricity of the Lambtons. I went to stay with the Homes at Douglas occasionally during the summer holidays. Douglas could not have covered more acreage than Rowallan but was a square, early 19th-century house of four storeys in which all the space was used. Pepper pots decorated the corners but the main block was fitted out with countless rooms and even the round towers below the pepper pots were usable. Just as well, as Douglas was full of people. There were the five sons and two daughters of Lord and Lady Home. Lady Home did not take up much room; viewing the scene with a quizzical eye from beneath the palm tree in the drawing room, she had, to use a slang expression, got out from under. Her husband, on the other hand, seemed to take up more room than in fact he did as he was excessively noisy. He made almost as much noise as my sister Gwyn and for the same reason: he was happy. He shouted and when not shouting he sang. He was small, round and sandy-haired. His life seemed entirely devoted to good works of an un-ostentatious and indeed rather boring sort. He would go hundreds of miles to open a jumble sale for some old sergeant he had served with. Since seeing Lord Home trundling off in plus-fours and a tweed cap with a bobble on the top I no longer believe that saints are elongated figures of ascetic habits and black hair. During these expeditions he would fall in with worthy souls whom he would then invite to stay. The summer parties which I attended at Douglas would therefore be composed of Homes and their friends of different ages; as it had very good grouse moors there would be a few serious shooters, though most of these had gone by the time I arrived; there would be some old habitués and the odd man or woman Lord Home had picked up on his peregrinations round the country. For the most virtuoso organiser it would have been difficult to manage. Lady Home had given up, as I have said, any attempt to interfere in the day to day tactics. Collingwood, the butler, seemed to be the prime improvisor. Usually some fifteen to twenty people sat down to dinner. The food and drink were ample but erratic. The wine, for instance, was dispensed by Collingwood on the relay principle. When a bottle or bottles were exhausted they handed over the next regardless of what stage the meal had reached. The first round of port might be exhausted by the time the meat arrived and like snakes and ladders we would go back to sherry. The meals were made more alarming by the wrangling of the Home brothers, occasionally interrupted by their father calling on Collingwood to throw them out. An even more alarming hazard for new and nervous guests was that on going to bed Lord Home turned off all the electric lights with one twist of a wheel. We were all supplied with candles but it was all too easy to set off on the voyage to bathroom or lavatory, perhaps a hundred yards or so from one's bedroom in a glorious blaze of electric light having improvidently left the candlestick behind. One flick of Lord Home's wrist and there one was at a critical moment far from familiar territory and wrapt in inexpugnable darkness.

The days at Douglas were devoted to slaughter. They began early and finished late. Alec was then a junior Minister at the Scottish Office. In his anxiety not to delay the shooting party some no doubt valueless correspondence was lost in the loo. Lord Home though well aware of the importance of shooting felt bound every now and then to suggest a pause. On one occasion desperate for some check upon his sons' appetites he was heard bellowing, 'Going shooting again, how do you know Grimond doesn't want to think today ?' I had some difficulty in living this down.

Towards the end of my time at Eton I made friends with boys in other houses, Guy Branch who was in Headlam's house and Lionel Brett. It is said that never in after life are the Eton swells such swells as they are at Eton. The public schools drain some boys of their vitality. Though I have never believed that life after fifty is necessarily more important than life before eighteen, yet to become obsessed with school triumphs is stultifying. My friends escaped the trap. Lionel Brett was Captain of the School. Since he was very well endowed for coping with the various estates of men he continued to be a swell at every stage, ending up as Principal of the Royal College of Art.

At this time I also fell in with Con O'Neill and Con's friend, Jasper Ridley. Jasper Ridley had an oval red face with forebodings of jowls, chestnut eyes and eyebrows which went up to an ogee-like point. If he was not so good an examinee as Con or Lionel he certainly had an active and eccentric mind—mind rather than brain. It was equipped like an intellectual Clapham Junction so that ideas, emotions, situations, were shunted off in surprising directions but without collisions. However, I knew him best at Oxford and to Oxford we must now turn. But before we get there I must mention Ireland.

I went on a wholly delightful visit with Dick Levinge, who was the Captain of my House at Eton, to his home at Mullingar. It was a holiday which was a success from start to finish, the drive to Holyhead through spring in North Wales, breakfast in Dublin and then a week in Knockdrin. Knockdrin was a gothic folly. One wing was a façade of Gothic windows with nothing behind them. The staircase was carved out of pine branches. Grass grew waist high around the house. The books and furniture had long mellowed and faded in the soft climate of Ireland. The first Levinge of importance had been Lord Chief Justice of Ireland in the 17th century. He left a terrible glimpse of the judicial mind. In his diary he recorded how he had gone for a walk in his park with 'the little dog, Top.' Top had chased a fallow deer which broke its leg trying to jump a fence. The last entry for the day in the Lord Chief Justice's diary ended 'I hanged the little dog, Top.'

Later Dick Levinge drove me to Oxford to sit for a scholarship. My first sight of the city was of the houses in Iffley Road. I experienced in a minor way some of the emotions Luther must have experienced on first seeing Rome. Oxford was awe-inspiring. Oxford was like a new planet swimming into my ken.

Nor were my expectations of Oxford disappointed. I am surprised that I found it on the whole so rewarding. For Eton, above all schools, had some affinities with a university. We had our own rooms, we were taught to work on our own, we were treated if not as adults at least as human beings and the boys to some extent ran their own affairs. Yet Eton was a closed society. Though you could escape from them, its bounds were strict. Its conventions and fashions appeared assured. And it encouraged as far as I and my immediate cronies were concerned a rather spurious success. We were not conspicuously good at games but that did not prevent us from being elected to the oligarchy of boys called 'Pop'. Games in my time at Eton were not as important as they had been. After reaching a certain position in the school we were encouraged to go our own way. This, as I have suggested, was much in tune with modern educational fashions. But in my case it meant that I relied on such faculties as I possessed without attempting what I found difficult. I could write essays whether I knew anything about the subject or not. My eyes lit up at 'Compare and contrast Boniface VIII and King Hagostrand of Hungary,' even if I had never heard of either. My father used sometimes to reprove me quietly for not attending to what I was doing. This habit grew more pronounced. I did not observe. I had always noticed how he would see birds which I did not. I did not attend to the meaning of what I was saying or writing. I soon got tired of any solid application. I lived partly in a world that I had made up for myself which could be extended and adapted as I wanted. These were of course characteristics of my particular mind. Eton cannot be blamed for them. But there were many boys like me. Should we have been forced more sternly to apply what minds we had? Against this could be argued that it would have been a waste of time: not only because of the nature of our minds but because we were too young. Eton taught no philosophy or economics, not even political philosophy. The nearest we got to abstract notions was Dicey (whose effect was rather spoiled by Headlam's custom of opening the Dicey lessons with song—'Dicey, Dicey, give me your answer, do'). This policy I believe was deliberate and there was a case for it, philosophy and the question 'why?', unless boys liked to raise such matters with individual masters, were left to the universities. But I believe we should have been taught more effectively to apply our minds. I say effectively because the teaching of Latin and Greek and mathematics was indeed intended as a mental exercise. This teaching was not entirely ineffective. I have gained something from it and many of my contemporaries have gained a great deal in ability to master and deploy arguments and order knowledge. The diffuseness of many men and women may be due to the lack of even an inkling of a classical education. But more could have been achieved. As I have said, education goes on too long. By doing so it annihilates interest—boys sense that many lessons are in-filling by rote of time which must be consumed. We were never told why we were 'doing' Greek or Latin. Mention would be made of their place in the history of civilisation, the importance of their literature, their role in improving the mind. But the precise relevance of the Classics to civilisation was not explored; if their literature was worth reading it was only after we had been bored stiff with classical teaching that any effort was made to read it as literature. And as for improving the mind, Scott, the St Andrews joiner, when I frequented his workshop would explain the point and excellence of his tools, would compare wood with wood, even if you were as bad with your hands as I was you could see the pleasure of doing carpentry well, the satisfaction and economy of the finished product. The same sort of satisfaction at some point between eight and eighteen ought to have been generated by a mastery of Latin or, still more, Greek. In my case it certainly wasn't. The most peculiar exercise in the classics was the construction of Latin verse. It was to most boys a meaningless penance. If it had to be done at all it should have been as the solution of a puzzle or crossword.

I have suffered a great deal from being disorderly. If only I were tidier and could find things I would have many hours to spend more fruitfully. Fecklessness may be attractive, disorder may be thought a badge to be displayed by the middle class—like the top hat was in Thorsten Veblen's time. But by the mediocre at least it is a disease to be avoided. In me Eton encouraged it.

During the war I was, as are most amateur commissioned officers, largely dependent upon NCOs. At one time in the Fife and Forfar Yeomanry my troop sergeant was a Sergeant Wann. Sergeant Wann had been a farm servant. Wann was splendidly organised. Everything was done in the right order. He knew where every tool was to be found and when found they were in apple pie order. It was a pleasure to see him doing anything. Our tanks at night were covered with large and heavy tarpaulins. I never could fold them. Wann, even in a high wind, would fold them as though they were handkerchiefs. He never had a classical education but for economy of effort and logical marshalling of what he had to do, no classicist could beat him. He had worked with horses and had been a ploughman at one time. Perhaps the routine of feeding, watering and grooming horses, the need to understand their characters and capabilities, the pride in them, and the care of their harness, had made Wann the even-tempered, skilled and economical worker that he was. My father, who was meticulously neat, never had a classical education. I suspect that some discipline other than the classics should be taught to most boys.

SOME OF THE GLOSS of Eton was rubbed off at Oxford and some of the deficiencies made good. The contrast of Oxford to Eton was the sharper because I read not history but Modern Greats which included philosophy, politics and economics. Superficially alike as they were, I found school and university very different places. Eton masters were masters—with the exception of James, and to some extent Marten, who were more like uncles to whom one was paying a visit. Dons lived in the same sort of rooms as their pupils and many led similar lives. The pattern of the day was at your command apart from a few fixed points such as reading essays—but very few. For Oxford, in spite of Eton, I was unprepared, except for a sort of reverent expectation. I found it an appointment. It is often small things which illustrate best big changes. My scout asked me if I would mind if he wore spats as his ankles got cold in winter. No grown-up had ever asked me for permission to do anything before. But the most serious change was to be treated as a person capable of thought, whose opinions should be taken seriously and who therefore should be serious in forming them. No longer was it enough to 'compare and distinguish' off the top of one's head. One had to show that one had some knowledge of Boniface VIII. More serious still, I was asked what I meant. I produced my usual well-rounded essays for Charles Morris, my tutor in philosophy, painted as I thought with an attractive broad brush, touching lightly on interesting opinions. Instead of responding to these generalities he would roll about like a harpooned porpoise, clinking the chain which ran to his trouser pocket against the money which it contained and ask me why I used 'but' instead of 'however' or what the word 'thought' meant. Philosophy came as a disturbing new element. I was not sure what it meant (nor am I now) but at least Charles Morris impressed the importance of concentrating my mind in a new way. However, I thought, history will be safe, cosy ground. But it wasn't. Humphrey Sumner sat smoking, his eyes closed, while I read my essay. He was not impressed. At the end of the tutorial he lent me two volumes in French about the Russian railway system. Equally invigorating were other Balliol dons—Roger Mynors whom I have already mentioned and Vivian Galbraith. Vivian Galbraith taught some of us for the preliminary examination of Pass Moderations. That an historian of his distinction should have spread his mind and its knowledge before entrants for such an examination was highly creditable. Galbraith not only knew no history later than about 1600 but disapproved of it. He was also an ascetic. Like my Aunt Jo, whom he rather resembled in his angular appearance and his disengagement from hum-drum life he had no hankering after either the luxuries nor the prestigious rewards of modern life. He was a favourite of Guy Branch whom I had known at Eton and who had rooms next door to his. Guy would inveigle Galbraith into discussing either contemporary Balliol or the study of modern history. On both Galbraith's views were, to say the least of it, detached.

Many people remember—or claim to remember—Oxford for its charm; the Cherwell, the smell of wallflowers on college walls, Peckwater quad at night or Magdalen tower at sunrise. These are literary reminiscences. They are true but they are selected because we read of them in other people's memoirs—Sir Edward Grey driving back to Oxford in the evening and winning his bet that every second tree by the road would be an elm, so leisurely was the pace of the dog-cart. Alas, he would not find elms there now. Other people seem to have filled their days with lunches and their nights with drink. I had my share of all these enjoyments. But they are not the clearest memories. My memories are of awakening, of probing new opinions and coming to believe that opinions might be important. I also discovered new friends or extended friendships already established. Guy Branch, as I have said, had been a friend of mine at Eton. No one, when he was there, would have seen him as a typical Etonian. Yet looking back he typified many of the attitudes of the pre-Second World War Etonians. While the dominant generation who grew up before the First World War seem to have been clever, rich, successful, arrogant and to have become swells at Eton, because they were good at games, Guy was clever but not rich and certainly not arrogant, nor did he attach much importance to games though he kept wicket for Eton. Before the first war public school nabobs could look forward to wealth, ease, safe seats in Parliament, accession to some almost hereditary offices. Some of them must have felt that after finishing their education there were no more pinnacles to climb. Some may have been so shocked to find that the world did not take them at their ancestral valuation that they decided to rest on their School and University laurels.

This would never have happened to Guy. He was rather more sophisticated than his contemporaries, amusing, detached, a discoverer of odd corners in life, whether in personalities or literature, sanguine about the future, engrossed in the present.

My other near neighbours in Balliol were Jasper Ridley, N. O. Brown and Con O'Neill. Jasper lived on the same staircase one floor above me. His father was one of the able, eccentric and rather choleric family of Northumberland Ridleys. His mother was a Benckendorff, daughter of the last Czarist Ambassador in London. Jasper's appearance was more Ridley than Benckendorff. His highly original mind, however, was a mixture of the two, perhaps predominantly Benckendorff. He enjoyed endless conversations of a Socratic sort, his society was a constant pleasure and a constant source of new discoveries. N. O. Brown was quickly unearthed and greatly appreciated by Jasper. He was a good classical scholar who had been born and largely educated abroad. At Oxford he was quiet and except among those who taught him his abilities were hardly recognised. After I went down he disappeared from my life until on a visit to Harvard a book *Life Against Death* by Norman O. Brown, a much praised psychologist and philosopher, was strongly recommended to me. Jasper and Con had been in the same house at Eton and were already friends. We all three lunched together every day. Con, who had an exceptionally efficient brain for any purpose, was never sure for what purpose he wanted to use it—or indeed if he wanted to use it at all. Gamekeeping in Ulster attracted him. His distinguished career has been punctuated by equally distinguished resignations. Having come to Oxford a year before Jasper and I he had already opened the series by resigning from the school of Modern Greats.

Jasper was reading Greats. The meticulous side of his nature enjoyed Latin and Greek as it did making toy furniture. His imagination thrived on music and talk. But both sides of his nature were irritated by philosophy. 'Reading Kant seems to me like watching someone else fishing. Colossal minute preparation of rod, line, cast and fly (one must limit oneself to pure *a priori* reason—it's no good using anything but a red cocker Stevenson on a day like this). Long, long periods of inexplicable casting and reeling in—"Now look, you must hold the rod and line like this, it must be synthetic *a priori*" then suddenly, click, burr, flop and out comes a magnificent 18lb. table of categories. God knows why. Now you try a cast, Mr. Ridley.'

I stayed frequently with Con O'Neill in Ulster and with Jasper in Suffolk. We also made expeditions together, indulging, largely under

Jasper's stimulation, in endless speculation. I still have some accounts of Jasper's social life. 'Christ, though, the house was full of stockbrokers—one of whom had, really, two pairs of eyebrows both in the wrong place and baldness where the one should have been; another, two aeroplanes.' Or after a hunt ball which he disliked: 'It was a riotously boring affair. On the way back we passed on the side of the road a car utterly consumed by fire. We discovered greatly to our satisfaction that it had contained hunt-ballers. I was unluckily unable to discover if they had been burnt to death or not.'

Jasper as well as playing the 'cello was a writer of light verse which should be collected, along with his letters, though many of them are too elliptical or ephemeral or both to be readily understood. Here is part of a poem he wrote on the Grid-Iron Club at Oxford—a rather fashionable resort of the fairly rich.

> Good Communist fathers forbid
> Their children to dine at the Grid
> Conservative spies as they justly surmise
> Would seduce any Marxist who did.
> For prudent Conservatives too
> To dine at the Grid is taboo.
> A sinister itch to dismember the rich
> Assails them whenever they do.
> For Liberals—well, they may try
> And yet they can hardly supply
> Enough of their kind to make anyone mind
> Either where they have dinner or why.

In other colleges boys I had known well, such as Lionel Brett, John Paton, William Home and Mark Pilkington were to be found and I saw a good deal of all of them. My friends and I had a great interest in personal relations and personalities. In this frequent assessment and reassessment of people Jasper played a leading part. But our attachments, male or female, were not violent. Oxford was short of girls and unlike our predecessors and successors we did not go much to London during term. But we saw plenty of girls in the holidays and occasionally at Oxford dinner parties.

I made two or three expeditions to the Highlands, during one of which Robert McNeile, who was a friend of mine from Eton days, later to marry John Paton's widow, Pamela, made the drawing reproduced. Bernard Fergusson, already in the Army, also came walking with us. I regret to record that the future hero of the Chindwin acquired a blister which necessitated a good deal of travel by bus while we, his supposedly softer companions, tramped the hills (he denies this but I think I am right).

For entertainment we were much indebted at first to 'Sligger'—F. F. Urquhart, who was still Dean of Balliol when I went up, though very ill. It has been easy to sneer at Urquhart—his primness, his mild homosexuality, his snobbishness, his apparent lack of interest in the general condition of the world. But such sneers are beside the mark. They imply that Urquhart was a dilettante. He was not. He had been the first Roman Catholic elected a Fellow of Oxford since the Reformation. His rooms were a place in which to meet and talk. His circle was constricted but had he attempted to widen it the tea would have been too weak: for Sligger was not a towering personality. He was wise to confine himself to what he did well and naturally, this was to help young men to get all they could out of the University, to work and exchange ideas, to behave as members of a community but not an inward looking community. He inculcated a serious view of education and of personal relations within Balliol but he also introduced students to Europe. At his chalet in the Alps he provided a haven for reading during the vacations which was complementary to Oxford. He was concerned with Catholic affairs though as far as I know he never proselytised. He taught us to take our obligations seriously, to handle our own lives and nurse our abilities such as they were with an eye to the contribution we could make to Balliol and far beyond. We now suffer from the dearth of unmarried dons, devoting themselves to their Universities, living in them, content to pursue the values which Universities should promote, impervious to passing fashions, never fretting for scholastic promotion or even recognition.

If the underlying lesson of Eton was that life must be taken seriously, Oxford reinforced this attitude. It at once tried to widen and concentrate the mind. 'Don't become paralysed by logic-chopping and the received wisdom' it said. 'Follow your intuition, question every dogma, but before you make up your mind make sure you know what you are talking about. By all means break the conventions but we will at least tell you what they are: by all means decide that Shakespeare is a bad playwright but read him first and be ready to justify your opinion. Use to the full whatever eyes and intelligence God has given you.'

I can't boast that I absorbed the lesson completely. But education made me look at familiar attitudes and places afresh and one of the places was my home town St Andrews.

It was the seat of the third oldest University in Britain, a University which with all its tribulations had preserved the genius of such places. If you want to learn about it you need go no further than Ronald Cant's *The University of St Andrews*, a book which also illuminates the general nature of Universities. Ronald Cant, one of the most distinguished historians never to become a professor, has showered upon generations of

St Andrews students teaching of the highest order in the best tradition of disinterested scholarship.

St Andrews has in its devotion to learning been in its moments of tranquillity the apotheosis of a University. A University is not merely concerned to train minds. Throughout the 17th and 18th centuries England had but two Universities—for long periods sunk in sloth, yet this was the age when her science and scholarship were held in high esteem. You can train doctors or lawyers in specialised colleges. Up to the middle of the 19th century none of England's great historians had read history. It is perfectly possible to have the finest teaching without Universities—look at the French *grands écoles*. Nor are Universities to be used—or rather abused—for the churning out of degree holders so that they can make a living from their paper qualifications. They should be centres of scholarship and teaching. They should embrace not one subject but all the main disciplines. They should broaden the minds of their students and widen their outlook. But above all they should nurse a morality—a personal morality and a moral criticism of the life of the country. In the past ages at Universities such as St Andrews this was achieved by the link between the University and the Church. Most Universities grew out of monastic foundations. Theology was not only a major subject on its own but permeated all teaching. When the grip of the Church weakened the liberal ethic, the teaching of the 18th- and 19th-century philosophers buttressed what was still an essentially Christian morality. Even atheists acknowledged that how you behaved mattered and mattered not only to you but to other people. This was what professors of philosophy in my time at Oxford taught, men such as Collingwood. Whatever you think of their worries about what to us are obscure culs-de-sac down which they trudged, nevertheless, if it does not matter how you behave, if a country does not require an informed and educated minority to guard and extend its best traditions and bring criticism to bear on the conduct of its affairs, the Universities have no reason for existence.

The face of St Andrews is Scots. But here Scottish vernacular architecture takes its place among the glories of Europe. The skeleton of the vast 14th-century cathedral, slighted by the Presbyterians, used as a quarry by the mean burghers, still stretches to heaven from above the harbour. It is the only great Gothic cathedral that looks on the ocean. It is seen at its best on wild autumn evenings when wind and rain have rinsed the sky and the sun sets behind its steeples like Turner's 'Fighting Téméraire.' Beside it stands the campanile of a still earlier church and below it on Sundays after chapel the students used to walk out to the end of the pier waving like a crimson pennant against the grey stones slapped by the sea. For St Andrews students flaunted scarlet gowns—proper gowns of flannel, stout protection against wind, not those silly travesties of gowns reaching only to the navel such as were affected by Oxford. The streets were filled with colour, here and there marked by the black gown of a Divinity student or a Professor sailing 'in amply bellying gown enormous through the sacred town.' There are few more becoming dresses for girls than a tasselled mortar board, gown and nylon stockings. If the Cathedral has been destroyed, the College chapel still presides, serene over North Street and with St Mary's College and the clusters of buildings which dignify the East end of South Street can claim for Scotland some of the best domestic architecture in Britain. With its main streets carrying on the ecclesiastical masterpieces at its East extremity, St Andrews was a mediaeval example of lay-out which modern planners should study.

But the city, the University and its golf course have had their ups and downs. In 1726 Mr. William Gib was allowed to keep his black and white rabbits on the links and for long the turf was at the mercy of townspeople casting 'feal and divot'. In 1697 the University was near as a touch moved to Perth on the grounds as quoted by Ronald Cant in *The University of St. Andrews* that the St Andrews air was 'thin and piercing' so that 'old men were instantly cut off and the inhabitants were brutish, quarrelsome and unscrupulous with a particular aversion to learning.' I dimly discern some truth in these generally libellous allegations. The air is indeed piercing. The habit of 'cutting' errant neighbours continued at least up to the Second World War. A celebrated bout of 'cutting' and counter 'cutting' reverberated through the town after Nancie and her sister-in-law, Ruth Hutchison, introduced a black male to the Ladies Club. As for learned men, they were treated with respectful curiosity or misgiving by some St Andreans.

In the city by the 18th century grass and middens defiled its streets, its population was small and poor. But perhaps this preserved it for what it was and is, a European town, for all its Scottish face. In its decay it escaped the pall of industry which draped Glasgow and Dundee with slums, it has not been raped by development nor is it threatened by the baleful embrace of oil. When golf woke the city from its sleep and set a new pulse beating at its Western boundaries it was to reverberate far beyond Scotland. Today the Royal and Ancient Club flourishes because of its international fame.

Scotland, if she is wise, will honour St Andrews as a jewel in the crown of Europe and make amends for the crimes she has inflicted on the city.

To return to family life: my father having died while I was at Eton, Nancie and my mother continued to live at 8, Abbotsford Crescent. Nancie was being wooed by Willie Black—a somewhat prolonged affair;

seldom has a girl played harder to get. The Grimond-Richardson blood has given rise to a certain indecisiveness though it is about small matters, such as whether to catch the 10.15 or the 10.30 train that I find it most difficult to make up my mind. I was very keen on Willie's candidature. Not only had he an aeroplane but an open Bentley two-seater even larger and faster than the car of the Spanish Count. He had the looks and figure of Clark Gable in his prime. All the Blacks were good looking though Willie and his sisters Ruth and Kay were pre-eminent. His children Tim and Mark inherited the exemplary character and looks of their parents. Above all, he combined competence with good temper and much entertainment. I usually found that people as well organised as Willie tended to be testy. Willie was never testy, at least not with me. He got on with young and old, indeed in many ways he would have been a more suitable Chief Scout than my other brother-in-law, Billy. If asked to go camping with one or the other I would have unhesitatingly chosen Willie. Billy, though he could not have been a better brother-in-law, I regarded as best attuned to indoor life. Nancie and Willie were eventually married and moved off into Fife where they bought a 19th-century Scottish baronial mansion, Teasses, which, like Rowallan, became something of a second home to me.

As I have mentioned, my great grandfather came from Blairgowrie. The children of his eldest brother, first cousins of my grandfather, still lived there. They were at this time in the thirties reduced to three unmarried sisters and a brother who died in 1931. When they died at the ages of 88, 91 and 93 respectively after the Second World War they must have been some of the last Victorians still living as they had always lived. They continued to do so until the middle of this century.

Their home was Oakbank, a small house up the river Ericht about a mile from Blairgowrie. The Ericht flows fast in a deep glen which made it a source of power for mills. Along it from Blairgowrie ran a road, little more than a farm road, which here and there was sliding into the river. About half way between Oakbank and Blairgowrie the Ericht crashes through a narrow gorge known as the Soldier's Leap after some soldier who was said to have baffled his pursuers by jumping across. His feat was rather devalued by my great-great-grandmother who, when first shown it as a young bride, remarking 'I could jump that,' hitched up her skirt and leapt across; the sort of behaviour to be expected from my elder sister, Gwyn.

Oakbank was cradled in wooded grounds above Oakbank mill which, like Lornty mill, was little bigger than a good-sized barn. Everything, like the road, was slipping peacefully into dereliction. But when I first went there the mill was spinning flax. Just beyond the mill were the mill houses, also gradually decaying. Further up were Ashbank and Lornty mills—still with their machinery but long disused. Everything was damp and rather dark like an old-fashioned engraving illustrating the works of Burns. My cousins owned three small farms, very steep and difficult to cultivate. Cousin John reigned over his little community dressed in black clothes, green and stained, topped off by a bowler hat which descended to my son, John, who wore it together with a corduroy jacket of my father's to visit his brother at Eton. Cousin John made a somewhat out of place, not to say disreputable, figure. At one time there must have been hundreds of small mill owners and farmers like him.

Years later I found Mr. Drever of Broch in Westray, Orkney, living something of the same life. But in spite of his appearance my cousin was a man of character and a stickler for the proprieties as he understood them. During his last illness he retired to bed and locked his bedroom door. His sisters, not unnaturally worried, persuaded the farm grieve to get a ladder and climb into his bedroom. Cousin John sternly ordered him to descend, rose from his death bed, dressed, no doubt, put on his bowler and appeared on the landing to enquire what the fuss was about.

When I inherited the property, piles of documents were crammed into every cupboard and chests of drawers. There were old accounts for flax, bills, bank notes and every kind of letter. My wife did valiant work sorting and tying them up. But many of them disappeared, to my great regret, for although they were no older than the 19th century I now know that they were of considerable interest. My daughter, Grizelda's, garage in South London is the last resting place for many of them. The most interesting were the records of employment at the mills. At Oakbank mill a hundred and fifty years ago some twenty or thirty adults were employed and nearly as many children. The employment of children in factories came to be regarded, rightly, as pernicious. Yet in many ways it must have been no worse to go off with your parents to work than to spend the day alone in a dark and no doubt damp house. I expect the children in these mills at least were not worked very hard. Like the railwaymen at Bowbridge they must have enjoyed a certain amount of larking around. But the terms of employment of the adults were in some cases horrifying. Those who got into debt seem to have been more or less indentured to the mills. However, whatever the conditions of work, and however poor the pay, it was not inhuman. The owners lived by the mill and everyone knew everyone else. By cousin John's time the housing was long out of date but my cousins charged no rent and no one was ever evicted.

The farm too was run in the same old way as ever and tilled by Percheron horses. No specialisation for the Oakbanks. The farmyard was full of hens, the fields were in crop of various kinds. Cows, sheep and pigs munched home-grown cereals. The barns were full of hay, straw and curious implements.

Cousin John's three sisters, Mary, Janie and Maggie, having never married, had lived all their lives in 'Blair'. Very occasionally they visited Dundee or Edinburgh. I remember indeed having lunch once with my cousin John at the old Metropole Hotel in London. He sent back the potatoes as others reject corked claret. Potatoes are savoured like wine in rural Scotland. His sisters dressed as they had always dressed, in long skirts to the ground. Unlike their brother, they were spotless and as neat as new pins. Cousin Maggie wore a tweed outfit, a stiff collar and a stock. Their gloves and shoes came from the most exclusive outfitters. There was gas but no electricity in Oakbank, a lavatory with blue decorated bowl and a wooden surround, little gold chairs in the drawing room and a bath off cousin John's study. Their amusements consisted of short walks, reading, sometimes a friend to tea. On the day of the Braemar Gathering they would go up to the drawing room to see the carriages, or later cars, driving up the road on the other side of the Ericht.

They were strict members of the Free Kirk. The clocks were one hour behind in summer (no tampering with God's time). Nothing could be done on Sundays after church except eat an enormous (and very good) dinner in the middle of the day, followed by a walk. For such walking they wore veils over their hats, gloves and highly polished button shoes or boots: as my mother said, they looked like three mice escaped from a children's tale. One hazard of staying with them as a child was that you might have walked to church in Blairgowrie and found that just as you were resting your weary legs an unnecessary note had been struck on the organ. My cousins would then rise and walk home. It was permissible to give a toot on the organ to signify the tune—but no more. The Oakbanks were the most happy and contented trio I have ever known. The notion that Free Presbyterians are gloomy was untrue in their case. On the contrary, it was visitors from another century who appeared out of tune, worried, unhappy and awkward. Nor, though they were in every way vulnerable, did anyone seem to take advantage of them. Cousin Maggie always gave money to anyone who called to ask for it. Their house was almost impossible to reach by car as the little gravel sweep in front, originally only intended for dog-carts, was over-grown by trees which no one was allowed to cut. In this jungle there lurked tramps and tinkers who came from far and near to collect 2/6d. or 5/-. Cousin Maggie sallied out to meet them at all times of day and dusk. Her tiny figure (they were none of them much over five foot) could be seen lecturing hulking vagabonds for, with the 2/6d, went a short Christian talk often with their huge paws clasped in her hands. No one ever robbed her. Nor did anyone make fun of them. After Cousin Janie had spoken in mildly disparaging terms of an advertisement featuring a girl in shorts the shopkeeper removed it without comment.

The Oakbanks also had the best taste of any family I have known, giving the lie again to the well known myth. Not all Victorians were ostentatious or brash. There was not a single object, piece of furniture, clothing or carpet they possessed that was not delightful. Cousin Janie, as an act of piety, had preserved the still smaller house in which their parents and my great-grandfather had been born. Lornty was like a doll's house. It had diamond-paned windows, deep eaves, a sundial in front and a garden up the hill beside it with a gean tree and semi-wild herbaceous borders. Unfortunately, it was in an even deeper cleft made by the Lornty burn than was Oakbank.

Inside the house everything was gleaming and again in excellent taste. An old woman, Janet, looked after it and Janie and I would walk up there for tea. Outside was a little round counting house, Lornty mill, a tiny lodge and all round the rush of water, for the mill dam (held up by wooden supports which eventually collapsed) was just above it. Janie played the harp and when over seventy learnt Greek. She also wrote a novel (unpublished) and was a frequent correspondent of the *Dundee Advertiser*.

Oakbank and Lornty were full of books, religious books, history books, Victorian novels. Janie was well read in Scots history and poetry. The Oakbanks were profoundly patriotic and there was nothing artificial about their patriotism. They lived in Scotland as they had always lived. They did not feel it necessary to prove their patriotism by exaggerated claims nor by attacking the English, or by indulging in revivalist political practices. No aggressive, drunken or self-laudatory Burns suppers for them. There is a streak of self-assertion and vulgarity in some of the Lowland Scots. But there is also the tradition the Oakbanks represented; among the farms and towns of the Lowlands there is still something like an underground which is declining but which has been good for the country.

Their line is gone. So almost from my life is that of my only other Grimond relations. Aunt Nellie never married. Her sister, my Aunt Amy, had one daughter, Moira, who is my only link with old Dundee days.

4

A T OXFORD I DECIDED that I would be a politician and a Liberal politician at that. I was a Liberal and saw nothing wrong in belonging to a minority. Certainly most politicians want to be Prime Minister. But every politician who feels there is any gravity in the business cannot be out merely for office. It is treating politics with disdain to opt for the party in which you guess promotion will come quickest. Politics are about much else besides being a minister in government. Nor did I, nor do I, concede that to toil as a Liberal is a futile weaving of the sands, an abject acceptance of exclusion, leaving one at best with one's nose pressed against the glass watching the world go by. On the contrary, Keynes and Beveridge were two of the most politically influential men of the last fifty years and both were Liberals to their dying day.

I made my first foray into electioneering in 1935. During the General Election of that year I spent a few days with Arthur Irvine, later Solicitor General in a Labour Government, who was the Liberal candidate for Kincardine and West Aberdeenshire. The constituency lay on either side of the Dee stretching down to the fishing villages south of Aberdeen. Inverurie, with a population of some 5,000 and railway repair workshops, was the largest and most industrialised town. The voters were for the most part dependent on agriculture with fishermen on the coast and a few small industries, such as paper-making. The number of farms and farm servants, though considerable by comparison with most constituencies, was not by itself overwhelming, but the shopkeepers, merchants and transport workers were largely connected with agriculture so that taken with its subsidiaries it was the largest interest. Although farms employed more men and women than they do today, the political weight which agriculture exerted was even then surprising. There was no Labour candidate:

My cousin Janie Grimond of Oakbank.

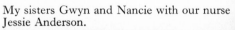

My mother.

My sisters Gwyn and Nancie with our nurse Jessie Anderson.

Cousin John of Oakbank.

My father J. B. Grimond.

My father and I playing golf on the Jubilee Course at St. Andrews.

the division which underlay differences in policy was between the lairds, bigger farmers, merchants and the professional people of the small towns on the one hand and the farm servants, weekly wage earners and some of the smaller farmers on the other. This was the old Tory-Radical division going back to Gladstone. The Trades Unions hardly entered into it. It is sometimes said today that we are ceasing to be one nation. It might seem that Aberdeenshire in 1935 was a much more homogeneous society than it is now. In some ways this was so. The dichotomy between the government and the governed was not as acute. Government in all senses was less ubiquitous. Local authority housing estates were smaller, the currency was stable. But at election times at least the conflict between Tories and Liberals was sharp. It dated from more primitive times when the lairds were a superior race which could be oppressive. They felt it was their natural right to rule. Meetings were relatively large and heckling brisk. Liberals suspected pressure on tenants and farm workers. It was said that farmers would visit the chaumers in the darkness of evening and undo all the good Liberals achieved at their meetings. The chaumers, or bothies as they were called throughout the rest of Scotland, were often large garrets in which the unmarried farm workers slept, the farmer's wife cooking their meals during the day. In point of fact, the main troubles of the Liberal Party were that it suffered in the North East of Scotland as everywhere else from its nation-wide decline and that even in this area where it retained a strong residue of its old following and had not been overtaken by Labour it had become dispirited and lacked new life and ideas.

Arthur Irvine did much to combat the depressing appearance of the party. Arthur was one of the best platform speakers I have ever heard. On or off the platform he was an easily recognizable figure, tall, rather stooping with an aquiline nose and a great capacity for entering into the endless talk and movement of electioneering. I made my first political speech as a warmer-up or supposed warmer-up at meetings under the cliffs of the coast at Johnshaven. It was not very warming. The carefully prepared passages, likening the National Government to an ill disciplined football team were heard with faint comprehension by rows of blue-jerseyed figures sitting immobile on hard benches in halls ill-lit by lamps. I found it difficult to strike much response from men (few women came to these meetings) who no doubt had difficulty in understanding what I said. The cold, the gloom and the gulf, small though it was, between the platform and the hall, all depressed me. My voice rang strangely unreal. I envied Arthur's ability to dominate the hall and to carry it with him. I still do not understand the art of public speaking. Orators with great reputations from Demosthenes to Churchill prepared their speeches with the greatest care but no practice before the mirror in the Palace Hotel in Aberdeen seemed to stand me in much stead when it came to the real meeting. Some speakers, such as Asquith, are said to impress by intellectual mastery, others such as Birkenhead, by scintillating phrases, some by the polish and rotundity of their speeches, others again charm by their very uncertainty. One of the worst orators in technical ability to deliver a script that I ever heard was Governor Stevenson, yet he was admired, even adulated, as a speaker. Speaking, I suppose, is an art which like all arts depends on hard work and an understanding of the material on which it is practised. But again like all art it can take many forms so that there is no pattern for success. For your own sake as a speaker, however, it is essential to have a message which you urgently want to deliver. Response will come if it is a message which the audience wants to hear but the appetite of the audience is not at the speaker's command. It is notorious that who you are and the general impression you create are more important than the message. Elections, in any event, are not won by speeches. Arthur had the better meetings but he was beaten, nevertheless, though not by so very much.

Aberdeen had, and still has, a strong Liberal tradition. Arthur Irvine's agent was Miss Ronald. I hope a place will be kept for her on some shelf of history for she was a woman dedicated without hope of advancement to all the decencies of life which I hold dear. In Aberdeen too in those days I first met Dr. Mary Esslemont. Dr. Mary was a doctor of high reputation. She was also a woman whose interests spanned many subjects and whose vitality was inexhaustible. She appears later in this book as does Tom Adam, one of the first Liberals to preach in and out of season that the only way to heal the rift in industry was partnership between workers and management. He too lived near Aberdeen.

Though my heart was with politics I did not intend to dive in at the deep end at once. I had finished eating dinners at the Middle Temple: the eating of dinners being the vestigial trace of the terms which pupils studying for the bar were expected to observe. The custom was exactly as described. Aspiring barristers turned up at one of the Inns of Court and ate a rather inferior dinner three times a year. The law interested me—up to a point—and seemed a suitable career for an aspiring politician to attempt. So now I spent six months in a solicitor's office at Ludgate Circus, which I enjoyed. The clerks who taught me, in particular Mr. Keys the head clerk, were as sharp and jolly and open-handed as only Cockneys can be. They mostly lived in the Eastern suburbs and seldom went West of the Law Courts. Once or twice a year, however, we would progress up the Strand sampling the beer as far as Trafalgar Square. After the solicitor's office I went into chambers as a pupil of Mr. Alchin, an off-beat barrister of scattered learning who occasionally arrived at the Temple in a caravan. I would have gone to the Scottish bar but I boggled at another three years at a University which this would have entailed— for the Scots insist that you know some law. I was staggered by what I found at the English bar: I did not know how men so able, so humane, so uncorrupt as lawyers could stride on, turning a blind eye to the enormities of their profession. It was, of course, a closed shop. It grew fat on restrictive practices far worse than those of any Union. The first money I earned was by sitting at a Board of Trade enquiry taking a 'noting brief'. No one read my notes. It was a sinecure—and there were others—of 18th-century vintage. No King's Counsel could enter a court without a junior— talk about the plumber's mate. Huge fees were charged and for them the wretched client sometimes did not even get the barrister he had hired. Briefs were won and the judges' lists manipulated by barristers' clerks who earned large salaries sometimes by dubious means and always without qualifications.

I was also brought face to face with crime and punishment. I was briefed as junior counsel to defend a man charged with murder. He was the skipper of a sailing barge plying between London and Ipswich. He worked it with a crew of one, his best, indeed probably his only, friend. After a week of work and danger they were accustomed to go drinking together. After one of these drinking bouts the skipper had shot his friend. Neither he nor anyone else knew why.

The law then closed in on its prey. We pride ourselves on the majesty and impartiality of our Courts. But the majesty of English law meant nothing to the wretched man caught in its toils. As counsel we explained to him the no doubt hallowed but to him incomprehensible working of the law. We coached him in all the palaver of the court, the standing up and sitting down, the 'Yes m'lud' and 'no, m'lud': how the judge all bewigged in grandeur was there to see justice done. All this was as remote from our client as a visit to the moon or an exegesis of Virgil. He was befogged about what he had done, probably he cared little what was to be done to him. I do not know. But I do know that as far as he was concerned the proceedings were an elaborate charade. I do not believe he would ever have repeated the crime. The only scintilla of justification for hanging him was that I could not think what otherwise within the possibilities of the time could have been done with him. To shut him up in prison would have been as cruel as to keep a wild animal in a small cage. His only pleasures were drink and women. The last word was his. He left us smiling, shook our hands and thanked us: behaved as a human being: the law with all its dignity did not.

Later I read *Weir of Hermiston*. The judge did not behave like the centrepiece of Stevenson's story but there was a terrible similarity between that tale and the tragedy at which I had assisted. If anyone is inclined to favour capital punishment they should read the chapter entitled 'Hanging of Duncan Jopp'.

'He kept his head bowed and his hands clutched upon the rail: his hair dropped in his eyes and at times he flung it back; and now he glanced about the audience in a sudden fellness of terror, and now looked in the face of his judge and gulped. There was pinned about his throat a piece of dingy flannel; and this it was that turned the scale in Archie's mind between disgust and pity. The creature stood in a vanishing point, yet a little while and he was a man, and had eyes and apprehension; yet a little longer and with a last sordid piece of pageantry he would cease to be. And here, in the meantime, with a trait of human nature that caught at the beholder's breath, he was tending a sore throat.'

Sentimental no doubt. But the passage struck home to me. Our client was not sordid. But he too was tending those infirmities which beset the human condition. The ultimate crime of the kidnappers, the middle-class thugs, the IRA is that they will compel a return to the death penalty for who can say that bombing and torture deserve pity or respect.

I also went on circuit as a marshal to Mr. Justice Lewis. Mr. Justice Lewis had recently been appointed. He was, surprisingly for someone who had been Junior Counsel to the Treasury or Treasury devil, a nervous as well as a kindly man. The assize opened at Caernarvon with the trial of three Welsh Nationalists who had burnt down an aerodrome which was being built, with some lack of tact, on Owen Glendower's birthplace. The town was packed for the spectacle. No embarrassment was spared the judge. There was an interminable wrangle about whether the proceedings should be conducted in Welsh. Mr. David Lloyd George's brother appeared and had to be ceremoniously greeted. The Defence then began objecting to members of the jury. I was an enthralled but detached spectator of these goings on when the Judge's clerk drew me aside to explain that if the Defence exhausted the supply of spare jurors it was my duty, the only one I had, to 'pray a tales'. I must rush into the street and, like a one-man pressgang, collar sufficient passers-by to make up the tally. I was appalled by a nightmare of myself in tail coat and top hat dodging after Welshmen like a clown trying to catch greasy pigs in a mediaeval fair. He must have been pulling my leg but I took it in no spirit of levity.

However, the danger passed. The trial began. The defendants looked like the mad hatter's tea party in so far as two were unabashed, not to say truculent, while the third, the dormouse between them, was obviously wishing himself far away. One defendant opened his own defence with a long eulogy of Wales starting well before Christ and enlivened by sweeping gesticulations, some of which nearly knocked the dormouse down. Mr. Justice Lewis bore this for some time before suggesting that perhaps we might soon approach the 20th century. To his dismay this appeared to cause a commotion in the jury box. It transpired that one juryman was stone deaf. As in snakes and ladders we had to start again.

I admire many aspects of the English legal system but I doubt if it is the envy of the world and I wish its acolytes would themselves clean up its blemishes. The Scottish system seems less extravagant both in its custom and its fees.

Meanwhile life was blossoming out. I became engaged to my wife, Laura Bonham Carter, on the road South from Dalnawillan near Thurso where we had been staying with the Sinclairs, the family of Sir Archibald, M.P. for Caithness and Sutherland where he owned much property. Dalnawillan was a shooting lodge far into the Caithness moors. I had first seen it and the Sinclairs a year or two before when I was staying alone with Mark Silkington at the next lodge, Glut. We were invited to take part in a hare shoot. My most notable memory of that shoot was of a vast and puffing gentleman heaving into sight over a rise in the ground, trailing his gun behind him through the heather. It was Crinks Johnston, a Chief Whip of the Liberal Party and friend of the Sinclairs and the Bonham Carters. He was not a man given to exercise even of the mildest sort.

Dalnawillan was a good deal more than even the best shooting lodge should be. Sir Archibald Sinclair by day in faded kilt and faded coat, lean, immoderately handsome, issuing orders, driving at a speed which threw the back seat passengers into the air as we plunged along the rocky road, was then Leader of the Liberal Party. By night he would sit low in a tartan chair conducting the conversation with a brandy glass as a baton. Even Violet Bonham Carter and Marigold, Sinclair's wife, no mean talkers, were hushed by his uplifted hand or cry of 'steady the Buffs', while he cross-examined his children or Jasper or me on some point about which he required information. The days at Dalnawillan started reasonably late with Sir Archibald pacing round the dining room eating porridge and thick cream from a wooden bowl. But once started the days were even more vigorous than shooting at Douglas. After bouncing across a singularly insecure swing-bridge we would mount ponies to ride to the rendezvous with dogs and keepers. All day we tramped from point to point after grouse. Lunch with cherry brandy and back well after six to tea from large cups enriched by green dragons: peat water in the lead baths and dinner which began late and finished near midnight or so. Marigold produced the best food I have ever tasted, grouse, lobster, and thick, pungent soups.

A feature of the season was the Dalnawillan games. The Sinclair children were four, Catherine, Elizabeth, Robin and Angus. They were all in different ways wildly good-looking. The other competitors were keepers and ghillies led by the formidable McNicol with a hook on one arm which did not prevent him shooting. Sir Archibald directed the proceedings with the panache of his army days when he was second in command to Winston Churchill in the Scots Fusiliers. However McNicol in fact dominated the events while Marigold made sotto voce remarks praising Robin, who was the apple of her eye, linked in her affections with Ginckel, her abominably spoilt dachshund. Catherine and Elizabeth were deeply in love with the younger ghillies. The guests were expected to toss the caber, run, and be knocked off slippery poles with sacks. Among other entertainments at Dalnawillan were plays in the nursery, written by Angus. Not only did my marriage start from Dalnawillan but it was while staying there that I first saw Orkney which, unknown to Laura and me, was to become our home.

The house which my future parents-in-law leased in the country was called Tilshead. It was on the edge of Salisbury Plain. The Bonham Carter family consisted of Sir Maurice, Lady Violet, two daughters—Cressida, who married Jasper Ridley, and Laura—and two sons, Mark and Raymond. Sir Maurice was one of the few people who was universally known by his nickname 'Bongie'. Bongie had been Mr. Asquith's private secretary. In many ways this job must have suited him admirably. He was intensely loyal, conscientious, unambitious, full of common sense and a painstaking draughtsman. I would see him 'Chinesing', that is, with his face contorted with concentration correcting his wife's writings which, though vivid, tended to run to dashes. As a civil servant, nevertheless, he must have had some minor drawbacks. It is difficult to imagine that he ever acquired that smooth machine-like way of disposing of business which I believe is the hallmark of the true mandarin. Though of the most saintly character he was full of prejudices and indeed of spleeny irritation. He also perhaps encouraged Mr. Asquith in some of his most sensible habits which however were fastened on by his critics. Mr. Asquith, so I have been told, worked extremely fast. Having despatched his work he departed from his office. He and Bongie then took a drive or engaged in some other congenial occupation. What a good example. I have no doubt that it improved their performance. But today and indeed some sixty years ago it was frowned upon. He had no idea of showmanship and once the business in hand was over made no bones about relaxing. Indeed, by the time I knew him he had a propensity for falling asleep. On going up to say goodnight to his younger children he would collapse snoring across their beds while they remained brightly awake. He also had the greatest difficulty in remembering names or indeed words, though he was brilliant at finding surrealist substitutes, as when at the annual meeting of a company of which he was Chairman he addressed the shareholders as 'the charwomen of the company.' After leaving the civil service he had gone into the City where he was a partner in a group including O. T. Falk and Keynes. His City career was erratic. He suffered bad luck culminating in the development of the jet engine. When none of the big financial houses, let alone the Government, would back Whittle, Bongie and some of his associates, including Dudley Williams, later the member for Exeter, put up the money. He should have made a million but in the war the project was taken over by Stafford Cripps at a derisory price—willingly accepted for patriotic reasons by Whittle. The whole incident is a good example of the vital importance of free enterprise in launching new inventions. He also backed television in its infancy and a concoction called atomised food products—a forerunner of Nescafé, etc.

He was the youngest son of a dozen brothers and a sister. They spread over the empire and the armed services—one was the Senior General of the British Army. I remember one of my wife's uncles starting some reminiscence with the throw-away line 'When I was running a small brewery in the Azores'. What set the Bonham Carters alight was a discussion about transport, geography and topography. At the end of a dinner, say, with Aunt Joan, the only sister, a controversy would break out as to how they were to get home. Nowadays the general confabulation would be described as a 'seminar'. Bus routes were rattled off, the virtues of the Underground discussed, some were even for walking, or taxis, though this was considered rather spoil sport.

At week-ends Laura and Cressida would invite their friends to Tilshead. We rode on the plain and talked endlessly, largely under the orchestration of Jasper. Blood sports did not figure much in Tilshead life. Personal relations were constantly discussed as they were at Balliol. Art, politics, gossip flourished. Among the many visitors, both to Tilshead and 40, Gloucester Square, was Desmond MacCarthy, whose 'Portraits' must be among the best collections of biographical essays ever written, talking away the time he should have given to book and theatre reviews. One evening at Tilshead Violet had spurred on Bongie to have a serious talk with me to ensure that their greatly valued daughter would be kept in the condition she deserved. He mumbled to me that he would like to have a word after dinner. Towards the end of dinner it became apparent that he had forgotten my name. As we left the dining room, his face contorted with fearful grimaces, he succeeded in shepherding not only me but Desmond into an empty and indeed little-used white sitting room. Desmond noticed nothing amiss. He regaled us with anecdotes of Dublin—how one of the street cries was 'stinking butter for sarvints.' Bongie eventually fell asleep. On his awakening we then trooped happily off to bed.

Desmond was a Liberal who professed all the liberal ideals including the brotherhood and essential equality before God of all men. But he had his reservations about the heaven to which the Left were actually voyaging. During the war he could not bring himself to join one of the popular front groups, 'Vigilance for Victory', full of admiration for Russia and equality. Laura wrote that he had visited the Bonham Carters after his refusal and confessed rather poignantly 'You see I've at last found my ticket; what I really am is a pluto-democrat. I do so hate this mowing machine that is going to cut all the blades to the same length.'

Bongie had a passion for ironmongers and chandlery—especially rope, twine and string. My wife records a journey with him: 'The moment we got to Carlisle I saw him restlessly scanning the horizon like proud Cortez for a string shop, which he eventually found and entered, Mark (her brother) and I being unable to restrain him, and left laden with skeins of quite unnecessary string and bearing a bow and arrow on the brim of his hat which had become unhooked from the ceiling. He entered a second shop in Wigton on our way to play golf and made further string purchases. I had the greatest difficulty in preventing him from buying a special kind of small hand sickle for cutting turnips with.'

I was on the whole well-received as a son-in-law though Violet always hoped for the best. She was in many ways Edwardian in spite of her achievement in coming to terms with each turn of the modern world. She wanted her family to be brilliant. They were to be immensely clever and beautiful, very well read and at the same time engage in the full round of week-ends and deb dances. She got her way with some modification introduced chiefly by her eldest child, Cressida. Violet shared a good deal of Margot Asquith's liking for worldly success and had a deep interest in people of all sorts and in ideas. She was also intensely loyal and generous-minded. So indeed was Margot. When Margot was told that Laura was engaged to me she remarked, 'Very rich, I hope, with lots of hunters.' When told that I came from Scotland—'Ah, grouse moors then.' She too came to Gloucester Square and I occasionally went to Bedford Square where she lived in some gloom. She frightened me rather. When some mutual acquaintance was mentioned she remarked casually, 'A dear friend but rather careless with her body.' In those days septuagenarian ladies seldom said that sort of thing to young men they had only just met. I remember her always dressed in black, haphazardly hung with a few bits of lace and jewellery and wearing a 'toque'. She held herself erect as any guardsman and her description of her Punch-like face was indeed very true—'I have no face, only two profiles clapped together.' Violet, I suspect, had been greatly influenced by her. Margot complained that the Asquiths 'lacked heart'. She accused them of shunning warmth both emotionally and physically—'skeletons with brains'. She remarked of her sleeping arrangements: 'Henry (Mr. Asquith) likes weight without warmth. I sleep under a Shetland shawl, he would like to sleep naked under a grand piano'. Her life was largely given to bridge which added to her money difficulties. When Bongie remonstrated with her, all she said was 'I hope to leave nothing but debts.'

The Tennant family has been famous for its women, endowing them not only with good looks—for all her Punch-like appearance, Margot was very good-looking—but with a refreshing tartness, like the best bramble and apple pies.

Later Anne Fleming, part Tennant, sometimes invited Laura and me to her houses in Wiltshire and London. Anne always had style, like Margot, though a different style, both older and younger. Sometimes she seems like the Spanish beauties with whom Beckford hob-nobbed in Madrid, natural, impatient, having lived all their lives in a small rich society without being impressed or engulfed. At other times she reminds me of the tunes played on gramophones of the '20s and '30s—'Room with a View', 'Dance, dance, little lady', 'Top Hat', 'Sous les toits de Paris.'

The Tennant of whom I have seen most is Margot's half-sister, K. Elliot. The Tennant blood must course with exceptional energy. Whether directing large parties of children at her home in the Borders or dealing with the House of Lords, local councils, good causes of all sorts, K. is indefatigable. I sometimes think that she should have been harnessed to some great enterprise—the Tennant chemical works perhaps—but on the whole it is better that she should spread her vitality and cast her generosity on a number of people and causes. So long as women like Violet, Margot, K, Cressida, Laura and Dr. Mary Esslemont exist it is difficult to see how dictatorship can take over the country. Women are a better bulwark against Fascism or Communism than men. And if, as is said, the family is returning to fashion, it is women like K. who keep families together.

Sir Henry Campbell-Bannerman called Mr. Asquith a 'sledge hammer' in debate. Campbell-Bannerman was exact and shrewd. I have no doubt that when he used this vivid phrase he meant it and that the cap fitted. Yet I did not detect anything hammer-like in his children. Violet, the most combative, was a rapier not a bludgeon in argument. Mr. Asquith has also been depicted as calm, almost nerveless. None of his children that I knew struck me as that.

73

But in his Bonham Carter grandchildren, my wife and her brothers, there is a streak of true Asquithian colour; or perhaps it is Carter colour. Their civic virtues may have come from those Empire builders, the Bonham Carters. Violet was so rivetted (like Megan Lloyd George) to the memory of her father that newcomers, such as I, might be forgiven for assuming at first that her children, on whom she justly doted, owed all their fine points to the Asquiths. Certainly they all had the mental sinew so evident in their grandfather. Unlike the Grimonds they were an intellectual family. In the days when books were more of a bond than they are now, they were, or were assumed by their friends to be, widely read. But they were certainly not cold, whatever Margot may have thought about her husband. Some have professed to finding in them a certain acerbity—but that is quite a different quality and indeed not predominant. The sharpest of them are easily melted by affection.

However, I must not go on in this vein. Nothing is more exasperating than being lumped together with your brothers and sisters dearly as one may love them. Nothing could be more misleading than to lump the Bonham Carters together. They were coins which each rang a different note. Raymond had he lived in the last century would have been the guardian into whose care each dying father would have wished to commit his widow and children. To Mark the widow would have turned for instant and particular support in predicaments where she was not sure of her ground when, for instance, her daughter had been not too unwillingly seduced. The Carters have what Winston Churchill called 'the canine virtues' one of which is loyalty to friends, particularly in foul weather.

For a family of such capabilities they were engagingly disorganised. But their foibles dove-tailed into one another. Violet nested among a litter of newspapers, periodicals and letters which her husband, though incapable of remembering his son-in-law's name, could marshal into reasonable order. Laura was addicted to unpunctuality as others are to drink. It pained her to be early. Once when we were abominably late for some engagement she demanded to know why I had not told her the time. When I defended myself by pointing out that I had—twice—all she replied was 'I know, but I didn't believe you.' She was also incapable of getting up. This she has passed on to our sons. When staying with friends in Washington I was complimented on the energy of Johnny, who they assumed had gone off sight-seeing before breakfast. At five o'clock that evening I found him still in bed. Cressida, on the other hand, was reasonably punctual but had a disarming way of knocking things over, thereby putting nervous young men at their ease. It is strange how human beings react with inanimate objects. In Laura's hand any pen or pencil flowed into the most readable writing; Cressida on the other hand appeared to have an endless supply of crossed nibs. Having known her, I am not in the least surprised to read that Mr. Uri Geller can bend tea spoons by looking at them.

Though sociable, Cressida was as allergic as I was to forcible enjoyment. While I was in America the coronation of George VI broke out provoking her to write: 'My state at the moment is faintly irritated—when this letter reaches you all this will be over and my normal vegetable placidity will have returned [this is a peculiarly unapt trope—anyone less placid or less vegetable than Cressida would be difficult to imagine]. London is a rash of Union Jacks, streamers, banners, pennants, etc. They have erected enormous stands in the park, royal blue and royal red with a streak of dark imperial yellow down the middle which are of a hideosity that one would have thought impossible to conceive or execute. Selfridge's façade is completely hidden under enormous plaques of appliqué statuary. Papier mâché painted gold representing the Dominions (in full relief) and papier mâché painted silver (in half relief) representing scenes from our history. These are rather puckishly chosen from before the Conquest, Boadicea, Caractacus and King Arthur with a swift and startling modulation through Magna Carta to the taking of Quebec. I long passionately to leave London but a tentative suggestion that I should abstain from watching the procession was greeted with such shocked horror and reproach that I daren't press the point further.' The filial understanding the Carters showed to their parents is proof in itself of their excellent characters. Cressida even participated in 'the Season'.

Before the war 'the season' occupied one summer of a considerable number of upper class girls and boys. They participated with some groans but also with some pleasure. Whatever their feelings, it was in those days considered necessary to humour one's mother. Further, social life which included Catherine and Elizabeth Sinclair, the Brett daughters, Juliet Henley who married Stuart Daniel, a friend of mine at Oxford, Nancy Jones and various other girls, was highly enjoyable. The orthodox entertainment of the time did not prevent Jinny Brett going off to a life of contemplation and rhythmic dancing to Switzerland. Nor did it in the lease inhibit critical astringency in her sisters, Nancy and Pinkie. Highly attractive girls did not need to be 'brought out'. Dances, a few of which they would have appreciated, when repeated night after night must have been a bore for them. Without all the dressing up young men would have sought them out, or indeed they could well find the young men they wanted. But looking round now I can see several males whose lives would have been much improved if in youth they had been forced to dress up occasionally, make polite conversation and dance.

MY OWN CHILDREN have been spared the Season. They have all liked social life, perhaps Andrew would have gained something from more compulsory enjoyment but I doubt it. All my life I have looked forward to the time when, whatever I had to do in the line of duty, I would be excused the obligations of compulsory pleasure. The time has never come. What I think my children have possibly missed is the society of their contemporaries' parents, but then possibly not. Despite certain tensions which were apt to arise, for instance, when Jasper Ridley would carry his gun at what is known in army circles as the trail, when shooting with Sir Lawrence Jones, I look back in gratitude to my friends' parents. I have written of Tilshead and Dalnawillan, of Bonham Carters and Homes and Sinclairs. There were also Bretts. Lionel's father, Lord Esher, was worth a guinea a minute. He landed on his feet in all company and any circumstances, Royal Courts, men-in-the-street, country neighbours, intellectuals, bureaucracies, all fell before him. And he was the best of company, particularly when talking about the characters of his children. 'Now take Lionel' conversation would start and we would all take Lionel for some time.

His wife Pom, or Christian as she was properly called, would conjure up rosy visions of his future for she was the most romantic of my contemporaries, a trait well suited to her Venetian looks. The daughter of Olive Snell, the artist, she was always a beautiful woman rather than girl and even in her teens had poise as well as glow. The Brett daughters, too, had poise and beauty but from a cooler palette. Nancy would roll her liquid eyes at Pom's flights of fancy and Pinkie, the youngest, quizzically regarding her sister-in-law plant some well sharpened dart in the general conversation.

Entertainments of all sorts were provided at the Bretts' home. Shooting at Watlington was very different from Dalnawillan or Douglas or indeed from later days with Pat Scott in Orkney. At about 11.00 a.m. small bags of cartridges would be distributed to the guests. We then surrounded a rhododendron bush outside the front door. Out of it scurried a few rabbits. After beating a few more bushes we retired suitably exercised.

Another girl of my youth, now resplendent in the Provost's House at Eton, was Gay Margesson. If Christian Brett was a Venetian, Gay one would have thought must be the original of 'Le bar au Folies Bergères'. The Margessons had a house in the Midlands where their mother underwent instruction in philosophy and from which the family hunted. Week-end guests, however, were not compelled to take part in either activity. Gay married Martin Charteris who, like his brother David, Lord Wemyss, was also a friend and indeed they were remote relations by marriage of my wife. Martin has now succeeded James as Provost: an imaginative appointment which I hope Eton appreciates.

Country house life has almost flickered out but I hope that for generations to come something will take its place.

The Jones' home, Cranmer in Norfolk, has been described in that masterpiece, Sir Lawrence Jones's autobiography. It would be a mistake to add to it. I am one of the many of several generations to whom his book *Georgian Afternoon* brings back the voices and sights and smells of a week-end at Cranmer and golf at Brancaster.

Everyone hopes that the best things they remember will be more widely spread. As we grow richer I would have liked more and more people to enjoy the comforts and pleasures that I experienced. It does not happen like that. In spreading wealth or education or entertainment we alter their nature. As science multiplies new possibilities she relegates old pleasures to oblivion. The old warts never vanish without taking the good features of old faces with them.

Let me give some examples of what I mean. One of the blessings which the Almighty has showered upon us is the invention of the motor car before we were all embraced in the grip of state bureaucracy. Had its advent been delayed fifty years we can see from contemplating the history of the aeroplane what would have happened. No individual would have been allowed to own a car. The National Automobile Promotion and Provision Institute would have owned all vehicles. They would have been of vast size, hopelessly uneconomic and run at a huge loss. Most of their passengers would have been civil servants and expense account travellers. The whole operation would have been kept going out of taxes for the benefit of its staff. Luckily we have escaped that. But instead of cars getting cheaper, simpler and more economical to run, as Mr. Ford hoped, they have become more expensive and filled with more and more gadgets which I personally do not want. Further, the motorist is destroying the very thing he loves—the proliferation of cars takes the pleasure out of motoring.

Or take boarding school education or the 'Season'. To go to a boarding school for a year or two might do many people good. To have a year between either school and further education or further education and their life's work would certainly do people good. But you still either have to spend five years at a boarding school or not go at all.

However, this is a side-turning down which I have been seduced. I was writing of the pleasures of staying with friends: there were also the pleasures of travel. I was getting to know the diversity of the English landscape. The green Thames creeping round the punts at Bablock Hythe. Wittenham Clumps like a crown against the pulsating sky of Summer. I relished it afresh when returning from abroad. In 1938 I went to America with Hugh Sharp, the son of my father's friend Fred. We travelled all over but our destination was San Antonio where the Alliance Trust Company of Dundee still owned large numbers of acres and cattle. Texas is a land of long sights, of earth thinly covered and often baked. When I came home England seemed a jungle. Dense hedgerows starred with flowers, intertwined so closely that the course of no stem could be followed, no light pierced the fragrant obscurity of the West Country banks. English roads were indeed tunnels of green gloom quilted with paler patches sometimes pierced by radiant shoots from the sun. No country in the world has so many greens as England up to the middle of June. In no countryside do the smells change so often from the heavy damp of earth after rain to the thin trails of flower scents in the wind. Yet just above these jungles and sunken lanes Salisbury Plain stretched like Texas rolling up and down, scarred sometimes by the white chalk outcrops. After my oral examination at Oxford I drove through the Summer evening from Oxford to the Ridleys' home, Mockbeggars in Suffolk where Cressida was staying with Jasper. 'The light in lances' lay on the village greens. Men and girls sat outside the village pubs against the background of dark chestnuts, like scenes from Watteau in rustic dress. Roads curved and dipped, white wash and thatch gave way to brick and tiles, all surrounded by luxuriant carefully tended gardens growing bluer and dimmer in the twilight. It seemed like a return to Keats's England, the moss rose and the pastoral eglantine.

My voyage to San Antonio and Suffolk both ended enjoyably. The Alliance Trust were engaged in litigation in Texas. The parties chose and, as far as I remember, paid the judge. The one we chose had brought back some English foxhounds after the First World War. His court, therefore, did not meet until midday as hunting could only be pursued in the early morning before the sun got too hot. The Alliance Trust had been represented in Texas for at least fifty years by the Drought family. The Dundee connection with America went back to the Civil War when the jute merchants sold sacking to both sides. Old Mrs. Drought told us that she could not get married until a director of the Trust came over to give his approval. He arrived off the coach with top hat, morning coat and umbrella exactly as he had left Dundee. She was a Southern lady with a drawl like a lullaby. 'I was a married wo-oman,' she told me, 'before I knew damnèd Yankee was two words.' In the evenings Miss Drought and I hired a small band as was the custom and toured the Spanish town of San Antonio.

As for Suffolk, with Wiltshire and Northumberland it is one of my favourite English counties. It was with the Ridleys that I first saw it.

The Ridleys are in origin a North Country family. Sir Jasper, my friend Jasper's father, played up the bluff, no-nonsense Northumbrian side to his nature. When his daughter-in-law proposed to call her son Adam he remonstrated against such a fanciful name, oblivious apparently to the fact that he and his son were called Jasper. In politics he was an irascible Conservative and if many of his opinions were conventional, too conventional perhaps for his son, he was a man of wide interests and young Jasper for all his originality was far from contemptuous of the life his parents led. Indeed, that life had much to recommend it. His father bought the paintings of Paul Nash, William Nicholson, Henry Moore and their contemporaries, was a friend of Belloc and Maurice Baring and was a lavish and genial host to all sorts of people. Though putting on the airs of plain down-to-earth John Bull as he stumped about the house he would every now and then burst into laughter at himself, pretending a non-comprehension of the young which was only partly sincere.

Jasper's mother was a Russian, the daughter of the last Czarist Ambassador to Britain. Superficially at least she was the opposite of her husband, where he was broad, high coloured and bald, she was thin with a complexion of ivory, a face which had it not been so expressive might have been the model for an ikon, with grey hair tightly swept from the forehead. My picture of her is seated at the end of their refectory-like dining room table eating jam with a spoon and cackling away at her own jokes. The Benckendorffs all have fascination and she perhaps most of all.

Cressida was not only the appointed wife for Jasper but a God-sent daughter-in-law for the Ridleys. Having notable originality mingled with the squirarchical temper of the Bonham Carters she appealed to both sides of the Ridley household. No wonder that her son has proved one of the abler members of his generation.

Years later in the House of Commons I got to know another Ridley, Nicholas, the son of Sir Jasper's brother and grand-son of Lutyens, who displays all the talents of that remarkable family. He has so far proved rather too strong a dish for the Conservative Party to swallow whole but his élan is most welcome in a House of Commons plentifully supplied with bores and he is a painter with an eye of his own.

As I regard Jasper Ridley and Con as two of the most notable of my contemporaries and find it difficult to conjure up their quality by mere description I shall again quote from some of their letters.

I wonder what my mother, who was very fond of the younger Jasper and indeed of the older Jasper in so far as she knew him, made of this letter from the younger:

'Dear Mrs. Grimond,

I am surprised, I must confess, by the badness of my manners, a surprise which is shared I hope by you and Mr. Ridley (i.e. his father). I keep on staying in your house and never a word of thanks. All I leave is a few belongings which you have the kindness (quite undeserved by me) to send on to so remote and inaccessible place as Caithness.

But even if gratitude increased at compound interest, fructifying in the rich mould of putrefying idleness I would not be thanking you enough, so let me turn a rapid corner (holding tight to my hat) and thank you simply (but, as they say and I mean, sincerely) for having me to stay in your house in a way so enjoyable and convenient for me but so haphazard and tiresome for you.

I felt a little embarrassed during your remarks on the social aspect of the crossword for I can only remember having supplied one word myself. Still, God bless me, I had the goodwill.'

Another letter from Jasper to me deals with a week-end at Lord Esher's house at Watlington. 'Nancy Brett is reported to have said that one of the reasons why you were so delightful was that you were so respectable . . . your physical strength I may say (what did you do?) made a very notable impression. . . .' Respectable I was; my physical strength has never been remarkable.

Jasper had also a more salacious side: he would have revelled in *Private Eye*.

As well as visiting them at home during these years I went to the continent several times with Con and Jasper and also with Tony Woozley, now a Professor of Philosophy in America. I was indeed motoring in Germany with Con on the 'night of the long knives'. We also all corresponded. My letters I fear from the replies were didactic. I early aspired to be the Polonius of my generation. Tony Woozley, as befitted someone who was to become an eminent philosopher sent patient answers. He and Con won Fellowships of All Souls in the same summer as we travelled.

Tony also became a Fellow of the Queen's College. It was not all port and talk. 'And now I'm so tired I must go to bed' one of his letters reads. 'The first day of term is always harrowing enough, fitting tutorials in like pieces of a jig-saw puzzle and today I have had a double dose because Franks (Lord Franks) retired to bed with jaundice which enables him to be perfectly still, feeling perfectly well and experiencing genuinely yellow sense data.' Con after nibbling at the Bar went into the Foreign Office. In due course I hope we shall have his collected correspondence in five volumes. From the Pension Piot in Paris where he was learning French Con wrote at the time of Italy's invasion of Ethiopia (he had heard that I had attended a Hunt Ball):

'I am pleased that you are keeping so much in the public eye. Here I scarcely fill my own. I am impressed with the triviality of my occupations and of their possibly successful conclusion. The futility of diplomacy is not to be hidden in the darkness of French obscurantism and no amount of demarches, negotiations and position treaties seem able to persuade this beastly nation that it ought to lift a finger for any purpose but to scratch Germany. As far as I can see, no one but rather extreme Socialists even doubts the justice of Italy's cause and I think if the government tried to take or even support any further action against the Italians the fascist leagues whose dissolution appears not to be going to be attempted would be 'dans la rue'. I notice I am writing letters like Frank Prince [a contemporary at Balliol and oddly enough a bird of passage like Edwin and Willa Muir through St Andrews whose poetry was, and is, greatly admired by Con and me]. Have you?'

'I have been here some three weeks, tomes of law, history and economics lie virgin on the shelves while I write daily French proses and essays which are a bore and whose benefit I don't yet see. The policy of my "Professor" is to wear down by constant attrition my tendencies to error but they are vigorous, numerous and continually re-inforced. My "professor" is very old, very slow, very charming and has coaxed innumerable persons into the Foreign Office. He has been teaching Englishmen, I suppose, for 25 years but speaks no English and reads it with an accent that is unbelievable. . . . My powers of speaking French vary from day to day, flag when confronted by the natives; but become excessively fluent, rapid, expansive, patronizing and confident when I subject them to a Japanese.'

I can vouch for the truth of this last paragraph. Con and Jasper were perfectionists, unable to utter in any foreign tongue before a native in case they made a mistake in gender. We were often saved from starvation in cafés by my brash disregard of ridicule. As for Con's dislike of the

French this was paralleled by his occasional distaste for most races in bulk though devoted to individual foreigners. I have a letter of three paragraphs, one of which reads: 'I think I hate the English more than the Germans and will eventually settle down in Dublin'. Even without jaundice he was liable to yellow sense data—though never too seriously, and never about his friends. The only time we visited Eire together (when at a farm where we stopped we were greeted in answer to our question 'Are you Mr. Black?' with the answer 'No, I'm his brother') I do not remember that his devotion to the Southern Irish was conspicuous. But I sometimes wonder whether if he had settled in Dublin—which he would no doubt have left—we might not now have another Joyce or Beckett. His letters carried a good deal of astringent comment, astringently meant. One tells me that someone had written a poem about me. 'But I thought you should know you have been immortalized in language which I for one thought undiscriminatory and excessive.'

My friends and myself, though not Conservatives, had a considerable admiration in home affairs for Mr. Baldwin. He not only shone when compared with the Press barons yapping at his heels; from afar at any rate he gave a feeling of reassurance—and indeed of strength (perhaps we were wrong but that is how many of us saw him). This may seem strange as he has been portrayed as a lazy old bumbler. His handling of Parliament, the Trades Unions, India, all seemed consistent and perceptive. The man who had given a fortune to reduce the national debt and who had come through the general strike, bearing ill-will to no one, had attributes lacking today in many who on occasion take a high moral line. Baldwin appeared to believe that politics was about something more than office. He seemed to aim at the national good not merely partisan success. He practised what he preached. All this appealed to us. I still think rightly so.

The heart-searchings of liberals in all parties on war have been well explained by Michael Howard in his book *War and the liberal conscience*.* We certainly felt the dilemma ourselves. As Howard says, 'Collective security . . . (was) widely regarded as a new ordering of international society . . . a serious and practicable alternative to the bad old ways of arms races and the balance of power.' Yet we were uneasy about collective security and the League of Nations. Even to us in the sweet ignorance of youth they seemed shaky bulwarks against the onset of more violent enemies. We had been taught to blame the Treaty of Versailles for most of the troubles of Europe. But fifteen years had passed since it was signed, surely it could not bear the responsibility for the growth of militarism which we saw from Japan to Germany? It rather looked as though some

*Temple Smith 1978.

82

arms were necessary, though we hoped still for general disarmament. The motion carried at the Oxford Union that 'This House refuses to fight for King and Country' was aimed not necessarily against patriotism but against it as an excuse supporting selfish nationalist purposes. It was not a pacifist vote but a vote for a wider loyalty to collective security and the League of Nations. As for the Fulham by-election the victor, Wilmot, was afterwards the Minister who in charge of the Ministry of Supply was responsible for the production of arms.

One week-end Laura and I were taken by her mother to stay at a rather grand party such as were common before the war when butlers and housemaids abounded. It sticks in my memory because Winston Churchill was among the guests. He spent much time upstairs dictating one of his many books: pacing up and down, I somehow imagine, in a bath towel. Downstairs, when the conversation turned to him, it was hardly prophetic. His brilliance was admitted but his faults were considered to make him unserviceable for any further office. He was then the Churchill of Die-hardism in India and of a quixotic but, in the common view, indefensible loyalty to Edward VIII. He was, in Conservative eyes, from a day which was done; he was unreliable and too fond of drink. I only remember one remark which he addressed to me: he demanded to know whether I was in favour of 'collective security'. Like Wellington and De Gaulle he wasted no time on small talk if he had other things on his mind. Years later Violet occasionally took me to lunch with him. On one of these occasions I ventured to say I was against capital punishment. 'What', he retorted, 'would you condemn young men and women to untold lustrums in the Dungeons of Pentonville?' I wonder if he always thought in the language of *The World Crisis*.

Nowadays, people deride pre-war politics. They are remembered by the slump, followed by appeasement. The National Government has been painted as a coterie of frightened and stupid men who failed to perceive the dangers of their time or to understand the means by which they could be met. This may have been true of their foreign policy; it was not a fair judgement on all their home policies. But what is grossly hypocritical is for the Left to make this judgement.

Neville Chamberlain fitted the Left Wing caricature of capitalists as warmongers even worse than Baldwin. He and his fellow Birmingham businessmen fully justified the 19th century view that free trade and a free market were the alternative to war. They were deeply opposed to violence. Their most virulent opponents, the Marxists and the Left Wing Socialists, were the people who contemplated bloodshed with complacency, if not relish. But in the face of Fascist threats Chamberlain seemed both arrogant and blind.

83

The Spanish Civil War was a catalyst for our opinions. It had an effect upon the young, not to be repeated until Vietnam. In that war where democracy and legality as well as Socialism were on the side of the Spanish Government, sympathy for the Republicans was felt by all liberals from Eden to the Labour Party. However, the difference between pre-war and post-war Left was obvious. Some enthusiasts for the Republic, even if they were only a minority, went to fight. They backed their opinions with their lives. As far as I know, few, if any, Americans and no British Socialists joined the North Vietnamese. Orwell now is the hero and prophet of the Spanish War. He is the participant who dealt honestly with the behaviour of the Communists. His *Homage to Catalonia* should have for all time taught us the rapacity of modern communism in international affairs, just as the successive terrors in Russia illustrated its methods of national government. How well Orwell stands comparison with later apologists for the USSR. How well indeed he stands comparison with those intellectuals who having fulminated against fascism fled to America or other neutral countries when war against it was declared—'Gone with the wind up' as was remarked at the time.

As the thirties advanced so did the hardening against appeasement. The Labour Party continued to combine calls for resistance to the dictators with obstruction of steps to rearm. Their attitude was not as dishonest as it may seem. They were entitled to demand that the Government must make it clear how they would use arms before they were encouraged to acquire them. Yet there was an element of hypocrisy, or at least timidity in their attitude. They wanted to pose as the defenders of democracy while retaining the vote of their pacifist supporters. Their best known pamphleteers were careful not to offend their capitalist employers. The same attitude could be found in the Liberal Party though by 1938 they had swung over to whole-hearted support of rearmament.

As for the unemployed, they too engaged not only our political sympathy but attempts at practical help. Undergraduates provided food for the hunger marchers. I made a small attempt with the aid of a Dundee clergyman to carry the fish landed at Pittenweem, which could not find a market, to the kitchens of the unemployed in Dundee, too poor to pay the full price. Compared with the present numbers there were fewer unemployed in the thirties. Socialists now seem remarkably complacent about unemployment. I do not entirely blame them for keeping so quiet when a Labour administration presides over the horrifying figures of today because neither they nor any other Party has an immediate remedy —and they indeed lack any long-term policy. But if a Tory government were in office today, as it was in the thirties, the clamour would have been orchestrated with every kind of abuse.

After I came down from Oxford I found much political discussion in my mother-in-law's house. She was ardently anti-appeasement, anti-Chamberlain and much engaged in work with those who thought like her, from Eden to Stafford Cripps. Pre-war politics were certainly not dull. They were about great and deeply-felt issues. Neither at Oxford nor later in London did politics mean only psephology, speculation on which party would win elections or examination of voting patterns. Dons like Cole and Laski (for whom I did some work) the two most influential teachers, were neither engaged in esoteric research nor in either joining the bureaucracy themselves or in creating groups to press particular expenditure on the Government. They were vigorously committed to formulating political theory and propogating ideologies. Men such as Richard Law were galvanized by the issues. I was a pupil in the Chambers of which Quintin Hogg was a member when he won the Oxford by-election. It was fought with fervour both by his pro-Munich supporters and the anti-Munich coalition behind Lindsay. Late one evening Desmond MacCarthy arrived in my mother-in-law's house from a meeting of the Other Club (a dining club founded by Birkenhead and Churchill) at which blows had been exchanged. In those days the rancour and asperity of political debate which the rules of the Club (drawn up by Lord Birkenhead) enjoined on its members were a reality: something they have never been during the time I have been a member. These great issues were intoxicating to Violet. She was embarking on a new political career. Now that her family were either at boarding school or grown up she was free in a way she had not been since the '20s when Winston wrote about her exploits at the Paisley by-election which her father won 'It must have been the greatest of human joys for Henry Asquith in his dusk—this wonderful being he had called into this world, armed, vigilant and active at his side'.

When not hurrying round to see Laura at 40, Gloucester Square, I lived, except for a short time when I shared a flat with Con O'Neill, with William Douglas-Home in lodgings kept by Mr. and Mrs. Crisp in South Eaton Place. Mr. Crisp was a Jeeves-like figure who had been Lord Durham's butler. Owing to this previous career I was able to attend King George V's funeral in the late Lord Durham's frock coat and made, I like to think, rather a striking figure. Mrs. Crisp was an admirable cook. And William indeed was an admirable companion. I have always liked people who are interested in themselves. William was much interested in his health. This involved giving an opinion on how he looked and occasionally gazing down his throat. He was then at the Royal Academy of Dramatic Art. He was also beginning his long series of plays in which most of the characters were drawn from his family. They were produced, if produced at all, at inconvenient theatres like the Q Theatre at Kew. I learnt quite a lot about the suburbs. He also had a series of girls of whom he was inclined to tire rather rapidly.

Another friend, a blaze of vitality and cheerfulness, who had a series of girl friends, was Hugh Boileau. He was in the Chambers where I was a pupil and, for a brief time, until the war broke them up, a member. There are people who, if I could call them back permanently from the dead, I would be bound to summon before Hugh. But I would very much like to see Hugh again. His appearance through any door, pushing his spectacles up his nose and demanding advice, was always welcome. He was doing well at the Bar, largely because everyone was always glad to see him. He had the courage and common sense which are often much more use in court than intellectual brilliance. One of the first conversations I over-heard in Chambers was our grumpy clerk telling Hugh that solicitors in Norwich wanted to consult with him before a case which was coming up at 10.30 on a Monday morning. He must therefore, the clerk said, go to Norwich on Sunday evening. 'Can't do that' Hugh replied, 'you know I always court on Sundays.' 'Couldn't you court on Saturday?' suggested the clerk. 'No', said Hugh, 'Hunt on Saturdays, court on Sundays.' His courting never ran smooth.

One girl he took hunting; when she fell off he jumped over her and continued at full gallop. He pursued one at some inconvenience on a Sunday to the Midlands, only to be entrapped by her uncle into driving him round the countryside while he shot rabbits out of the back of the car. However, he had great success with 'Bola—my panther woman'. We were never allowed to meet Bola, in fact I sometimes wonder if she existed. If she did she presumably spent her life on a bear skin wrapped in a leopard toga, flashing her eyes and tossing a great mane of yellow hair. She would hardly have been in place in our chambers in the Temple. Hugh's dress, and indeed his life, were, when away from the Temple, harum scarum. He is said to have lost Barbara Yeatman-Biggs, who would have been a notable prize as a wife, because of his abominable turn-out while paying his respects to her parents. However, she got Frank Sykes instead, an old friend of ours, than whom no one could be a better husband. So no harm was done even if the story is true which it probably is not. I can hardly credit such stories about him. After five minutes everyone fed out of his hand. When my mother had recovered from a passing frown at his arrival to stay at St Andrews in sand-shoes, she doted on him and so did Violet who pronounced his name as in French—as she pronounced 'hôtel'. One of the nice traits of my mother-in-law was that she was always discovering new aspects of life, such as policemen and people like Hugh who had no pretensions to intellectual ability but in whom she found depths of delight which she believed no one had plumbed but herself. In spite or probably because of her sophistication she was curiously innocent, a trait she shared with my mother. I listened one day to a cross-purpose conversation between Winston and her: Winston was treading not too delicately on some affair of a mutual friend, which he thought had been too blatantly conducted. 'I was brought up never to do it in the office' he mumbled, looking at me slyly. I could see Violet had no notion what he was talking about.

My happiest days at the Bar were spent motoring round the North half of the South Eastern circuit with Hugh in his open Daimler which he was always willing to let one drive. To stay at Bury or King's Lynn was delightful; better still, driving on summer evenings through the wide Norfolk and Suffolk landscape, moths flitting in and out of the headlights' beam and the now departed elms crowding over the roadway.

Meanwhile Munich came and went, leaving a smoke-trail of dread behind it. I remember Alec Home telling how he had been shut out of the lift taking Chamberlain and Mussolini up to see Hitler at one of the meetings so he had run up the staircase which spiralled round the lift and at the first floor Mussolini's large bald head with a boil on top had slowly risen past him. I was staying at the Travellers' Club as Laura was in the North, and I looked with apprehension at the entrenchments in St James's Park. But Con was in Berlin, gnashing his teeth against the Nazis and British policy.

'I sit here listening to the wireless and as the voice of the BBC announcer sinks, overwhelmed by the menacing barbaric squeals and thumps of the bugles and drums of Nuremburg into a gradually more total inaudibility, I turn the knob and find in swing music from the States or Scandinavia a blessed token of civilisation.

'Goering made a speech today the juciest parts of which I shall not be able to read in the German press. But the BBC tells me he called the Czechs ridiculous dwarfs and someone who heard him on the wireless tells me he said Germany was prepared for 30 years of war. If that is so, why all this hurry to begin? Let me give you an extract from a third source, a Berlin evening paper. This quotes him as saying (I think my translation is correct) "The Germans have always been shooters, but never shits." There seems to me something wrong with the proposition.'

Almost exactly a month after he wrote this letter Con resigned from the Foreign Office. 'After Munich I was so disgusted with the attitude and arguments of most of my Embassy colleagues and particularly with the behaviour of our notorious Ambassador that I wrote to the F.O. on October 3rd asking for leave to resign the service.' I congratulated him and urged him to campaign vigorously after resignation. This, perhaps wisely, he refused to do. In spite of being asked to reconsider his decision

87

he stuck to his resolve—made the more difficult by being forced to stay on for three months. As he said—'It is harder, if you will permit me a gruesome image, to drown oneself in cold blood.'

In retrospect Con's resignation seems even more creditable than it did at the time. Modern bureaucrats seldom, if ever, resign on principle. Indeed, I wonder what would make any of them do so? Con and my contemporaries who fought in Spain had views which governed their behaviour. Their attitude is largely a thing of the past. Indeed not only do bureaucrats in and out of the Civil Service show a lack of principle—they have no scruple in practising the very opposite from what they preach.

When I was at Oxford I made a short tour with David Astor and Adam von Trott. Adam von Trott was a young German Rhodes Scholar who epitomised the dilemma of his compatriots. David was convinced that Britain must guide more of her better brains into industry: he himself worked for a time in Mavor and Coulson, makers of mining machinery. Adam wanted to see something of the industrial North. I may say that his enthusiasm for sharing the life of the English working class quickly wilted. After a luxurious night at Cliveden he announced that we must spend the next night in a lodging house settling however for the Birmingham Station Hotel. On reaching Manchester he wished to call on Mr. Vinogradoff, then the foreign editor of the *Manchester Guardian*. As he was by then suffering from a painful boil, my first experience of the lift at the Cross Street building of the *Manchester Guardian* was poor Adam in agony as the usual horde of passengers bumped into him.

In a letter written to me from China in 1937 which he was investigating by river boat, Adam wrote 'we seem to turn mad or mediocre in Europe nowadays. It is an awful mess and looks very bad from out here. We nice, post-war people were brought up to believe that the right things always win and that therefore it was only a matter of discovering and stating the right things—if we weren't even convinced that there could be anything but perfect rightness in the society we happened to be living in. So we thought that Europe was right to consider itself an entity of culture and interest and forgot to bring this about and now that the explosives have accumulated again we turn amoc or defeatist. The present show disquiets and in that sense I am probably the typical post-war product does not stir me to action. The present current has to be substantially modified— which at present I feel in no position to do—or destroy the whole fabric of European life after which destruction there may be room again for rational effort. I refuse to be just a passive part of that general drift—and both the amoc runners and the defeatists are.'

Indeed Adam was no 'passive part'. He died, by hanging, for his courage in anti-Nazi conspiracies. His dilemma was one his British friends never had to face. He was a German, and for all his wanderings, could never be anyone else. How then was he to behave when the government of his country violated all his beliefs? Count Benckendorff and countless other Europeans have found themselves in a similar predicament. Years later De Gaulle in Westminster Hall, speaking to British Parliamentarians, pointed out that no one had for hundreds of years questioned the legitimacy of the British State. Most of the audience, I suspect, did not grasp what he was talking about. But within the last fifty years the legitimacy of many European states has indeed been questioned and German, Russian, Italian, French and Spanish patriots have had to make up their minds whether or not they owed loyalty to their countries when under Hitler, Stalin, Mussolini, Pétain and Franco.

Adam was restless, he was insatiably curious about people, philosophies and countries. This was what made him so attractive—and so misunderstood. Coming from a deep-rooted and conservative German family he could examine dangerous thoughts and strange countries from the solid ground of someone who was not frightened, though often worried and depressed. He carried the ballast of old German liberal traditions which kept him on some sort of an even keel in the stormy waters he tried to navigate, even so he was driven into some queer channels. One can see why, 'My superiors, with intense and uncomfortable disapproval view me as a die-hard reactionary with some rather paradoxical inclinations—definitely not "trustworthy" '.

He suggested to me, 'Perhaps we may still meet again in the South of France or in Egypt or even, if you really break loose from your law for a while, in the wilds of Africa which we might explore together?' Endearing but odd. Why the South of France? And it is difficult to imagine two less intrepid explorers of the wilds of Africa than Adam and me.

It is strange but praiseworthy for both him and them that British Ministers took a young German without any position so seriously.

It is strange too, but hardly elating to compare our behaviour towards Communism with pre-war attitudes to Fascism. The Russian tyranny is as evil and more prolonged than that of Hitler.

6

B Y THE NEPOTISM of my brother-in-law, Willie Black, I was smuggled
into the second Fife and Forfar Yeomanry three days before the war
broke out in 1939 (for this I received the Territorial Decoration for long
service—an example of the general inflation or debauchery which has
devalued British titles, appointments, medals, etc.). It is one of my themes
in writing this book that too little history is written by those who endured
and did not direct our affairs. War, in particular, in my experience was
not at all like the description of it. These descriptions tend either to be
histories of the great events, memoirs of generals and politicians or
accounts of the experiences of those who suffered in the front line or who
perpetrated acts of exceptional daring. Some excellent books, e.g. *Good-
bye to all That, Undertones of War, Memoirs of an Infantry Officer* have
been written about the First World War and some evocative novels about
the Second. But then their authors were exceptional—indeed, they were
professional writers. The First World War too must have been very
different from the Second. Seldom in the Second War did British soldiers
undergo for long anything that can compare with the frightfulness of
trench warfare. Even I can vaguely remember the columns of casualties
which appeared in the newspapers. Many people, myself included, who
on the face of it served during the Second World War in the armed
forces, were in little danger throughout. Others only for short though very
unpleasant periods risked being killed. Others again went through a hell
comparable to 1914–18. So if, to borrow a phrase used by Diana Cooper
about one of Evelyn Waugh's books, what follows sounds like Mrs. Dale's
War Diary—that in fact is what much of the war for me was like.

I spent the first months in the 2nd Fife and Forfar Yeomanry in Fife.
Life was peaceful. We had a few light tanks and one or two Rolls-Royce

armoured cars—superb vehicles whose engines rather inconveniently could only be repaired by Rolls-Royce mechanics. The higher command seemed, as far as we junior officers were concerned, to have forgotten us. Practically the whole regiment came from Fife or Dundee. We were not at all keen on incomers. Not that we were particularly pleased with ourselves or idle but we had our habits, illustrated by an incident at a pre-war camp. Our second in command was Fergus McIntyre, a popular officer but in appearance un-military. When the regiment was in camp near Barry in Forfarshire it was warned to prepare for inspection by some General. Fergus having been told to make himself scarce went off with an NCO and a Lewis gun, ostensibly to undergo a little instruction in the sand hills. It being a fine day, the General decided to take a ride. He was somewhat surprised to come across an officer asleep in the dunes with a Lewis gun pointing to heaven. Fergus, having been prodded awake, the General demanded what he was doing. 'Well, since you ask' Fergus replied, 'we're hiding from you.' Fergus was apt to be off-hand with Generals. Even in the war he came into the mess one evening and failed to notice that another inspecting General was having a drink and announced with a sigh 'Now all that nonsense is over I'll just pop upstairs and slip into something loose'.

Meanwhile my brothers-in-law though older—old enough indeed each to have won the Military Cross in the First World War, were soldiering more actively than I was. Willie Black was a Brigadier in charge of anti-aircraft guns. Billy, in spite of a rickety and sometimes painful leg, having gone to France in command of a pioneer battalion marched and fought with his men all the way from the Maginot Line to England.

Regimental life, though I have no desire to return to it, was at first surprisingly relaxing. I made new friends, such officers in the Fife and Forfar as Alistair Grant and Graeme Hutchison, with whom I later joined in a brief excursion into publishing and caught up again with old ones such as Teddy Lee. Alistair, Graeme and I must have been the three most unmilitary looking officers in the British Army. Alistair had some excuse as he was rather lame and showed great spirit by joining up at all. Graeme and I were incurable. We always looked as though we had slept in our uniforms. We were appointed gunnery instructors but our inability to assemble the lock of a Vickers machine gun (with which the 2nd Fife and Forfar were armed in so far as they were armed at all when the war broke out) led to our removal from that perplexing office. But war brings sad separation; harder to bear when you are young. I was touched by a letter from Lionel Brett in 1944 recounting how he made an effort to see me. 'I located you when your Corps Headquarters were at Eindhoven and we were temporarily in the same Corps. Since then I have kept an eye on your whereabouts and awaited a day when I was free and you reasonably near. Today looked reasonable on the map but was not so on the ground. . . . My journey towards you was a nightmare, one of those landscapes which return to one years later and give one a sinking feeling inside. Apart from the usual mud and pouring rain and sappers looking mediaeval in their leather jerkins, and pinched and pale civilians, there was a horrific quality of desolation about the landscape which was unique even in Holland.'

At the time of Dunkirk I was on a course. Places familiar from previous wars cropped up in the news, Sedan, Arras, Mons. The German advance was unbelievable. Surely it would be stopped? Or was it possible that the Nazis had sparked off a new era in which the old countries of the West would be annihilated? That it was alarming was undeniable. Alarming is too mild a word, it hit one in the pit of the stomach. It was not a simple fear of military defeat. As far as I remember the feeling was compounded of several fears, one ingredient in the shock we suffered was a fear that the Nazis with all their cruelty and imbecilities might be the harbingers of a new politic destined to rule Europe. We had watched corruption and despair wax in the politics of France, while clarity of purpose waned in our own. Democracy seemed to have grown distracted and feeble. Might the Nazis, like the Goths or the Moslems, be the scimitar which could cut through the floundering politics of the West? Had they not the 'un-conquerable will and study of revenge, immortal hate'?

But no one contemplated surrender. This was not heroism but simply that there was no reason for it. Britain still seemed to have troops and guns, birds sang, larks and British aeroplanes flew overhead. The collapse of France shattered the dream on which our superiors had fed us: the invincible French Army and the impregnable Maginot Line. But at the back of my mind at least there had always been small doubts. I could not understand the reputation of the French Army, which since Austerlitz has few victories it can claim for itself and a history starred with defeat. Nor could anyone fail to notice that the end of the Maginot Line hung in mid air. Never should anyone be taken in by authority when contradicted by experience and common sense.

A tide of exhausted men swept over Southern England. They slept in railway stations and barracks, in commandeered halls and sometimes by the roadside. The war seemed to pause, not knowing what to make of this dramatic change in our future. The 2nd Fife and Forfar Yeomanry were ordered to Northern Ireland.

When we first arrived in Northern Ireland the Fife and Forfar were attached to the 53rd Welsh Division. We were stationed at Dungannon. The officers' mess was set up in a house called Killymeal owned by Mr.

Newton 'the Bosun' a character who might have stepped out of Somerville and Ross, though I do not remember that he ever mounted a horse. Despite the nefarious attentions of the IRA we lived in considerable comfort. Wives were allowed to join us. Those who lived in Killymeal were well looked after by the Newton family. It was a snug house, agreeably shabby, the few regular soldiers attached to the regiment kept us in reasonably military condition. Those regular sergeants and adjutants attached to territorial units deserve to be remembered. Our adjutant at that time, Captain Sutherland, an Australian, certainly deserved high marks. He fitted so well into our way of life that he might have been born in Fife. At Killymeal he chose to get married. I was his best man; as he left for his honeymoon we discovered that neither he nor I had any money but the Newtons provided. I hope they got it back.

Soon afterwards I was sent off to be a staff officer Grade III. The divisional commander was General B. T. Wilson who looked very much a general with a benign presence and infinite patience—sorely tried I fear by some of his officers. One of them, a lieutenant who had been put in charge of ABCA (The Army Bureau of Current Affairs—one of the foibles of the higher command) called upon the general one Sunday afternoon. General Wilson and his wife entertained this somewhat unexpected guest with their usual courtesy but after an hour or two decided they must be rid of him. On showing him to the door the General was alarmed to find a taxi waiting, the clock on it ticking up from £15.8.6 to £15.8.9. He was even more alarmed when the guest got in on one side, out on the other and doubled back into their house. On enquiries being made it was discovered that the lieutenant had gone a little potty. His ABCA lectures consisted of an exposition of his family tree. The troops had taken it all in their stride, not for them to question the whims of their superiors.

Ill-advisedly, I was put in charge of the Generals' Mess. My job was brightened by having to deal with the Commander of the Royal Artillery, Brigadier Christie who signed his name Xtie, wrote plays, professed Left Wing opinions and when orthodox pleas for the removal of one of his staff failed himself wrote 'For God's sake take Captain — away, he makes me so unhappy'. The letter had the desired effect. I also had to deal with 'the camp'. This was the unit which looked after Divisional Headquarters. It was in charge of Captain Thomas, a mordant officer of exceptional delight, and Lieutenant A. D. Powell, the author of *A Dance to the Music of Time*. I need hardly say that dispatches from their office were both pointed and hilarious. There were, for instance, complaints that the milk was sour. Either Dennis Thomas or Tony Powell sent back a short note alleging that the milk was fresh when it left their premises. 'You must have a witch in the Mess, suspect A/Q' (the Colonel who was assistant adjutant and quarter-master general). They saw to it of course that the message fell into that officer's hands.

At that time *How Green was my Valley* was widely acclaimed among the Welsh. When we were issued with a new greyish blanco in place of the verdant shade then in use, Captain Thomas was heard lamenting 'alas, alas, how green were my gaiters'. General Wilson much enjoyed the goings-on in the camp, retailed to his wife by Tony Powell's wife Violet, including the incident of the English orderly officer who on asking the routine question during meals 'Any Complaints?' was nonplussed by my Welsh batman who replied 'Thank you sir for leave to speak, the food is delicious'. However my own downfall as mess secretary was encompassed by the visit of a senior general on a day when we were supposed to eat no meat. As General Wilson and his colleagues fished around for protein in a cauldron of nauseating vegetable stew the mess waiter lent over and with a horrible leer hissed at him 'Don't you know it's a meatless day'. 'How can I be a General without meat?' came an anguished cry. I was relieved of my post to the mutual satisfaction of myself and the General of whom I have fond memories.

Meanwhile Laura was living a much more difficult life. Her letters though amusing, tell of moves, discomfort, uncertainty and hard work. She had to make all the dull and difficult arrangements war entailed, such as getting our furniture moved out of London, suddenly dashing off to stay with me when living with wives was allowed and all the time looking after Andrew, our eldest son born in 1939, and giving birth to our daughter Grizelda. At the beginning of the war the Bonham Carters took a delightful house, Fellside, in Westmorland. Here my mother-in-law continued her unflagging activities, not only political but also as a governor of the BBC. A letter from my wife gives a picture of one of the more comfortable of her numerous moves and also the effect of war on small children. 'Mama and Raymond (her younger brother) were borne off in a taxi by Mr. Tyson, the carrier, this morning in true Bonham Carter style—the car crammed with dilapidated suitcases and odd parcels and Miss Law (my mother-in-law's maid) squashed against the Irish cook, dimly discernible through a bunch of rowan berries at the back of the car. They have left the usual welter of *New Statesmans*, *Spectators* and wads of the BBC journals and typewritten reports behind. Ray (Raymond) has already made Andrew (our eldest son) militaristic in the course of three short weeks and he now marches round in front of the house with a Woolworth tin hat and Lord Kilbracken's blunderbuss. Raymond has innumerable 'war books' and spotting books for planes and ships where he makes Andrew say which ships or whatever it is, are good, and which bad, according as to whether they are ours or the German ones. Poor Andrew

94

was rather bewildered at first as he thought the *Altmark* looked quite nice and the *Cossack* (the destroyer which caught and boarded her) only moderate and Raymond made him change all his opinions.' Laura stayed for long periods with my mother, not the easiest of arrangements for my mother was not unnaturally upset by the war and even St Andrews was not free from alarms. 'The sirens went about 11.30 this morning. I was having my hair permanently waved and was pinned beneath the apparatus.'

Miss Law must have more than a passing mention. Had she chosen to desert Violet she would have made a fortune on music-halls, or television had it been in existence. For the cockney music-hall which might seem an appropriate theatre for her would have been too large for her elegant talent. Her cleverness was such that she could beat all the intellectuals at after dinner games. However, it was at riddles that she really excelled. She and Violet engaged in a long-running 'turn'. Violet barking at her and Miss Law shrugging her shoulders with a martyred look returning from foraging among Violet's cupboards with unlikely hats, gloves etc. before with perfect timing producing like a conjuror whatever Violet had lost. Like all cockneys she revelled in both London and the country. I fear she may have loathed the Irish cook but she would have willingly endured the rowan-berries. Her brother, Fred, was the best clock-mender anyone could find. His old age has been spent in a Peabody flat—comfortable and near to his friends—filled with fascinating furniture, pictures and ornaments, many made with his own hands—just the sort of building planners and developers itch to demolish.

In her letters to me Laura made some pertinent comments on the conduct of the war, showing that there was not that universal admiration for the Allied governments with which in retrospect they sometimes seem to be endowed: showing too that a great deal of information was available to the public—thanks I believe to Walter Monckton and Brendan Bracken. 'What do you think of the American fleet squashed tightly into Pearl Harbour instead of being on the High Seas with a war imminent? I can't understand it, still less that no American patrol reported Japanese aircraft carriers in the neighbourhood.' I must say tho' I think conscription the only fair way of getting women. I think Winston's speech contained some very questionable statements after what one hears of mismanagement in production. Also, I should have thought it was Bevin's business to announce a thing of that kind—it is rather pathetic the way all Lab ministers incline to shelter behind Winston knowing how they will be made hay of if they try to say anything themselves.' She was also scathing about the retention of old appeasers in top jobs.

The British Press has always derided the bravery of the Italians. No doubt the hearts of many Italians were not in the war but that they did not always deserve the insults and jokes thrown at them is shown by the account Nigel Irvine (son of Sir James Irvine, the Principal of St Andrews University, later killed during Naval service), given to Laura of the capture of an Italian submarine: 'He says the Itis are not to be despised by any means and that the submarine which surrendered to the *Moonstone* had been hit repeatedly by 4-in. shells—her Captain had been killed and she could not submerge.'

For a few weeks in the war Laura stayed for a time at Limekiln with the Count Benckendorff, Jasper Ridley's uncle. Limekiln close to Mockbeggars just outside Ipswich, is now the home of Natalie Brooke, Connie Benckendorff's daughter, and her husband Humphrey, at one time Secretary of the Royal Academy to whom should be given much of the credit for its post-war revival. In those days it was enclosed in a jungle of grass and briars where lurked a biting dog. Connie Benckendorff's father was as I said earlier, the last Czarist Ambassador in London; he himself had served in the Russian Navy both under the old regime and Bolsheviks. It was said that he was in a small ship in some North Siberian port when the Russo-Japanese war broke out. Unfortunately, no one had told his ship that war had been declared. On sighting a Japanese vessel they hurriedly changed into full dress and were drawn up on deck playing the Japanese national anthem when struck by a torpedo. As a publisher one of the very few books which I published in partnership with Martin Secker and Graeme Hutchison at the Richard's Press was Count Benckendorff's autobiography. But that was in the fifties. In the meantime we listened to Connie's stories of life in Russia, in the country, in gaol and as an Admiral in the Soviet Navy. He remained intensely patriotic. He too had tasted the doubts and dangers which were the diet of liberal Western Europeans in the thirties and the war.

When I read of the hardships suffered by the families of M.P.s it strikes me that the hardship of war-time wives was incomparably worse. M.P.s choose their careers and only too many rivals stand on the touch-line eager to take their place. Their ridiculous hours are their own fault. If the future of many is uncertain, at least while they are Members they know where they have to work. Many, many wives in the war and not only the wives of servicemen, traipsed from relative to lodging house, from Scotland to Brighton and many, of course, never saw their husbands for months and years.

Early in the war Lady Glen-Coats who had been the prospective Liberal candidate for Orkney and Shetland gave up. She had made a considerable impression in the islands but even before the war found travel around them tiring. In those days it was entirely by small boat. On one occasion she had to be carried pig-a-back a considerable distance through the surf—

Laura, my wife, and Margot
Asquith playing leap-frog.

Laura and her sister Cressida.

Golf was a way of life at St. Andrews.
My sister Nancie in the flower of her youth.

an experience I have also undergone. She very kindly suggested me as her successor. It is to her in the first place that I owe twenty-eight years as their Member. Had Lady Glen-Coats not recommended me to the Liberals there, I should never have been adopted—and probably would never have been an M.P. at all. I am profoundly grateful to her.

I wanted to be a Member of Parliament but only for a Scottish seat and, if possible, for a seat in the North.

I never went abroad in the war, unless you call Ulster abroad, until 1944. I was by then Deputy Assistant Adjutant General of the 53rd (Welsh) Division, a high sounding title with little to it. We landed a fortnight after 'D' Day. The salient was quite deep. It was strange to be chugging across the Channel on a sparkling day on what might have been a holiday trip. Strange to see the Norman country with its gnarled trees and gnarled cattle. Strange too to find traffic driving on the right. I had no sooner landed than I was knocked over by a motor bicycle. Life in the countryside and at Bayeux was comparatively normal. Frank Wilson, the Deputy Assistant Quartermaster general, and I slept in peace and safety in a tent within, I suppose, four hundred yards of the Germans, feeding on Camembert cheese. I lunched with a French landowner still living in his château. He told me that he preferred occupation by the Germans to that of the British who apart from their looting habits were very careless about burials, both of men and cattle.

Under the Norman apple trees too I first met Harald Leslie who was a colonel on the legal staff at Corps. He was an Orkneyman who later became a close friend. In Normandy he was infiltrating Scots Law into the Advocate-General's department. He finished a distinguished legal career as Lord Birsay, Chairman of the Scottish Land Court.

In the war I learnt something of fighting—though I did not fight myself. No one wants to be killed. Absolutely fresh troops are naturally panicky. Then comes a period of maximum utility when battalions fought with the greatest gallantry. Once veterans have survived many battles they become deeply determined not to die. I cannot believe that Napoleon's veterans were any different. What I find quite astonishing is how battalions went again and again into the trenches and over the top of them in the First World War. I once went with our General to discover why we had received no news from a brigade which was supposed to have carried out an attack. The reason was that though ordered to attack no one had moved.

The other striking feature of the war of 1944 in France and the Low Countries was the gulf between the first line and those behind in the risks they ran. The 53rd Division was not in the forefront of the invasion, compared to some other divisions we were not so very heavily engaged. Yet within a few months the officers of the infantry battalions had turned over twice. Only one Colonel of an infantry battalion, I think, survived un-wounded and half were killed. But once you were behind the infantry you were as safe as in London during an air-raid. Even the gunners suffered very few casualties and our long tail practically none.

The reason for this was not far to seek; the Germans, except in the Ardennes, were in retreat. They had very little artillery which could reach behind our lines, even their nasty, big mortars did not have much range. They had a few Tiger tanks; in spite of their small numbers we had nothing to match them and these frequently held us up.

The Free French fought valiantly in many campaigns and there were heroes and heroines in the French underground but I could not find much evidence of French Resistance in our advance through Normandy. Although farmers were still working, the villages seemed only half popu-lated, a Rip van Winkle feeling pervaded the countryside. The French seemed in no hurry to get life going again. The most conspicuous activity of the Resistance was the shaving of girls' heads.

The Belgians on the other hand had their services running, cranked up their trams, produced food and knew exactly what accommodation was available. I suppose long practice in being occupied had helped. In con-trast to the French we had seen, they were full of courage and activity.

Antwerp, where we were held up for some weeks, was, on our arrival, unscathed. The Germans were on the other side of the docks but life in the town went on much as usual. Scent and silk stockings were readily bought and the Opera was going. I was there during a performance of 'Carmen' in Flemish when the roof was hit by a small shell which, burst-ing a pipe, deluged the stage in water. The chorus retreated to a dry patch and continued at full blast. Frank Wilson and I were hospitably enter-tained by a Belgian family. After tea one of their children, a boy of fifteen or so, would come in to have his military overcoat done up, he would then be kissed by his mother and despatched to join a sort of Home Guard which exchanged shots with the Germans across the canal.

Unfortunately, before we left, Antwerp was devastated by buzz bombs.

While I was in Belgium Jasper Ridley and my brother-in-law, Mark, escaped from the camps in which they were imprisoned in Italy—Mark after showing great courage and enterprise eventually reached the British lines. Jasper was tragically killed, blown up probably on a land mine almost within sight of safety. His death was a disaster, felt for ever by his friends and most of all, of course, by Cressida.

I believe that much that is wrong with attitudes and organisation in Britain stems from the war. I have mentioned that no one I ever met con-templated giving in after Dunkirk. What we did feel was that Dunkirk had been a shattering defeat due to the incompetence of the British and

French governments and war offices. Yet in retrospect the British have almost turned Dunkirk into a victory. Publicists and politicians constantly harp on the unique courage and determination we showed after it. Churchill has been placed on the top rung of heroes, without him it is suggested even the magnificent British might not have pulled through. I have no wish to denigrate the courage shown at Dunkirk nor the leadership of Churchill. Both were magnificent. It is, however, absurd and insulting to suggest that Britain with the tank trap of the Channel as her moat and her airforce intact would have caved in when Holland, Belgium and Norway resisted, not to mention Poland in spite of a stab in the back by Russia. It is also no service to Churchill's memory to suggest that but for him we might have surrendered. And, of course, once America joined in the war, let alone Russia, we were bound to win. If anything is remarkable, it is remarkable that it took so long. Yet we came out of the war being told we had saved the world by a unique act of courage against fearful odds. We naturally became convinced that the world must see that we were natural leaders of the West entitled by our deeds of valour and skill to rest on oars as far as work was concerned and owed a debt, indeed a living, by our neighbours.

It was in the war too that we first became accustomed to a top-hamper of staffs and hangers-on. This was particularly obvious in France in 1944–45. As far as I could see, most of the fighting was done by some three or four infantry divisions and the armoured divisions. Yet we had two Corps Headquarters (as well as the Canadian Corps and the Canadian Army Headquarters), an Army Headquarters and an Army Group Headquarters. Even in 1939 it was being said that the British Army was composed of Generals and 3-ton lorries. Around these large staffs dangled the forerunners of the modern quangos and advisory bodies, civil government, ABCA, liaison officers, etc. It was in the army too that I first noticed the absorption of public officials, at this time regular army officers, with their allowances, perks and badges of office.

From the lower ranks, the war did not seem to be very well conducted. I never understood the strategy which ended at Arnhem. I cannot understand why Montgomery chose to advance at a tangent to the main axis virtually up a single road to a place where the Rhine had to be crossed, not once but three times. Patton seemed much more sensible in going straight for it and getting across. Afterwards in Parliament I knew Montgomery a little and liked him. To junior officers he had the immense virtue that he seemed to want to keep us alive. We laughed a bit at the old show-off but his antics were useful in that at least we knew who was in charge. His insistence on getting plans explained was also well received. But as a strategist or tactician he did not seem so good. Since he reached high command he had been lucky or wise enough always to have over-whelming material superiority. And the discipline on which we are told he prided himself was a hoax. His headquarter's staff at a time when trans-port was said to be in great demand, was alleged to have sent off lorries to collect brandy from Cognac—so much for the spartan life Montgomery was rumoured to impose. The British too were notorious for their looting. They did not touch occupied houses or their inhabitants but if a house was empty it was turned upside down within an hour or two. Nor did they confine their attentions to valuables. I once saw a soldier on a very hot day driving a bulldozer, stark naked in a top hat—a French top hat I suppose.

What makes me think particularly well of General Montgomery was his appointment and support of our divisional commander, General Ross. General Ross did not fit in with the public relations portrait of General Montgomery. I can imagine no one less likely to go for a run before break-fast. His main interests outside the Army were poker and good food, which his ADC, when we were in England, with the General's whole-hearted approval, bought in the black market. Nor did he conform with the standards of the Army. He had never been to the Staff College, he there-fore lacked those 'qualifications' which have been the stamp by which the second-rate have come increasingly to rule Britain. He had spent much of his time in the Sudan. There he had retreated for most of his career, reading *The Times* three or four months out of date but in order. He maintained that so long as you did not cheat by looking ahead (as one is tempted to do in detective stories) it did not matter how out of date the news was. I have always suspected that 'First with the News' was a bogus slogan. Montgomery must be accorded very good marks indeed for ignor-ing his own reputation and the conventions of the Army in promoting Ross. The promotion was entirely justified. General Ross understood, or at any rate could manipulate, the devious abilities of the Welsh. He in-inspired devotion. We knew which of our superiors were cardboard figures. We knew Ross was a creature of flesh and blood who hadn't ex-pected to get as far as he did and didn't care a damn about conforming so as to get any further. He also knew what mattered. But he was under-standing to those who had to deal with things which did not matter. High among these he put the affairs of my department. Certain documents which passed through my hands had to be signed by him. I used to ask if I could come to see him. 'Yes,' he would say, 'come at a quarter to one'. On looking out of my caravan at twenty minutes to one I would see the dear General scurrying over to the mess. When I arrived there he would beam upon me and suggest a drink. Like all Generals he did, however, take a considerably interest in medals and awards. We had a vast allocation for mentions in despatches. Eventually as we were scratching our heads having mentioned every man in the Division who could have conceivably qualified, I suggested he should recommend me. 'Of course,' he replied, 'what a brilliant suggestion, put yourself top of the list.' I am curious to know what happened to all the other soldiers, Indian Civil and Colonial Civil servants like General Ross. Ross was of course primarily interested in the fighting qualities of his brigades. But he also knew a good staff officer when he saw one and he saw one in my opposite number, Frank Wilson. Frank ran the supplies of the division, first under Rex Cohen and then Robert Neilson and then by himself with easy competence. The relationship between General Ross and his amateur staff officers is a good example of the regular army's freedom from jealousy and eagerness to use civilians—if good at their job.

Looking at its remains from the outside, the British Empire and its demise puzzles me. When I was at school and we celebrated Empire Day by singing 'Land of Hope and Glory' around a flagpole, when St Andrews had its retired nabobs and the maps were red, I imagined thousands of Aunt-like over-energetic spinsters running every aspect of Africa, Asia and innumerable islands. I now know that there were comparatively few. They interfered little but competently. Men like Ross and the Bonham Carters wrestled to the satisfaction of the natives and their own government with problems of every variety in half a dozen continents.

What has happened to all the District Officers and those they taught? Some like Harold Shearer in Orkney have been absorbed into home life. But what is as strange as the demise of the Empire is the evaporation of the skill which made it one of the world's most astonishing feats of government. Since there is no particular merit in sticking to chronology in a book like this, I may here insert that the same thought struck me with force twenty years later.

In 1964 Dr. Banda, whom I had known in London, invited me to the celebrations of independence in Malawi. It is the only time I have ever been in Africa south of the Sahara. I found it surprising. From the sky, which was resting on the tree tops, drenching rain swept round the shivering bare legs of the Africans. It was like home; only in Shetland have I seen such a combination of mist, cold, wind and rain. Dr. Banda's chief guest was a Portuguese from Mozambique who was on excellent terms with everyone. The African and British seem to share the same humour, perhaps this is what draws so many Britons, for instance, my son Johnny, to Africa. Dr. Banda in one of his many welcoming speeches suddenly embarked on a passage which looked certain to cause a Diplomatic Incident. 'We will hang Welensky' his voice rose to shriek, then perceiving trouble it dropped a decibel or two, 'if he comes across the

Limpopo (a word certain to make the British laugh) we will hang him from the chandelier.' A variant on the lamp-post I suppose. He was constantly acclaimed with cheers, laughter and songs whenever he appeared. The welcoming chant of 'Who do the trees belong to?' greeted with the resounding response 'Dr. Kamusu Banda' and succeeded by many other verses; 'Who do the hills belong to?' etc. had somewhat Hitlerian overtones until the final 'And who does the whole world belong to?' 'Dr. Kamusu Banda' at which the whole audience rocked with laughter, as they did when the head of his fly whisk flew off as he did a triumphant tour of the arena. I also heard that a British trader had been disarmed by an African who explained why the new roof of his store had vanished (it had in fact been given to the store keeper's family, by the single word 'lions'. What fun African children must have, taken everywhere on their mother's backs, how easy life appeared as compared with, say, India. But what struck me as most surprising was how little the British appeared to impinge. Beyond the garden of the Governor of the Bank of Malawi, who kindly had me to stay, an encampment suddenly sprung up. No one knew who they were nor what their 'rights' might be. Outside the province of law and a certain amount of order and the administration of some aspects of life, the British seemed to have shrugged their shoulders and contemplated African life with tolerance and little itch to interfere. What they did, the British did well but they did not attempt too much. How wise: though perhaps rather Turkish. It has meant that until it built New Delhi in the sunset of its days the British Raj has hardly left an imposing building behind. But that too is lucky considering the standard of British architecture.

The British have been slated for exploiting the Empire. This may be so. I do not know how, if any balance sheet could ever be drawn, the debits and credits work out. They can be faulted for interfering too little, over education for instance, and for being slow to hand over their responsibilities. But all the colonial administrators I have known seemed to have ungrudgingly trained the natives of the countries they served to take their own jobs. No, it is the apartheid in social behaviour, our keeping of ourselves to ourselves and the presumption of superiority which gave offence —and one can well see why. But that only partly explains why we falter so unsurely in the twilight of Commonwealth.

Our restrained regime was supported by intelligent and dedicated men organised into services of which they were rightly proud. Almost as surprising as their self-restraint is their disappearance and apparently all they stood for. How can we have made such a mess of Rhodesia? What has happened to the genius which ran India, economically, efficiently, humanely?

Apart from being a prospective candidate I naturally took little part or interest in politics during the war though I remember going to see Sir Stafford Cripps to whom I had taken a fancy, partly for what must now seem the strange view that I found him friendly. Officially he has been docketed as a cold fish. That is not my memory. I have vague recollections of finding him in his shirtsleeves willing to discuss politics (and some suggestions of mine about tanks) when he was presumably feverishly busy. But what I certainly did was to pursue some Scottish Nationalist ideas to which George Malcolm Thomson had introduced me before the war. I had always been something of a nationalist. The first political meeting I ever attended was addressed by Eric Linklater, the Scottish Nationalist candidate in the East Fife by-election of 1935. I then fell in with the MacEwens of Inverness, Sir Alexander and his son Robin and so with George, then high in the hierarchy of the *Daily Express* but in the war attached to the Lord Privy Seal. In those days Scottish sentiment was fragmented. I felt the elemental desire to see one's country in control of its own destiny. I then had no clear idea how this should be achieved. In 1945 George wrote to me saying that he had thought of an 'immediate programme' for Scotland consisting of:

1. Administrative autonomy, i.e. the filling out of Scottish Departments so as to take in Transport, Works and Buildings, Forestry, the internal activities of the Board of Trade and suchlike including any 'planning' activity.

2. Legislative devolution corresponding to the above. He went on to suggest that those propositions be put to all candidates for Scottish seats.

While not over-estimating the likely effect he believed that such an exercise might focus public attention, particularly as a recent Gallup Poll had shown 53% of the Scots in favour of Home Rule and 8% for sovereign status. Looking back I believe he may have been right but the chance was missed and the Covenant launched some years later was mishandled.

Meanwhile Orkney was submerged under the armed forces. At one time in the war there were 100,000 servicemen in islands with a population of 18,000. Scapa Flow, that sheet of enclosed water where the Norse fleets had mustered a thousand years ago was once more bristling with warships. From Shetland the Norwegians raided their native land. I had never set foot on the islands which were to be my main interest for most of my life. This may be the place to give some account of the Northern Isles and their history.

‘THIS BLOODY TOWN'S a bloody cuss,
  No bloody trains, no bloody bus,
And no one cares for bloody us,
In bloody Orkney.

The bloody roads are bloody bad,
The bloody folk are bloody mad,
They'll make the brightest body sad,
In bloody Orkney.

All bloody clouds, all bloody rains
No bloody kerbs, no bloody drains,
The Council's got no bloody brains,
In bloody Orkney.

Everything's so bloody dear,
A shilling for your bloody beer,
And is it good? No bloody fear,
In bloody Orkney.

The bloody flicks are bloody old,
The bloody seats are always sold,
You can't get in for bloody gold,
In bloody Orkney.

No bloody sport, no bloody games,
No bloody fun. The bloody dames
Won't even give their proper names
In bloody Orkney.

The bloody dances make you smile,
The bloody band is bloody vile,
It only cramps your bloody style,
In bloody Orkney.

Best bloody place is bloody bed,
With bloody ice on bloody head,
You might as well be bloody dead
In bloody Orkney.'

Such was the opinion of the sailors, soldiers and airmen, shanghaied in their tens of thousands to Orkney during the wars. This new 'Orkneyinga Saga' had become a much relished piece of Orkney lore. Mr. Hugh Crooks, assistant editor of the *Shetland Times* was himself in Orkney in the army and confirms at least the description of the weather. 'We were billeted in the area surrounding the old distillery in Stromness. Billeted? Yes, in tents. Running water? Certainly, the icy cold stream which flowed between the tents—and the rain which seemed to teem down incessantly.' No wonder the services' paper which Gerry Meyer edited before he took on the *Orcadian* was called *The Orkney Blast*. We have all suffered such weather in Orkney. But those who stay longer soon find out that Orkney and Shetland have another side to their climate and their life.

Many people think that Scotland is far north and more still think that within Scotland you have about reached the limit of the known world when you get to Inverness. A curious combination of oil and seals have half-awakened Southerners to the existence of regions even north of Caithness. It is to be expected, I suppose, that I have received a hundred times more letters about the killing of seals than I have about any other matter: not threats of war; not changes of Government; not the future of our Commonwealth; not taxation; nor of course torture in Russian concentration camps or massacres in South East Asia have provided anything like the volume of letters I have sustained on seals. Three letters made up my total post-bag on the Bill for Scottish Devolution, more than thirteen hundred on seals. I received petitions bearing some twenty-five thousand signatures.

But in spite of oil and seals little is known about the regions of the north. A hundred miles north of Inverness the maps usually end with Caithness, the most northerly county of the Scottish mainland, but that is by no means the end of Britain and the British had better raise their sights for much now depends upon the oil coming ashore in Shetland and Orkney.

Orkney lies off the north coast of Caithness across the Pentland Firth, a savage piece of water through which the tides building up round Britain race to and fro between the Atlantic and the North Sea. One of the two main sea routes to Orkney runs between Scrabster, a harbour near Thurso, and Stromness, a town on the mainland of Orkney at the north-west end of Scapa Flow. When I first went to Orkney the journey was made in one of several generations of *St. Ola*'s, a steamboat of old-fashioned design on to which cars were driven over planks and in whose saloon burnt a coal fire. She rolled and bucketed and wallowed. But my memory is that she got across the Firth in weather which now causes her far larger and more sophisticated successors to skulk in port. Her skipper, Captain Swanson, was a man of independence and character, red of face and large of body. It was said that he had many brushes with the military who ran the harbours during the war. One story runs that having taken his ship out of Scrabster more or less in defiance of the Guards' officer in charge of the port, he picked up his megaphone and bawled at the exquisite but slightly absurdly turned out figure on the pier, who must have indeed looked rather like a commissionaire, 'I have seen better dressed and more capable dummies than you outside cinemas.'

If the weather allows, the *Ola* sails outside the island of Hoy. In a westerly gale she takes the longer route through Scapa Flow. Either way you get a dramatic introduction to Orkney. Hoy is more like Shetland than the rest of Orkney, being relatively high, heathery and wild. Yet it is different from Shetland. The red cliffs to the Atlantic could not be Shetland cliffs. The crofts, even the deserted crofts, could not be Shetland crofts. Orkney and Shetland, so alike in many aspects of their climate, people and history, are yet always distinguishable. Both have their own individual character. Though the gales blow as fiercely in Orkney as in Shetland, indeed there is less to break them, Orkney is a little further south and being more fertile than Shetland makes a rather gentler impression. The land lies in long sweeps, across horizontal slabs of flag-stones—or so it appears—I am no geologist. The North Isles seem so low in the water that a high tide might sweep over them, and even the higher ridges are much wider and milder than the Shetland hills. The Hoy hills at the north-west end of the island of Hoy are the exception, a big expanse of heather running up to 1700 feet with sheer cliffs to seaward.

The pastures of Orkney have been broken out of the heather over countless generations. Even in the days of the Vikings Orkney farms were already established. The import of white clover in the 19th century is said to have given Orkney farming its most lasting boost. The Orkneymen then set about ploughing out the hill, a laborious business with oxen. Up to the First World War oxen were common and so were beremeal and salt meat and salt fish. The grass and clover grew well in the long summer days and black cattle from Orkney farms came to be in demand. So the landscape changed and is changing. Lord Thurso has the diary of a man who came year after year through the middle of the 19th century to shoot on the Sinclair estates in Caithness. He sometimes crossed to Orkney and records bags of thirty and forty brace of grouse to his own gun in Harray. His gun was, at least when he first came, a muzzle loader and as he had to sail across the Pentland and back the shooting time must have been short. Today I don't suppose there are five brace of grouse in the whole parish of Harray. Most of the heather is gone and the hoodies and black backs patrol what remains. When I first came to Orkney the fields and farms were dotted with hens. Orkney in spite of her tiny size produced more eggs than any other county in Scotland. Every year she shipped off eggs worth more than her whole rateable value. Now all that is finished; Orkney imports eggs. There is less grain now than there was thirty years ago, bere has dwindled and there is more barley than oats. The harvest has diminished too—silage and combines have taken the place of stooks. Row upon row of oat stooks used to line the landscape in September, sometimes remaining out during October and November. Beautiful they were, but hard work. There are still stooks in Orkney but they have grown fewer every year, though how it pays farmers to buy combines for perhaps a week's work in the year baffles me. I know many of them are rented out to several farms, but in Orkney good harvest weather is precious and everyone wants the machines at the same time. Even if they are used for a month in the year, they must stand idle for eleven.

So the typical Orkney landscape is of green fields of grass with here and there a field of barley, a glint of water and herds of cattle. Now the small black Aberdeen-Angus are mingled with the white faces of Hereford, the fawn-grey Charolais and many other breeds including rarely a specimen of the Highland breed aptly christened 'Dog Cows' by my second son Johnny. The middle of the West Mainland is taken up by two large lochs and there are many more. There are a hundred or so dairy farms, relics of the wars when the services needed milk.

Orkney farms have got bigger but there are still many small farms— most of them are run by the family, most of them are owned by the farmer. It makes the islands look comfortably populated. The nights are studded with the lights of farms and farm cottages. When I first came to Orkney the houses seemed to me very stark, standing straight up from the fields: for the salt winds make the growing of trees a slow and difficult business. After twenty years the few dozen trees I planted round my house are perhaps twelve feet tall. But I do not now notice the lack of trees. Orkney farmers don't work with hedges—stone dykes and now barbed wire enclose the fields. The farm buildings were low and built of the thin, grey stone which also served for the roofs. In the last thirty years they have been largely rebuilt with concrete blocks and roofed with Welsh asbestos slates or asbestos. And there has been a great increase in gardens. More around the cottages and in the towns; the farms too now have a halo of daffodils in spring and annuals and perennials later on. But the country-side is still bare.

Bare but not now to my eyes bleak. Orkney is full of change and colour. The sea in summer can be of a blue which makes the Mediterranean look a washed out grey. The sunsets splurge across the sky colours which no painter would dare to use. But the point of Orkney is not dramatic. It is the light lying across the sea or the swathes of different greens, ochre and grey rocks, yellow beaches meeting the arching sky. In spring the prim-roses grow on the banks, later in ungrazed corners wild lupins and many other wild flowers flourish. Before the stupid and expensive cutting of the verges the roadsides were thick with clover and cow-parsley. Below my house there are banks of yellow whins and beyond them the hill is purple when the heather is in flower. So free from frost are we that fuchsia springs up round every house, supplying with the wild rose, veronica and elder what little shelter they get.

To these islands people came a long time ago, some eleven thousand years after the Ice Age, probably around 2000 B.C. The first people who have left traces behind them seem to have been the same race as built Stonehenge. It is supposed that coming from the Mediterranean they gradually made their way up the west coast of Spain, Brittany and Britain. It is also believed that, at least in Orkney, they were still dependant on stone—having no metal tools. But they apparently grew crops, for traces of a primitive form of barley, of which Orkney bere is a descendant, have been found. Why they set out on these travels or why they did not follow the east coast of Britain, I do not know. Their migration is as inexplicable to me at least as that of the ring doves which appeared in Orkney only a few years back and have now sent scouting parties to Faroe and Iceland. But our generation, so used to land and air voyages, must remember that for centuries by far the easiest way to travel was by water.

Orkney is dotted with ancient tombs and underground rooms. The best known surviving monuments to these people are the village of Skarabrae, the Standing Stones of Stenness and the Tomb of Maeshowe. Skarabrae is by the shore of the Bay of Skaill on the West side of the West mainland of Orkney. Here the sea has been eating away the land for centuries so that it is likely that much of the village is beneath sand and water. On the links above high water mark some eight or ten subterranean houses have been excavated. They were only discovered a hundred and thirty years ago when a storm shifted the sand which covered them. They are connected by a passage or underground street two or three feet wide and perhaps fifty yards long. Each 'house' is a single room with the remains of stone 'boxes' of different sizes, some filled with heather or straw as beds, others apparently used for keeping shellfish which to judge from the contents of the middens seem to have been the chief food of these people. The walls of these 'rooms' are rather cunningly bent inwards. Presumably after being excavated they were closed by laying slabs across the top of the in-curving wall and covering them with stone slabs, sods and heather. Life at Skarabrae must have been dark and dank. In mid-winter light only comes after 9.00 a.m. and, if the sky is overcast, begins to disappear soon after 3.00. The air at the best of times is laden with moisture and on the shores of the ocean sea-gust whipped up by Atlantic winds adds to the damp.

The standing stones of Stenness are a circle of monoliths between the lochs of Stenness and Harray—the site is hardly so dramatic as the landscape of Stevenson's poem 'Grey recumbent tombs of the dead in desert place, standing stones on the vacant, wine-red moor' but it has something of the same atmosphere. It is the subject of a very effective picture by Arthur Melville, the best painter who ever painted in Orkney.

Maeshowe is for me—and I am no archaeologist—the most impressive of the antiquities of Orkney. It is a grass-covered beehive tomb, now empty. For a thousand years or so it stood inviolate, containing no doubt the bones and personal possessions of chieftains. The entrance faced west so that the rays of the setting sun on the shortest day of the year shone directly into it and were aligned by a row of standing stones stretching down to the loch. The walls were expertly corbelled inwards—superior work to Skarabrae but of the same type. One side of the entrance passage is formed of a single block of stone, perhaps 18 feet long, showing that the builders must have had some means of quarrying and moving considerable weights of stone. But in the 12th century there gathered in Orkney the Viking contingents going to or from the Crusade. Crusaders had no respect for the sacred places of Paganism (nor indeed of any other religions; the contempt of the Italians for their Christian Allies and their churches was shown by the appalling destruction of Constantinople): they broke into the tomb and looted it, or so it is said. In any case, Maeshowe was certainly broken into by the Norse. Round the walls they carved with their axes the largest surviving collection of runic inscriptions. They also carved the Maeshowe Dragon and one or two other beasts. The fir-tree like writing and the tiny creatures—the dragon is about three inches from head to curled tail—are done with a delicacy which is extraordinary if they were really cut into the stone by axes. The inscription as translated by the guide is a stilted eulogy of some maiden. It may, however, be that the popular version has been bowdlerized and the graffiti are in the traditions of rude remarks scribbled by troops since time immemorial.

But this incursion into Viking times has taken us out of the sequence of Orkney history. After the primitive people of Skarabrae who bequeathed us numerous other earth houses and chambered cairns came that mysterious race, the Picts. As a boy I was taught that Scotland was inhabited by the Picts and Scots and assumed that these two races lived jumbled up in a unified kingdom. I gather now that this was not so. Some historians believe that the Picts came from Brittany or at least that a branch of them lived in Brittany. Dr. Hugh Marwick in his book *Orkney* in the County Books series (Robert Hale) suggests that they came across from Western Gaul about 300 B.C., made some incursions into South West England, could not make much headway there and continued on to North Scotland, Orkney and Shetland. At any rate, if, as is generally supposed, they built them, their surviving monuments are the brochs. As Dr. Marwick says, these round towers were like squat lighthouses. They vary in size but follow a uniform plan. The best surviving specimen is on the island of Mousa in Shetland which, though its top has been knocked off, is 40 feet high and of considerable diameter. The broch was hollow, probably to allow cattle to be driven in. The very thick walls contained small chambers or galleries, presumably for human use. It is thought that they were for defence against the attacks either of the existing local inhabitants or from pirates. The Picts presumably retired into them when attacked and did not live permanently in the cramped conditions of the broch. They are invariably found on the low land near the sea. The Picts were for their time fairly successful farmers, judging by what has been unearthed around the brochs.

The most curious feature of the brochs, and one which must throw some doubt on the story that the Picts came from Gaul where Caesar met with considerable resistance from seafaring tribes which seem to have resembled them, is that they only exist in the north of Scotland and mostly in the far north. Of the total estimated number of brochs—495— some 200 are in Orkney and Shetland and a further 233 are north of Inverness. Very few, if any, were built south of the Forth. Did the Northern Picts—perhaps through the genius of some early architect— invent the broch after they had left Brittany? Or were they in fact a development from Skarabrae—they exhibit the same inward-curving walls, perhaps a joint effort by the earlier inhabitants and later immigrants? It seems to non-historians like myself that it is unlikely that there were such clear divisions between different eras and ways of life as we are apt now to assume. As Dr. Marwick points out the brochs themselves resemble later feudal castles with their central keep and surrounding ditches and subsidiary dwellings.

Dr. Marwick finishes his chapter on the Picts with the following quotation from Dr. Anderson's translation from the Latin of the *Historia Norvegia*: 'One race, the Picts, little exceeding Pigmies in stature: they did marvels in the morning and evening in building towns but at mid-day they entirely lost their strength and lurked through fear in little underground houses. But at that time the islands were not called the Orchades but Petland, whence still the Pict sea' (now Pentland Firth). From this is seems as though the people described were the inhabitants of the low, semi-underground houses of Skarabrae. Eric Linklater indeed concludes that the brochs were not built by the Picts—but against them—by the earlier inhabitants. Others point to the use of 'oppidan' or 'urbs' by the Romans to describe both the construction of the Western Gauls and of the Orkney Picts as showing a common origin. Personally, I suspect that the inhabitants of Orkney may have been as muddled up ethnically as earlier historians were intellectually. 'The Orcades' are mentioned by several Roman historians and a Roman fleet sailed around Britain through the Pentland Firth—which they found so calm that they thought the water must have been as heavy as lead.

King Brude, a Pictish king from Inverness, devastated Orkney in the 7th century, as did various other unwelcome visitors, including perhaps Hengist.

At the end of the 9th century the Vikings, who had no doubt been raiding spasmodically for many years, took over Orkney and Shetland and for the next 500 years Orkney became one of the Norse earldoms, for 2/3 of this span one of the great fiefs of the Vikings. Most of our place names are Norse, the old language was Norn and our history is celebrated in one of the cycle of Sagas written down in Iceland—The Orkneyinga Saga.

Considering its importance in their own history the British have paid singularly little attention to that of Scandinavia. The leaders at the crucial battles of Stamford Bridge and Hastings were all Norsemen of Scandinavian origin, Harold of Norway, Harold Godwinson of England and Duke William of Normandy. William the Conqueror was a direct descendant of an Earl of Orkney and two Earls of Orkney fought at Stamford Bridge with a contingent from the Islands.

From Orkney Viking expeditions raided the rest of Britain and Orkneymen went as far afield as Nijni-Novgorod, Palestine, Byzantium, Spain and France. Sweyn Asleifson, who lived on Gairsay which I can see from my house, captured Dublin. In his house on Gairsay he would feast two hundred men. Now there is one family there.

Orkney can also claim two saints, Rognvald and Magnus, with possibly a share in a third, Olaf or Ola, an Orkney saint by adoption. Rognvald in the 12th century started the Cathedral which still stands in Kirkwall, a magnificent memorial to his uncle, Magnus, murdered in Egilsay. The

Celtic church had brought Christianity to Orkney and Papa Westray and Papa Stronsay, islands where hermit priests lived, commemorate these early Christians. Later the diocese of Orkney owed allegiance to Trondheim. Before the Cathedral at Kirkwall was built the bishop officiated at Birsay in the west mainland.

No mean inheritance for the few thousand Orcadians of today. For though Orkney has been part of Scotland for some five hundred years and though more Scots than Viking blood must flow in Orkney veins, her inheritance is to a great extent Norse. That is to say, she was and is distinct from Scotland. Certainly Orkney and Shetland have had no truck with Gaeldom—except through the early church. Gaelic was never spoken, clans and tartans were unknown. No kilt flapped around the legs of Norsemen.

Orkney came to Scotland as the forfeited security for the dowry of Margaret, Princess of Denmark who married James III of Scotland—those 50,000 florins of the Rhine which figure so prominently in Orkney history. Orkney looks with nostalgia to Scandinavia—might she not have profited had gay and easy-going Copenhagen been her capital rather than dour Edinburgh? From time to time too the Danes are reminded about the slip they made in virtually selling her. Worse still, they reckoned Shetland was only worth 18,000 florins. But then the Danes have constantly sold colonies. They appear never to have had much pride in Empire; blessed people free from the canker of prestige. And is there not a palpable link here between Orkney and Shetland and Scandinavia?—a link which sets them apart from the British—a lack of prestige-seeking and all that goes with it, waste, ugliness, dissatisfaction, class divisions and the rat race.

The Scots, or Scotch as I was used to calling them having been brought up by unselfconsciously Scotch people, got a bad name in Orkney and Shetland, particularly the Stewart Earls and their grasping followers who collared much of the land. Lairds and merchants are seldom popular but may have been necessary. Certainly so far as Shetland is concerned, Hance Smith in his book *The Making of Modern Shetland* suggests that their overbearing behaviour may have been off-set by some usefulness to the Shetlanders. In fact, they were the pivots of the Shetland economy.

Orkney having much better land than Shetland farming was the staple way of life. I have mentioned the introduction of wild white clover in the 19th century—clover, white and purple, is intertwined with the sight of Orkney and the summer smell of heather and grass. Up until the thirties I believe Orkney moors were grazed by cattle, sheep, pigs and geese. Then the rising fertility of the enclosed fields left the moors to sheep, clover and grass took over much of the landscape.

Orkney life was old-fashioned up to the First World War. Even after the Second World War when I arrived and after the invasion of troops which the war brought and the agricultural grants and the breaking out of the hill land, you could sense the solid, old-fashioned 'bone' beneath the new changes. Once out of Kirkwall you feel Orkney to be an agricultural land in a way that the feel of agriculture has been lost in most of Britain. Much of Britain is still wild but it is mostly poor soil given over to few people, big estates and grazing; much too is intensively farmed but increasingly as a business rather than a way of life. Orkney by Highland or even North of England standards is not wild. Thirty years ago oats, bere, hay and neeps, called turnips in the south, were grown in quantity, poultry abounded and black cattle were the main crop, no longer loose upon the hillside but well tended in green fields.

We first lived in Orkney in a cottage by the loch of Harray belonging to Eric Linklater's sister, Elspeth Cormack. Their father had built himself a grander house nearer the loch but the cottage was snug and more in keeping with the low landscape.

Between 1945 and 1950 I did not spend much time in Orkney and Shetland though I had done a tour in the summer before the Election. Meetings compared with today were crowded in those times. Just before the Election I had persuaded Sir Archibald Sinclair to come across from Caithness. The Kirkwall Town Hall which seated perhaps three hundred people was packed with a hundred or so standing. Sir Archibald was not a short speaker. But by the time he had finished there were no signs of restlessness. Then the questioning—the heckling—began. It ranged from the national misdeeds of the Liberals to Northern Scottish and local affairs. Two incidents in particular I remember. Someone asked Sir Archibald if he would press for the reopening of the branch railway line from Wick to Lybster. Sir Archibald luckily said that he thought the line could not be justified and therefore it could not be reopened. 'Indeed it canna' came a voice from the back of the hall belonging to one of Orkney's best known and most popular dealers, John T. Flett, 'I have the sleepers'. The other incident arose from a confused hubbub at the back of the hall. The Chairman asked the questioner to come forward so that Sir Archie could hear what he was saying. Down the aisle there swayed a well-known docker well primed for a political evening. With difficulty reaching the front, 'What Party do you belong to?' he asked. 'The Liberal Party' of course responded Sir Archibald. Whereupon Mr. Annal flung his cap to the floor and with a shout of 'The good old Liberals' collapsed and was carried out.

In those days the great majority of the farmers and crofters had been born in Orkney as had their fathers and grandfathers: the Robertsons at

Lyking, the Ritchs at Kierfiold were strong Liberals. Such farmers were the backbone of my support. I first began to think that I might be elected when it was reported to me that Mr. Corrigal of North Bigging, who had of late shown signs of backsliding into Conservatism, proposed a vote of thanks to me. When taxed with this sign of grace he replied 'I am too old a rat not to know when it is time to leave the sinking ship'.

The best of summer days in Orkney is evoked in Edwin Muir's poem on his childhood in the island of Wyre:

> Long time he lay upon the sunny hill
> To his father's house below securely bound,
> Far off the silent changing sound was still
> With the black islands lying thick around.
>
> He saw each separate height, each vaguer hue,
> Where the massed islands rolled in mist away,
> And though all ran together in his view
> He knew that unseen straits between them lay.
>
> Often he wondered what new shores were there,
> In thought he saw the still light on the sand,
> The shallow water clear in tranquil air
> And walked through it in joy from strand to strand.
>
> Over the sound a ship so slow would pass
> That in the black hill's gloom it seemed to lie,
> The evening sound was smooth like sunken glass
> And time seemed finished ere the ship passed by.
>
> Grey tiny rocks slept round him where he lay,
> Moveless as they, more still as evening came,
> The grasses threw straight shadows far away,
> And from the house his mother called his name.

At Election times heckling at the main meetings would go on for over an hour, sometimes longer. The verb to 'heckle' comes from the heckle which hecklers or hacklers used in the flax and jute mills. Hacklers in Dundee were renowned for the vigour of their political opinions. Stromness in Orkney and Lerwick produced even more dedicated hecklers than Kirkwall, probably because in each there was a small but vigorous Labour Party. Meetings were then a serious business and the candidate's performance was considered to affect his chances of election, certainly it greatly affected the morale of his supporters. The hecklers too took their duties seriously, standing at the back of the hall and listening in silence until their chance came. Jimmie Paton, the leader of the dockers in Lerwick, was a constant attender. The heckler was a great asset to politics. The mixture of serious questioning and joking, the rapid change of subject and the response of the audience made a good meeting. Nothing could bring out the flavour as well as the policies of the candidate as this questioning could. I remember giving wholly inaccurate answers—but then I went away and did better next time. I learnt never to underestimate a questioner. In the days before television groups of people in Orkney and Shetland would take up some interest and by constant discussion become expert on it. One such group in Eshaness on the extreme north of Shetland mainland had in 1949 been studying the writings of Major Douglas, the Canadian inventor of Social Credit. My opponent, Sir Basil Neven-Spence, went to Eshaness and was suddenly confronted in the mellow light of a Tilley lamp by a series of searching questions about credit, the trade cycle, etc. His efforts to shrug the matter off were not well received. I was luckily warned. So at least I gathered together what little economics I knew and made some response. Such a favourable impression did this make that several of the Social Creditors accompanied me on motor bicycles to the next meeting to continue the discussion. At Burravoe in Shetland there was a debating society in which a crofter called Rendall played a prominent part. He was of far Left opinions and a keen atheist but also an advocate of slavery. Before ecology and manure-grown vegetables became fashionable he practised the simple life (with the help of national assistance) digging his small piece of ground with the Shetland spade. He was an unusual man but not one I would have liked to be dependant upon. In the island of Eday in Orkney a surprising interlude was caused by an incomer, a Cornishman, who rose and asked if he could read a statement. On being given permission he read a short document blaming the ills of the world upon the increasingly important role in public affairs played by women. At the end of it he sat down in silence, a silence not even broken by any of the two or three women there and the meeting continued as though nothing peculiar had happened.

Years later, when Leader of the Liberal Party, I took part at a General Election in one of a series of televised meetings at which journalists fired questions about the policies of the parties. As I fired back my encapsulated answers I became conscious that the questioners were not interested; their heads were down considering the next question. It was a strange experience, like stepping off a cliff into the void. How very different from a Lerwick meeting at which each questioner asked his question because he himself wanted to know the answer and intended to follow it up.

No glib rejoinder would satisfy him or the audience which surrounded him.

There was another feature of meetings in Orkney and Shetland which still persists in some of the islands. At the end of the meeting the Chairman instead of proposing a vote of thanks to the candidate or just closing the meeting, rises to his feet and asks if anyone will propose a motion 'that Mr. Grimond is a suitable person to represent Orkney and Shetland in the House of Commons.' This is usually followed by an embarrassing silence. However, eventually someone is prodded into proposing the motion. The Chairman thereupon calls for a seconder. An even longer pause follows. If performer and seconder are obtained the Chairman then asks if there is any counter motion, whereupon half the hall spring to their feet to propose a contrary motion. When this first happened to me I was sufficiently alarmed by this time to see no end to this public exposure. The end indeed is disconcerting. The motion is presumably debatable—it is certainly liable to be put to the vote, though I have always had chairmen of sufficient skill to announce the original motion carried before anyone can demand a count. This custom must go back a long way, I suppose to the days when electors numbered a score or so in any district. Or is it an Orkney and Shetland peculiarity? It was not until the 19th century that Shetland had an M.P.; up till then there were no voters with the necessary qualifications. Another custom, perhaps dating from the same time as the motion of confidence, was that at election times in some parishes a leading man, often the County Councillor, took the chair no matter what his party. I had at least one excellent Tory Chairman.

These anecdotes throw light upon some of the characteristics of Orkneymen and Shetlanders. The characteristic that struck me most agreeably was their tolerance, their lack of abrasiveness. Politics were to be conducted in a reasonable way without rancour. I found this all the more agreeable as from reading some of the correspondence in the local papers before I had visited the islands I had an impression of some considerable ill-temper. I seem to remember a letter suggesting that Churchill was a war criminal who ought to be sent for trial and another that someone who advocated a certain rig for racing yachts ought to be hanged. But I have since learnt that writers to the papers are often a race on their own, usually untypical and frequently non-native. Seen against the Orkneymen or Shetlanders the Scots seem an assertive and quarrelsome race.

In the hotels where I spent much time as I travelled around the Scotch visitors were usually identifiable by a coarse volubility; not always of course, but few of the people of Orkney and Shetland, even those locally described as 'bigsy', had the blend of patronage and assertion noticeable among visitors—the English no doubt as well as the Scotch.

Since the Reform Bill of 1832 Orkney and Shetland had been loyal to the Liberals—of various persuasions. Once or twice the tradition had been broken but often the feuds had been between different camps in the Liberal Party. Arthur Anderson, the Shetlander who was among the founders of the P. & O. Company had been the Member from 1847 to 1852. Apart from representing her in Parliament he had been foremost in the economic history of Shetland. He had introduced new methods of organisation and had founded the Shetland Fishing Company which revived and extended the Shetland trade with Spain in dried fish. One of my most popular predecessors had been Cathcart Wason. Wason was a New Zealander who had sat in the New Zealand Parliament, changed his Party and been evicted for corruption. He won Orkney and Shetland as a Liberal Unionist in 1900. Repeating his New Zealand career he changed to being a Liberal and remained as M.P. until 1921.

Even in the fifties tales about him lingered on. He was said to have knitted in the House of Commons. An extremely sensible way to pass the time but did he do it in the Chamber itself? I have been unable to find out. I doubt if nowadays it would be in order. He and his brother Eugene (who was also an M.P.) were enormous men, the sight of him landing in streaming and gleaming oilskins from the 'flit' boats which used to put passengers ashore was stamped on some childhood memories of men and women I have met. Children, though below the age of voting, were serviceable to him in other ways. He is said to have carried to Orkney and Shetland other habits from his New Zealand days: when kissing babies he would slip a half sovereign from his mouth to theirs. If the story is true his constituents' wives must have been adept at turning their small children upside down to extract the coin.

Orkney and Shetland were natural Liberal territory. Trade, and in Shetland the fishing industry, had been in the hands of the lairds and merchants but there was, by the standards of the South, no big Conservative class. Though evictions took place, important differences marked the islands off from the Scottish Highlands. In Shetland men were valuable, indeed essential, to fishing. In Orkney the land could sustain a proportion of small farmers. The clan system did not exist. The lairds or their agents did not carry out wholesale removals. As for the people themselves, the Poor Law Commission of 1843 found that as they were too poor to emigrate, sea and land provided the alternative. In Orkney and Shetland as elsewhere in the Highlands and Islands the Crofting Acts cemented the loyalty of the people to the Liberal Party. To the economic advantages bestowed by these Acts and such other Liberal measures as the Old Age Pension was added the moral fervour associated with 19th century Liberalism reaching its height in the populist appeal of Gladstone.

In 1945 Laura drove to the poll in Lerwick an old lady who told her she would vote for 'Mr. Gladstone's man'. She could remember the visit of the Napier Commission to her father's croft whose rent was subsequently reduced to £12.

Sir Basil Neven-Spence told me a story which also illustrates the grip of Gladstone. At the time when Sir Basil lived on the island of Uyea in Shetland, one of the few inhabitants was an old lady whose Liberalism he accepted and never tried to change although they were good friends. However, in the thirties when Liberalism was patently on the wane he said to her, half joking, 'You'll have to vote for me this time', and she promised that she would. When the Election was over he asked her if she had done so. Embarrassed, she replied that she had put on her bonnet and coat and was just going off to do so 'when I looked up and saw him' pointing to a plate with Gladstone's face on it, hanging over the door. 'I couldna' do it.' When I read of the popularity of the T.V. stars today I realise that none of them has the power that Gladstone had over people who had never seen or heard him. To vote Tory was like leaving the true Church. It was a betrayal.

Nor did Socialism have much appeal to people of independence. They were not proletarians. Though dismally poor and extremely badly paid— Hance Smith in *The Making of Modern Shetland* reckons that out of the £20,000 profit which the herring exports yielded in 1837 the fishermen got £4,500 or £1 16/- per man—the Shetlanders had their own life and self-respect. Only among the merchant seamen and dockers did Trades Unionism find many adherents.

Though they shared so many characteristics and so much history there were and are considerable differences between Orkney and Shetland. Shetland is a wild country, the Old Rock, round which the wintry seas curdle and clash. Though it has a myriad of skerries and small islands the inhabited islands are fewer than in Orkney—Yell and Unst, virtually extensions of the Shetland mainland to the north, are larger than any Orkney island except Hoy. Shetland, though not mountainous, is sharper than Orkney; you feel the rocks like a skeleton under the thin heather; it does not lie in such gentle sweeps, as in Orkney. Long, dark fingers of land stretch into the sea and you come upon deserted voes, lurking like Norwegian fjords between the rocks. The light too is different, reflecting Shetland's affinity with the sea. It has a liquid, mauve sheen with skies mussel coloured and lochs with the iridescence of seaweed and sea pools— Yeat's *Mackerel-crowded seas.* Apart from the southern tip of the mainland where there is lime and the central valley of the Ting, the ancient Parliament, it is covered in heather and peat except for green patches round the croft houses—or where croft houses once stood. Shetland is a lonely country. When I look out of my house in Orkney at any hour of the night I see lights in the houses and lights moving on the roads. In Shetland you can wind round the moorland roads and see no lights but the moon or stars (if showing) reflected in the innumerable little lochs or the long voes which cut in from the sea. One night I was driving back to Lerwick at about eleven o'clock in a car I had hired when it stopped on the main road to the north of Lerwick. I could not get it to start. It was pouring with rain, I knew nothing about the car, not a house in sight. So rather than get soaked by trying to tinker with it I thought I would wait until a passing car would give me a lift to Lerwick. I waited until 7.00 a.m. Not a soul passed either way all night.

I have often thought of building myself a cottage in Shetland close by the sea with the hill behind. Many sites in the world have a magic beauty on certain days and nights and Shetland is among them. It is a savage but not a forlorn landscape. Before men polluted the moon and found it to be dust they must have imagined the moonscape like Shetland, treeless, floating in a framework of sky.

But for many of those not born there—and for some of those that are— it is too strong meat for an all-the-year-round diet. Mixed in with the beauty are those weeks of drenching rain and howling wind. The immediate outlook in Shetland—as in Orkney—can be squalid. Shetland architecture is now not of a high standard; the crofts are apt to be surrounded by debris of day-to-day living, from fish heads to old motor cars.

The low croft houses crouched under their thatched roofs with the byre and mill at one end and the living quarters at the other were one with the landscape and the 'Lodberries' (house and store) of Lerwick at right angles to the sea with one gable in the water so that goods could be lifted from the boats were well built and a pleasure to look at. Even Shetland gales are tamed by the narrow streets in which all traffic is slowed to walking pace, there being plenty of pedestrians and no pavements. But many of the old crofts languish abandoned in favour of more commodious concrete cottages and traffic, unfortunately, is prising open the old towns of Shetland and Orkney.

Lerwick has its jetsam of newspaper and old cans and its council house estates as dreary as any in Scotland, which is saying a lot. The middle class, to which I belong, hanker for a bogus cottage existence, spotlessly clean but unpretentious, small in scale but everything in its place. But it is a dream, especially in cold, inhospitable climates when even keeping life going requires extra effort. The wide landscape of Shetland, though it lacks the drama of the Alps, the romance of the Highlands or the subtlety of the farmed countryside of England or France, has a purity of air and light and colour which the north can give but it also has its drawbacks.

119

It must, however, be a good climate for people. I have an unscientific theory that history is full of flukes. I see no evidence that any rigorous attention to history will produce much evidence of inexorable economic forces. If human success depended upon economic forces Russia with its vast natural resources would be the richest country in the world instead of one of the poorer. In the long run, climate, the selection of the fittest, the pressure of changing conditions, may well determine the very long tides of human development. But within the horizons of a thousand years or so chance seems the determinant. Shetland for some reason seems to breed a tolerant, decent people. The Vikings were apparently anything but this. How account for them? Because, I suggest, they were a fluke, a chance or mischance. They no doubt contributed to the Shetland character but do not dominate it. And by chance Orkney and Shetland seem to have got the best of the Viking blood. When I first became an M.P. a salvage company asked me if I could find them some Shetland sailors. They wanted them not only because they were good seamen but because they did not quarrel. They could be left for months alone on or near a wreck without going berserk. They would over-winter in the Antarctic. One skipper once said to me that he found the Shetlanders very odd, they seldom fought and they never threw coal at the seagulls. I suggest that Shetland has evolved through the Vikings. Like all races the Vikings no doubt had difficult sides to their character, some of which have been ignored, others over-rated, by history. The Shetland and Orkney Vikings when at home seem to have got on rather well together. If the absence of fortified castles means anything they must have lived in comparative peace with one another. Nor do they seem to have wanted to enslave other people. Yet it was the branch of the Scandinavians that settled in France, the Normans, who built huge, frowning castles. It is they who behaved with such brutality to their victims, the English for instance. It may be that for long voyages in open boats the present day Shetland virtue of tolerance was essential. Perhaps the Normans gave up voyaging and took to castle building because they lacked this virtue. It seems odd, however, since they were of the same stock. What seems at least possible is that the native stock which the Vikings found in Shetland continued. The characteristics of this stock had no doubt been formed over the years by the nature of the islands. Although the population must always have been small and mixed the process no doubt continued and continues— those Viking qualities which are unsuitable or unnecessary are bred out— or those with them go elsewhere. I suspect for pure application of any such theory the time is too short but I find it difficult to reconcile the accounts of Viking raiders and Norman barons with the present traits of the Shetlanders (or Orkneymen).

But one trait certainly went back to Viking times, the skill of Shetlanders in boats. There is some truth in the hackneyed old saying that a Shetlander is a fisherman with a croft (and the Orkneyman a crofter with a boat). Shetland is anchored in one of the most prolific fishing grounds in the world. How long it will remain so as nation after nation dredges up the fish is an open question. But for centuries the North Sea has produced great harvests of fish. The first nation to launch fleets of fishing boats capable of riding out to sea were the Dutch. Their 'busses' came by the hundred to fish from Bressay Sound to the harbour of Lerwick. In the European wars these fleets were attacked by Holland's enemies. The Dutch fishery declined sharply after their fishing fleet was burnt by the French in 1703. But the Dutch continued to visit Shetland until the First World War. An old woman told me that as a girl she was woken by the wooden clogs of Dutch fishermen going down to their boats. The Shetlanders used open boats, the smaller and older rowed by four men, later sixerns—six rowers. The fishing was carried on from sandy beaches all round the coasts. The fishermen lived for the season on or near the beaches. The boats were launched from the sands sometimes across halibut then apparently not an esteemed fish and the catch dried on the stones. The smaller boats caught codling in the voes, the bigger boats, the sixerns, rowed and sailed out of sight of land 'Rowan Foula Doon' i.e. rowing out until even the island of Foula was below the horizon. It was a summer fishing but even in summer Shetland is often caught in sudden and fierce gales. Terrible losses were suffered periodically from 1832 to 1888 after which this type of fishing declined. The far 'haaf' fishing was for white fish. But herring on which the Dutch fishery throve were also caught by Shetlanders using larger half-decked vessels—though for the Shetland seas they were still very small. Around the turn of the century these Shetland smacks were replaced by 'fifties' and 'zulus' as used on the Scotch coast. I have photographs won in a raffle on the fishing island of Burra showing the old herring fleet putting to sea. The boats look perilously fragile. The last zulu boat, the *Research*, fished successfully until about 1970. Her skipper told me that he and his boat were the same age—over seventy. She was the top catcher in the sixties. In old days Shetland white fish were dried and sold on the continent. In the 17th century much trade was carried on with the Hanseatic League. The more enterprising lairds in the 18th century opened up markets in Spain and Portugal. The herring and other fish were salted. Salt therefore was a most important commodity. The beaches on which the fish were dried were also valuable. A man in Unst told me that his first job as a boy was to carry stones to repair the roads. The stones had to be gathered below high-water mark so as not to damage the beach. He got I think 2/6 per ton gathered, carried and delivered to the road. By the 19th century there were numerous herring stations—wooden piers—all round Shetland and hundreds of girls came to salt and pack the herring.

Mrs. Lennie of Stronsay in Orkney who died last year at 102 told me that Hamnavoe Olnesfirth in Shetland was the most beautiful place she had ever seen. I was rather puzzled as I could not place it. I discovered that it was an old herring station where she had worked in 1890. Baltasound in Unst was once the largest herring station in the world. So there have been big economic waves sweeping across Shetland and bringing in folk from the south before oil.

Whaling too was a considerable Shetland industry from the 18th century to the beginning of the 20th and whaling stations dotted the coasts—all gone. In Shetland after the Second World War fishing was largely confined to Lerwick, Scalloway and the islands of Burra, Whalsay and Skerries. Perhaps it survived on these islands because there was no other means of earning a living. Certainly they are some of the more barren parts of Shetland nor do the shores of Whalsay or Burra provide conspicuously good anchorages though Whalsay is known as the 'Bonnie Isle' which indeed it is today with the fishermen's houses all painted and gay in their new prosperity. When I first went to Shetland few of these islands had piers at which even the larger fishing boats, let alone the coasters, could tie up with safety. Whatever the reason for the continuation of fishing from these islands, it certainly made them the most thriving districts in Shetland, at least in numbers. While Whalsay was bustling with some thousand inhabitants, the population of the neighbouring island of Fetlar, over twice the size and much more fertile, fell to under a hundred. Why did a fishing community survive in Burra, keeping the population at roughly the same size for a hundred and fifty years, while only four families lived on Trondra next door? I have remarked elsewhere that I believe fishing provides some conditions which human beings like but are seldom taken into account. The men and women separate during the day. Fishing satisfies the gambling and hunting instincts. It also calls for skill. It provides excitement, not to say danger. Crofting by comparison is dull, plodding work, done in isolation, yet mixed up with domesticity. On a fishing boat there is camaraderie. You never can tell how the day or night will turn out. No one could say that life on the old fishing boats was comfortable. These boats were little changed from the 'zulus' so called presumably because they were first built at the time of the Zulu Wars. The bunks were stacked round the cabin like chests of drawers. They reeked of fish and diesel oil. Nor was the work easy or safe. The herring fishing meant putting to sea in the evening, bucketing out perhaps five, perhaps fifty miles, shooting the eighty or so drift nets then having a short rest until the early morning when the nets had to be hauled and shaken out. I find an hour or two of pulling and shaking, balanced on the nets as they pile up in the hold, quite enough. But it needed more than four hours to get them all aboard. Meanwhile the boat heaved and tossed, usually in rain. Back in port the catch had to be disposed of and by that time if the herring were very far out you had to put to sea again. The winter seining for white fish (haddock, whiting, and ling etc.) was worse, though you might get more rest. The boats sailed in the early morning, pitch dark and bitterly cold. When the seine net came aboard the fish were gutted live on deck. I suppose the hands of the fishermen got used to the cold, mine never did. Until prices rose in the fifties the returns were poor. One old fisherman told me that he had never finished the season with more than a few hundred pounds in his pocket. Sometimes the boats ran to Aberdeen to sell their catch. But the life was friendly, large mugs of tea and meals of fish livers (for those with strong stomachs) were the rewards for good appetites.

The smaller islands were often served by missionary school teachers who took the church services, taught the children and often looked after any visitors. One of the best of these in my time was Mr. Alex Doloughan in Fair Isle—a man who deserved an honour if anyone did. On the larger islands we stayed in lodging houses or small hotels, homely places where the guests soon gravitated into the kitchen. Many cups of tea I drank in the Fotheringhames' kitchen in Stronsay. Now, with oil, hotels are becoming more pretentious and much more expensive and much less homely.

It was at sea, above all, that the good nature of the Shetlanders was most striking. Radio meant that the fleet could exchange news of their luck, gossip, pick up the calls of foreign boats. Yet, for five minutes, or so, in the evening everyone kept off the air so that one particular fisherman could sing a psalm to his family on shore. The boats were owned co-operatively, every member of the crew and some merchants on land had a share; this spirit of co-operation permeated everything. This spirit was indeed essential to island life. You relied on your neighbour to help you, the fishing boats took the women to Lerwick, collected messages or took the doctor to islands where there was none. The most remote islands, Fair Isle and Foula, only fished for lobsters or occasionally for haddock and whiting for their own consumption. There were only some thirty to forty people on each of them. The mail boats crossed to the mainland about once a fortnight, weekly from Fair Isle. Often they were held up for weeks by weather. Though they were supposed to have postal votes these islanders hardly ever succeeded in recording their votes, the weather nearly always intervened. When you arrived at the pier on Foula you would be met by two or three men with wheelbarrows—wheelbarrows peculiar to Foula—a flat board with a large wheel. When anyone went out they would usually take a barrow in case there was something to be collected. They were the shopping bags of the islanders. So exposed were the havens on these islands that the mail boat had to be drawn up by a winch or crane and stowed on land.

The old travellers whom I used to meet on my rounds have also departed, Mr. Pearson, the Shetland dentist, who carried his instruments on his motor bicycle and the oculist, a 'stickit' oculist, I suspect, but old people swore they never had such good spectacles as he supplied. His name was C. Franklin, his slogan was 'If you can't see, C. Franklin'. Toothache could be a terrible scourge in the outlying islands—often the best hope was the doctor and a pair of pliers so children sometimes had their teeth out as soon as they grew up.

Until oil came, life in Shetland was hard. But the Shetlanders seldom complained. And it had its compensations.

I was travelling one Saturday by bus from Lerwick to Scalloway with a party of fishermen going home for the weekend. I remarked on one who was conspicuously merry. 'Aye, aye', my neighbour replied, 'Walter's a grand fisherman. He drinks every penny he gets, but with thae subsidies the money's aye gaining on him.'

On the crofts, the spring, Voar as it was called in Shetland, was a busy time. Oats and potatoes had to be sown, peats cut and lambs received into the cold wind, for spring is usually cold and windy in both Shetland and Orkney. Lambs and knitwear were the cash crops. Shetland women were famous for their knitting (and in the island of Trondra also for their rowing). They did much of the work on the crofts for the men were often away from home, fishing or in the Merchant Navy. They carried the peats and much else in baskets, kishies, on their backs leaving the hands free to knit even when walking. The needles were stuck in their belts. However, knitting machines were coming in: in the late fifties units of some dozen knitting machines were established which provided more companionship for the knitters. These units and the fish-processing plants which were also being set up were a tribute to the enterprise of the Shetlanders. They were mostly locally owned, not only merchants but schoolmasters and doctors took a hand in managing them. Mr. Tait in Whalsay, Gibbie Johnson of Vidlin, Dr. Dowle of Hillswick and the three Tulloch families and John Laurie among many others deserve to be remembered as does, for a different craft—silverware—Mr. Rae who came to Shetland as a missionary and gave valuable employment as a silversmith.

By mid-summer there is hardly any darkness on a fine night. At

Kirkwall a golf competition used to start at midnight. Football too is a summer game in the far north and often played in the late evening. Bands abounded. Weddings went on all night, sometimes for two or three nights. Whalsay and Skerries weddings have a high reputation. Very exhausting they must be for the bride and groom. The ceremony is in the afternoon. The whole island down to babes in arms then adjourns to the village hall, the bride still in her wedding dress. In Orkney the bride's cog, a beautifully made wooden vessel like a small milk churn, is passed round and round by the bridesmaids. Everyone brings something to drink. Dancing goes on till morning with a supper of potatoes and mutton around midnight. Then some sleep through the day and sometimes back to the hall for another night's dancing. As the lancers, reels, valetas and other energetic dances are the main items you get well exercised and all too thirsty.

The autumn too is busy with thousands of lambs jostling down the pier at Lerwick on their way south, the harvest to be gathered and the pony sales in Unst and Lerwick. It is the season of Willie Peterson, the Shetland auctioneer. No pop star, even with electrical aids, can galvanize an audience like Willie. He rattles prices out of the most wary dealers until with a bang the lambs, as bemused as their buyer, are shuttled out of the ring. So when I first became an M.P. the old trades carried on and the old ways absorbed the Shetlanders.

Even after the war various nations stuck to their traditional catches. The Swedes with their white hulled boats came every summer to catch ling. They even had their own church in Unst. The Belgians fished for mackerel, the Spaniards for hake. So there was a kind of rationing. The boats were limited in their catching power by their size. Now we have huge fleets from Russia and Eastern Europe anchored out to sea with their parent ships and catchers sometimes to be seen at night like the lights of a city on the horizon. Some years ago I was told that during a spell of bad weather there were four thousand Norwegian fishermen ashore in Lerwick. It is amazing that the stocks have lasted so long—they cannot sustain this slaughter for ever. Fish of every species and size are hauled aboard to be boiled down for fish meal or fertilizers. It is a free for all. The most fertile fishing grounds in the world for good quality fish are being wrecked. Knitwear too is subject to change in fashions. Hand-knitted Fair Isle patterns are expensive. We have lost the name 'Shetland' which now appears on garments made in the Borders, the Midlands of England or even Japan and South America.

But this is to anticipate. In the late fifties and sixties though there were clouds in the sky the Shetlanders were getting a bit more money in their pockets and the small green shoots of prosperity could be seen in the new fishing boats and knitting machines.

125

Transport charges were the great handicap. Though the Western Isles got an annual subsidy which even in the fifties ran into hundreds of thousands of pounds, Shetland got nothing and Orkney very little. They were penalised for the hard work of their inhabitants. We had no trunk roads and though the sea was our trunk route we got no government help in crossing it.

These were the islands and their anxieties with which I was to live. Still, I had not seen them. I was in the Army pursuing other thoughts.

8

WHEN THE WAR ENDED I was in the Atlantic Hotel in Hamburg. The circumstances were not what might be expected in a defeated and disrupted country which had suffered the vilest tyranny ever experienced outside Russia. The 53rd Division had taken over the Atlantic Hotel from some German formation which had apparently been living in style right to the end. The building remained as it must always have been, a first class hotel of the old sort, high rooms, gold and plush, waiters, housemaids, restaurants etc. and a hall porter who went on functioning in his braided uniform as the best hotel porters do. Particularly was he useful in telling us the way to get around Hamburg. The city was full of bits and pieces of the German army asking for orders. Their discipline was good, too good to be sensible perhaps. Several companies of old gentlemen who had been repairing roads or engaging in some such unwarlike occupation reported to me. I had no idea how to dispose of them so I told them to wait in a football stadium. I then forgot about them for many hours, meanwhile it rained. When I eventually remembered them they were still standing in their ranks in the middle of the football field. They had not even taken shelter in the stands. I still believe that German army training and discipline and courage, from the little I saw of it was excellent. I am not one of those who deride it as mindless and mechanical and I cannot believe that it was achieved by sheer brutality.

But what can anyone who admires and likes many Germans make of the horror of the concentration camps? When we took over Neuengamme it was neat, clean, orderly with the ashes of the victims in cardboard boxes. It is the incongruity between the homeliness of the Germans and the behaviour of the Nazis that is so sinister. The Germans still cherish the skills we have lost. Their vaunted efficiency does not rely on new technology or profligate expenditure. They win because they make the most of what they have—horse-drawn transport if that alone is available. But this thrifty, admirable application to the job in hand is all the more gruesome when the job in hand is the running of an extermination camp.

It was at the Atlantic Hotel that I saw the best cabaret I have ever encountered, including a man who balanced on one finger. Here too another incident occurred revealing the curious attitudes of some of the higher command.

The senior officers had gone off to Corps or Army Headquarters on some pretext. This was a favourite pastime of theirs rather like the penchant which councillors and officials have in peace time for trips to London for conferences. We junior officers were having a cup of afternoon tea off the fine porcelain of the hotel when a soldier appeared and announced with boredom that a car had been stopped on some bridge and found to contain Seyss-Inquart. What was he to do with him? Seyss-Inquart was notorious for his cruelty both in Austria and Holland where he had been Gauleiter. The consortium of Majors present, of whom I was one, decided we had better ring up our superiors, which we did. We were told that he was to be treated with the utmost consideration and despatched to Army H.Q. in a staff car. This we considered more than a bit thick. Our superiors had pinched nearly all the staff cars and we were not going to have a Nazi going off with any that remained. We saw no reason why a notorious murderer should be treated with special consideration. So we gave orders that he was to be kept under guard outside the hotel while negotiations continued. We still had with us two Dutch liaison officers with whom we were on excellent terms. With their collaboration we told higher authority that we would carry out their instructions if they insisted but we must have them in writing as the Dutch liaison officers must inform their government that Seyss-Inquart was to be cossetted as a V.I.P. No written orders were forthcoming. We then treated him as an ordinary prisoner. Protesting violently he was searched, (just as well as he had a knife strapped to his thigh) and put in a military police cell for the night. After that he was collected and whisked away, ultimately to stand trial at Nuremberg.

While enjoying a suite in the Atlantic Hotel news came that I was to be returned to Britain as a political candidate. I had largely forgotten about this. However, as even the delights of the Atlantic Hotel were wearing thin, I jumped at this chance of going home. Looting, as I have said, was one of the hallmarks of Montgomery's army. Even humble, well, fairly humble, Majors had their perks. I was driven to Calais, or it may have been Boulogne, in a Mercedes. A wheel flew off as far as I remember but otherwise nothing of moment happened. Who drove the Mercedes or what happened to it I don't remember.

Johnnie back from school
at the Old Manse.

Grizelda, Johnnie and I sailing from Vidlin on
the mainland of Shetland to the islands of Skerries.

Grizelda and Fiona Corbett dressed in the
clothes of the Oakbank Grimonds.

Unloading goods from a flit-boat at Papa Westray, Orkney.

Aerial view of St. Andrews, 1929.

So I turned up to fight the 1945 Election. There had not been a General Election for ten years but there had been the war. Everyone was out of touch with elections, not least the electors of Orkney and Shetland. I arrived in the islands for the first time to find that political interest and organisation were both low. Peter Goodlad a local lawyer, who had been Lady Glen Coats's agent, asked me when I first called on him for what Party I proposed to stand. Peter afterwards did me great service, nor was this as naive a question as it now sounds. The General Election of 1945 began in a muddle. Many people in and out of Parliament wanted the coalition to continue. The machines of the Conservative and Liberal Parties creaked into motion with some difficulty. In two Highland constituencies, Ross & Cromarty and Inverness, it was at first uncertain whether the Liberal candidates were independent or National Liberals. Jacko MacLeod who won Ross & Cromarty as a National Liberal told me afterwards that he had intended to join Sir Archibald Sinclair, but unfortunately Archie was beaten.

In Shetland, apart from Peter Goodlad, the first person who befriended Laura and me was Alec Tulloch a knit-wear merchant now Convener of the Island Council. He carried us off to the island of Yell where he had a house on the edge of a voe—one of those arms of the sea that are such a feature of Shetland. There he and his wife entertained us most hospitably. I think the first meeting I ever addressed in Shetland and Orkney was with him in the Mid Yell hall. The big hall was fairly full. Nowadays an election meeting is a dozen old stalwarts in the small room above the hall.

I had to gather up the remnants of the old Orkney and Shetland radicals. Among these were many thoughtful and scholarly men. William Tulloch, my Chairman in Orkney, was the schoolmaster in Finstown, where three of my children subsequently went to school, and a very good schoolmaster he was. He had started his connection with the Liberal Party at an early age. Late in the 19th century a riot had broken out in the island of Sanday where he was born. It was said that the stick with which the Tory agent had been beaten was hidden in his pram. In Finstown too there lived Ned Sinclair who divided up the world according to their political beliefs (Tories were usually referred to as 'rank', Liberals as 'grand') and supplied me with a list of Members of Parliament for Orkney since the Union of Scotland and England. Looking back I see my campaign was somewhat sporadic. But I had little to go on.

I was, however, greatly helped by the existence of local Liberal papers. Without them it would have been impossible for a Liberal to win the seat. They and two Conservative papers were widely and closely read. They carried leading articles on national and local politics of a high standard. The *Shetland Times* belonged to the Wishart family: as the young Wishart son, Basil, had not been demobilized it was still being edited by a cousin, a chemist by training, Johnny Laurenson. He was another well-informed and well read Shetlander who taught me a lot about his native islands, looked like the photograph of Giuseppe de Lampadusa, author of *The Leopard*, and had abilities to match his looks. Though Peter Goodlad was my agent in Shetland, Johnny travelled round a good deal with Laura and me. He gave us most valuable advice, as well as support in the paper. Congenial companions are very necessary during election campaigns and I was lucky to have Johnny and Peter Goodlad in Shetland and Cecil Walls and later Jackie Robertson, both local solicitors, in Orkney. Jackie Robertson is still going strong, Orkney's leading criminal advocate: but Cecil is dead. Many hours did I spend in their hospitable houses tossing over to islands under their guidance (agony to Peter who though a Shetlander was a poor sailor) or motoring to parish halls. Cecil and his grey Daimler car were known all over Orkney. They were well suited to each other, old-fashioned, spruce and reliable.

A candidate's nerves are often set on edge, the most even tempered need soothing. I was far from phlegmatic as well as knowing little about Shetland. Johnny did me a lot of good as did Edwin Eunson, my first and strongest supporter in Oban, now Alec Tulloch's opposite number as Convener of Orkney Islands Council. I fear such men as the two Tullochs, Ned Sinclair, Johnny Laurenson, Mr. Fotheringhame another school-master and Mr. Learmonth, are a dying breed; books no longer play the part they once did. Fewer schoolmasters are now content to remain turning out excellent teaching in village schools. Independent radicals have become bureaucratic state socialists.

What thoughts did the 1945 Election provoke? In retrospect sound reasons have been found for the Labour victory. Some say that though Winston Churchill was popular, the Tories were still held to blame for 'appeasement'. Some hold that servicemen and women had been quietly making up their minds to set off on a new course. It has been suggested that Churchill's 'Gestapo speech' lost many votes. It has also been suggested that while the Tories had let their organisation rust while they attended to winning the war, the Labour organisation had been kept well oiled. None of these reasons was obvious to me at the time. I did not find the Tories particularly unpopular or much worse organised than anyone else. I remember buying the daily paper in which the Gestapo speech was reported. Other people in the paper shop seemed to find it amusing rather than offensive. Recently I came across what seems to be an extract from a letter written later by Duff Cooper to my mother-in-law. He had apparently been asked to write a biography of Winston Churchill to be called *Man of Vision*. 'I refused', he wrote, 'I think he has the vision of a bull—he sees one thing very plainly, larger than life, and goes straight for it. Just now it happens to be red.'

In the election campaign I spoke of 'power in the hands of the people'—forestalling a Liberal slogan of the sixties. I was also prepared to go into a coalition if the election results made it necessary.

I never expected to win Orkney and Shetland. The general opinion was that while Neven-Spence would win even in a straight fight with a Liberal, the candidature of a Labour candidate for the first time made it certain. So low did I rate my chances that I did not go to the count (which took place some weeks after polling day). I was astonished to hear that I had got within 329 votes of victory. I kick myself for not having made the extra effort and in particular for having wasted time early in the campaign paying long visits to people who would never vote for me. As I was unknown I should have spent every available moment showing my face around the constituency.

It was during the run-up to the 1945 General Election that I went to lunch with Miss Balfour, a staunch Tory. From the point of view of politics the visit was a waste of time. But she told me an interesting story. She was almost the last of a branch of the Balfour family originally from Fife but long established in Orkney. She lived in a 19th century castle on the island of Shapinsay, full of beautiful and interesting things, now dispersed. In the 16th century the Balfours inhabited a more northerly Orkney island not far from Fair Isle, which lies between Orkney and Shetland. In 1588 one of the supply ships of the Spanish Armada was wrecked on Fair Isle. Scotland and Spain were not at war; even if they had been I doubt if the Fair Islanders would have known it. The Spaniards and Fair Islanders got along with some friction during August and September but when winter approached the islanders pointed out that there would not be enough food for everyone. So unless the Spaniards could arrange their own removal they would be obliged to push them off the cliff (Eric Linklater suggests that some may have already been pushed). The Spaniards were in fact taken off, many to Shetland, where they were hospitably treated and sent home. In this good work the Balfours apparently took a hand. In the middle of Miss Balfour's dining room table there stood 'a Tazza,' a cup with a lid. On one side it bore the arms of the Balfours, on the other, the arms of the Duke of Medina Sidonia, the commander of the Armada. It had been sent by the Duke as a gesture of thanks. I can visualise the cup and can hardly have made up the story but no one in Orkney that I can find can remember the cup. It has disappeared.

Certainly there was a breath of radicalism around. So there has always been after great wars. But after 1815 and 1918 it had virtually been swamped by jingosm and had only become apparent some years after these wars ended. Looking back we can now see Attlee's virtues, but at the time he struck the public, in so far as he struck them at all, as something of a sheep in sheep's clothing—to use a phrase attributed to Winston. He and his lieutenants, Ernest Bevin and Herbert Morrison, offered however, an alternative government suitable to the circumstances. They had been effective members of the war-time coalition so could be trusted to finish the war with Japan satisfactorily, at the same time they held out some promise that things would be different and better at home. At any rate they offered an alternative—something which did not exist in 1918. The Conservatives did not impress as a Party which had much to offer at home. Winston sensing this tried to talk of homely things, rather as Henry IV of France spoke of a chicken in every pot. But he did not convince nor was he adequately supported. Managerial politics were taking over.

The nationalisation measures introduced between 1945 and 1960 were essays in public management. They were State Socialism on the lines laid down by Herbert Morrison and the creators of such monopolies as London Transport. Keynesian economics relied upon the manipulation of demand to ensure full employment by financial and budgetary means. The Beveridge Plan and the National Health Service assumed that sound paternal government was the way to run a country where the evils of poverty would be abolished. Planning was much in vogue. It would be absurd to say that Liberals opposed the trend towards managed economy or foresaw its results and its failures. The *Yellow Book* had been an important pioneer in exploring possibilities of better state management. But Liberals at least raised the possibility of more democratic participation. Not only was the main stream of political and economic theory a state socialist stream but the war had shown that all sorts of things could be achieved if the state mobilised the resources.

Little wonder then that we were all to some extent Socialists. That was not wrong. But it should not have excluded, as to a large extent our Socialism did exclude, debate about what sort of socialism. Liberals tried to insert some participation by the workers into the nationalisation Bills: but the Tories were not seized of the need for this. They might oppose or modify the trend but they did not press for alternative means either political or economic to expand democracy. The Labour Party for their part were so indifferent to what is now called industrial democracy they abolished profit sharing in the Gas Light & Coal Co when it was taken over.

After the 1945 Election I was ordered to report to Catterick to finish my time in the Army. To be sentenced to Catterick filled me with dismay. My escape from it gave me further experience of how the world works.

A French friend of my father-in-law and mother-in-law, who had been particularly kind to Laura and me on our honeymoon, Toto Morhange, was, I knew, working for UNRRA in Portland Place. For some reason which I have forgotten I went to call on him. In the course of conversation I mentioned the fate that hung over me. Suggesting that I might find a job in UNRRA he sent me off to see Colonel Whiteley, the Director of Personnel for Europe. I remember Whiteley staring out of the window at the BBC and on hearing that I had been a Deputy Assistant Adjutant General in the Army, a post which dealt with personnel in a humble way, saying over his shoulder, 'I suppose you wouldn't like my job?' I accepted at once. Whiteley, who was keen to get back to Tootal Broadhurst and Lee, left as soon as he could get his luggage packed. By such curious expedients was the staff of UNRRA recruited.

The United Nations Relief and Rehabilitation Administration had been set up by the Allies to assist the countries devastated by the war and to help refugees. We sent missions all over the world to lift shattered nations onto their feet, we also ran refugee camps chiefly in Germany and Austria. The plight of the refugees was heart-rending. Torn from their homes, treated as animals or slaves, some had been battered into despair, others had lost all track of their roots and others by fierce necessity had become all too resourceful in looking after themselves. Many were frightened of returning to their countries, even if their countries would have them. UNRRA's highest hopes sometimes miscarried: but we did at least stave off some hunger, give some hope and distribute a great volume of goods. We provided medical services and expert assistance of various kinds. By far the greater proportion of aid came from the USA. The European and Mediterranean operations were run from London and we recruited from all over the world. Many of our staff worked themselves to exhaustion coping with unpredictable and sometimes insoluble problems. The real tough work of the organisation lay in central Europe and the occupied countries. I cannot write of it because I was ensnared in a London office. But I was well aware of the devotion shown by the best of our staff.

In our European Regional Office I found myself in Bedlam. It was like trying to swim in a pool constantly flooded and drained by the waves, round which curious pieces of jetsam swirled. The top of the organisation at that time was Fiorello La Guardia, the late mayor of New York, quite capable of causing chaos single-handed. But he was in fact ably assisted in this work. The headquarters were in Washington, but the European Regional Office in London looked after all the operations in Europe and adjacent continents. We were expanding rapidly in accordance, or sometimes not in accordance, with constantly changing plans. We were also under constant pressure from Governments, Central Banks, Army H.Qs, and other such malevolent institutions. Orders and people trickled erratically downwards. Soon after I arrived, for instance, I noticed a curious difficulty in getting the personal files of anyone whose name was low in the alphabet. When I could find no details of anyone before 'M' I made enquiries and eventually discovered that the moles in our subterranean registry were busily despatching the personal files by batches to France in accordance with some casual injunction thrown out apparently at a conference of the Director of Administration.

That taught me the importance, not of minutes, but of some short, sharp record of action required as a result of these endless conferences. The next lesson I learnt was to beware of bureaucracies bringing gifts in the shape of their superannuated brethren. We all know that the British Civil Service is the best old boy employment net in the world. Some at least of our troubles since the war have been caused by putting unsuitable civil servants in charge of nationalised industries, boards, etc. When I was still innocent in these matters I was informed that the British Treasury with condescension would lend us as a special favour Sir Somebody Something, an accountant of stupendous renown. He turned out to be quite useless and indeed involved us in the recruitment of several secretaries, working accountants, etc. to bolster his self importance during the few hours he spent every day in his office.

UNRRA had a capacity like a poltergeist for spreading confusion in its offices. When I arrived we were in hot water with Sir Frederick Leith Ross over some dismissal or refusal to appoint. Being new I was despatched to placate him. I found him in an irritable mood but with his usual courtesy he ordered tea, which he upset, no doubt infuriated by my ignorance, all over his desk and into an open drawer. Tea spread over his documents and dripped from drawer to drawer. By the time we had finished crawling around with handkerchiefs and blotting paper he could hardly remain angry.

The second in command of the personnel division was a British civil servant called Mr. Kearn. He was the firm mooring round which chaos swirled. He showed no resentment at my appointment though he was far better qualified than I was. I suppose he had for years nursed incompetent chiefs and wayward ministers. Nor did the diet of crises on which we lived upset him. As we were about to leave one evening a message arrived saying that twenty Peruvian doctors unordered and unheralded had been off-loaded at Southampton. Mr. Kearn arranged their lodging for the night and sped them off to somewhere—goodness knows where—in the morning. Then there was the affair of the Ethopian ploughs. UNRRA was much entangled with American politics. I was constantly summoned to carry on telex conversations with the head of personnel in Washington about complaints made to senators or congressmen by their constituents or to find posts for prominent Democrats. One of these latter, the formidable female chairwoman of a powerful committee had elected to go, most unsuitably, as head of mission to Ethopia. There she found a shortage of ploughs. Ploughs were ordered. Minutes, telegrams, telexes (UNRRA seldom operated by anything as cheap and simple as a letter) waded through the machinery and back to America. Eventually a consignment of multiple disc ploughs suitable if drawn by caterpillar tractors for breaking up the prairies, arrived from Chicago in Addis Abbaba. Apparently it was the custom in Ethiopia for the women to carry ploughs on their heads. At the sight of these juggernauts a female revolt broke out. Our representative, a staunch champion of women's rights, found her name not revered but execrated in female society. Then there was the case of the Sephardic Jews. They had apparently been expelled from Spain in the 15th century or thereabouts. Ever since, they had lived in Salonika. When the Germans advanced through the Balkans the Spanish Government, to its credit, offered them asylum. It now wanted them to be moved home. Washington hired a Professor at some Mid-Western university, who was said to be an expert on Sephardic Jews, to superintend their removal. Expert he may have been on paper, unfortunately it was doubtful if he had ever seen a Sephardic Jew, nor was he well versed in the ways of the Mediterranean. As there was a shortage of shipping he led his charges, like the Pied Piper, along the Northern coast of Africa. Silence descended. Then an eruption of cables descended upon us from Egypt. He had apparently collected a good many hangers-on of unsocial tendencies. Some of these were not at all keen to leave Alexandria where they were engaged in mild rioting, petty crime and profitable black market activities. But Mr. Kearn smoothed it all over.

And of course we were always losing people. Kearn would appear in my office, a cigarette dangling, brushing tobacco from his waistcoat, with a file twisted into a tube (a habit of his) to remark how interesting it was that someone we had hired as a refugee camp superintendent in Germany had turned up in China. I acquired an undying admiration for the aplomb of such civil servants as Mr. Kearn, their nose for likely trouble and their footwork in side-stepping it.

I thought doom had overtaken me when it was announced that efficiency experts were to examine the administration of the London office. I knew my department was both inefficient and over-manned. However, they reported that all would be well if we had a 10% increase in staff. Since then I have remained sceptical about efficiency audits. The outcome of this was that I received a second deputy, a charming, cute and tactful girl called Carol Laise who afterwards became the American Ambassador in

Nepal. By that time she had married Elsworth Bunker who was Ambassador in Vietnam. Surely the only husband and wife both to have been Ambassadors at the same time.

I was now bolstered up by a team which hid my shortcomings. In addition to Carol and Mr. Kearn there was my American secretary, Miss Kane, appearing as though she and her clothes had just emerged from a Fortnum and Mason band-box who would soften even the most crotchety clients, and Jimmy King who was an American long resident in England, a figure out of Scott Fitzgerald's novels whose speciality was taking irate Generals (of whom we had a superfluity from many nations) and girls parted from their boy friends, out to lunch. Over excellent lunches for which he paid—we had no expense accounts—Jimmy would listen spell-bound to the Generals' reminiscences and compliment the girls on their hair-dos. We were also lucky in having a chief, Bill Howell, in Washington, who was not only capable but popular. I always looked forward to trips to Washington.

When I first went to work in UNRRA a constant cause of trouble was the hiring of staff without authority. To stop this the Organisation and Methods Division decreed that every office must have a Budget. Within this Budget every member of a department's staff must be carried on a Line. This led to a constant minuet based partly on jig-saw puzzles and partly on musical chairs. When some enquiry was launched by O. & M. or Accounts it was vital not to be left without a line. Mr. Kearn was a grand-master at the lines game. He was also a humane and wise man. Heads of Mission, Generals and other big-wigs were always sneaking ADCs and female car drivers onto their pay roll. Mr. Kearn used to appear announcing that so-and-so had been caught with no line for his favourite girl. 'He is really doing rather well' Mr Kearn would explain. 'It is much better that he and his car should be under the eye of his old ATS or WAC driver. He will then get into less trouble. Now that we are supposed to be establishing friendly relations with our old friends or enemies I would much rather he had her than locally recruited girls. I find the Montenegran mission has a line for an assistant security officer which is unfilled. I will pop his girl onto it and note that she is on leave.' By the time O. & M. or Accounts got round to Montenegro Mr. Kearn had translated Miss Swinging Hips elsewhere.

The people who absolutely refused to play Lines were the French. When I went to see M. Morhange on these crucial occasions, which I felt bound to do in person, as he had got me my job, he would smooth his elegant grey hair and break into that tolerant smile which I had seen him adopt when asked to take part in some childish after-dinner game at a week-end party. If Accounts were rash enough to beard his division of

Finance they were referred to Miss Walder or Miss Parker who were seconded Treasury officials, from whom they would retreat somewhat dishevelled. I doubt if the Treasury have ever suffered accountants gladly.

There was a tradition in UNRRA, if you can have a tradition in an institution aged one, that only the United Kingdom, Canada or very occasionally Holland, could supply accountants. I have sometimes wondered if the accountancy scourge has not been a factor in the poor performance of British industry since the war. I hope UNRRA by helping to make the dread disease endemic in Britain and discouraging the breeding of accountants in Germany did not play a small part in the process.

Besides M. Morhange there were rather few French in our organisation. They were interested in the top Lines only. I remember one Inspecteur des Finances. When I went to see him he was sitting alone resplendent in an office looking as I imagine an eagle-owl might look if disturbed when taking its mid-day nap. When I murmured something about his staff he lifted his hands slightly off an empty desk and gazed out of the window. Paris, however, was a popular post so our mission there was of considerable size. It was under the command of an ex-military attaché who later lived in Shetland, Brigadier Fraser. He was somewhat provoked when on entertaining a newly arrived recruit from across the Atlantic he courteously admired his revolver; the next thing he knew was that three bottles had exploded behind the bar, picked off by our new recruit to show how effective as well as decorative was the weapon. However, here again, the Americans showed their ability for producing the right man or woman for the job. They sent him Mr. Cramer. Red Cramer was a professor of history who was well up to French cultural standards while also well able to handle those quick on the trigger. He was a good choice, a man whose looks, like President Lincoln in the prime of life, reassured his compatriots and awed all Europeans.

M. Morhange's Finance Division was in close alliance with the General Counsel. This last office was an American importation, usually I believe, filled by a lawyer. What lent undoubted strength to the holder, Mr. Dudley Ward, was that he was not a lawyer. He hired an able legal deputy, Max Cohen, to whom he referred all technical matters. Dudley Ward, like Morhange, had contrived to remain outside the Organisation Flow. He had before the war been an international banker. The snarls of UNRRA were, I suspect, unexacting compared to the negotiations of Balkan loans. As the top brass of UNRRA were quite keen on international social success he hinted that M. Morhange if not a survivor from La Belle Epoque had at least been a member of the Jeunesse Dorée in Paris while in return Toto would from time to time draw attention to Dudley's friendship with famous, though mostly long dead, European statesmen. The General Counsel was a delightful man always ready to help. He never enquired into how mistakes had been made, he expressed no moral indignation nor even surprise. He simply took snuff and settled matters. He had a high regard for the charm and ability of Carol Laise, so on receiving, say, a frantic telex from my superior, Bill Howell, that a favourite son of the Democratic Party was either in gaol or, worse still, had not been promoted, I would ask Carol to see Dudley and all would be well. I learnt several lessons from him and Toto Morhange. Never have a large staff. One or two very able people are enough. I was lucky in getting Carol, Kearn and King. But nearly always there is one able person within capturing distance. Capture them, then hang on to them, refuse all other recruits and resist promotion boards. In later years, for instance, I clung to Pratap Chitnis. Also, Dudley had a most effective presence at the innumerable UNRRA meetings. He never attended unless personally summoned. He would then arrive a little late and if possible resist any invitation to sit down. By perching on the table and taking snuff he would not only establish a certain superiority but impress on us all that the crisis under review was no responsibility of his and that though anxious to help he had more important work elsewhere.

Among other lessons learnt at UNRRA I was taught to See Us as Others See Us and to take care in attributing motives. Those were the days when no one was allowed to spend more than three consecutive nights in an hotel (believe it or not): one of our Russian mission chiefs having come to London for three days found, as so many have found, that his flight home was cancelled. On returning to his hotel he was ordered to leave. As he sat reproachfully on his luggage in the hall he clearly was convinced that Stalin had nothing to teach Britain. As for the attributing motives, this again arose from a Russian incident. A Russian lady wanted at a conference was nowhere to be found. We were all convinced that she had been spirited away for some dastardly motive. In fact, we later discovered that she had gone to pray—it being the anniversary of her son's death.

I also learnt that officials stick together. We had the greatest difficulty in persuading the Bank of England to part with any currency. The Russians were avid to be paid in sterling. I thought that at least I should have the support of the Russian state bank for a small float of sterling. Not at all, they stood shoulder to shoulder with Threadneedle Street.

At UNRRA too I discovered that most American foreign activities are an extension of their home politics. This is why so much of their foreign policy is mistaken. It accounts, for instance, for their bungling in Africa, particularly over Rhodesia.

Of the field work of UNRRA, as I have said, I saw very little. I do not know what assessment has been made of its success or failure. We did something, I hope, to help the refugees. We made their lives a little more tolerable. But while it seems surprisingly easy to rebuild cities and industries, you cannot rebuild the lives of people driven from their homes.

Of the internal workings of the organisation I saw quite a lot. Apart from some scepticism about efficiency experts I noted one or two other lessons.

The difference between the British and American personnel was marked. The British were on the whole reticent and dowdy, the Americans extrovert and smart. The senior Americans were embedded in their political system like ants in an antheap. The British did not connect their jobs with politics. If they looked at their jobs from the point of view of their careers outside UNRRA it was for the possibility of getting jobs in other agencies. The lower paid British employees seldom if ever came to ask for a personal rise in pay or grade. Sometimes a whole grade would ask to be upgraded but personal ambition was low. The Americans constantly appeared alone to point out how good they were and how well qualified for better jobs. If refused they went away cheerfully and came back in three months.

I also watched the smothering of the British system by the American. Mr. Kearn would scribble a few notes on the left hand side of a file, the Americans would circulate twenty copies of a memorandum. They would then refer the matter to a committee. I was watching the start of the office equipment explosion—which has a lot to answer for. One of the most efficient operators on the Liverpool Stock Exchange before the war confined all his notes to his shirt cuffs—so a highly efficient senior staff officer once told me. Those days were passing. But the American methods did not suit the British. First, the British love their beds. This cuts down the time available for committees. They have not the spare energy or personnel for this prodigal outlay on paper and talk. It all bolstered the growth of the bureaucratic top-hamper which I saw in the war.

I knew little about personnel management when I went to UNRRA, but my experience makes me doubt the present trends in personnel handling. Largely at the instance of the Americans I was pressed to issue various manuals and regulations (the size of a novel) to new personnel. My inclination was to resist this. I saw no reason why we should not engage people subject to agreed notice on either side. Instant dismissal for misconduct was a different matter. Misconduct needed to be spelled out and an appeals procedure instituted. But I do not believe it to be in the interest of an employer or an employee to prevent them from ending their association with due notice (or pay in lieu) and no reason given. If employers (as under the Employment Protection Act) feel that their discretion to get rid of unsuitable employees is limited, they will be chary of engaging just the sort of people who should be given a chance. If reasons for dismissal have to be given this may damage the long-term chances of the employee. I am also against allowing everyone to see their files. If reports have to be made on the work of an individual, he should usually see such reports before they go to other departments etc. But that he or she should always see remarks in confidential files which do not leave personnel departments seems to me dangerous. I personally would rather that people should make rude remarks behind my back—if they must make them at all. The American system led in some cases to endless wrangles. The deficiencies of individuals had to be set out in detail. They inevitably leaked. They harmed the individual's self-confidence and his reputation. In my experience more harm is done by keeping unsuitable employees than by marginally justified dismissals. But then international organisations attract some odd applicants. One of the reasons they do so is their high rates of pay. The result is to draw foot-loose characters who are not doing too well at home, as flies are drawn to a honey pot, and to provoke jealousy from local employees. Finally, simplicity in wage rates saves endless trouble. The complication of wage rates and allowances in British industry leads to friction.

After I was demobilised I left UNRRA. From the law I had been too long parted to contemplate with any gusto the prospect of beginning again the exacting task of climbing the ladder of the English bar. Also I wanted to work in Scotland and was still the prospective candidate for Orkney and Shetland.

Between 1947 and 1950 we lived in Prestonpans, a mining village outside Edinburgh. Through the good offices of Robert Hurd I was appointed Secretary of the National Trust for Scotland. Robert deserves much of the credit for the growth of interest in Scotland's art and buildings during the last twenty-five years. Hamilton Dower House where we lived was a 17th-century building belonging to the Trust which with other relics of the old village had survived among the new housing estates. Andrew and Gelda were at school, Johnny aged about three was beginning to run about. He was already showing signs of happy originality. One morning he flung himself into our bed whispering 'lady, lady'. He claimed to have met her in the passage. Sure enough the house was haunted by a lady. He is the only person I know who can claim to have seen a ghost. This despite a night spent with Henry and William Douglas-Home at Borley Rectory before the war which was said to be choc-a-bloc with ghosts and poltergeists. Henry was there on behalf of the BBC who intended to broadcast the moanings of the spirits. He became a well-known observer of birds but I fear his rather downright manner may have put off the ghosts: we drank a great deal of beer but neither heard nor saw any ghosts. This was not the only evidence of second sight which Johnny evinced; when we were on holiday in Wiltshire he saw a vision of Prestonpans in the sky. This bears out two of my theories. The grip of the places where we spend our childhood. Prestonpans was hardly beautiful but had something of the same effect on my children as St Andrews had on me. And just as saints may look round and red like the late Lord Home and not as they are depicted in stained glass windows, so those with second sight may not always look like warlocks. I am afraid that in growing up Johnny may have lost touch with the other world.

From Prestonpans we made expeditions to look at National Trust property. Sometimes Johnny would be left behind. One day when we went to bed before one such expedition we found a note which read 'Toad (which was his nick-name) musn be left out.' Among our neighbours were two Miss Cadells—a modern version in some ways of my Oakbank cousins. Late in life they had become accomplished gardeners sending gentians all over the country: part of the Scottish underground. They first introduced us to the paintings of Gillies whose talent Laura at once perceived. This started me on buying pictures—particularly Scotch pictures—which I have done in a small way ever since then.

9

I NEARLY DID NOT fight the 1950 Election. The outlook for Liberals
was bleak. I was due to go to work for Collins, the publishers. In
preparation for this I put in a few weeks with a printer in Edinburgh.
Ever since then I have sympathised with the anarchism which machine-
minding engenders. After an hour I was bored to distraction. I went to the
lavatory as often as possible. I was tempted to throw spanners in the
works. Talk about clock-watching: I looked at my watch every ten
minutes.

Now I am very glad I did fight the election. The opposition was strong.
Sir Basil Neven-Spence, the sitting Member, was a Shetlander, well-
liked and deservedly so. He was rejected for no better reason than the
electors thought he had been in Parliament long enough. The Labour
candidate was Harald Leslie, the Assistant Adjutant General of my war-
time experience, an Orcadian devoted to his home islands, with a delightful Orcadian wife who had been the doctor on an Orkney island. For any
other Party he would certainly have got in for Orkney and Shetland and
as a Labour candidate for many other Scottish constituencies but he
wanted to be M.P. for his native islands and they were not inclined to his
Party.

The 1950 General Election was fought largely on the record of the
Labour Government. The Labour Party said little about the future—
particularly, as usual, they played down the prospect of more nationalisation. During the Election I said that the advice of some of their spokesmen
to the electors seemed to be to 'Pull down the blinds, draw up their chairs,
warm their toes at the embers of the Welfare State without worrying
about the next bucket of coal.' It has been their attitude ever since. By
1950 the confidence of the Tories had sprouted again. For national appeal

they could still rely on the war leaders, Winston, Eden, Woolton and others. The Liberals always had to contend with the taunt—'A Liberal vote is a wasted vote' or 'Don't let Labour in'. As the Labour Party had no hope of winning Orkney and Shetland this last was not a particularly effective accusation. At subsequent elections I suggested ironically that as they dreaded the 'split vote' above all things the Tories should withdraw as I was now the sitting Member. They never did. At this election I raised a demand for a highland development corporation, which was eventually set up as the Highlands and Islands Development Board.

In view of what happened later over the Scotland Bill it is interesting to read that of my meeting in Kirkwall, the *Orkney Herald* reported 'The heartiest rounds of applause came for his (my) backing of the policy of Home Rule for Scotland and his (my) outlining of the Liberal plan for the development of the Highlands and Islands.' The history of Home Rule is made more bewildering when you consider that the independent candidate who stood on a Home Rule platform in the Western Isles and Argyll both lost their deposits, the latter scoring 490 votes out of some thirty thousand. Both these seats were by 1977 held by the S.N.P.

It is also interesting that in those days before the opinion polls the Tory and Labour press were quite capable of raising scares at the last minute, often on the theme that the Liberal vote was collapsing. It is symptomatic of the changed relationship between Tory and Labour parties—the latter having now become the establishment, that it is the Labour party which now tries to scare the electorate with warnings about the dire consequences which may follow from right wing Tory policies.

If you read the speeches of that time they have a familiar note. The pound, Tories and Liberals pointed out, was only worth 10/9d. in pre-war values—freedom was in danger—out of every five days work, two were done for the government. The Labour Party claimed to be the party of 'fair shares'; they stood for subsidies and bulk buying. My Labour opponent said that the rise in the cost of living was due to the war and had been 'kept in check' by Labour policies.

The history of the last thirty years shows that the same factors have been at work: too much money chasing too little production. I am glad to say that at the 1950, '51 and '55 General Elections I stressed the need for more production.

What was absent in the fifties was any widespread fear about Russian Imperialism or the power of the Trades Unions.

The election meetings in 1950 were the most crowded I can remember. Not that any were large but four times a night I would find several rows of black-suited and black-capped crofters waiting in the halls or schools. They sat patiently, often in desks designed for the infant class—like large birds on small nests. There were no air services round the islands in those days nor vehicle ferries between them. In Shetland candidates went to Yell and Unst either in launches or in the *Earl of Zetland*. *The Earl* was a comfortable enough ship but in rough weather she bobbed about like a cork. She is the only vessel plying around Orkney and Shetland on which I have been sick (and that only once). I was sick on a fishing boat but that was due to an unwise tea of fish livers in the hot and diesel-fume laden cabin.

During the '50 Election which was held in March the weather was rough. Sir Basil was out of action for twenty-four hours while the *Earl* was hove-to behind an island for shelter. To smaller islands the voyage had to be made in hired boats. We were once accompanied by a killer whale, no doubt with hope that we would capsize—but he (or she) was disappointed. There were few piers at which the *Earl* could tie up. Passengers, cattle, sheep, crates and numerous cargo of all kinds were ferried ashore in undecked 'flit' boats, cumbersome affairs in which you could get very wet. For an evening meeting you had to spend the night on the island. As there were some twenty parishes each on the mainlands of Orkney and Shetland in addition to the outlying islands the programme was pretty heavy. I addressed over a hundred meetings. In Orkney the northern outlying islands were served by two small steamers, the *Earl Thorfinn* and the *Earl Sigurd*. They took all day to get round. At times this was inconvenient but many farmers enjoyed the trip. At each pier they had time to chat to their friends and even take a cup of tea. The South Isles of Orkney were served by two old naval drifters. The skippers grew old along with their boats. I was travelling in the wheelhouse one day when the skipper let out a piercing shriek down the speaking tube. 'The engineer's a bit deaf' he explained 'When he hears that he knows it's time to stop.' Speaking of the companion ship he announced, I thought, 'that she was "done" '. When I said that she didn't seem to do too badly 'It's not the ship' he explained with disdain 'It's the skipper, his legs are done'. The islanders of North Ronaldsay voted on the neighbouring island of Sanday. The custom, illegal I suspect, was that the candidates clubbed together to charter a boat to take him to the polls. Sanday had a pub: North Ronaldsay did not. It was probable that many of the visitors did not vote. North Ronaldsay had, and has, another peculiarity. The sheep except at lambing time are kept outside a dyke which runs round the shed just above the water mark. They feed on seaweed and marram grass. Like the Shetland sheep to whom they must be related, by life-style if not by parentage, they have grown athletic. They can be seen leaping about the rocks like chamois.

As one might expect, the essence of Orkney and Shetland is distilled in the outlying islands. They are free, or were free, even from the urban taint of Kirkwall and Lerwick. In the island of Sanday in Orkney the Chair was taken by the schoolmaster, Mr. Mackay. Mr. Mackay was a man who never exposed how he voted. However, he was a glutton for political discussion. He had never been to a university (I am not sure that in these degenerate days he would be allowed to teach). He had lived all his life in the North Isles, having been born on the little island of Papa Westray. All his life he had bought books. They cascaded from cupboards and stood in stacks around the furniture. Before the meeting it was customary to partake of a high tea provided by his admirable housekeeper. During this meal Mr. Mackay discoursed and questioned upon literature, politics, Orkney and education. In Skerries, which are two rocky islets to the east of Shetland, the schoolmaster used to drive every available inhabitant to the meeting (there were only a hundred all told). All the dogs and babies had therefore to come too. They sat round the hall like one of those Victorian paintings—say by Sir David Wilkie.

I never canvassed. To ask anyone how they were going to vote would have seemed impudent to many of my constituents. Laura once approached the subject obliquely by asking a man how he thought his Papa Westray parish would vote. She got a terse and dusty answer. 'The folk in this parish will vote as they think fit. They will vote Liberal if they be of that mind.' If you called at a house you were expected to stay for a cup of tea or a 'refreshment'. To bang on a knocker, thrust a pamphlet and run away would have been considered rude. So most electioneering was done at meetings, sometimes, if time was short, a meeting at the piers speaking from a barrel while loading or unloading proceeded.

There were, as I have said, four local weekly papers, two in Orkney, two in Shetland. They were violently partisan, two Liberal, two Tory. Indeed, the last issues before polling day of the Orkney papers were largely given over to propaganda and abuse of the other parties. This has gradually died out as our papers have been reduced to two and the Labour Party and S.N.P. have to be accommodated. Also, I fear, apathy and television have smothered local enthusiasm. But the standard and leadership of the local papers under Gerry Meyer and Basil Wishart remains very high. I was much helped by Basil Wishart's brilliant journalism in Shetland, particularly in the lay-out of my election addresses, and by the Twatt family, owners and editors of the *Orkney Herald*. The Twatt sons were both expert in what is now called electronics. One of them went south to work for Marconi. When I met him some years later I found he was called 'Watt'. On being asked why, he said that people in the south couldn't believe his name was Twatt so he had obliged them by dropping the 'T'. A nice example of Orkney goodwill. My Orkney Chairman too, Mr. Tait, showed the same freedom from pride and selfishness. On going one day to his dignified Victorian mansion which he rented in Kirkwall I saw that the garden had been flattened and laid out for council houses. He was head of the largest merchant's business in Orkney. In Scotland any such local big-wig would have thought it an insufferable affront to his privacy and position to have his home surrounded by council houses. When I commiserated with Mr. Tait he was much surprised. He had asked the council to build on his garden, he claimed he was too old for gardening and, anyway, he wanted near neighbours.

The pursuit of status is one of the most childish and contemptible of post-war British inanities. Orkney and Shetland were free of it. Long may this remain so but I fear that along with envy it is seeping in—'Look, he's got a bigger car or more pay, or a higher sounding title than I have'—we would be well quit of such follies which are the antithesis of the old ways which made Orkney and Shetland such happy places in which to live.

When the poll was declared on Monday, 27th February 1950 (polling day having been the previous Thursday—so long did it take the boats to bring in the boxes from the outlying islands) I could hardly believe that I had been elected. I had long wanted to be an M.P.: for a Liberal that was in itself a remote possibility: now I was not only an M.P. but M.P. for Orkney and Shetland which to me was the most romantic of all constituencies. After the declaration of the poll I drove round Orkney, coming down the road into Stenness from the Orphir hills, seeing the lochs lying all peaceful in the fading light and thinking that even if it was only for a few months it was well worth it. By that time it was known that Labour would have a small majority. The *News Chronicle* doubted whether a government could survive with a majority of eight or ten. Even then, though I was under no illusion that I had done it all myself. Laura deserved most credit at that election as at subsequent ones: Laura and such supporters as Edwin Eunson, the Tullochs, Charles Tait, Basil Wishart, the Twatts and the contributors to *Liberal Orkney* a paper which Ernest Marwick and others produced during elections. It was significant that in the 1970 Election when Laura was away I did not do so well, being saved from doing much worse by Grizelda. My children and others were particularly good at designing posters which were a feature of elections in the fifties and sixties. 'Vote for Grimond—disregard the ex-Spence'; one Tory poster simply said 'Don't fiddle—Ban-Jo'. Jackie Robertson, who was my Agent for so long, thought of 'Vote for Jo—the man you know'— which adorned many an Orkney gatepost.

When I reached Westminster I knew none of my Liberal colleagues in the House of Commons. The Party was, not surprisingly, disappointed by the Election results. As repairs were still going on in and around the old Commons chamber the Commons were sitting in the Lords and the

Liberal rooms were at the end of a long, winding, subterranean passage. Clem Davies was our Leader. Frank Byers, the Whip, had been defeated. The most notable among the nine survivors of the Election were Hopkin Morris and Megan Lloyd George. Within three days of being elected I was made Whip and soon found myself struggling in this far away basement with the disputes which divided us. There were a number of small cracks and knots in the Liberal Party timber but the fissure which caused the most trouble was between Hopkin and Megan. It did not exactly split the Party. For one thing the split was already there and had been for over twenty years. For another, Hopkin would never have dreamt of calling himself anything else but a Liberal and Megan was already so much in love with Labour, the Party she eventually joined, that no new bone of contention was likely to make much difference. Nevertheless, the disagreements were deep and exhausting. Clem bore the main brunt. My job was made easier too by the great charm and kindness to me of both Hopkin and Megan. Hopkin was the most delightful and original man I met in Parliament. Dark, thin and good looking he had been a figure in Liberal politics for 30 years. During all this time he had upheld the purest doctrine of traditional Liberalism. A staunch follower of Asquith he had been the only dissentient to the election of Lloyd George as Leader when the two wings of the Party were once again co-operating in 1930. Hopkin would neither manoeuvre nor compromise himself, nor had he much tolerance for those who did. He had no ambition for office, nor indeed even to hold his seat on any terms other than his own. Carmarthen, for which he sat, was largely agricultural with a sizeable pocket of miners in one corner. It was said that when the farmers asked for his support for guaranteed prices he replied with scorn that the phrase was a contradiction in terms. When the miners asked him about his policy for the coal industry he told them that if the mines did not pay they should be closed. His hold on Carmarthen was a great tribute to himself and his constituents. I should like to think that it was entirely due to altruism and respect for his integrity. It must be said however that, as the Tories did not oppose him, he was the only alternative to Labour.

Whether there were ever many men of such intellectual purity as Hopkin in any House of Commons I do not know, but it was interesting to notice that when he made one of his rare speeches from the extreme end of the bench on which the Liberals sat, it was the older Labour Members, ex-schoolmasters or Welsh Trades Unionists, who listened most intently though everything he said was anathema to Socialists. At his arguments deduced from first, and often remote principles, a few bald Labour heads could be seen nodding in appreciation, if not in agreement, while the Tories with whom he usually voted sat in impatient non-comprehension.

Many of the older generations of Liberals and Labour supporters shared a way of thinking. Christian Socialism and Gladstonian Liberalism (though I sometimes wonder if Hopkin would have unhesitatingly supported Mr. Gladstone) had not only religious and often non-conformist beliefs in common but an admiration for integrity and a dislike of ostentation, material ambition and blowsiness which no doubt came from their similar education and family upbringing. The brassy streak in the Tory Party was disliked by them all.

As Hopkin was immovably opposed to government direction, subsidies, restrictions, planning, everything in fact that the Labour Government stood for, the most that could be hoped for was that he might be persuaded to abstain on votes when Clem and his colleagues wanted to support the Labour Government. It was a tricky job to negotiate his absence, made in some ways more difficult by his relationship with Clem and Megan, both of whom he regarded with affectionate contempt: great affection for themselves, contempt for some of their politics.

Clem was a man of extreme good-will. He never showed the least impatience at my idleness and incompetence as Whip. Years later when going to his funeral in Montgomeryshire the ticket collector told me how much the railway officials would miss him. He also told me that as he travelled to and from Montgomery all sorts of people would buttonhole him about their troubles. He would listen patiently and invariably did what he could for them. He had a good brain but he was a natural barrister, good at picking up a brief and this, plus his desire to be accommodating, led him into contradictory attitudes.

When the future of conscription was under discussion at a meeting of the M.P.s during the 1945 Parliament Hopkin delivered a powerful attack on it (though by no means a pacifist—he held the M.C. and had a distinguished war record) arguing as usual from first principles. Clem was convinced. On his way, however, from the meeting of M.P.s to that of the Liberal Party Committee he met my mother-in-law, Violet Bonham Carter, who asked him what he was going to say about conscription. Clem replied that he was going to make it clear that conscription was incompatible with fundamental liberties, that no government had a right to impose it in peacetime and that it must be ended forthwith. Violet expressed amazement at this. For Britain, she insisted, to stop conscription would be regarded as a betrayal by all European Governments, for him to support such a decision would spread dismay among our Liberal allies on the continent etc. Clem absorbed the new brief instantly and to Hopkin's dismay delivered a powerful defence of conscription to the committee. Loyalty, gratitude and admiration bound me to Clem but I was never quite sure on what branch he would finally settle.

Hopkin not only inspired respect but he had a certain innocent quality, he seemed to have gone through life never shedding a fawn-like appearance and a wild eye. This made him very attractive, and so was Megan with her Pekinese face. I never saw Asquith, Lloyd George, Amery, Birkenhead, Bonar Law but I have known their descendants and some day I think I shall write a book deducing their ancestors from their children. I do not believe that the conventional picture of Bonar Law as a rather dull man can be true, having known Dick Law. I find it difficult to trace the traditional Lloyd George in Gwilym or the Roman aspects of Mr. Asquith in his children and grandchildren. But that may be because we leave out their mothers. But I saw Lloyd George in Megan, and with a difference. Never was Megan unresponsive. Never was she overbearing. Never was she dull. On occasion she would fix me with her protuberant eyes and like a cat upon a wall tell me to tell somebody else to do something. But never was she careless or rude. She was perpetually young, perpetually unfulfilled. And the difference from her father—who I am told could make people feel that they were the only people in the world who mattered, which Megan too could do—was that she was nervous and idle. Or perhaps he was too; if so, history has not recorded it. It was difficult to persuade her to speak in the Commons, when she did you could feel her nervousness if you sat on the bench with her. Yet she always got a good hearing from the Labour Party and spoke very well. But not for her the perusal of white and blue books or a swarm of statistics.

Dealing with Hopkin and Megan—though Clem bore the brunt of it—taught me a bit about political ways. All organisations, the Army, a business, a village, a football team, differ from one another. The motives of their members differ and so do the pressures upon them. In a political party some of the motives and pressures are obvious, ambition, for instance, and the pressure of the herd. Even in the Liberal Party which was unlikely to reward anyone with high office and where the herd was peculiarly centrifugal these motives and pressures applied in a modified extent. No Member of Parliament, even in a safe seat, let alone any Liberal, can afford to ignore his or her constituency. But in addition M.P.s have to shake down with their colleagues in their Party. The Palace of Westminster has been likened to a liner at sea. Nowadays most M.P.s spend long hours in it, as cut off from the outside as passengers on the ocean. Their food and amusements are provided. Their companions are not of their choosing but they must get on together. Though there is a fair amount of conversation between Members of different parties, yet the parties for the most part sit at the same tables to eat and, of course, constantly meet in committees. Personal relations are important, particularly within the party, but also sometimes between Members of different parties. Megan who in general was reluctant to vote in the same lobby as the Tories had a considerable regard for some individual Conservatives. Osbert Peake, for instance, was a favourite of hers. It was easier to persuade her to vote with the Tories if he had been a leading spokesman in the debate—like pushing a restive horse over a jump by getting its stable companion to give a lead. Megan had endowed her father with a liking for the Labour Party and a loathing of the Tories which he never evinced when living. She seemed to have forgotten that even before the first war he had nibbled at the notion of a Liberal/Tory coalition, that his chosen associates were Tories and that he never was Prime Minister except on Tory votes. Then M.P.s are for the most part in politics to contribute some view. The cynics who believe that office, prestige or a quiet life obedient to the Whips are all that they want, are wrong. Even if their opinions are disregarded M.P.s want to express them. Even if they are over-ruled, and indeed know in advance that they are going to be over-ruled, they must be allowed to argue their case. The most important part of a Whip's job is to divine how the minds of his flock are working and if he has reason to believe they may not back the Party line seek them out and find how they can be accommodated or persuaded. Neither Clem nor I as Whip had any sanctions. But the sanctions of expulsion, pressure through the constituency party and withdrawal of patronage though they existed in other Parties are usually measures of last resort. In recent years the most important sanction has become refusal of office. M.P.s' salaries are low and most of them are now career politicians. But in the fifties there were still a number of Tories, usually sitting for counties where they held a personal position, who did not want office and were impossible to browbeat. On the Labour side their counterparts were some of the Trades Union Members and Left-wing independents, instinctively suspicious of any government and nursing their rights to speak as they pleased from the back benches. In a period when the Party machines were tightening their grip these Members were valuable and the Tory and Labour Whips if they were wise were tolerant towards them. But the lesson of the three Labour Members who had been expelled in the previous Parliament and all lost their seats in 1950 was clear. Very few M.P.s could expect to hold on for long outside their Parties. In a Parliament where the Government has a small majority —and in the 1950 Parliament its majority was only five—the power of the Whips is increased, for even the most thrawn backbencher will think twice before deserting his Party in such circumstances. But, equally, in modern conditions, every vote is important. In the fifties governments could not stomach defeat even on minor issues, an attitude which I am glad to say has to some extent changed. The narrow margin between the

Labour and Tory Parties lent importance to the Liberal vote. If dissentients could be persuaded to abstain instead of actually voting in a different lobby from their colleagues that could often ease a difficult situation. By listening rather than talking to the disaffected this could often be achieved. Though all Parties are coalitions there is common blood flowing in the veins of most members of a Party. Of late the boundaries between the Parties have become more blurred, several members of the Labour Party could well sit on the Conservative benches and one at least has crossed over, but distinctions remain. In 1950 the prevailing mood was to accept a large degree of state intervention. The form which this intervention was taking I discuss later. Here I shall remark merely that this prevailing climate did not erase Party differences. These were as often seen in Party reactions to events as in the Party philosophies. Whatever our differences in the Liberal Party, there was a common outlook springing from individualism. From this common angle from which most of us in some degree looked at events it was possible to appeal for unity. Shortly after I was elected John Strachey asked me why I was not a Conservative, saying that were he in my position with strong feelings for freedom and enterprise he would be one. I replied that apart from ideological differences I knew that if I became a Tory I should always be tacking up against a wind from the right. I should find that on all those unexpected issues which crop up in Parliament and whose significance to Parliamentarians it is hard for others to appreciate, I should have a different instinctive reaction even from those of Tories with whom in general I agreed. He accepted this. In many ways the High Tory instincts of John himself, which had been overlaid by Marxism, were asserting themselves. I have mentioned the element among Labour M.P.s which put a high value on their right to argue cases out of focus from the main beam of the Party, these were the Sydney Silvermans, Leslie Hales and Fenner Brockways of the Party. There was also the High Tory element. I deliberately use the word 'High'. They were people assured of their position, both materially and intellectually, usually educated at fashionable schools and the best universities, often appearing arrogant and the best of them eccentric. They were not universally popular in their party but they bucked it up and gave it confidence. Their patronising, sometimes almost contemptuous attitude to the middle ranks of the Tories cheered up their colleagues when suffering from bouts of social inferiority. John would be seen gazing down at the Tories as they went into the division lobbies looking like a llama, or at least Belloc's description of one, 'with an indolent expression and an undulating throat.' In fact, they were some of the most able, and generous Members. I admired John Strachey himself (in spite of his lamentable worship of Russia between the wars) and two others of this sort became friends of mine, Woodrow Wyatt and Reggie Paget. Reggie later, when well into his sixties, took on the Mastership of the Quorn. Two Labour Members in my time were Masters of Foxhounds, Reggie and the admirable Phillips Price who before being an M.P. had been the *Manchester Guardian*'s correspondent in Russia during the civil war. One of many happy memories of Woodrow Wyatt is of his wandering down the Labour benches complaining in much bewilderment that none of his fellow Socialists would vote for his private Member's bill to abolish surtax; nor indeed would the Liberals. Nor was his reply when taxed with eating off silver plates 'So much easier to wash up' considered quite adequate by those Socialists for whom Socialism was said to be about equality.

With many individuals in other parties I found a great deal to agree. But I never doubted that I was a Liberal. The circumstances of the time, however, had affected the sort of Liberal which I then was. I was convinced that Socialism as an all-embracing creed, and that is what it claims to be, was wrong—morally wrong and practically inefficient. I believed then as now in some form of co-operation or syndicalism within a free market. I believed that only individuals had any ultimate value and that therefore any system such as communism, which treated them as means and subordinated them to the state, must be evil. But the Tory creed also, though to a lesser extent, subordinated the individual. I disliked its hierarchical aspects and its resistance to new thought until that new thought was put into practice when it accepted it too readily. A state of affairs in which the only pressure for change came from socialism seemed to me dangerous. The Tories would gradually accept more and more state control. Tory new thought did not amount to much. In areas which one might have expected to be particularly their own, they showed no imagination. For instance, the Commonwealth seemed to me to have great potential if developed laterally. By that I meant that the dominions and colonies should take a share, a big share, in running it. The paternal, or maternal, role of Britain could not last. Britain could not solve many of the problems facing new nations. While her children might be sentimentally attached to her, and might like visiting her, they must like all children dislike being kept in leading strings. Further, this affection was felt most acutely by the white children; the black children might tolerate her but they were not deeply involved in her policies. Moreover, her parental role smothered new initiatives and retarded the use of some commonwealth resources. For instance, it seemed to me that a French-Canadian Governor might well be better able to cope with Malta than a British Governor. Apart from sharing the same religion he would have appeared at least to share some of the aspirations of the Maltese to be free from Anglo-Saxon heritage. Canada too should be encouraged in extending her interests in the Caribbean. India and Australia had much to contribute to each other and to the Far East.

But I accepted many restrictions. The war was only five years away and in the interval there had been the nationalisation measures of the Labour government. We had grown used to rationing and other infringements of freedom. At the same time I experienced the pressures of modern politics. All politicians, even Liberals, feel these pressures. The politicians must tell the electorate that their condition can be improved. This is so even if his or her party is in office. Much more so if in opposition must he or she promise change. The only instrument at the politician's disposal is the machinery of the state. When a Party announce that if elected they will do this or that, they mean that they will try to use the machinery of government to do it. Usually this means that they will increase the activity of the state; at least they will pass new legislation.

This tendency for all politicians to enlarge the power of the state and its satellite public bodies was strong in the forties and fifties. An obvious way to bring work, population and prosperity to the Highlands was to suggest a Highland Development Board which, as I have said, I did. Had not the Tennessee Valley Authority and other New Deal measures proved a success? As the Member for Orkney and Shetland I knew the need for roads, piers and housing. Roads, bridges and indeed harbours had been built in a matter of weeks, sometimes days, by the army during the war, why not by similar methods in peace? Everyone, apparently, accepted that the great increase in social services recommended by Beveridge were possible. No one disputed that Roosevelt, Beveridge and Keynes were liberals—the last two with a big 'L'. They had all fathered more action by the state. Centralization, the way in which governments and public bodies acted—their delays, extravagance and inefficiency certainly seemed a menace even immediately after the war. But that it would be prudent to call a halt to all further government expansion was not so obvious.

The old balancing feat between freedom and order continued in the effort to balance what were felt as the advantages of planning against the claims of diversity. In Orkney and Shetland too it had struck me as absurd to apply the same rules all over Britain. In one of the Shetland islands some dozen houses had been built at the end of a bone-shaking road. The road remained without tar but a hundred yards of tarmac pavement was laid down outside the houses. In Middlesex this would have been sensible, on a Shetland moor it was not. The pavements proved, however, very acceptable to sheep.

At this time, too, whatever misgivings were felt about nationalisation and centralisation, the efficacy of Parliament, more particularly the House

153

of Commons, was hardly challenged. Outside centres of power were not felt as a threat. Nor were we or our institutions subject to violence. If many things were wrong there was nothing which could not be put right through the better use of the British political system.

Parliament and Government believed in themselves and in what they were doing. The Parties and the diverse groups such as I have described within the Parties hardly questioned Parliamentary government, as it existed. That Parliament and the Government could solve the problems which faced us was taken for granted—difficult though those problems were considered. The Western world had tackled the aftermath of the Second World War much better than it had the aftermath of the first. America, Germany, France, Britain and Italy, let alone the smaller and much admired North European countries in their different ways had settled down to running their affairs with reasonable stability. Their people seemed content with their lives but I must guard against hindsight. To most people, and not least to politicians, who as I have said have an interest in promoting discontent, the past seems more attractive than the present. Certainly at the time the rate of inflation and taxation, Russian intransigence and other difficulties seemed real enough. But there was confidence in our institutions. Nor were we plagued by the gluts and famines of the pre-war era, or the maverick strikes of the seventies.

The self-confidence of the House of Commons could be detected in its behaviour. The Conservatives, who still had a lingering faith in their destiny as the natural governors were scenting the sweet smell of office. It was a sweet smell. They were baying at their exhausted Labour quarry.

The Liberals always sit in the middle of the opposition; thus we get to know the habits of the other Parties. Behind me sat a Tory Member who became Lord Mayor of London. When ministers were answering questions he let out a howl from time to time. The ability of M.P.s to lash themselves into a bogus fury whenever one of their opponents says something critical about their views or their Party has never ceased to astonish me. You would think that after a year, let alone twenty years, in politics you could let pass the routine jibes—but not at all: old Party hacks and hackles rise in indignation. These howls were emitted with no detectable cause other than that a Labour minister had opened his mouth; they often contained no identifiable words. The Tories kept the government up late at night objecting to almost every order that came before the House. Crude as these tactics were, they wore down jaded ministers. More serious opposition was offered in the debates. The House was usually full both for the opening speeches and the wind-up. There were accomplished debaters such as Captain Crookshank, as well as the stars, such as Churchill. Foreign and Defence affairs were still of importance. Bevin for the Government and Eden and Oliver Stanley—a most elegant and effective speaker—ensured a full house. The fall of Britain from her old place in the world is nowhere more obvious than in the eclipse of Foreign Affairs as a House of Commons subject. Bevin was dying as was Cripps. But they both retained authority. Bevin stumbling to his place followed by his cherubic minister of state, Kenneth Younger, was like a polar bear followed by her cub—giving rise to Oliver Stanley's remark about Kenneth Younger—'The minister who plays Brumas to the Foreign Secretary's Snow White'—Brumas being the cub lately born to Snow White a polar bear at the zoo. No one would have claimed that Bevin was a great orator. But orating in the House of Commons is misunderstood and comparatively unimportant. Churchill with his carefully read or memorized speeches was not always a conspicuously successful House of Commons performer—certainly not a great debater. But the sort of speech you make and its success or failure depend upon who you are and what your job may be. A minister opening a debate must speak from a prepared brief, whatever the standing orders say about reading being out of order. And Churchill certainly enlivened his set pieces with well-turned illustrations and distinction of language. The care he took over preparation was in keeping with the respect he invariably showed to the Commons and its traditions. For instance, when a vote is taken Members troop past two pulpits in which sit clerks ticking off their names. In case the clerk does not know you there is a direction that you should give your name as you pass: you might have thought that Churchill could have relied upon recognition by even the newest clerk but he invariably paused and announced 'Winston Churchill'. If he was sitting near a Member due to make a maiden speech, he would not leave until he had made it and he never appeared in the House except in black clothes and stiff collar.

After the opening speeches, leaders of minority Parties, such as Liberals, or groups within Parties are bound to give the views of such Parties or groups rather than taking up points already made. Most backbenchers want to make points which will appeal to their constituents when reported in the local papers. None of this conduces to good debate. By the time the wind-up is due the Commons in the 1950s at least was ripe for knock-about or real debate—according to how you view it. Captain Crookshank and Herbert Morrison were adept at mixing the two. In the fifties, victory for government or opposition in debate counted for more than it does now. Not that it changed many, if any, votes. But it cheered up the Party. Probably too Hansard was more closely read by M.P.s and speeches which appeared to have had no effect at the time, might help later to change the climate of opinion. Another restriction which limited the effect of debate was the rule of 'Buggin's Turn'. Although in theory those who 'catch the Speaker's eye' are called to speak, in fact the list of speakers is settled in advance. M.P.s let the Speaker know that they want to speak. He is bound to give them all a fair turn in the arena—however bad speakers they may be—and he is also bound to call those who have a special claim, e.g. because their constituency is affected or they are being personally attacked. So Buggins, not the Member most qualified to carry on the debate, is called. This custom, inevitable as it is, not only damages the debate but drives out of the Commons individual Members whose views might be valuable. I remember a debate on the steel industry when I was sitting next to Sir William Robson Brown, a director of a steel company who knew something about the subject. But it wasn't his turn. He sat from 3.30 p.m. to 9.00 p.m. hoping to speak and then left in disgust.

What would happen if we went back to the old rule which forbade the reporting of speeches? In theory it should improve debate by eliminating those speeches designed purely for the press. In practice perhaps few would speak at all. For another lesson which M.P.s soon learn is that they can save much time and trouble by writing to ministers and publishing the replies. Why bother to put down questions or sit through tedious debates when you can pursue your business and fill the local press by dictating a letter in a few minutes?

Nevertheless the House of Commons, though it has been ousted by television from its old position as the main political battlefield, was to become busier than ever as M.P.s became more bureaucratic. It provided a spring-board from which they launched out in broadcasting or in press. As a platform for reaching the nation it was and is still useful. (While some Members well-known to the public or making substantial incomes seldom attend.) Nevertheless, it can be a centre of influence. Many Members and groups, I would include the Liberal Party, appear to have been weaving sand for decades yet their toe-hold on the political process has given them influence. Had there been no Liberal Party, in the wings at least, and spasmodically making some impact from the stage, the Tory and Labour Parties would, I believe, have been different. I at any rate find that I am from time to time impressed by what is said in Parliament. Even if it does not alter my immediate vote, it enters into my thought. I have no reason to believe that in this regard I differ from many of my colleagues.

The interplay between the Government, the House of Commons, the Press and Television has been increasingly important. The House of Commons in common with the Press and Television likes what it expects.

A new thought seldom strikes home, a new uncomfortable thought will certainly be ill-received. At a time when the publicists in and out of the House were even more than usually anxious to find good in Russia, I remember Churchill himself making a speech advising caution, particularly in regard to Soviet foreign policy. This deviated from the euphoria which though dying still blinded honest perception about Russian intentions. He got little applause and one prominent Tory stalked ostentatiously out of the Chamber. This is not to say that polemics are not well received. But abusive speeches in the House seldom say anything new. It is the familiarity of the invective which tickles the Party and Press palate. The British love the jokes they know and the Aunt Sallies they know. The reception of speeches in the House is unpredictable. Mr. Herbert Morrison during his brief spell as Foreign Secretary made a speech which went down badly—a Tory back-bencher tossed a penny for the organ grinder onto the table before him. But it wasn't such a very bad speech. The Press Gallery import their opinion from the reaction of the House. So, as in Mr. Morrison's case, a speech which is either ignored or disliked by the House will receive the same treatment in the Press. At the same time the process is self-perpetuating. The House finds its opinion—which may have been transitory—confirmed by the Press and so Mr. Morrison was branded as unsuitable for the Foreign Office.

The Press likes to represent politics in terms of a fight. I have sometimes been amazed at the headlines describing some exchange between the front benches. 'X slams Y', 'Uproar', 'Z lashes the Tories' etc. Again, action causes reaction. Some M.P.s soon discover that the way to get into the Press or on to television is to take the offensive, or at least put up a barrage of questions and speeches hoping that some will stick. In itself this may not matter much, though it gives a distorted view of the relative importance and good sense of Members and debases the news. It has added to what seems to me an unfortunate tendency. It means that leading figures in government and opposition are constantly expected to put on a gladiatorial show, particularly when the Prime Minister answers questions. We are not discussing politics in terms of prize-fighting. Commentators treat them as a horse race. Their columns might be written by tipsters or by racing addicts diagnosing why a horse won or lost. Only a few analyze the issues, explain the background of political events or deal with the content of politics. British politics has suffered from the absence of a Lippman. I must not forget the leading articles in some newspapers, but it is not through the leading articles that the public get their political news. The Opinion Polls have accentuated this view of politics. Every leading politician is for ever being marked up or down—usually for reasons remote from what he or she is doing. And he or she must forever be saying something—for ever be on the screen or in a photograph. I suspect that this has seriously damaged some leading politicians to the detriment of the country. It must be extremely wearing for the nerves. The burden of detail on modern ministers is heavy enough. To be under continuous but erratic examination as well must for some be unbearable. It is not that the issues today are more difficult—it is that those who grapple with them at the top must be for ever on show. It is perhaps that as British parliamentary politics become less significant—certainly in world terms—detail, triviality and appearance become more important. I remember saying to Julian Amery some twenty years ago that being in office must be very exhausting. 'My father', he replied, 'always said that it was not nearly so exhausting as waiting to get into office.' I wonder if his father would say so today.

Although the full shock of modern publicity had not struck the Government in 1950 I mention this now because even then the strain was destroying Bevin and Cripps. This was taken at the time to be the result of continuous strain running through the war and the 1945 Parliament. But, looking back, though their long stint undoubtedly wore them out, there were even then other factors at work.

When first elected for Orkney and Shetland I lodged with my mother-in-law, Violet Bonham Carter, at 40, Gloucester Square. As a home in Orkney, we bought, in 1951, the old Church of Scotland Manse of the Parish of Firth, about five miles from Kirkwall. Like many Orkney manses it is unnecessarily tall. Since it is perched on a spur of high ground it catches the full force of all the gales—and there are many. As it is largely one room thick the wind rushes through, no window or door will stop it. But it commands views, south to the long, dark, heathery flank of Keely Lang hill and north over the Bay of Firth. The greatest assets have been our neighbours who live in the Glebe Farm, cheek by jowl with the house. When we first came the farm was run by Miss Sinclair, her nephew, Mr. James Brown, and one farm servant, Ronnie Moar who, with his successor, Billy Nicolson, tragically killed in an accident, became great friends of our family. Indeed the implement shed at the Glebe Farm still bears an inscription in indelible white paint 'Billy Nicolson is a clot' inscribed by my daughter. The farm extends to some 110 acres. It is typical of the Orkney farms. Twenty-five years ago the farmyard was full of hens, two horses, Peggy and Dick, were kept for carting. Now all these are gone. Mr. Brown concentrates on cattle and sheep. Silage has largely taken the place of hay and a contract combine does what little harvest remains. Ronnie and Billy have been replaced by the Slaters, admirable neighbours too and breeders of ducks and bantams.

Below us to the north lies the island of the Holm of Grimbister, one farm, reached at low tide by tractor but at high tide you must go by boat. Beyond, under the vault of the northern skies lie other islands among which boats wander on fine evenings, crossing the currents of green and blue which, when the wind is down, shimmer and tremble across the sun-streaked sea.

A mile or two away, down the hill by the sea, is the village of Finstown, improbably named after an Irishman called Finn who once lived there. In Finstown my three younger children went to school and in Finstown we did our shopping, indeed we still do. Our shop was kept by Andrew Baikie, one of the great breed of Orkney merchants. In true rural life dealing is endemic. Andrew was for ever buying up consignments of crockery, implements of all sorts and old baths to be used as troughs when water reached the farms. Between the farmyard, Andrew's shop and Miss Helen Taylor, who for more than twenty years has come off and on to help in our house, we have never lacked for news. I have remarked elsewhere that life in Orkney and Shetland is full of events, so many that not even the *Orcadian* and the *Shetland Times* can cope. News is still spread by word of mouth and sometimes I think by telepathy for people who seem seldom to leave their houses are often remarkably well informed.

A community breathes by local news and we are lucky to have local radio. The directors, Howie Firth and Jonathan Wills were respectively S.N.P. and Labour candidates in the General Election of the autumn of 1974. They therefore have wide interests in national affairs as well as intimate knowledge of the islands. Howie was a travelling teacher of mathematics, in demand at all sorts of junkets for his wit; Jonathan ran a croft and was boatman to the most northerly lighthouse in Britain after being the first student Rector at a Scottish university. It may not be easy to find their like again. But local radio has come to stay. It cannot, however, replace the local papers which in addition to saturating the islands by their circulation reach many exiles and many such as myself who have to spend much time away from home.

Too much indeed. Rewarding as the life of an M.P. may be, it also has anxieties. To the normal hazards of election were added in my case the uncertainties of communication between Orkney and Shetland and between either of them and London. It is not only that when you must vote in a division the plane may be cancelled, sometimes the mail is held up for days and to motor through the Highlands may be difficult. It is about 135 miles from Inverness to Scrabster where you embark for Orkney. One January we found the road across the Ord of Caithness covered with a skin of ice. It took us two hours to cover fifteen miles. We missed the ferry and had to spend the night at Thurso. On occasions like that it is an advantage to have a wife with strong nerves and phlegmatic children ready to console. As he got into bed in the Pentland Arms, Johnny remarked reassuringly 'A big town like this is sure to have a Salvation Army band'.

But my constituency had a personality: two personalities indeed. What rapture when flying home to spy Copinsay with its lighthouse standing out in the Pentland tides or shafts of sunlight striking into Scapa Flow between black clouds over Hoy. As you flew further north across the North Isles of Orkney 'Lily upon lily which o'erlace the sea', Fair Isle, Sumburgh and Fitfull Heads would swim out of the mists. From Sumburgh to Muckle Flugga in the far north of Shetland was a community with its own pulse and history, not some arbitrary slice of a southern city.

I have spent too much of my life in airports and aeroplanes. The smaller of them are cosy enough places with friendly staff but the big ones get more and more like abattoirs. The passengers are first stupefied and then herded through, the loudspeakers spew out the same announcements. 'We hope the delay has not inconvenienced you too much.' Of course it has. 'Please ensure that the arm rests are down.' Why? 'We have enjoyed having you on board.' Nonsense. 'We hope you will fly with us again.' But there is no alternative. Why not have a gramophone, or at least a well-trained parrot. The girls on aircraft cannot be such dolts that they can only be trusted to mouth these incantations nor should the airlines show such contempt for their staff and passengers.

But it would be churlish indeed not to salute the exertions of the airport staffs at Grimsetter in Orkney and Sumburgh in Shetland. Messrs. Ridgway and Burgess toiled and sweated in the service of their passengers. Jack Ridgway was a gifted impoivisor. He bent over backwards to keep the traffic moving, even chartering boats if aircraft could not fly. And of late we have had Loganair to fly us round the islands and to Wick and Inverness. Loganair has supplied not only pilots but a pilot in the shape of Andy Allsop who is also a guide to Orkney and its wild life, especially the seals for which he will make a detour so that his passengers may descry them reclining like bananas on the rocks.

The troublesomeness of travel to Orkney and Shetland was not so much the time it took, though by British standards it is a long way: it was reckoned that I travelled 75,000 miles a year between Parliament and my constituency. How true was Magnus's answer when asked by a visitor to Orkney what his father did. 'Och, he just gangs aboot.' Since Captain Fresson had pioneered the air services you could fly from London to Glasgow, Edinburgh, Inverness or Aberdeen and on from there or you could take a sleeper for part of the journey: London to Aberdeen is a pleasurably long night. The trouble was that the planes once they became

160

Lornty, near Blairgowrie, Perthshire, the original home of the Grimonds.

Grizelda, Jimmie Brown and Johnnie in the square (farm-yard) at the Old Manse.

The old *St Ola* which plied between Stromness and Scrabster.

Spring at the Old Manse with the Holm of Grimbister and Damsay in the background.

relatively large were frequently delayed or cancelled. Wind, fog, strikes, breakdowns, were all hazards. Fog was the most frequent cause of disruption all the year round, indeed the summer haars off the North Sea were the worst of all. I have also been held up by sea-gulls hitting the propellers, sick air hostesses, and snow cutting off the road to Sumburgh airport.

Representing the constituency, however, was made a great deal easier and pleasanter by the hospitality of a Shetland doctor, Dr. Hamilton, and his wife. To spend too many nights in hotel bedrooms becomes wearisome. It is as far from the South of Orkney to the North of Shetland as it is from London to York, so that if I went to Shetland from Orkney or indeed to any outlying islands I could not get home that night. But week-end after week-end the Hamiltons put me up. They also joined the dedicated band of Liberals who got me in at the General Elections. Janet Hamilton was a woman of imagination and of considerable energy. Dr. Hamilton whose practice consisted of the South end of Shetland plus Fair Isle was very much in the best tradition of Scottish doctors, able, dedicated, firm with silly or hypochondriacal patients. They were both in my mother's phrase 'immaculate'. He was in addition a very neat carpenter, his work, particularly his model of a life-boat, was much admired. Dr. Hamilton was indeed fond of the sea. He enjoyed visiting Fair Isle. And as if living above the bay at Levenwick was not enough, he occasionally spent a holiday as a ship's doctor.

If Orkney and Shetland have been lucky in their schoolmasters, they were also well served by their doctors. When we first went to Yell and Unst they were looked after by two celebrated old men, Drs. Taylor and Saxby. Dr. Taylor wrote *A Shetland Doctor*. Dr. Saxby went on far into his seventies. In a snow storm in the winter of 1947 a woman started a difficult birth in the South end of Unst, some ten miles from Saxby's house. He and the Minister, who was a mere 71 or so, and a cart horse started off from Baltasound to Uyeasound. After a few miles Saxby sent the horse and minister back as the weather in his view was too bad for them. It took him, I believe, twelve hours to get through.

In the late forties and fifties Orkney, and more particularly Shetland, were depressed, assailed by depopulation and an absence of any alternative employment to agriculture, fishing and knitwear.

But by the sixties the outlook was better. The effort which achieved this renaissance was a communal one flowing from many sources. But, since we are all now much concerned about how to provide more jobs and a more satisfactory life, it is worth looking at some of the sources which can be identified. One source was the small but essential number of local entrepreneurs. They were the merchants who dealt in knitwear, such as my Chairman, Arthur Irvine, a Shetlander born and bred who had no wish to become a tycoon or leave his home at Hillswick in Shetland. When orders for knitwear began to pour in he felt in danger of drowning. I remember him bemoaning the impending arrival of his American agent 'with all his ulcers and telephones'. There were men I have already mentioned like the Tullochs and there were the founders of the Shetland fish processing industry.

On the official side there were Bob Storey and Bob Innes. Bob Storey, the Shetland Development Officer, before such offices grew to their present size, was one of the first to see that development must be all-round development. Jobs were not enough. Communities had to be rebuilt. They had to be rebuilt by the members of the community. Bob's secret lay in his sensitivity. Sensitivity is not encouraged by bureaucratic habits. It does not flourish among files, committees, memoranda and flow charts. A particularly depressed part of Shetland at that time was the island of Yell. We organised a conference about its future. Conferences have become hackneyed. But they were less so then and the gathering of people in Yell did make them aware of its troubles. We also had the advantage of the flair of Basil Wishart, editor of the *Shetland Times*. Yell had no electricity. One week Basil arranged that every Member of Parliament received a post card which read 'Yell for Light'. Next week they got another post card 'Light for Yell'.

Bob now works for the Highlands and Islands Development Board which no doubt is an appropriate job for him but he ought in addition to be in charge of the training of development officers. I have happy memories of moving majestically around the Shetland moors with him in the days when the roads were of gravel with passing places, ensconced improbably in his car which was a Rolls Royce upon which his grandfather had mounted what, if attached to a house, might be described as a patio.

In Shetland at about this time the further education officer was Bob Innes. He was responsible for practical training. Bob had a great advantage as a schoolmaster: he had never hankered after academic life. He was a crofter's son from Caithness. He described how he had been happily working in the sun and the harvest when he descried the local schoolmaster coming with his father down the edge of the field by the dyke. His heart sank with a premonition that he had got into a university—which turned out to be true. He must be one of the few schoolmasters who has built his own house. He is exactly what Scottish education needs and though Shetland has suffered, he has now found a broader field at Stirling University.

The recovery in the native Shetland industries was overtaken by oil. But the lack of training after school and the failure to see the need for

the all-round development of communities still cause me concern. We
need another Bob Storey, another Bob Innes.

MAGNUS WAS BORN IN 1959. So the late fifties and early sixties was the only time my family were often at home together.

In London we lived at 71, Kew Green though Andrew had a flat of his own not too far away in Sloane Street. After coming down from the university he worked in the merchant bankers Singer and Friedlander. I never remember my parents trying to influence me about what I did, nor did we attempt it with our children. Andrew and Johnny leant towards politics but it is not too easy if your father is already a politician. In some ways Andrew suited the City but it did not entirely suit him. All my sons at some period have been journalists though I do not remember any of them having such ambitions at school, indeed I do not see that they possess the characteristics which journalism is said to require. Andrew was certainly no extrovert. Johnny and Magnus can hardly be described as tough, gin-drinking, investigatory hacks of the conventional legend.

But they had some gift of description—Johnny as a small child described something as 'hot as a cooker'. They came through school unscathed by jargon. In Johnny's case we had made a lucky shot in the dark by pitching on Westminster Under-School, of which Mr. Campbell was then the Head—and a very good Head he was.

Magnus too has been inoculated against the flummery of Public Relations. Is this due to innate good sense or Stromness Academy or *Private Eye*? I do not know. But I enjoyed the note he sent to me as a boy, about the renewal of my car insurance:

'The Rt. Honourable Member would be well-advised to have an earnest personal interface situation with his insurance media so as to prevent the termination of his insurance cover on July 13th. At the same moment in time he should indicate to the insurance operatives that there has been an error in the visual interpretation of the distinguishing numerals of the personal transportation medium. Hoping that we can continue our ongoing and meaningful personal relationship.'

Gelda was at St. Paul's. St. Paul's teaching was as good as Winchester's but Manners Makyth Man (or woman) was not its motto. Parents, if not pupils, were treated as potential delinquents. I thought of gently pointing out when peremptory demands arrived from the High Mistress's secretary that even the Prime Minister found time to sign his letters. I like being paid the small courtesies of life. I resent, for instance, when someone wants to speak to me on the telephone, being told to hold on by their secretaries for long periods while they are fetched or connected. I would not claim to have outstanding manners but I recognise them when I see them. 'Good Manners are perpetual letters recommendatory.' At the time I found St. Paul's appeals to the 'Honour of the Hat Band' more alarming than the solidarity of the Old School Tie. However, lately I have felt somewhat chastened about jokes over the hat band and the old school tie. If more people showed some esteem for the uniforms they wear and the associations of which they are members we might get along better. When, say, airline pilots, dressed to ape services with a long history of devotion to duty and the public, strike like petulant children because an aircraft is diverted to help passengers at a time of difficulty, a little more regard for the traditions of public service would be no bad thing. So good was Gelda's education that she got an Exhibition at St. Hugh's at 17. She had perhaps been forced rather too hard but at Oxford she had a welcome relapse from intense intellectual endeavour. Just as well, as girls are, if not entirely flippant, apt to be over-conscientious. She soon recovered. Now she is the most executive of my children. Her visits to the Old Manse result in a noticeable lift in the 'quality of life'. Her mother lives in some awe of her disapproval. A sharp intake of breath by her daughter when arriving at the Old Manse is apt to fluster my wife: about the only thing which does. However, Gelda's character confers great credit on her parents, or perhaps she has been issued with a 'new soul'. Anthony Squire, son of Sir John Squire, used when we edited a paper together at Eton to account for the excellence of character displayed by some of our contemporaries (as against others) by citing Madame Blavatsky who apparently believed that there was an issue of freshly minted souls in this century.

To straddle Orkney and Kew was awkward at certain seasons of the year. Parliamentary and school holidays do not synchronise. So, although after the cradle my children had no permanent nurse, they were in the charge of a mixed bag of attendants. If only four of these appear in these pages it is not because we are ungrateful to the others but because the Grimond family are so much in debt to these four. First was Miss Ray Russell of Prestonpans. She came with us when we first went to Orkney. She helped to dig the garden, heavy work among the couch grass and brambles. Her equable temper soothed us all in the days when we first began gadding from house to house and were not sure how to cope with all this flitting to and fro. The next was Didon Howard who married Mike Faber. She was near my children in age—as the years wore on almost a contemporary. Before Laura and I came south after the summer holidays she took charge at Kew. Why, I am not very sure. By which I mean I don't know why she did it, it must have been a risky undertaking. I can think of few jobs I would back away from with more speed than meddling with other people's children. But it turned out very well—as far as we were concerned.

The third was Helen Taylor who has already popped up in this book as a fountain of information in Orkney. She and her family have been mixed up in our lives for a long time. She only came to London once or twice but is often still to be seen peering out of the windows at the Old Manse to keep her eye on Jimmy Brown or gossiping with Magnus about Orkney affairs.

And the fourth, Miss Dora Gidney, specifically in charge of Magnus in the days when he deigned to visit London. With Laura much in Orkney and I myself at the House of Commons for most of the day Dora and Didon were virtually in charge of our Kew house. The duties of an M.P. divorce him or her from a family for much of the time. I do not see how this could be avoided—in my case, at least.

Opinions differ as to the duties of an M.P.; indeed they differ as to the very nature of the animal. The public, led by publicists constantly confuse M.P.s with the Government. They would hold Hopkin Morris, for instance, to blame for actions of governments which he had totally and constantly opposed. Many M.P.s would indeed like their job to become an amalgam of civil servant and researcher with a dash of welfare officer thrown in. They press to be given assistants, duplicating machines and offices to work in, all the trappings indeed of the minister or bureaucrat. They thrive on a diet of paper. They follow a career and ape the responsibilities of Congressmen and Senators in America. My view has always been that the work of a British M.P. differs from that of a Congressman and even more sharply from that of a member of a government or public official.

The House of Commons came into being to provide some check upon the government. Members were sent to Westminster by the communities to keep an eye on the executive, to criticise it, to prevent it becoming too powerful. The government on its side summoned the representatives of the Commons—the communities—to get them to supply money: hence the importance of supply days. The Commons traditionally demanded the rectification of grievances before it would supply money. Supply days are still the occasions on which the opposition chooses the subject for debate. In short, M.P.s were elected not to govern, but to stop the government doing too much. If they became ministers the civil service was there to serve them. But most did not become ministers. If the executive was behaving with reasonable propriety they had no business to hang around Westminster unless their constituents wanted grievances raised. If the government was lax in its duty or their constituents' grievances were not met, the remedy was to refuse supply, to deny the executive the money with which to govern. Ultimately, in theory at least, the government could be thrown out. Even if that was often impossible it could be subjected to harassment, questioning and hostile publicity. But in no circumstances did the House of Commons take over the government. It was an anti-government institution. Nor was it a legislature as is Congress. The Government initiated all major legislation. Why then did Members need rooms, secretaries, filing cabinets? Why indeed. They were supposed to speak from the heart. It is in theory out of order to read a speech in the House of Commons—though ministers nearly always read. There should be no need for desks in the chamber. Most significant, for most of the time there should, according to the old view be no need for all Members to attend. So only some half of the membership can be seated. Being an M.P. was meant as a part-time occupation. M.P.s should be representative citizens sharing the troubles of their constituents, making most of their living outside Parliament. Such was their traditional role.

Of course the position of the M.P. had changed steadily over the past hundred and fifty years and was changing even more rapidly. More and more M.P.s looked on it, especially if they were Labour, as a full-time job. More and more M.P.s and, this was particularly apparent in the Labour Party, wanted to be members of the Government. Even before they could achieve that they wanted to be in touch with government policies. They were by nature insiders not critics. The number of teachers and lecturers among the Labour Party had swollen. They were keen readers of blue books and writers of monographs. The great research industry invaded the House of Commons. At the same time the field of government expanded. Government impinged more and more on the life of the ordinary person so that the 'welfare' work of Members increased and with it their correspondence. I was asked to sell an old man's silver watch for him. I was asked by another constituent in Orkney if I could help him as his house was haunted. When I demurred on the grounds that I doubted if any minister of the Crown was responsible—would not a minister of religion be more appropriate?—my constituent pointed out that he had lately been given an improvement grant so surely the Secretary of State should be vexed by the deplorable behaviour of his ghost which banged about inside and out, certainly impairing the value of the house and perhaps even the fabric. I sat in his house for an hour or two; nothing happened.

Unquestionably the trend of politics made more services and more money essential for M.P.s. But it may be carried too far. For one thing, though the pay was poor, other aspects of the job were gratifying. I would not have gone to sea on a trawler for five times the amount. How do you fix the pay of M.Ps., university lecturers and other jobs which have long holidays (I know that neither M.P.s nor university lecturers are entirely free to do nothing during the holidays but the holidays provide a change and to some extent they can choose what they do during them), variety and interest and in which you are your own master in a degree unusual in life? In addition, the Houses of Parliament provide many of the minor comforts of a club. What job, above all, would provide free travel between Orkney and Shetland to London? If M.P.s don't like the terms there are always others willing to take their place who would be just as good. Secondly, we are in danger of losing the main purpose of Parliament in the by-ways of specialisation. There is great value in keeping the simple traditional job of the M.P. though it may well need new instruments for its performance and other roles may be added to it. Indeed they must be added to it but the older role must not be extinguished.

If they are to discharge their functions back bench Members and indeed the whole opposition must not be seduced into the arms of the executive by expectations of government employment. Fear that this might happen to the Liberal Party was one reason why I opposed the 'Lib-Lab Pact'. Members of Parliament must maintain their independence. It is threatened from various directions. The executive has immense powers of patronage. Seventy or so M.P.s hold offices for which they are beholden to the Government. Many others hope for office: a hope which may inhibit them from criticism of the hand that they hope will feed them. Then there is the increasing volume of legislation which keeps Members in the Palace of Westminster immured together and isolated from the world outside. This too makes them think of themselves as professionals. To many this is a welcome thought. They have been brought up in a bureaucratic world. But politics is a vocation, pompous though it may be to say so. It is not just another way of making a living. To survive you must be interested in people as well as power. This is true of everyone wrapped up in political life—not only of M.P.s but of their supporters and sustainers.

During my first years as Liberal Whip Miss Revel Guest was my only helper and abetter, a part-time secretary in a poky office on scandalously low pay. That she and, after her, Catherine Fisher, coped with the multifarious trials of an M.P.s secretary must seem a miracle. So it was. She did it because she was fascinated by politics—her family had spawned several M.P.s and she herself stood as a Conservative candidate. My luck with help in the House of Commons showed once again how quality in staff overshadows quantity—indeed the latter is the enemy of the former. Some M.P.s want a pool of secretaries for Parliamentarians. It will be a sad day if they ever get it. The next move will be a uniform. The very marrow of Parliament, deep-seated in the bones of that imposing and complicated piece of machinery, are the secretaries, clerks and librarians. Each displays in varied guises dedication, cunning, mastery of a number of crafts and diplomacy of a high order. They like the House of Commons and so do I and I do not believe that you can do a good job there unless you like it. Secretaries recruited from a pool might come to treat their work impersonally. The ties, not only between the Member and the secretary, but between the secretary and the Member's constituents would melt. The independence of M.P.s has already been chipped. Let them at least pick their secretaries upon whose endeavours they so heavily depend.

The independence of M.P.s is curtailed too by what is happening to their constituency parties. But we must keep this in focus: in the focus of what is the prevalent attitude to politics and in the focus of a consistent view of how M.P.s should be chosen, which in turn depends upon what you think their job should be. The break up of the class divisions in society and the rejection of oligarchy has led not to a wider interest in politics but rather to the disappearance of an informed political public with a persistent interest in political questions. Political discussion such as echoed round my mother-in-law has been stilled. At the Other Club, for instance, political argument as against political gossip or talk of ephemeral political events is uncommon. In Orkney and Shetland at least the old parties have fewer active members than they did twenty years ago. Mr. Mackay of Sanday and the Lerwick hecklers have few successors. This alters the pressures upon M.P.s. Insidious temptations to succumb to bureaucratic assaults are nibbling away at the roots of democracy which can only thrive when refreshed by enthusiasm among the people at large.

Commentators have complained about attempts by their constituency parties to dislodge sitting M.P.s. But M.P.s have no prescriptive right to be a party candidate or a Member for ever. Nor should Liberals complain if those who dislike the views of their M.P. get a majority on the executive. Liberals should complain that apathy and the lack of an informed and politically interested electorate result in the electors, like sheep, obeying a small minority from whose views they dissent. Certainly this points to the decay of the Liberal suppositions behind democracy. But the remedy is not to give M.P.s a freehold in their constituencies. If they are not re-adopted by their party and if they cannot hold the seat by a direct appeal to the electorate this is a consequence and not a cause of the decay of democracy. It is an example of the manner in which through our own volition we are ceasing to be a Liberal country. Another example of illiberalism is the withdrawal of its grants by the government to firms which flout its policies. This may be deplorable but is inevitable in a country which demands that the government should interfere here, there and everywhere. The piper calls the tune; if you ask someone to give you a grant do not be surprised if conditions are attached. If you put more and more power into the hands of government do not squeal if they use it. If you abandon general rules and the idea of the common good by re-turning to a mediaeval warfare in which organisations of all kinds set out to coerce the government do not be shocked if the Government hits back. In fact, if you are not prepared to practise Liberalism do not expect it to survive. It will merely be exploited by authoritarians. I am astonished that so many people are so lethargic about the nasty necessities that creep in when you jettison Liberalism. But then a previous generation was blind to Communism and Fascism.

The pundits tell us that even if M.P.s want to control the executive they cannot do so today. If this is so it is our own fault. The machinery of the modern state may be complicated. But it is far more complicated than it need be because of the absence of principle behind our politics and an acquiescence in office-seeking and bureaucracy. In so far as some complication is inevitable, control could still be exerted did the public distinguish between what is the proper function of government and what is not. Modern methods if directed to the proper ends should make con-trol easier. Discipline in the Army has not collapsed because weapons are more sophisticated. At the moment there is a demand for more open government. With this go allegations that civil servants conspire secretly to bully the public. That the civil service has become an interest or series of interests on its own is true. By so doing like all other such organisations, it attempts to further its own interests at the expense of the general interest and often to extort what it can from the public. This is a serious retreat from Liberalism to corporatism. But I have not found that the officials of the central government (I have no comparable experience of local government) act illegally or harry individual members of the public. I must be careful what conclusions I draw from this. I am an M.P. and dispute the belief that M.P.s are despised, in fact they are a privileged class who get rather good treatment (though less privileged than many other classes). M.P.s may be sheltered from the ugly truth. Many ordinary individuals believe that civil servants are arrogant and arbitrary. Some experiments show this may be so. But in this book I have tried to describe my personal experiences, not what I read or am told even by people better informed than myself. In twenty-nine years in Parliament I have only come across two cases in which civil servants seemed to have definitely misconstrued or twisted the law. One of them was put right by Richard Wood, then a Minister. The upright and amiable side of British politics are illustrated by Richard's readiness to reverse his Department's decision, once convinced it was wrong, without any anxiety about loss of face, and incidentally by a small story concerning his behaviour to my son John.

Richard lost both of his lower legs in the war. Lately I came across a letter from Johnny, then at Eton. 'The other day I found a very handsome black walking-stick leaning against School Hall so I picked it up and took it home and then just put a notice up on the school notice board saying that I had found it. The next day I got a message from the headmaster to say that it belonged to Richard Wood, the ex-Minister of Housing or something, who I believe is crippled. Anyway, he was coming down to Eton and wanted to thank the person who found it. However, when he heard that I had found it he said he could not face seeing a Lib so soon after the Election. Instead he wrote me a v. nice letter enclosing £1.'

To turn back from this irrelevancy to my defence of the public service.

I am constantly amazed that the Inland Revenue makes as much sense as it does out of the entanglements of tax legislation. It may well be that senior Treasury officials bear some responsibility for the ludicrous state of our tax laws. But governments cannot evade shouldering most of the blame. And I have no doubt that junior members of the Inland Revenue groan under the torture of the tax laws as loudly as anyone else. As I write it has transpired that certain ex-officers have been defrauded of part of their pensions. That is indefensible, but it is notable how few such cases have been discovered, bearing in mind the load we have placed on the Civil Service. I am surprised that the Ombudsman has not discovered more irregularities. My fear is for the future as the standards and outlook of the Civil Service will be eaten away by its increasing size and the fading of Liberal assumptions. But up to now I have found civil servants fair and uncorrupt.

Let us have more open government but do not let us delude ourselves that by opening up government we are going to cure its defects. No amount of success in opening the stable to inspection will get the horse back once it has got away with the bit between its teeth. M.P.s should certainly strengthen their powers of inquisition, through the Public Accounts Committee, into what governments have done. For this purpose that committee may need more staff of its own. More comprehensive and rapid monitoring of government action should be followed by more searching inquests into failure (accompanied by some punishment of the guilty). Checks too are required upon the initiation of legislation. One of the most deleterious changes in my time as an M.P. has been the attention afforded to the manifestos put out by the parties before each General Election. The disease of the manifesto has been aggravated by the supply at the expense of the public of party research workers and political advisers (who also have contributed to the congestion of the order paper of the House of Commons with questions more suitable to a Polytechnic than a Parliament). The Manifesto contains a string of bribes designed to win the votes or money of different organisations. It ties a series of legislative proposals round a government's neck. A party should put before the electorate the principles upon which it will act. It may set out one or two major areas for legislation. But that at each election every party must promise more legislation is absurd: it is not only absurd but damaging when a list of measures is produced to please its backers. A freeze on legislation would do more good than sporadic freezes on prices. Many of these measures for which legitimacy is claimed because they were in the manifesto prove irrelevant or harmful when introduced. They too are symptomatic of a misunderstanding of democracy. Because a party has a proposal in the manifesto and because, say, a third of the electorate have voted for that party at a General Election is no good reason for putting that proposal into effect, regardless of whether it is beneficial to the nation or relevant to the country's needs.

Before a law is brought before the House of Commons the principles might well be examined by a committee. The public should have a right to appear before this committee. Public hearings could establish how far there was a case for the legislature, what public support it might have, what its effects were likely to be and what was the probable cost.

I do not support the general use of the referendum (see *The Referendum* by Grimond and Neve). But in the present state of our democracy it has a part to play, at least until we get electoral reform. It might well be used to test public opinion on those issues where change is difficult or impossible to revise or reverse. Incidentally, no one seems to have paid enough attention to the head-on challenge to our form of democracy and parliamentary traditions posed by the threat from some socialists that certain laws should be 'irreversible'. Another change which is certainly worth considering is the separation of the Government from the House of Commons. By that I do not mean that Ministers should not appear to explain and defend their policies; but that they should be elected separately. This would to some extent be a return to the days when Ministers had to stand again upon appointment and in others the adoption of the American system.

I do not believe that all that democracy comprises can be summed up in one person one vote and the divine right of a parliamentary majority. We must reinforce the Member of Parliament as our defence against the growth of Government. M.P.s today have a more exacting task than ever they did if they are to study the pretensions of the state and confront it on behalf of their constituents.

But an M.P.s life is of incomparable interest. What other occupation can compete with the fascination of Parliament? Add to this the pleasure of living in Orkney and Shetland and the variety of local and personal matters in which M.P.s become involved and it is difficult to think of any life other than that of an artist which can be so absorbing and varied. The life of an M.P. even when Parliament is sitting is not confined to the chamber. You are always on the job, Sundays and Christmas Day, at home as well as at Westminster. If to be perpetually on call is sometimes irksome, not least for one's wife and secretary, there are compensations. I count myself lucky to have been round the world at the public expense.

In 1952 Richard Law, Dai Grenfell, a clerk of the House, Mr. Cocks, whose apposite remarks would figure in this book were they repeatable, and myself were despatched to present a Speaker's Chair to the Parliament of New Zealand and a Mace to Australia's House of Commons. The original Australian Mace was said to have been carried off by a Member and lost in a brothel. Perhaps this accounts for the much stricter discipline enforced by the Speaker of the Australian House of Commons compared with our own. I was having a drink one day in the hotel at Canberra where in those days most of the Members lodged. At the bar I found the Australian Liberal Party's Chief Whip, who had been attached to the Fife and Forfar Yeomanry in the war. It was not long before the House rose for Christmas. I knew that important debates were going on so I asked him why he was not at the Parliament. 'Oh', he replied, 'I have been suspended for the rest of the sitting.' The suspension for several days of a Chief Whip here would cause a sensation.

I found popular superstitions about Australia untrue. Everyone we met was kind. I admired their cities. Sydney was like London even down to the notices requesting you to put no more than four inches of water in the bath, and some of the accents which were a variety of cockney. The strongest cockney I have ever heard was that of an inhabitant of Tristan da Cunha who came to see if Shetland would be a suitable place for his people to settle—they found it too cold—he spoke as I imagine Londoners did in the time of Dickens, even saying 'welly' for 'very'. Melbourne was delightful with its distinguished buildings. Adelaide seemed like mid-Western American towns in old-fashioned movies with wide streets and white wooden balconies.

The Australian countryside, on the other hand, I found frightening. I don't hanker after eucalyptus trees. All around fields were dry as tinder, waiting apparently for the fires a hundred miles long which were approaching. The big and rich wool producers near the cities seem to have a life rather like Ascot on a vaster scale, much bridge and many Rolls-Royces. They were very hospitable.

What struck me most forcibly about Australia, however, is how with a small population of some fourteen million people, it has created a personality of its own. Also, the extraordinary ability it has produced. What country founded, as far as Europeans are concerned, only about two hundred years ago can claim such singers, writers, painters and athletes? Sir Robert Menzies was also a remarkable politician. Meeting him (he used occasionally to come to the Other Club in London) confirmed me in my opinion that we should have made far more use of Commonwealth leaders throughout the Commonwealth. We did not lose an Empire and then fail to find a role. We lost an Empire because we never developed its role.

New Zealand was restful. Its towns were like what Dundee must have been before the First World War. Friendly as everyone was and pleasantly familiar as was the way of life, I felt a long way from home: remembering Orkney and Shetland I feared that the freight charges must be killing. To be given a new *Times* ten days old rubbed in the lesson. I don't much care for freaks of nature which are a feature in New Zealand. Boiling mud, for instance, does not appeal to me. But the ordinary New Zealand country must delight any farmer. The grass in some parts grows all the year round. We met one professor whose college was far removed from his farm. All he had to do was to go over at the week-end to move the electric fence. Seasonal work, shearing, etc. was done, as I believe it is in Australia, by gangs hired for the purpose. It seems strange to me, used to the all-purpose Orkney farms. Everywhere the development of farming seems to me odd. Orkney with its bad climate is intensively farmed. The east coast of America with huge city markets to hand contains hundreds of square miles of uncultivated scrub. In some parts of the shores of the Mediterranean terraces have been laboriously cut in every hillside, in others you can walk all afternoon and never see an olive, a vine or an animal.

New Zealand was enjoyable but the most enjoyable thing about the trip was Dick Law. He was an ideal travelling companion: equable and thoughtful, always wanting to walk, stop walking, drink and eat just when his companions did. As a politician he was as honest as Hopkin Morris whose views he shared. The compromises of post-war politics saddened him. He could respond to a battle about some issue such as appeasement but the politics of corporatism bored him. Before we set out on our long voyage I remember that one day when I was asking during a debate in the House of Commons for help with transport charges to my constituency he had replied 'It is nonsense enough to pretend all men are equal, don't let us further pretend that all places are equidistant'. He held laissez-faire, free trade, views of the most robust order—he expressed approval that the trawlers of Hull, part of which he represented, got no subsidies. In those days his views were unfashionable in the Conservative Party. It is a pity he retired from politics before they became more acceptable.

Later, I spent an idyllic few days sailing with Dick across the Channel and down the coast of France. He once also inadvisably took me to the Clyde with the idea of bringing south a boat he had bought. I did not distinguish myself on these expeditions. The voyage south on this occasion never got past Bute. I nearly dismasted the boat. On the final morning when we were back at our moorings in the Holy Loch it was blowing quite strongly as we prepared to go ashore in the dinghy to catch the train south. I let go inadvertently. We were whirled down the loch leaving Dick's shoes and socks on the boat. When we reached the Central Hotel in Glasgow, Dick in bare feet was refused admission even when we explained that he was the son of Glasgow's only Prime Minister. Luckily, that ever-helpful man Brendan Bracken appeared and got us in.

In 1954, I made a tour of the Middle East at the invitation of Mr. Emile Bustani, a Lebanese who had made money contracting for the oil industry. He was generous enough to take many politicians round the Arab States. Though he openly did so in the hope of making converts, he never deflected us from seeing anyone we chose.

Here again, I was lucky in my companions. I put Patrick Gordon Walker with Dick Law, the Kees and Sir Nicholas and Lady Henderson in the highest class of fellow travellers. Patrick like Hugh Gaitskell was a paternal social democrat. In other days either might well have ruled as imperial nabobs. Many M.P.s were escorted round by Emile Bustani: the Middle East is hardly as fascinating and unexplored as it was fifty years ago so I see no point in describing the tour. But one or two comments may be germane to this book.

The Arabs are the worst advocates possible for their own cause. They have been wretchedly treated. In many ways they are less blood-thirsty than the Europeans (they came better out of the Crusades). They have not succumbed to the American way of life. They have dignity. And yet, and yet, after hours of strident harangues, the goodwill of the most fervid pro-Arab must wilt. And though I kept on reminding myself that, if you are glad, as I am, that someone is standing up in the path of the American cultural steam-roller, then you must not judge them by Western standards, yet the frequent compound of Cadillacs and mediaeval superstitions topped off by belly dancers I find hard to bear. Unfairly they are at an immense disadvantage in making their case against the Jews.

In Qatar we were drinking coffee with the Sheikh when the far end of the salon began to fill with a crew of cut-throats armed with assorted weapons from long, ivory-butted rifles worthy of the Victoria and Albert Museum to Tommy guns. On enquiring the significance of this menacing but operatic chorus I was told that the Sheikh's uncle had been seen in the neighbourhood. Uncles in the Gulf States were apparently often a sign of trouble and few Sheikhs of Qatar have died in both office and their beds in the last hundred years. Patrick then learnt that some British officers on secondment were conducting a small war on behalf of the Sheikh. We pricked up our ears at this news which we had not heard about before. The weapons for their exploits were apparently bought on the Colonial Office vote. The laudable operation had been quickly and quietly completed. This showed that the British are still capable of handling such matters with skill. Larger and larger staffs and information officers will soon choke such initiatives. Nor am I sure that open government will help.

The skill of the British was also exemplified in our Embassies. We learnt how easily politicians on quick tours can burn their fingers. Syria was then under General Shishakly. Having talked with him, Patrick and I were impressed. We concluded that he was a pillar of stability whose advice should be accepted. The Ambassador demurred but arranged that we should see him again. This we did and came away more certain than ever that we had found the touchstone of the Middle East. Three days later he disappeared for ever from Syria.

The making and seeing of friends is a constant bonus from membership of the House of Commons. After the ten-o'clock vote you could be fairly sure of finding Christopher Hollis in the bar which he called the 'Spanish lavatory'. It was a large, tiled room giving on the terrace. The tiles gave Christopher's voice an even more penetrating resonance than usual. He combined most excellent manners with startling and spontaneous remarks on whatever came into his head. It is said, for instance, that one day he put his head round the drawing room door at Mells, the Asquith house in Somerset near to which he lived: the room was full of distinguished people but not those whom Christopher had come to see. 'Per not here? Helen not here? Trim not here?' he remarked, 'Nobody here' and withdrew. The 'Spanish lavatory' tinkled and rang with Christopher's comments about his fellow M.P.s several of whom were usually in the room. Then there were Lord Hinchingbrooke, Fitzroy MacLean and Hugh Fraser. Hinch had been a leader of the young Tories of his generation. But he would have had a better chance of scaling the upper reaches of the slippery pole a hundred years before. In spite of the huge proliferation of patronage the growing thickets of Quangos, there seem no jobs for such as Hinch. Patronage is too much reserved for whey-faced conformists. Hinch would have been just as competent at governing the BBC or running the steel industry (after all many people can lose £1 million a day) as some who are appointed to these jobs and in addition he would have lent panache to such bodies. I once promised Roger Fulford if I was ever Prime Minister he should be Master of the Buckhounds—failing Fulford, Hinchingbrooke. Anyway, he and such as Christopher kept Commons debates alive. But I must confess that a headful of off-beat opinions is not always the most serviceable luggage for a politician. Fitzroy was much more usable and indeed was used. He was not, however, conformist, especially about the Army over which as a junior minister he presided. I have reservations about his Yugoslav predilections, our treatment of Mihailovic seems one of the most disgraceful betrayals but he was the best and most amusing of companions. Promotion in the Tory party remains something of a mystery to me. The party was not really so rich in talent that it would leave such members as Hinch and Fitzroy on the back-benches, nor did it use the debating powers of men like Derek Walker-Smith or John Boyd-Carpenter to the full. I sometimes think that some Scottish Members have never got office because their speeches were too short for their Scottish colleagues. A nation which describes a bus company as 'Scottish Motor Traction', is unlikely to take to anyone who can say what they think in five minutes (incidentally, why do Tories get through their speeches so much faster than Labour Members? Why have questions and answers got longer and more ineffective, why is Scottish question time, above all, so slow?—decline of classical education?) Christopher and Hinch, like Sir Will Y. Darling were in danger of becoming House of Commons characters—fatal—no one takes wit seriously in Britain. I remember Christopher beginning a speech 'The Hon. Member's remarks are as bizarre as it would be to speculate whether if I had been born a female horse I would have won the Derby'. That did not enhance his claim to office. Whether by nature or education Scots like to spell everything out in more detail than the English. They actually admire sonorous phrases running into several paragraphs. What the

English would dismiss as long-winded the Scots consider weighty. Perhaps as you get further north minds work more slowly. I notice too a tendency in my compatriots to bolt in middle age like cauliflowers, suddenly they sprout quiverfuls of opinions on which they dilate at length.

During the fifties Michael Astor lent us a house in the grounds of Bruern where he lived. Michael was not an enthusiastic M.P. In those days it was the custom to debate the Finance Bill in committee through the night. Finance Bills cannot be guillotined (another relic from the tradition that an important function of the Commons is to examine government expenditure). I did not find occasional all night sittings wholly disagreeable: getting up early has always made me feel rather ill about mid-day but to come out into London with the catalpa trees in New Palace Yard coming into bud ('Neither catalpa tree nor scented lime' is one of those lines in British poetry which I find irrationally moving like 'Come unto these yellow sands'), to find the streets fresh and empty in the air of early June is to see London at its best. But Michael loathed such nights and fled as fast as possible to the country. Jakie Astor was also an M.P. and also unenthusiastic. He did not share my mother-in-law's view that he was cut out to be Prime Minister. It was indeed the only political office for which he was fitted. Dinners at Downing Street, had he attained it, would certainly have been hilarious. Both Michael and Jakie, as well as their brother David, had a talent for politics which in their case never found an appropriate outlet. Sad. Nor was their case unique. The House of Commons repels as well as attracts and as, at least until Life Peerages came in, it had a near monopoly of national politics, those who found it uncongenial usually cleared out of political life.

In the sixties I also used to go sailing with Reggie Paget. Like Dick Law he was a wonderful host but not as peaceful. Indeed John Strachey described him as the Captain Bligh of the Channel. I used to cower in the bows. Reggie would roar directions which I seldom understood, but luckily he could not let go of the tiller to chastise me. The ultimate ignominy was to be sent with a boat hook to pick up the moorings. It reminded me of a nursery game in which you had to pick up boot buttons with a bent pin on the end of a string. Time after time I missed the wretched thing in full view of Reggie's yachting associates. But in spite of the lapses those week-ends in the Solent were very happy. Reggie's generosity was boundless. He had defended Field-Marshal Erich von Manstein at the Nuremburg trials; he was always helping those in all sorts of need. Disappointed as he was at never being a Minister he should take comfort from the delight he gave many friends, while enlivening life in the House of Commons. The Labour Party has been invigorated by bonnetfuls of odd bees. I would not put Reggie in the class of one of his Labour colleagues of whom it was said that the only things he cared about were the abolition of income tax and the restoration of the Czar, but he did suggest that I introduce a Bill to abolish the rearing of pheasants as pheasant shooting interfered with fox hunting.

Another by-product of becoming an M.P. was the Rectorship of two Universities—Edinburgh and Aberdeen. I was elected Rector of Edinburgh University in 1960 through the good offices of David Steel, then a leading student. The office of Rector has a history relevant to recent student happenings. At one time, at least in some of the Scottish universities, the Rector was head of the university, elected by all the students and staff. Eventually the staff rebelled against being swamped by students. The Rector was left to be elected by the students, still retaining the Chairmanship of the Executive, that is the Court, but third in the hierarchy after the Chancellor and Vice-Chancellor or the Principal. Up to the First World War Rectors tended to be elected on political lines. They usually only appeared once or twice during their three year term, the great occasion being the delivery of their Rectorial address. That strange man, Lord Rosebery, whose hold on the Scots was so tight, is the only man I think who was Rector of all four Scottish Universities. Strange at least he seems to me, the darling of London society, the winner of the Derby, the power behind Gladstone's Midlothian campaign, one of the greatest of populist triumphs, the recluse of a tower on the Tay. His popularity in Scotland is highly creditable to the Scots but difficult to reconcile with their usual predilections. Anyone less like Bruce, Burns or Scott it would be difficult to imagine. Margot Asquith records that long after he ceased to be Prime Minister she found a crowd at a railway station and on asking for whom they were waiting was told 'Rozzberry, Rozzberry'. Why, by the way are Robert Adam, Adam Smith and David Hume so under-rated in their native land? The heroes of the Scottish intellectuals are a rum lot.

I usually attend the sittings of the Court of both Edinburgh and Aberdeen Universities. Appleton was the Principal when I was Rector of Edinburgh. He endeared himself to me by drawing me aside and enquiring anxiously 'I trust that you are not going to be a working Rector?' I reassured him. But I turned up two or three times a term both at Edinburgh and Aberdeen, giving small parties as well as attending the Court. I found Edinburgh stimulating but exhausting. There was a tension about it—admirable on the whole but perhaps a strain for Rectors and some of the students.

The latter were scattered about up stone staircases in Portobello or in the Pollock Halls of Residence (financed by Sir Donald Pollock who had

179

made his money by raising the German ships in Scapa Flow). Aberdeen was more sedate. Universities have suffered in esteem since I was a boy at St Andrews. The modern world is more inclined to hand its hat to professors than take it off in the street when it meets them. Vice-Chancellors are perpetually in committee or incomunicado. The Lad o' Pairts is looking for a safe job in the civil service. In garrets good students fret their youth away in doubt what to do or how to behave. Some spin out their education as long as they can extract grants to support them. Others jump at the first job offered and find themselves with no means of escape. Although at first sight more sophisticated, today's students are often more naive than my generation. Fewer have ever been away from home. The battering they receive from television hardly equips them to think for themselves, yet the world has uprooted most of the signposts. Boys and girls are entitled to find some fences to show where their elders think they should go. If they want to climb over them, so much the better but fence-jumping should be seen as a serious step by the adventurous and the less adventurous should be able to pray behind the fence if they do not want to stray beyond it.

In their treatment of the towns in which they are lodged Scottish Universities have much of which to be ashamed. You would think that they would be contrite about the demolition of the old buildings of Glasgow and St Andrews. Yet the new Students' Union at St Andrews is well down to the lowest standard of modern architecture and Edinburgh University has only recently completed the catastrophic destruction of most of George Square. All the wreckers of football trains put together have never perpetrated such vandalism.

At Aberdeen I encountered the wave of student protest. A Rector has the right to appoint an assessor to the University Court. I was asked if I would appoint a student. I replied that I would if I could find a suitable one, preferably a girl. As half the University was female they should have had more representation on its governing bodies. They would also bring with them a welcome breath of independence from hierarchic ambitions and cast a new eye on the University. The male students demurred, this was not at all what they had in mind. In spite of diligent searching I could not find a girl for the post. They had the good sense not to waste the golden hours of their youth on University administration when others would do it for them. They were not bemused by whatever accolade membership of the Court might be imagined to bestow. Their good sense buttresses my contention that we should have more women in public life. I did, however, appoint a student, Kenneth Chew, the first I believe to be a full member of any university governing body, and very well he did. On the Court I found Dr. Mary Esslemont and frequently stayed with her when in Aberdeen. Women's Liberationists might contemplate her career. She passed her medical examinations during the First World War. She was President of the Students' Representative Council some fifty years ago (and the only woman to hold that office up to now). Ever since, she has not only had a most distinguished life as a doctor but has travelled the world for good causes. She does not yearn for recognition; just as well for considering her performance she has had strangely little from her own sex or the other.

I have had pleasurable dealings with two other Universities besides Edinburgh and Aberdeen. In 1970 I was asked by the Vice Chancellor, Sir Robert Hunter, to be chairman of a committee set up to look into the constitution and working of the University of Birmingham. Dr. Hunter had attended my mother when a professor in Dundee. He was an astute and justly popular Scot well able to cope with the students who occupied his office. He promised that well-known British medicine for all ills, a committee. He also felt that after sixty years or so since its foundation, Birmingham University should look again at its constitution. Joseph Chamberlain had founded it on the flood-tide of early 20th century civic pride. It now catered for students from far beyond Birmingham. He was wise enough to get Sir Maurice Dean to run the committee over which I nominally presided. It included two students, as well as Professor Dorothy Hodgkin and Sir Peter Venables, who had just retired from the Vice Chancellorship of Aston University.

How fickle are modern moods. Seeds spring up and wither. Is it because the modern world and particularly its education is shallow and stony? If universities offered the rich soil which they did in my time it is hard to see why students long to sit on committees or take sabbatical years to play at politics, or worse, to become premature bureaucrats. Yet I found that Edinburgh, Aberdeen, Birmingham and later Kent offered a great deal so I conclude that the fault lies not with the University but with the country or with education in general. I am all for handing over the running of student affairs to students. Students in the Scotch Universities run their Unions rather well. Courts, Councils and Senates can digest some student members and gain by doing so; by shouldering some of the burden of administration students may free some of their seniors from stupefying and time consuming tasks. But students should not be more than part-time administrators.

In all four of the Universities with which I have had some dealings the Secretary or Registrars have not only run their offices admirably but have rendered general services with a devotion seldom recognised.

The student assertion in the 1960s was also a symptom of the new lack of confidence among the British. Everyone has to be reassured by being given some office or title. The different attitudes of British and Americans which I noticed in UNRRA were illustrated by a small incident when I was reconnoitring other universities to find out how they ran their affairs. I told a professor from Harvard that one of the questions thought momentous at Birmingham was who should run a department and how the Deans were to be chosen. He agreed, saying that they found it hard to get anyone to take on these jobs at Harvard so the most junior lecturer was usually designated. This was not at all what I meant. At Birmingham everyone wanted to be head of the department: even in some cases if it meant less time for their own research and teaching.

We then came up against the conservatism of British organisation which is part of the same parcel as their itch for tampering. The Faculty of Social Science which was combined with accountancy was in disarray. We suggested that it should be associated with law in one faculty. Lawyers might impose some discipline on sociologists and social workers: while to mingle with such people might extend the interests of lawyers. But while both lawyers and sociologists were quite keen to extend their own houses they were most unwilling to settle down with each other.

Almost half the University of Birmingham was in one faculty—that of Science. On paper this looked unbalanced. But just as it did not matter at Aberdeen that theology with few students was a faculty on its own, so it did not seem to matter at Birmingham that one faculty was so much bigger than the others. 'Untidy' like 'small' is sometimes beautiful.

Our committee was also bound to consider schools embracing several subjects as an alternative to single subject departments. The solution seemed to me to have both: to have a 'vertical' division into faculties and departments, so to speak, and a 'horizontal' grouping across these departments. I was also attracted by the notion of leaving some subjects floating outside departments. Any or every department might design courses to include them—for instance, Greek, and Moral Philosophy.

In 1970 I was elected Chancellor of the University of Kent, mounted on a magnificent site overlooking Canterbury. A Chancellor's duties hardly exist though he is nominal head of the University: his opportunities are somewhat greater. I used my expense account to entertain some staff and students in or near the University or at the House of Commons. With the decline in personal entertaining due to its expense people in all walks of life get isolated from those who may have no axe to grind and can speak freely to them. Mr. Asquith I expect ran across many more people who talked freely to him than do Prime Ministers today. It can have done him no harm either to watch the fare ticking up on the taxi in the days before government cars. So I hoped to contribute a little towards understanding by arranging a few dinners with professors, politicians and others.

Kent is a collegiate University. The colleges of Kent are not self-governing or self-financing institutions. But they are worth while. As the University expands—and I hope it will not expand too much or too quickly—they will provide a skeleton which monolithic universities lack. Kent treats its Chancellor well, whether it gets much in return from him I am not so sure, but it certainly does get a lot from the pro-Chancellors and other laymen who sit on its council and court. Both Sir Paul Chambers and Robin Leigh-Pemberton tended to its affairs with a dedication and expertise which universities are lucky to be able to attract. Even so a Vice-Chancellor's time is too mortgaged to committees. Geoffrey Templeman, the Vice-Chancellor of Kent, would be even harder pressed if he could not count on such lay assistance. As it is, he and the other founding fathers can be proud of an institution which is largely their creation. At Kent as in Shetland I have been fortunate to find a family always ready to put me up, entertain and arrange my appointments. Without Professor Bryan Keith-Lucas and his wife I could not have done even the little I have. The university too owes much to Bryan for bringing to it the Oxford and Cambridge tradition of interest not only in the work of the students but in the students themselves. It is appropriate that a man from the same intellectual stock as Darwin—and indeed related to that network of Cambridge families to which he belonged—should have been head of the college named after the great scientist.

When the Government proposed to merge the Art Colleges into the Polytechnics I organised a small conference at the University of Kent on the teaching of art (and to some extent music. Mrs. Cecil King, a most stimulating music teacher, attended.) I had as an amateur been impressed by British art in many forms since the war. The Arts Colleges could claim some credit for this. They had so far escaped the bureaucratic age. Such principals as Mr. Brill of the Chelsea School of Art and John Barnicott of Falmouth, blessed originality and their pupils were free to work no set hours and no set pattern but always under the discipline of strict standards in technique. Many artists felt absorption into the Polytechnics would threaten a field, one of the few, in which Britain since the war had gained a high reputation. At Patrick Heron's request I had introduced a delegation including himself, Henry Moore and John Piper to see Mrs. Thatcher, then Secretary of State for Education, to protest against the merger. We did not win her over. For me the most stimulating event at the conference was an introduction to one meeting by Patrick Heron. Patrick is not only a notable painter in several styles, he is also a purveyor of new thoughts, a trader in ideas and a kindler of enthusiasms. I shall not forget him talking about the central importance of art, how it is not a peripheral amusement secondary to the real business of life but the focus of life. The way we see and do things we learn from artists. He took illustration apples and human faces as painted by Rembrandt, Cézanne and others and showed how each artist had made subsequent generations see the world anew.

British art since the war has shone with unwanted effulgence. From Mary Quant to Henry Moore, if indeed that is a progression, in the visual arts and music and design and dancing, Britain's reputation has stood higher internationally than ever before. As always, it is difficult to identify the many impalpable factors which led to this renaissance—or naissance. Perhaps it is not important to do so. But one such factor seems to have been a fruitful alliance of public money and private initiative (another example of such an alliance is in agriculture). The Art Colleges, the Public Galleries, the Arts Council and its protégés, such as Covent Garden, can surely all claim some credit. Perhaps I am too morbid when I see love of size and the bureaucratic attitude creeping into this Eden— but I do. Art is a personal, elusive, living, unpompous affair which certainly needs patrons but must take care not to be suffocated by them.

I rebel against all this guff about our National Heritage, that is to say, Italian pictures, French furniture and German porcelain for which we are told the taxpayer must cough up huge sums so that they can be stuffed into museums for the greater glory of the curators. I am prepared to let most of it take its chance in the bogus art market. Do not let us pretend that the piling up of foreign paintings and antiques has much to do with British civilization. I do not believe that our magnificent public galleries will be embellished by more Titians. They have already a glut of exhibits all of which they cannot show. What would redound to the sincerity of national-heritage-mongers would be to persuade the public collectors to return some of their stock to locations where it would be appropriate. What a delight it would be to visit some Canalettos on the Grand Canal. No one is going to smash china or tear up paintings if they leave this country. But all too many people are standing with their pick-axes at the ready to tear down buildings which really are part of our heritage. Every year such buildings are demolished or their contents collected for specific and specifically British settings, torn out and dispersed. All the great London private houses have vanished. 'Country Life' carries lists of country houses which have likewise been demolished or stripped of their contents—the latest being Warwick Castle.

It is in saving buildings and their furnishings and in fostering living artists that I would like to see money concentrated. But then I am an ex-Secretary of a National Trust. It was in that capacity that I first learnt to appreciate the work of the Royal Academies. They never bleat for public money and they hold excellent exhibitions without being exhibitionists. At present in particular under Sir Hugh Casson and Sir Robin Philipson they are models of how such institutions should behave. In Scotland in particular the R.S.A. has kept a home for the visual arts which has contributed to their recent successes—remarkable for so small a country.

BETWEEN 1950 AND 1956 while I had been juggling as Whip with the internal discussions of the parliamentary Liberal Party the country had experienced Churchill's last administrations, the half-hearted 'dash for freedom'—that is to say, freedom from socialist controls—and the death throes of imperialism. The dash for freedom was quickly replaced by what *The Economist* called 'Butskellism'. Messrs. Butler and Gaitskell seemed to stand for more or less the same economic policies. They straddled the middle ground of politics. Under their guidance a 'mixed' economy of privately and publicly owned industries was to operate within a regulated market. It was at best only a modified success.

I believe now that the Liberal Party accepted 'Butskellism' without sufficient questioning. They should have been more inquisitive about its workings. They might have foreseen that unless sharp limits were put on it government interference would stifle enterprise and foster inflation. However, I was not in charge of the Party even had I formulated the views I shall later describe.

When we parted for the Summer holidays in July, 1956, Clem had made no mention of any intention to retire. Indeed I suspect he had none. I told him that I had been asked to visit America late in September. He readily agreed that I should start at the end of the Liberal Assembly.

Liberal Assemblies in those days were occasions for the Party in the country to express their opinions. Today they are more like sounding boards for the proclamations of the leader, M.P.s and the policy panels. M.P.s attended spasmodically, some of them not at all. Clem descended like Zeus in a shower of gold—just before the annual financial appeal on the Saturday morning and gave the farewell oration. The mainsprings of the Party in the country in those days were Philip Fothergill and Frank

Byers. They both deserve to figure largely in Liberal history. Frank has sustained the Party and its leaders throughout the post-war period and will I hope long continue to do so. Philip is dead and here seems an appropriate moment to talk of him. It is a tragedy that he never got into the House of Commons and that Life Peerages were not invented in his day. It will be sad if his services are forgotten. He came from Yorkshire where he had a woollen business. But he spent a lot of time in London and as he had been in Edinburgh during the war he knew Scotland. His business prospered and since he was capable and commanded loyalty—which he thoroughly deserved—from his staff, it seemed largely to run itself. Philip devoted himself to the Liberal Party. He possessed a quiverful of political qualities, including, alas, gout. This made his movements uncertain though in other ways his vitality gave him the appearance of some small, round, furry animal. Like all such animals he was always busy. I never knew anyone with such a palate for politics, theory, argument, strategy, tactics, money-raising, publicity and, above all, personalities. He was always eager to hear political gossip and exchange political ideas. The *Guardian* once referred to him as 'Foster Fothergill, the Liberal Fire-brand'. The zany misprint and the incongruity of the phrase makes it stick in my mind—for though it is incongruous to think of Philip, with his liking for good food and good company, as any lean and hungry rabble rouser, yet he did more than anyone to keep the Liberal fires alight. He was intensely generous and friendly, many are the dinners he provided for friends at the Ivy, his eyes glowing with pleasure at the prospect of a pleasant evening, more like a caricature of a French bourgeois than the usual picture of a Yorkshire Puritan. To the older generation of Liberal leaders he behaved like the best of family butlers, to us of his own generation he was a favourite cousin or uncle. Britain is lucky to have had a succession of people who are always prepared to be helpful. On the national scene, I think of Brenden Bracken, Walter Monckton, Lord Goodman and in the Liberal Party, Philip. It is essential if you are to be helpful, and indeed it is essential for politicians, that you should be interested in people. This Philip certainly was. A streak of mischief too is an advantage. This Philip had too. He enjoyed launching senior Liberals on delicate subjects likely to cause trouble. His solid ability, acumen and devotion to his friends and the Party were set off by admirable manners so that he never gave offence and everyone was glad to talk with him.

When the Party gathered for the conference in 1956 Philip was of course there. The possibility of Clem's retiral had been mentioned and was indeed, I believe, raised at the press conference just before the conference opened. A change of leaders is always tricky and no Party has devised a wholly satisfactory procedure. At that time in the Liberal Party there was no procedure at all. The onus fell to such as Philip and Frank Byers to take soundings and if necessary bell the cat. Not that in this case the cat was at all disposed to bare its claws. Nothing was said or done during the first two days of debates. I made a speech on behalf, somewhat strangely, of the Merton and Morden constituency, moving a resolution in their name. On Friday evening I left for London to pack my bags. On Saturday morning I was installed by Clem in absentia as leader of the Party. In his speech he announced his intention of 'handing over the wheel and going below'.

I mention these haphazard goings-on because the leadership of Parties and the way in which leaders are chosen has become a matter of some moment in British politics. The change-over of leaders in a Party of six Members was not in itself of much account. But the Liberal Party, though small, was essentially a beast of the same breed as other Parties and some conclusions of general relevance can be drawn from its be- haviour. As there is no statutory limit on the time anyone can lead a Party and seldom any moment which all those involved see as the right moment to resign, a great deal depends on the character, judgement and good-will of the leader. The leadership had come to Clem owing to the defeat of Archie Sinclair at the polls. Had Archie won in 1945 he would unquestionably have continued to lead the Party. At least among my friends he was accorded deep loyalty. His second defeat by the margin of 269 votes in 1950 left Clem as the undisputed choice for the job. Hopkin Morris would not have wanted it. Even if he had, the Party would hardly have plumped for him or Megan: they were too far out on the wings. In any case, by 1956 Hopkin was deputy Chairman of Ways and Means and Megan had joined the Labour Party. Frank Byers, who in addition to having served as a forceful Chief Whip, had made a considerable impact on the House of Commons, would have become Leader had he too not been defeated. In these circumstances Clem might have claimed to go on for more than ten years. Indeed, as I have said, at least up to a month or two before he resigned, he clearly intended to continue. It does him credit, therefore, that he accepted with such good grace the suggestion that it was time for a change. All Party leaders are in a strong position, if they want to stay. It is always difficult to dislodge them and much harm may be done to the relationships of those who run Parties if a struggle develops. Nor do I believe that new methods of election will necessarily circumvent this. As far as the public is concerned, however, it seems to me that a contested change-over is often beneficial. The Liberal Party at least only makes headlines in such circumstances. For all Parties there is the extra publicity, the excitement of the race and curiosity about the victor when he or she emerges. A new Leader too gets the advantage of goodwill. There is no evidence that the contest of 1975 in the Tory Party did Mrs. Thatcher any harm with the voters. I even question the generally accepted view that it is a bad thing to change Leaders close to a General Election. But if it is, then it is rather that the contest will have left unhealed wounds in the Party hierarchy than that the electorate will be wary of a new and untried figure. Of course, I accept that unfamiliarity may be more of a consideration when that figure may be the next Prime Minister.

To have disinterested and trusted men and women of standing in the party—but not themselves in the running for the crown—is a boon in times of change. They are the fly-wheels which keep a party running steady. The Liberal Party is too small to need a 1922 Committee, the committee through which the elders of the Tory Party operate, but whether it is with a formal committee or with influential individuals a leader does well to act in close concert with such elders if he can find and trust them. I know that Sir Nigel Fisher's account in *The Tory Leaders* of the events leading up to Mrs. Thatcher's victory is disputed. But it certainly seems from that book and other sources that some Tory leaders were either not on the best of terms with any such figures in the Tory Party or disregarded their advice. One person upon whom any leader must rely is his Chief Whip, who in turn would want to be in constant touch with M.P.s, peers and other leaders in the party. But the Chief Whip alone is not always enough.

My first weeks as Leader of the Liberal Party were spent in America where I have been on one pretext or another quite often. When I arrived in September, 1956 the Presidential contest between President Eisenhower and Governor Adlai Stevenson was in full swing.

My itinerary was carefully worked out. I merely recount the following to show how America works. I went to call on Bill Howell, my friend of UNRRA days. He said that I must come with him to dine with Katie Locheim, an old UNRRA acquaintance. After dinner Katie told me it was absurd for me to go round looking at factories or talking to schools. I must go to Chicago where Adlai Stevenson was about to start a tour of the West. She would arrange that I accompanied him. So, in a rather too well entertained state, I agreed. The people who had arranged my now cancelled tour were providentially accommodating. Next evening I arrived at the Drake Hotel, Chicago where no-one had ever heard of me. In the morning Stevenson's circus flew off to Great Falls, Montana, a marvellous morning of sun and Majorettes. I felt happily relaxed, so although still rather early I accepted the offer of a Manhattan, indeed several Manhattans. Sitting there, as we sped west, I asked my companions who provided the comfortable plane in which we were wafted through the radiant air. 'The press', he replied, 'what paper do you represent?' The truth began to dawn on me. 'How much does it cost?' I enquired. '$250 a day.' I had an allowance of $15. I foresaw difficulties. I was not the only one. When we arrived at Boisy, Idaho, the day was even more golden. Back-slapping broke out with convivial heartiness. Then everyone realised that the candidate was not with us. Eventually there appeared at the top of the stairs leading into an aeroplane a bemused figure in a Burberry—Adlai himself looking like an untidy country vicar. He tottered down evading two synthetic Red Indians and started his speech. 'As I gaze upon your wonderful green pastures enclosed by the great panorama of the Rocky Mountains.' He looked round nervously. As far as anyone could see the landscape was flat and brown. The Rockies may have been behind him but they were certainly not in front. If he had read his speech before it was not apparent. At the end of each page there was a nasty jar as happens to those who come downstairs thinking that there is one more step than there is. After this ordeal a beaming woman state senator clapped a musket into his hands and a helmet over his head— to equip him for shooting elephants, the symbol of the Republican Party. Unfortunately, the topee came down on his nose like a candle extinguisher.

After the meeting a member of Stevenson's entourage said how glad they were to see a British politician in these foreign parts. I told him that he had better take a good look as I had already run up a bill I could not pay and was about to walk back to New York. He appreciated my predicament. The only solution, he said, was to get into Governor Stevenson's aeroplane: Stevenson, he said, had no idea who was in it and would think I was one of his speech writers. I protested that I was once bitten twice shy about getting into strange aeroplanes but, as he pointed out, I had little choice. So for three or four days I joined the Stevenson flying camp. I stood up waving in the motorcades; I sat with my feet dangling over the platform in various Rose Bowls. It was highly entertaining for me but not, I fear, for Adlai. 'Happy days are here again' and 'The Side Walks of New York' reverberated. Nothing was spared the Governor. I happened to be near him when on leaving a meeting at Oakland a mother thrust forward her baby, presumably to be kissed. I have never actually seen a politician kiss a baby. Adlai with a glazed, punch drunk expression and routine reflex held out his hand. To everyone's astonishment the child solemnly held out his (or hers). 'Good God', said Stevenson, 'it looks as though it actually enjoys it.' One day he clambered into his open car to discover the back seat occupied by a girl in sky-blue shorts and bra wearing a revolving top hat on which was emblazoned 'I'm madly for Adlai'. As she pinned him with a furious embrace on the back seat it seemed doubtful if he was madly for her. American electioneering is fun, though it goes on far too long and includes such bizarre information as a detailed report on Eisenhower's stomach with which I was regaled at breakfast when I spent a day at his headquarters. In the autumn of 1956 when I was just finishing my tour in America Eden began his operation on the canal. The Suez crisis had begun in the previous July.

Just before Parliament broke up for the holidays in 1956 I was for once in a way present in the House of Commons on a Friday morning when Eden made a statement on the seizure of the Suez Canal by Nasser. It was a fairly tough statement which was greeted with approval by Gaitskell who said:

> 'We deeply deplore this high-handed and totally unjustified step by the Egyptian Government. Has the Prime Minister in mind to refer this matter to the Security Council? . . . Will he bear in mind the desirability of blocking the sterling balances of the Egyptian Government?'

Obviously the Middle East was going to be the main summer topic. I saw Clem just before we went home. Even by then Gaitskell was damping down his first reaction due in part at least to the alarm of his party at anything smacking of gun-boat diplomacy. Liberals too had reservations about the Eden line but we agreed to hold our fire until the smoke cleared a little. By autumn the Liberal Party was aligned with the opponents of the Government's Suez policy. Our armed intervention brought me home. Before I left Washington I called on various politicians and ambassadors. The most enlightening I found to be the Australian Ambassador. He impressed on me the hostility of the Americans which he made no effort to minimize. I returned to find the House of Commons in frequent uproar. The atmosphere was unlike anything I have experienced there before or since. It was like being in a ship bumping from rock to rock, frequently out of control. The rules of procedure seemed in danger of being swamped. Sittings were suspended. Then after a cooling off period we would return to hear another statement about the operation. The Cabinet would shuffle in behind the table looking like a gang of schoolboys who had been caught stealing apples. No government ever looked more shamefaced. The only one of them who looked as though he knew what he was about was the Prime Minister himself. It has been said by those who saw much more of him than I did that he was in a state of high tension—as well he might be—and swept by bursts of violent temper. All I can say is that looking across the Chamber he was the only minister who gave me any confidence. I made a speech suggesting that whatever our views of the Government's policy it would be unwise to jeopardize the operation just when the troops were landing. I was given some good advice by Donald MacLachlan, the editor of the *Daily Telegraph*. In the forties and early fifties the *Economist*'s reputation had soared under the editorship of Geoffrey Crowther assisted by Tom Kent and Donald. Tom and Donald were a remarkable pair to find as assistant editors and to them liberalism with a small 'l' was greatly indebted. Liberalism with a big 'L' too benefited from their advice: as it did from many other economic writers such as Graham Hutton. Tom in particular gave me a lot of help before he went to Canada. Once as we were trooping out of the House I found myself close to Eden who, having heard I had been in America, asked me to come to his room and tell him my impressions. He seemed relaxed but surprised that I had found the Americans so mad at us. He went so far as to say that he must go over there—apparently with the thought that he could put things straight by some sensible talking. Too much notice should not be taken of what Prime Ministers in a hurricane say in passing—but I was astonished. Not for the first time I wondered how much information reaches our rulers.

I have always wondered how the Government and particularly Eden and his Foreign Secretary got away so easily with misleading Parliament. There can be little doubt that there was 'collusion' with the French and the Israelis. The truth was not told. While I personally rather welcome the veil which has been drawn over this incident—there may well be occasions when ministers must lie in the national interest—yet the contrast between the treatment of the dissemblers on this occasion and the way that others have been expelled from public life for lesser offences, is strange to say the least of it. The House of Commons is notoriously incompetent and wayward when it tries to deal with moral issues, offences against the supposed customs of the time or even plain dishonesty or negligence by its Members or servants. It is just as well, therefore, that it should not go sleuthing around unnecessarily still less whip itself into an ecstasy of indignation. The temptation is often strong. The Press like a scandal and will publicize those who fulminate with righteousness. Debates involving personalities are more attractive than those on abstract principle. And in those days there were always at hand some Members claiming that they acted with reluctance, and only at the call of public duty, who were willing to demand enquiries or statements about alleged wrong-doing. But it is surely time that we considered the proper procedure for pursuing mistakes or omissions in government. It has often struck me that we do not monitor our government, or review the working of Acts of Parliament in general. The handling of crises such as Suez received little or no attention once they had passed from the headlines.

Suez culminated in the resignation of Eden. Eden's reputation at present stands lower than I believe it should. Strangely this is so in the Conservative Party itself. Yet Eden after the war was the hero of that

Ronnie Moar, Johnnie, Grizelda, Jimmie Brown and his uncle from Canada.

Johnnie. Photograph taken at Finstown School.

Impression of a walking tour – drawing by Robert McNeile.

The old Shetland herring fleet sailing from Lerwick.

Laura, Grizelda, her daughter Katharine, self and Kate Grimond, Johnnie's wife.

Party in the country. By the fifties he could draw bigger crowds than Churchill to a Tory *fête*. He has been the subject of a sort of denigratory *mélange* concocted of alleged idleness and aloofness, dependance on others cleverer or more resolute than himself, dullness as a speaker and an inability to conduct government effectively. Donald MacLachlan's article in the *Daily Telegraph* demanding the 'smack of firm government' had even before Suez aroused misgivings about his judgement. It was also alleged that Eden knew nothing of home affairs. These criticisms have eroded the high regard which his diplomatic work earned him before and during the war.

I did not know Eden well but I had some chance to observe him in the House of Commons and after he had retired I spent a couple of days at his home in Wiltshire. In my experience the criticisms I have mentioned are not valid, if they can be justified at all it is by singling out some aspects of Eden's performance. They will, if not countered leave a misleading impression about the whole of it. It is true that his speeches lacked the wit of Oliver Stanley or the telling phrase of Churchill. 'Clich, Clich, Clich' they may have been as Bevin remarked. But he held the House of Commons. He made Foreign Affairs appear important and British foreign policy as explained by him seemed of weight and significance. No one else could do it as well. Speakers have a right to be judged by the purpose of their speeches and their suitability to the occasion. I have seen his eyebrows rise and his forehead pucker a little like a spoilt child crossed by his nurse—but usually as far as I could judge his irritation was justified. His ascendancy over the House of Commons was partly due to his good manners towards it. I remember how he turned on a singularly silly interruption and instead of tearing the questioner apart or ignoring him—as he deserved—used the occasion to explain again with courtesy the point he was making. He was an admirable host, not only in supplying excellent food, drink, comfort and amusement but in, at least as far as I could tell, his freedom from self-pity or self-glorification. As for his intelligence: he took a first and if that does not impress you read *Another World* 1897–1917 (Alan Lane) an essay on childhood and war strongly to be commended. Pictures, books, gardens, cattle breeding, he had a great variety of interests and of friends.

What about Suez then? I still think it to have been a mistake. Some have suggested that Eden needed to prove himself after the attacks of the original Suez rebels. There may be something in this. The school solution is that Eden was determined not to repeat the appeasement of the thirties. That is largely right. But that hardly disposes of the matter. Eden must have realised that 'going it alone' and thereby risking a clash with the United Nations and the Americans, let alone giving the Russians a chance to make mischief, was highly risky. He had heard Gaitskell demanding collective, not unilateral, action, indeed the cavalier treatment by Chamberlain of the Americans had been a main cause of his pre-war resignation. He has given his account of Suez. Unfortunately, it is not convincing. Each new Leader or Prime Minister wants to make his own mark. Eden may have disregarded the advice given him. Whether this was so or not he seems to have been misled about the reaction of our allies and the capacity of the British. This may well have been the fault of the Foreign Office. Over-estimation of a country's strength and reliance upon forces only tested in circumstances different from the current crisis have again and again proved fatal. An enquiry into the circumstances of Suez would be valuable now to establish how the misjudgement came about rather than to apportion blame. It need not wait until the archives are opened. Eden felt let down by the opposition at home. Tories often feel injured by the failure, as they see it, of a Labour opposition to give them the support which they claim they provide when in opposition to a government taking essential measures. They have a case. Eden's support had been invaluable to Bevin. The Labour Party scarified Heath for pursuing the sort of economic policy of wage restraint which they themselves have had to introduce. But Tories pass over the Curragh, of course, and their pre-1914 encouragement of rebellion—old, far off days perhaps, now admitted even by Tories to have not been particularly happy. In the case of Suez Eden felt particularly grieved at Gaitskell's behaviour. Gaitskell was always regarded as something of a traitor to his class. The Tories like to maintain that they get on better with the 'genuine working class' e.g. Maxton, or J. H. Thomas, though how far any of their heroes remain working class after a spell in Parliament is open to doubt.

Britain was lucky to escape as lightly as she did over Suez. No doubt it made easier the Russian's brutal and typical attack on Hungary. The Russians have shown that they do not need excuses to sit on their neighbours and satisfy their imperial ambitions. No doubt Britain's prestige took a further twist downwards. While our international horns were inevitably being drawn in I doubt if the pace was much accelerated. Eden was right in his deep suspicions of the USSR which continued to his death and were wholly justified. But the Russians have not so far advanced in the Middle East to the extent he feared.

The damage of Suez has been chiefly felt at home. We have not learnt the lessons. One simple lesson is the acute difficulty, if not impossibility, of facing serious international crises with a divided Government and an unprepared nation. Any international crisis of a sort which threatens war is certain nowadays to come from communist aggression. At present there is a substantial minority of the Labour Party in the country which will always find excuses for the communists and their allies. This element in our politics is bound to be reflected to some extent in the House of Commons. It will make it difficult for a Tory government to handle such a crisis. The nation has to be taught where the main danger lies just as it had to be taught about the Nazis before the war. Then too there was a faction in our politics which was ready to find excuses for the menace which threatens us. The Germans had been badly treated at Versailles, it argued, Hitler was interested in establishing a new economic order at home, not in expansion, so the arguments ran. There were also pacifists. I always maintained that we could have stopped Hitler when he sent his troops into the Rhineland. But I confess that the story of Suez raises doubts. I wonder what the public and the parliamentary Labour Party response would then have been if we had retaliated with force in 1933? The position is worse today. There is an even more dangerous disposition to excuse or play down the threat from Russia.

What has Suez taught us about the conduct of our foreign policy and our relationship with our allies? Britain has never found it easy to prepare for storms. The Liberal Government has been criticized for its dealings with France and other countries before the First War though in my view it played its hand well. But at least in the 19th century the choices in diplomatic strategy were clearer. We were not ashamed to defend our interests. Since the Second World War the Western world has been riddled with masochism. To some extent this has an honourable origin— hope for the U.N. and disarmament. But the U.N. as an umpire has proved too biased. It is absurd to treat every country in the Assembly as equal. The majority of countries are hardly imbued with a righteous desire to act in a judicial spirit, still less a liberal one. It is astonishing to see how meekly the Western nations, who provide by far the greatest part of the resources of the poorer countries and of the international agencies, accept the abuse hurled at them, while Communist countries, who stir up violence, invade their neighbours and subscribe little to development funds, escape unscathed. So while we have to a large extent stopped regarding the pursuit of national interest as the aim of foreign policy, we have found little to put in its place. We share this vacuum with the rest of the Western world. Indeed in some countries in the Western world the majority, or at least a vocal and influential minority, seem to consider that any policy which defends the interests or indeed the ideals of the Western world must be wrong. Take Vietnam, for instance. The American defence of South Vietnam may have been badly managed. Prudence might well have suggested that it should never have been under-taken. But it was launched from good motives. If there was an element of national interest in it, since America no doubt does not want South East

Asia under Communist domination, the chief element in the mixture of motives was the desire to resist aggression and defend liberty. I have always sympathised with some of the American misgivings about Vietnam, but I have never understood the force of their feeling of guilt, nor the condemnation which their attempt to stand up for freedom incurred in most of the free world. The French may well blame the Americans for their failure to help in Indo-China due to the usual American nightmare about Colonialism. American foreign policy is too often the slave of vote-gathering at home. The Americans no doubt misconceived the position in Vietnam, they may have been bungling and corrupting when they got there but I am not convinced that the motive for their intervention was immoral. I do not believe that even Chile under a right dictatorship competes with the horrors perpetrated by Communist dictators. I cannot see why Cuban forces in Africa are excused their part in suppressing popular revolts while a few white mercenaries rouse cries of horror. This masochism engenders a liking for defeat. Success embarrasses many Liberals, failure earns their applause.

I do not believe Eden knew about the new mood of masochism. We can see how much he was affected by the First World War—indeed who would not have been? But, appalling as was the experience of the First World War, and disillusioning as was its legacy of disappointed hopes, unemployment and international mismanagement, his generation were not masochistic. They believed that the only way to come to terms with the horrors of trench warfare and its aftermath was to cling on to the belief that the world could be made better so that the mud and bombardment had not been wholly futile. In their view, the First World War was ill-conducted. But ill-conducted as it may have been, they believed that we were right to fight. Terrible as was the war, a German victory would have been even more atrocious. Perhaps it was this pre-Second World War outlook which persuaded Eden that Britain had a part to play and should play it to success. His successors learnt a lesson—the wrong lesson. They became adept at saying one thing and doing another. Or in saying something and doing nothing. We entered the years when our leaders thought that making a speech was taking action: the years when the British learnt to lie back while Prime Ministers told them how well they were performing, reassured them that they were great and respected, while the rot continued. We were under the command of statesmen who walked backwards while claiming to advance. At least Eden, mistaken as I believe he was, did not behave like that.

More disastrous even than the charade in foreign affairs that followed Suez was the inertia in home affairs. For a moment the causes of our poor economic performance could have been tackled. For Suez excited not only the House of Commons but the public. The public was shaken from its complacency. It might have responded to new departures. And the economic and financial climate was favourable. But the first post-Eden Conservative government was intent on hushing us back to sleep.

However, before we get to that phase, I had an awkward corner to turn. Hopkin Morris, who had been a supporter of Eden's policies, died in November, 1956. This meant a by-election in Carmarthen. Megan was the Labour candidate. The Liberal Association adopted a candidate who was in favour of Suez. Should I disown him? At a General Election it is quite easy to embrace a few heretics. In a big Party and in a seat which the Party has no hope of winning, such nuisances can be brushed aside. But to have one of the six Liberal seats contested by a candidate in opposition to the Party line on a major current issue, was, to say the least of it, awkward. Looking back, I should probably have disowned him. But it would have been to take a gamble and flown against most of the advice I received from my colleagues. In the end I spoke for him but did not attempt to paper over our disagreements. It was an unhappy affair. How grateful I was to Jeremy Thorpe for his support. We addressed some meetings together and his good humour made the whole experience more tolerable.

We lost Carmarthen. From then the fortunes of the Party improved. This was largely due to events outside the Party's control. When the tide has ebbed for a Party there is bound to be an upturn. The Tories looked in bad shape in 1945–50 and again by the end of 1955. The Labour Party should not, on the cards which the Tories held in 1973, have won the election in Spring, 1974. Labour looked down and out in 1977 but quite perky by the Spring of 1978. Of course these resurgences may be temporary. There may be a long-term swing against a Party with occasional ups and downs. But the long-term swings in the British system over the last hundred and fifty years or so have been more likely to affect the system as a whole than the Parties within it. If the reason for the existence of a Party disappears, as happened to the Irish Nationalists when the Free State was set up, that Party will disappear. But there remains a reason, so long as the system remains, for the Tory, Labour and Liberal Parties. There have been elements in both the Tory and Labour Parties which would like to take over the Liberal Party. Though the idea of a permanent arrangement, whether pact or realignment, with elements of the Labour Party has been more popular in recent times, it is the 'Left' Tories (if the word 'Left' has any meaning in this context) who have looked most enviously at the Liberal position. From the Liberal Unionists and Joseph Chamberlain, through Lloyd George, to the National Liberals, such coalitions as have actually taken place have been with the Tories.

The case of Lloyd George is particularly instructive in this regard. In the popular eye he is figured as a radical. Yet before the First World War he favoured co-operation with the Tories and his premiership depended entirely on their support. The relationship of the three Parties is on the face of it full of paradoxes. While the younger Tories of the fifties wanted the Liberals out of the way, so that they could claim at least part of their inheritance, it was the Tory Party which by withdrawing their candidates made it possible for us to hold Huddersfield West and Bolton West. While the Liberals had made it possible for the Labour Party to get its original toe-hold in British politics by recognising that it should be represented in the House of Commons, and allowing it straight fights, the Labour Party in no way reciprocated. Yet the dominant sentiment within the Liberal Party inclined to Labour rather than Conservatism. It is possible that more Liberal voters, whatever the Party organisation felt, were inclined to the Tories than Labour. At least when Tories are in office and therefore attracting the odium which all governments incur, the voters who swing away from them vote Liberal in greater numbers than do disaffected ex-Labour voters when that Party is in power.

So in 1957 the time was ripe for some improvement in the fortunes of the Tory and Liberal Parties. It was also likely that later on when the pendulum swung against the Tory government we should gain. And so it turned out.

The Conservative government after Suez hoped to kid everyone that all was well. It didn't look for the longer term causes of Britain's decline. It made no effort to take advantage of the favourable economic conditions, nor did it try to counteract the growing greed which could only lead to inflation. It was careful to soothe the public into believing our political system needed no reform. Perhaps it was the last chance any government had of shaking the British lethargy. The public, alarmed by the Suez fiasco, brought up short against loss of power in world affairs might have responded to a lead which accepted the new situation and led us in a new direction. The government deliberately turned its back on any such courageous departure from the grooves of decline. On the contrary, as I have said, the Tories assured us that all was well, all as before, we need do nothing but enjoy our prosperity.

Gaitskell unwittingly contributed to this somnolence. While the Tory Government wanted to lull the voters back into a conservative sleep from which Suez had disturbed them, Gaitskell assured them that they could trust the system if only it was in the new hands. He was of the stock from which great and good administrators had come. Huge provinces of India might have lived in tranquillity under his beneficent rule. Several such pro-consuls *manqués*, finding the Empire closed to them have made their careers in the Labour Party. Brought up in the self-confidence of Winchester and Oxford, imbued with public spirit, excellent brains and the best of good manners, the outward sign of an excellent character, he was convinced that the country had only to be entrusted to men (and indeed women) like him and all would be for the best—and he was prepared to fight for his convictions unlike some other social democrats.

At this time the orthodox parliamentary system still seemed to be capable of working. It was led by politicians who believed in it. Suez seemed like an aberration. We could return to government by dialogue between the main Parties. Gaitskell was a true social democrat.

In the late fifties the leadership of the Trades Unions still lay with Bevin's collaborators and successors. Inflation was low by subsequent standards—around 3-5% and shortage of labour was more prevalent than unemployment. Taxation was high but it was not considered to be so high as to do serious damage. The Kennedy–Gaitskellite belief in the public authorities had not been challenged. For those who held this view the instruments at the disposal of Western governments were perfectly serviceable, their Cabinet procedures and popular assemblies, their home and foreign civil services. Bureaucrats grew in numbers and power but they did not seem so overwhelming as now. Parkinson had published his books. Everyone took his point. No one minded enough to do anything about it. If anyone had suggested in the fifties that Northern Ireland would be rent by thugs not for a week or two but ten years, they would have been laughed at as mad. If anyone had suggested that the prosperous middle classes of Europe would breed criminals of the Baader Meinhof–Red Brigade variety they would have been reminded that growing wealth and the conquest of unemployment and poverty had cured even the poor of such appeals to violence; as for it breaking out in the middle classes it was as absurd as to suggest rabies among the Quorn foxhounds or a return of the Black Death. Some political economists suggested that a country in which inflation rose above 10% or in which more than 35% of the GNP passed through the hands of the Government would become unmanageable. The response, if there was any, was to say that if this were true it was in itself a guarantee that inflation would not go over 10% nor government expenditure over 35%. Beveridge in the conventional thinking of the ruling classes was considered to have shown how to cure poverty and Keynes how to run the economy without unemployment. The Commonwealth might take a new lease of life, if there were doubts about that, then we could turn to Europe.

This was the background tapestry of the late fifties. Suez was swept behind it. Leading politicians found a new diversion in a supposedly special relationship with the USA and a new political plaything in Europe.

199

I speak of these diversions cynically because only a few years before the same politicians and civil servants who were now swinging towards Europe had dismissed the suggestion that we should join the new European institutions. As a result we had lost the opportunity of being in at the start. As for our relations with the USA, Suez had shown how little our common heritage had meant when put to the test in a particular crisis. If war and peace were to be tilted by the dislike of an Eden and a Dulles for each other or the bonhomie of their successors, the relationship could not be deep. At home the economy took a turn for the worse. We were rebuffed by De Gaulle. There was the night of the long knives in 1962 when a third of the Cabinet was sacked in a panic. The political battle took a new turn which brought the Liberal Party close to the gun-fire.

B Y 1957 THE LIBERAL PARTY was on firm ground from which to advance. It offered a non-Socialist alternative; an alternative which people who had voted Conservative could contemplate without alarm. I had planted a sub-heading on the *Liberal News*—'The non-Socialist radical Party'. The Party had little money but one or two first-class officials: high among these were Harry Cowie as the co-ordinator of policy and Pratap Chitnis as an organiser. The *Liberal News* itself had Christopher Booker and William Rushton on its staff. We could also tap the best intellectual resources in the Universities and professions, such academics as Professors Alan Peacock, Victor Morgan, Roland Oliver, Hugh Tinkler and Paul Bareau and such tax experts as George Wheatcroft and Hubert Munro and educationalists such as Jack Peterson. Gaitskell for all his intelligence was not a fountain of new thought: he believed too much in the system for that—and was too involved in internal Party battles. We also had, considering our small size, some excellent M.P.s, candidates and local Chairmen. If I mention only two or three that is not because they were unique. Arthur Holt was an all-round politician, deeply loyal to the Party and its principles and most competent. He took on the *Liberal News* and made it a simple statement of what we stood for. We had been criticised for not making this sufficiently clear—this is a perennial criticism of the Party. The *Liberal News* therefore carried in a conspicuous box in each issue a statement of some aspect of our policy, relevant to immediate issues. I sent out regular letters giving the Party line. We attracted some interest among the young, Ludovic Kennedy, Robin Day, David Steel, James Davidson, Emlyn Hooson, Robert Oakeshott and many others made up a telling list of candidates, enterprising and humane. Geoffrey and Heather Taylor for instance, names unsung in political histories, were the first to demand more comfort for the old and cold. Hypothermia was a word they coined. We were particularly lucky in our candidate in a by-election at Torrington in March, 1958. No doubt anything I say about my brother-in-law, Mark Bonham Carter, is prejudiced. He seems to me one of the most under-used members of his generation. Britain is guilty of mis- or under-using some of its best material. The Liberal Party could be criticised for side-tracking talent which should have been working in the main power houses of our affairs. It is not the only such organisation—consider the Foreign Service—and I like to think that the Party has exerted some leverage in spite of its devotion to a cause offering little chance of power. But Liberals in Britain have been denied the obvious opportunities open to Members of other Parties. Few have been lucky enough to serve long in Parliament and with several exceptions those who have not been so lucky have been excluded from major jobs in public life. However, this has been mitigated lately—for instance, Life Peerages have enabled some to play a part in the House of Lords. Mark was invaluable to the Party in the House of Commons for he has an incisive brain. He delves down to the bones of problems, marshals arguments and proposes right and often original solutions. He had already stood for a Devon seat. Now the chance turned up again. He seized it. He and his wife, Leslie, proved attractive campaigners. No trace of that 'effortless superiority' which, his grandfather, Mr. Asquith, said was the mark of Balliol men, intimidated his rural audiences. He writes and speaks with a clarity which is indeed superior. But no husband and wife could be more friendly and relaxed at village meetings as I saw for myself. Nor was anyone better equipped than Mark for the various sides of political life. His speeches had a cutting edge and his advice fertilized the thinking of the parliamentary Liberal Party.

In the 1959 General Election the Liberal Party more than doubled its vote to 1,600,000, gained one seat, North Devon, won by Jeremy Thorpe, just failed to get Edwin Malindine in for North Cornwall and lost Mark. This was a heavy and by me unexpected blow. But Torrington had long been a safe Tory seat and Mark was unlucky in coming up against a Conservative exceptionally well suited to the constituency. I was cast down by the result of the General Election but within a couple of years things looked up again.

The Tory Government disappointed many of those who voted for it. The swing to the Liberals continued. In March, 1962 we scored a success at the Orpington by-election. Eric Lubbock turned a Tory majority of 14,760 into a Liberal majority of 7855. I could hardly credit it when it was announced. The negative aspects of Orpington have since then been emphasised. But it should be remembered that the Liberal Party held the rudiments of a positive alternative to Tory and Labour parties.

It should also be remembered that Eric Lubbock who won the seat interwove in his personality and outlook several Liberal strands not always found together. He was not only convinced of the truth of Liberalism, he constantly put his beliefs into practice. He was active in all sorts of causes concerned with the condition of the people and the freedom of the individual—and still is. He is a sensitive person, but he suffered from none of the inhibitions which often make Liberals too diffident in pushing their views. He was widely and rightly regarded as a representative of a new generation—Orpington-man—the generation which was classless, understood technology (Eric Lubbock was a trained engineer) was free from the patronising airs of the old Eton and Oxford hierarchy and intended to apply to the management of the country the principles of modern science—political engineering—but from strong Liberal conditions. What was much less often remembered, the Lubbocks were an old Orpington family. They had been the Squires of Orpington. Eric still lived in what had been their home farm deep in the woods where the bark of a fox was as common as the hoot of a motor horn. These woods had been presented to Orpington by his father. It was, I believe, the only local authority which employed a gamekeeper. He was in every way an appropriate descendant of the Lubbocks, one of those banking families which, like the Peases and the Gurneys, contributed so much to 19th-century Liberal England. He and Pratap Chitnis ran a brilliant campaign against an able Tory opponent. Indeed it was at this by-election that Pratap established himself as one of the most acute and capable organisers in politics.

Given the political climate in the late fifties and early sixties and the personalities the party had attracted, could we have advanced more? The answer is probably 'yes'. Perhaps I did not grasp the opportunity firmly enough. Perhaps I did not realise it could be there. I believe it may have been there then, even though we were nowhere near the balance of power. Perhaps it recurred ten or fifteen years later but I shall come to that. Looking back I fear I was not sufficiently on the offensive. That was one mistake. I could not believe that a Party with six Members in the House of Commons could achieve much immediately. I did my best to keep my small army on the field of battle. Liberals have a tendency to depart to their tents where they indulge in their own wars. I tried to keep the head of the Party to the wind and concentrate our fire on the main issues. But while the role of the Party was clear in my mind—to offer a non-Socialist radical alternative—I believed that we could on our own only capture a limited number of points of vantage. I looked to the day when there would be a realignment on the Left. Liberals would then be the centre of a Party which included many Labour voters or potential Labour voters and many Tories or potential Tories. I was right, I believe, in telling the Party that it could not by some miracle of parthenogenesis spring from six M.P.s to a majority in the House of Commons. It would have to go through a period of coalition. The prospect of coalition in those days scared Liberals out of their wits. They became as restive as a horse asked to pass a steam roller. And for the same reason. They were frightened it would flatten them. I also believed that the process of widening the non-Socialist Left, of getting our elbows going and barging our way through was to be achieved not only by tactical victories at by-elections but by a policy campaign.

This strategy had grave defects. It was ahead of its time. Perhaps it would never have had its time. At any rate, time was not to be afforded it. The British were not interested in longer term unfolding of new politics. In this they had the press wholeheartedly on their side. The Nuffield school offered one example of what was going on in all universities, except Manchester; they were not interested in the content of politics. To the detriment of the country most political academics had swallowed the bait of 'psephology', the collection and interpretation of statistics about who was going to win. They had become racing tipsters. They analysed the votes of bakers in Leicester. They, with their newly dis-covered toys, computed from the latest Gallup Poll what would happen if there were a General Election tomorrow. That there was not going to be a General Election tomorrow did not greatly worry them. Racing tipsters at least pay some heed as to whether there is to be a race or not. The academic psephologists shaded off onto the journalists. Indeed the attrac-tion of psephology was that you could get on television and become a journalist. Many modern academics yearn to be something else, some-thing which will bring them publicity. Inflation has not only debased the currency. Every rat-catcher is now a rodent officer. In Scotland, the first division in football is now the premier division. The only result is con-tempt not reverence. The journalist must for ever be boosting or denigrat-ing politicians. Prices on the Stock Exchange at least are what someone is prepared to pay. But the assessment of the Prime Minister or the Leader of the Opposition is what makes a good story. Most journalists make no attempt to recount what politicians are saying. Fewer still are capable of examining it. In America, Lippman was a serious examiner of the content of American politics. Here there have been no Lippmans among reporters though we have had some wise editors and two or three shrewd and thoughtful political correspondents. So the British public has been led, like drug addicts, to regard politics as concerned with who will vote how next week. And they got a Prime Minister who thought a week was a long time. The notion of getting any space or time to discuss the content of politics as it might or should be over the next ten or twenty years was an illusion.

The opposite plan of campaign might have achieved something. We have seen how the press and television fasten avidly on the National Front though it gets few votes and the content of its policies hardly exists. The National Front is largely a creation of the press and indeed of its extreme Left opponents—its own mirror image—which has used the publicity which Fascism has now to boost its own repulsive doctrines. Several of the 'newsworthy' names of far Left organisations stand for no significant view or number of people and have never been elected to anything on any public ballot. Liberals might have cashed in brazenly on their success as a Party of protest. We have seen lately how effective lobbies and protest can be. The SNP have panicked the Labour Party into introducing preposterous Bills in the hope of bribing the electorate. I did not realise how hollow was the building behind the façade of Labour. A more vigorous campaign by the Party as a whole in the Colne Valley, for instance, in 1962 might have toppled that party. We might then have elbowed Tory and Labour out of our path.

We were ahead of our time in another way. We advocated, for instance, a reduction in direct taxation. That is now the accepted wisdom of the City of London. We got little support from it then. We were in favour of joining the Common Market when to do so made sense. Now, when the initial opening has been missed, it has the enthusiastic support of the top people. Then, it was explained to me (by one of our diplomats in Europe) in a manner used to teach the ABC to the children, that it was absurd for the British ever to join the EEC. He later—too late—became a leading, deeply respected and much quoted enthusiast for the EEC. We plugged partnership or co-ownership. But it was not running strongly in the political race.

All this sounds like that well-known trick of excusing oneself by self-accusations of not being nasty or stupid enough. And so it is. But not entirely. A Leader who had grasped more firmly the *Schwerpunkt* of politics could perhaps have achieved more; a Leader perhaps who had more confidence in his and the Party's destiny. Though I have suggested that in some ways, for instance, in gaining long-term adherents to his or her party, the power of the Leader is over-estimated, yet in the short-term the Leader is pre-eminent. In modern politics at least and perhaps in politics for the last hundred and fifty years the tactical possibilities are opened by the Leader grasping the moment to attack. This is because the Leaders get the publicity. Their speeches may be written for them. The real or shadow Cabinet may put their thoughts into his or her head. But they must decide what is to be fed to the public. The newspapers, radio or television are concerned with what the Leader has said or blessed. 'Spokesmen' get publicity, so do a few mavericks, but politicians with a serious suggestion which has neither the blessing of the Leader nor the recommendation of insanity get little attention. It is no good, therefore, my blaming the admirable lieutenants that I had. They could not speak for the Liberal Party and were not barking enough to command the attention of journalists on their own.

A second, minor, mistake, or perhaps not so minor, was our disregard of patronage. I did not realise the greed of the British not only for money but for honours. I could not believe that civil servants and others having led well-paid lives topped off by bountiful pensions indexed to the cost of living, supplemented by directorships often taken without blushing in companies to which they would contribute little, would as icing on the cake hanker after GCMGs and KCMGs as well. The Liberal Party had no patronage. At the time it did not strike me as a grave disadvantage. It does now.

We were also under the illusion that it was enough to state a fairly obvious proposition. Excellent as were some Liberal M.P.s and officials, they had not the staff to back their work with endless statistics. But now it is not enough to maintain that two and two make four. This must be demonstrated by a research team or confirmed by consultants. No one has a right to enjoy Mozart unless they are a D.Phil student with a grant and no one has a right to an opinion unless they can back it by graphs. Finally and most significant we did not realise what a threat we had become. We were a threat because we did not want office above all else. That struck at the root of modern life. The playing of roles which is the essential of the modern bureaucratic society is threatened by those who won't play. Politicians ought to want office. Never mind what they do when they get there, they are letting the side down if they whisper that office only matters if you have some idea what you want to do with it. In the eyes of the bureaucrats of politics a politician is a politician is a politician, and a politician wants office, wants office, wants office, and that is that. We threatened those who had staked their future on the Tory Party being able to peg out their tents on the Liberal ground. We disrupted the smooth to-ing and fro-ing of the Party system. We were seen as people cashing in on the mistakes of the Conservative Party, with no standing on our own. We threatened, therefore, not only the system but the apparatchiks of the Tory Party who unconsciously relied for their position upon being employed by the party which was the only recipient of non-Socialist votes. If the Tory Party had looked to the interests of its supporters it would have made us an offer. It had done so in earlier days or at least received favourably the overtures of the National Liberals. The electoral mistake of the Tories was to leave the Liberal Party as a contender for the non-Socialist but non-conventional vote. It is easy to see why the Tory M.P.s did this; less easy to see why their supporters in the country allowed them to do so. Proportional representation would have been to the Tories advantage; the suggestion of some electoral toleration would have embarrassed the Liberals. At this time the Tory Party proposed neither.

As for the content of Liberalism at this time, I wrote two books, *The Liberal Future* and *The Liberal Challenge* which set out my ideas. The argument ran in outline as follows. We should aim at a liberal society. A liberal society allowed every individual the maximum range of individual choice. The limits were set on the Mill principle at the boundary where individual choices clashed. Here impartial law intervened. Impartial in the sense that such law was laid down by Parliament in the general interest and rested upon principles with which governments did not tamper. It was not tailored to suit the most powerful interests. The general interest took account of minority interests. Further, Parliament should only intervene in the individual's life when this was necessary to arbitrate between individuals and give effect to the general interest. The individual must not be regarded as a tally in a total. He or she was a participator with a part to play in the community. I asserted the rights and duties of the individual as part of a community. The rights of individuals did not depend on their work. They did not depend upon joining a particular profession or Trade Union. The political process worked upwards to Parliament which reconciled their rights and defended them. It seemed to me quite natural that the social services should flow from this view of society. They did not hedge the rights of individuals. They made it possible for individuals to make use of their rights. I then went on to examine education and other services and, above all, Parliament to see how they contributed to the maintenance of such rights and responsibilities.

I thought even then, in the hey-day of Kennedy–Gaitskell confidence in the ability of Winchester–Oxford–Harvard scholars to run our affairs that much needed to be changed. Though I was a greater admirer of the Party system than I have since become, I had serious reservations about it. I had more serious reservations about Parliament and Government. I believed that Parliament had not adapted itself to deal with its managerial functions, the handling of the nationalised industries, for instance. I was impressed by the Quaker conception of the 'spirit of the meeting', though with qualifications, having watched how it could be manipulated by resolute personalities. I wanted to see the same principles which had been translated into our political institutions given effect in our industrial institutions. The free market was the most efficient, the most satisfying and the most democratic way of running the economy but it offered obvious advantages to few people, too few people, and therefore industrial democracy must be extended. I accepted more readily then than I would now a mixed economy, though even then I had doubts about the possibility of running the nationalised industries. I did not see as I do now that the main threat came from the bureaucratic attitude. I supposed, like most people, that Keynes was broadly right, that we should release more money and credit to ensure a wider use of resources when they were under-employed. I issued a pamphlet under the influence of Harry Cowie, possibly at his dictation, of which the title and theme was *Growth not Grandeur*. That is to say, Harry and I suggested that effort should be directed to those activities which produced wanted goods, and not to prestige products. How right we were, when we consider Concorde. But we were once again ahead of our time. We, at least I, did not see at that time the depressing effect which the Trades Unions and other self-interested organisations would have upon the life and economy of Britain. The strength and weaknesses of government which were to become apparent in the next fifteen years were then veiled. But at any rate we fixed our attention on the content of politics. Twenty years later the Conservative Party is finding it necessary to do the same sort of thing. For twenty years there has been no comparable exercise by the Labour Party with the result that some of those who should be their natural supporters have slipped into mindless violence or nearly as mindless so-called neo-Marxism. This stagnation in Labour thinking is not fortuitous. Either state socialism must become authoritarian or it must desert its bible which teaches that all the means of production, distribution and exchange and indeed all education and all news reporting must be under public control.

Another suggestion Liberals pursued in and out of season was home rule for Scotland and Wales. In every Election address I issued I proclaimed it. We made some headway in Scotland and Wales by being the Party which had a particular interest in their affairs. We published a policy for the Highlands. In the early fifties I had recommended a Highland Development Board.

In some ways the Highlands and Islands Development Board was a pioneer. It was the forerunner of other Boards. I am not sure that these have been good for the country and I now believe that much of the capital needed in the Highlands could have been provided by lowering taxes and channelling local savings into local investment. But at the time the Board seemed necessary. A promise was made that it would be temporary (we should have known better than be taken in by any such promise). There did seem a shortage of risk capital in the North.

As for Scottish Home Rule, I never guessed that it would take the form of an additional tier loaded onto a country already bent double under too much government. I always assumed that it would go hand in hand with a reform at Westminster and a smaller British Parliament and Civil Service. Nor in the fifties and sixties had we tasted the burgeoning of local government, the multiplication of officials nor the additional regulations pouring out of Brussels.

The Liberal Party, free from too close attachment to either employers or the Trades Unions, could look at the industrial scene with an impartial eye and recognise that what it saw was not good. We did not realise—how could we?—that the Trade Union members were so intent on cutting their own and everyone else's throats as afterwards appeared. Our cure for the disease of bad industrial relations was to make workers employers, make them feel that they employed the managers and so had an interest in good management. This eminently sensible and liberal solution struck few sparks then. When it does it may well be too late. British workers have learnt by unpainful lessons that the easy way to increase their nominal pay is to strike. Strikes must be called at the moment they will do most damage. So far strikers have seldom, if ever, lost. Leyland workers, the most inefficient motor-car makers in the world, have boosted their paper earnings and their share of the national income to which they contributed nothing but losses. Though, like everyone else, greedy workers will suffer from inflation, in the short run they exploit the rest of the country. Newspaper printers who are as skilled as newly trained typists now by dint of wage demands and restrictive practices are paid four times as much for working half the time of typists. The British air services with their swollen staffs are stopped by sudden strikes which wreck the lives of the ordinary public. The money that such workers grab is worth less. The standard of life in the country declines, but what do some of them care? They have more banknotes in their pay packet. For this, above all else, the Liberals provided a solution. But it was not seen as necessary in the late fifties or early sixties. Even today resistance to new methods, go-slows, over-manning, and strikes official and unofficial are not seen as the menace they are. The public acquiesce in them. But when that happens liberalism may look down. For that is the present dilemma. Do liberals with a small 'l' fight illiberalism with illiberal weapons? If not, how do they fight it at all? But this, the great decision facing liberals is only beginning to emerge from the fog of apathy. It was imminent but hidden in 1960.

In the late fifties began the policies which are now familiar—incomes policies, guide lines, government boards to steer or stimulate industry. They were Tory inventions. They were the heralds of the new anarchy in which each bureaucracy, Trade Union, organisation or group of workers pressed its claims regardless of whether or not there is the wealth to meet them. That was the time when British government first despaired of Britain's putting its own house in order and of British workers doing as good a job as those abroad. The Tory Government turned to Europe to save us. By learning to compete in the European market British industry would be forced into greater efficiency. By having a bigger market it could reduce its overheads per unit of output. For years Britain had lagged behind America in investment and in horse-power at the disposal of the workers. But it was not yet admitted that a good reason for this short-fall was the poor use the workers made of the existing machines at their disposal. The nationalised industries proved a sink down which savings were poured. It is no good saving and then wasting the saved resources. To save time, for instance, and then use the saved time in digging holes in the ground may be good exercise but it is not investment. Yet that is to a large extent what happened. Bureaucracies, restrictive practices, the nationalised industries, wasted the country's savings as surely as if a proportion of them had been poured into the sea. It was never envisaged by Keynes when he spoke of the importance of investment that so-called investment would thus be frittered away. We began to suffer too from the 'bigger is better' fallacy which reached its peak under the next Labour government. Somehow it was believed that by throwing three inefficient companies together efficiency would increase. The buying of companies to strip their financial assets became one of the few ways of making big money. Labour as well as Tory financial manipulators engaged in it. Inflation, though it was to be kept within limits, 5% or so per annum, became the accepted way of life with all its consequencies. It was accepted too that under no circumstances should anyone ever take less, on the contrary, everyone must have a rise every year. There was to be no surgery, the British economy was to be soothed with poultices and state controls. No structural change was contemplated. Politicians and ministers warned of the consequences of living beyond our means. But their words were not backed by deeds. The British people snapping off their hearing aids announced that these warnings must be meant for someone else. The late fifties and early sixties were a turning point. The Tory Government encouraged the British to take the wrong turning, which they gladly did. After Suez it is possible that the British would have responded to new methods. But the Tory government gently stroked the public instead of applying the spur: the economy grew feebler as it staggered from crisis to crisis. The government assured everyone that they could go on as before, so long as we exercised reasonable care. It put on acts abroad with Kennedy and Europe which diverted attention from the sapping of our strength at home.

The Liberal Party belaboured the need for increased efficiency, better use of resources and an increase in goods and services which people wanted and for which they were willing to pay. Professor Paish, one of our principal economic advisers, constantly drew attention to the danger of stimulating the economy too fast by using the drug of more currency. As he pointed out, increased demand working through the supply of money, led to inflation and bigger imports before greater productivity was achieved. He advocated the unpopular policy of keeping some resources, including labour, unemployed. 'Over-heating' was indeed a danger. But I don't think we appreciated the extent to which restrictive practices and monopolies had ensured that the economy, even when fully employed on paper, was unemployed in practice. However, Liberals constantly demanded that steps should be taken against these monopolies and restrictive practices. Little was done. Paish and the other Liberal economists, such as Alan Peacock, were more sympathetic than most of their colleagues to monetarism. But monetarism got no support then. We were still in the days of demand management and the fine tuning of the budget. I always thought this a policy of little significance. Arthur Holt pointed out that no one could find any close correlation between fine tuning and the way in which the economy behaved. No one indeed bothered to follow out in detail whether the Chancellor's prophecies of the effect of 3d. here and 6d. there, came true. All we knew was that the spring 'budget strategy' usually proved wrong and often had to be reversed in the autumn. We realised that the engines and rudders were not working but we did not realise that this was a permanent defect. We stood up, as far as we could, for the consumer against the growing strength of producer interests. On the principle that people should determine their own future and that those concerned did not see their future as part of a federation, we opposed the Federation of Northern and Southern Rhodesia and Nyasaland. We advocated Scottish and Welsh self-government within the United Kingdom and the setting up of specialist committees in the House of Commons. Electoral reform was a permanent plank in our platform though perhaps not given enough emphasis. I myself was attracted by the single member constituency and the simplicity of the British system. I wanted if possible to keep the tie of the member with the community in one chamber of government. Votes cast would be reconciled with seats won in a second chamber. If such a reform was too much for Britain to swallow then, regrettably, the single member constituency must be scrapped. I saw that electoral reform could not be introduced without altering the traditional working of Parliament. To me this was an ad-advantage. But many of those who cried most loudly for electoral reform were also the most adamant against any coalition with other Parties. If electoral reform led to the results for which Liberals hoped and which statistics foretold, that is the fifty to seventy M.P.s to which our vote entitled us, then if government was to be carried on, coalitions of some sort would often be essential. Miss Enid Lakeman was even then conducting her expert and tireless campaign for Proportional Representation. Her method was to chip in with definite proposals when a problem arose which P.R. could solve. She wrote clear, concise and well-argued letters to the papers about national elections, local elections, the dilemma of allowing for different views in a Party without disrupting it. Continued over at least a quarter of a century it was a remarkable performance.

Perhaps our most distinctive and justifiable policy was over Defence. Britain, we said, should no longer attempt to keep a presence 'East of Suez'. It is strange to look back on the days when Tories argued that the West would collapse if we withdrew from the canal zone—and when we had done so, that we should never withdraw from Cyprus. Liberals also opposed the independent nuclear deterrent. We held that Europe must be defended by conventional forces and by the American alliance with an American nuclear deterrent. When Labour went back on their anti-nuclear policy begging people not to send their Foreign Minister naked into the conference chamber I pointed out that over the Cuban–American crisis we had not got into the conference chamber, naked or clothed.

We had been the only party which offered to join the new EEC from the start. This had been Clem Davies's policy and remained mine. We were much ridiculed for this previously. But we held a steady course. We warned that Britain would suffer from her complacent obstinacy which had denied her the influence of having been a founder-member—she has indeed suffered over the CAP and Fishery policies. Clem Davies must get the credit for his advocacy of British adherence to the Coal and Steel Community, Arthur Holt for his courageous declaration that we should have proclaimed our whole-hearted support for the EEC and then started on the details of negotiation.

With these policies and considering the calibre of our candidates, staff and advisers we had a chance of breaking through to a new plateau. The crux came in the West Derbyshire by-election of June, 1962. Col. Ronald Gardner Thorpe nearly carried the day. He would have done so but for a frantic last minute scream from the Tory press. As it was he lost by 1200 votes. A Herculean feat in a constituency where Liberals had not stood since 1950. If he had won, such a victory coming after Orpington and after George Scott in the same year had doubled the Liberal vote in the industrial seat of Middlesbrough West might have changed the balance of politics.

We were showing that we could win big votes in industrial constituencies such as Colne Valley, Rochdale where Ludovic Kennedy had come within 2700 votes of victory at the 1959 General Election, and now Middlesbrough West. No longer could we be treated as a fringe party. But we leant heavily on the quality of active Liberals. Our resources were small even for those days and would now be considered tiny.

The organisation of the Party at that time was simple. I had a secretary, Miss Catherine Fisher. It now seems incredible that she coped with all my correspondence, visitors, filing, typing of articles, speeches, etc. I have never received the volume of correspondence to which other M.P.s and my successors lay claim. My mail looked big. It was padded out by all the circulars with which the public relations industry justifies its existence, 90% of which can go straight into the waste paper basket. Then there were the letters from lunatics, people with bees in their bonnets, memoranda about running the country. These did not need long answers. Whatever their shortcomings in other ways, I found ministers and their civil servants sure and prompt in dealing with constituency cases. These are not the trouble they may yet become if the civil service is overloaded. Many complaints too were not my business or the business of ministers; they were complaints against local authorities or nationalised boards and industries, or big private monopolies. Such complaints comprised well over half of constituency cases. Just as I have nothing but praise for the fairness and care of civil servants, so I have found that the great majority of ministers are conscientious about individual claims. The picture of ministers anxious only about their careers and always seeking out publicity and popularity is not true to life. Unpublicised and with no possible gain they take a great deal of care over individual cases. Orkney and Shetland had a small and undemanding electorate. Except on their way through occasionally, on their summer holidays, they seldom visited the House of Commons. So no doubt my life was comparatively easy. It remains a miracle nevertheless that Catherine Fisher handled it all. She more than deserved the MBE which Jeremy Thorpe with thoughtfulness obtained for her.

For a time Christopher Layton acted as my personal assistant. He is another able man who has been under-used, though he did important work in the Commission at Brussels as Chef de Cabinet for Industries and Technological Affairs. Perhaps I should say he was under-used by me and the Liberal Party. He is one of those who were active in the Party in the fifties and sixties who never found a Liberal seat and naturally looked to other pastures. I could have used his capacity as a political economist to greater advantage. I find it difficult to make use of researchers; difficult too, indeed impossible, to deliver other people's speeches. I don't think I have ever delivered a speech written for me—or even partially written.

This is a failing. Other people's speeches would often have been better than my own. In any case, it is a waste of talent not to make use of speech writers and a waste of effort—as well as being rather presumptuous—to insist upon writing your own. At election times some articles appeared over my name written by other hands but, otherwise, I wrote my own.

In the Houses of Parliament just off the inner lobby there was the Liberal Whip's office in two small rooms. Here sat the Whip, in turn Donald Wade, Arthur Holt and Eric Lubbock, with a small outer office for his secretary. Tommy Nudds was the official who ran the Whip's affairs. He was frequently at the House of Commons but had his own office at Liberal Headquarters. In the fifties the Liberal Party was lucky in having devoted servants whose experience went back a long way. When I was Whip I was amazed how Nudds produced the weekly programme and kept us generally informed with no apparent effort and certainly no assistance from me. I must have been the idlest Whip of any Party at any time. We had one bonus: Sir Charles Harris who ran the government business, had been an officer of the Liberal Party. I have always found the Whips of the larger parties helpful and friendly but of course they did most of their business with each other: Sir Charles ensured that the Government Whip's office was scrupulous in keeping us informed. The running of the Whip's Office was made more difficult because it became the meeting place and club of the Party. In bigger Parties this would have been impossible. But thirteen Liberals could just about squeeze into the office and into it senior Liberals were inclined to infiltrate their secretaries.

Outside the House of Commons the Whip had a shadowy organisation known as the Liberal Central Association. It had been established originally to deal with such delicate matters as honours and patronage generally. Into its coffers some money chiefly from industrial backers found its way. It dealt with candidates but in my time had little in the way of funds or staff.

The Liberal Party in the country was run by the Liberal Party Organisation. This was controlled by an elected council and executive. For some of my time as Leader it was under the brilliant direction of Pratap Chitnis. At its core were three women, Miss Deborah Allaway, a king-ping of the organisation: Miss Phyllis Preston, who was the best ambassador to the Press a party ever had, superb not only in her grip on what journalists demanded as news but as a first-rate organiser and, finally, Mrs. Evelyn Hill who still continues to run Liberal Publications so expertly on a shoe-string. After the retirement of W. R. Davies, a Secretary in the old style, methodical, loyal, self-effacing, whom everyone trusted and who had grown wise in the service of the Party, it was thought necessary to have someone more like a general manager. Political parties need good management but they cannot be run as businesses. Most of the work in the Liberal Party was done by volunteers. We could offer neither good pay nor rewards or punishments. Associations were kept going by dedicated women who worked as volunteers. They could at any time down tools. I am astonished at how long and hard many of them worked. M.P.s' wives, including my own, were very much in the forefront of the voluntary slave battalions. W. R. Davies and Tommy Nudds understood this perfectly. Senior officials, not only in London, but such as Albert Ingham in Yorkshire and Arthur Worsley in Manchester were masters in cajoling, jockeying and smoothing ruffled feathers. To get the party to work you needed the skills suitable for the game of croquet in *Alice in Wonderland*, for the balls might uncurl and depart and the sticks were very much of flesh and blood. Those trained in different schools of management found it hard to adjust to this tempo. Philip Fothergill, though not an official, was adept in keeping the party running. So was Pratap Chitnis who, like Philip, added political flair to his competence. Some idea of the slenderness of our means can be gauged from the figures. Chitnis at most was paid £3000 a year, Albert Ingham who ran Yorkshire £2400 and the staff at LPO numbered thirty in all. Within the LPO was Harry Cowie's small research unit and Phyllis Preston's miraculous Publicity Office from which flowed not only hand-outs but a stream of general helpfulness both to me and the press. Phyllis was held in special regard by newspapermen and journalists although she had so little material to offer.

In addition to the council and executive there was the Liberal Party Committee. The members of this committee were chosen by the Leader. This undemocratic procedure was, I believe, essential. With only six M.P.s and no new creations of Liberal Peerages (we were allowed one hereditary peerage all the time I was in Parliament) many leading Liberals were outside Parliament. Nor were they all members of the Council. The Liberal Party Committee met about once a fortnight or three weeks for a couple of hours or so. It was concerned with policy, not the day-to-day voting in Parliament, nor usually long-term policy, but the attitudes of the Party to major political issues. In addition to all M.P.s, leading Peers and such prominent Liberals as Violet Bonham Carter and Sir Andrew MacFadyean it contained our expert advisers. I also spent some time in going to see academics and industrialists in their lairs to pick their brains. In theory there could have been some clash between the Committee and the Party council but I do not remember that there was. The executive was concerned largely with organisation and the council, so to speak, married the policy recommendations of the Party Committee to the practical work of the executive, though this arrangement was neither explicit or recorded. As we had no Trade Union levy and no big sub-vention from industry we had to raise all our money by voluntary work. That we have done so for so long is a remarkable achievement by the Party workers.

By the 1960s our strategy depended upon the Labour Party or some part of it being convinced that, as a socialist party committed to public ownership of all the means of production, distribution and exchange, it had a poor future. The state of public opinion pointed to a realignment. There was a hope that the full-blooded socialists would split off to the Left leaving a radical party on the Left of the centre of politics but free of socialist dogma. In this the Liberals could play a part. I constantly re-minded those who saw no future for us in a two-Party system, that in fact Britain had never had only two Parties. It had had a two bloc system. On the Left the Liberal and Labour Parties and the Irish Nationalists had co-operated for many purposes. The division between Tory and Labour no longer corresponded to the differing views and interests in our society. Few people were committed to the policies of any one Party right across the board. Party loyalties were weakening. The working class was changing its nature and losing its solidarity. The Labour Party would even then have been forced to close if it had lost the Union levy and been thrown back on what funds it could raise.

The 1964 General Election was crucial to this strategy. Had the Labour Party lost it I believe that it might have split. Labour won by a hair's breadth. By doing so it was enabled to appear the Party through which ambitions could be satisfied. It achieved office with all the patronage and hope that went with it. It had lost the previous three General Elections, the loss of a fourth would have brought damaging frustration. I do not claim that the split would certainly have occurred but I do claim that there would have been strong forces working for a realignment.

If the Tories had played their cards better in the last week of the election they would have won the few vital extra seats. In spite of the scoffing of some of the publicists, Sir Alec Douglas-Home impressed many floating voters. He was a thoroughly professional politician for he had been at it all his life except when laid low by a cruel illness from which he recovered with determination. He liked and was liked by the ordinary Tory. He seems to have run the Party well. In addition he was trusted. He may have appeared too aristocratic for upper middle-class intellectuals. But it was not for nothing that he had originally been elected for a mining seat. While other politicians often seemed to pay too much attention to their 'image', to be too worried about what impression they were making, Sir Alec made no effort to be other than he was. The election started under bad auspices for the Tories. Some ministers had refused to serve under Alec. There was something of a hang-over from the leadership struggle. The abolition of price maintenance, one of the most courageous and positive steps the Tories had taken, may have lost them some support. Sir Alec himself had been out of the Commons and was said to be out of touch with the modern world and particularly its economics. But as the election went on it was obviously going to be a close thing. During the last Monday and Tuesday I was touring in Aberdeenshire. I heard that the Tories had chosen to finish by putting on some of their more cantankerous spokesmen at the final press conferences. When I heard that one of them had said that anyone who voted Labour must be bonkers, I guessed they would lose. Such remarks, trumpeted by the press, were out of tune with Sir Alec's campaign. They were not likely to appeal to the uncommitted. The Tories should have made a more sober appeal to the undecided in the last few days.

The Labour Party was returned with a very small majority but a majority nevertheless over the other Parties combined. Liberals did not hold the balance of power. We were baffled. I do not see that much could have been done between 1964 and 1966. Certainly we had to make a showing in the political fray. We had to pretend that we could influence events. But our influence on immediate events was very limited, if indeed it existed at all. We made a mistake in not stumping the country preaching devolution. We could have exploited to better advantage the work of Professor Keith-Lucas and others on local government. We should have stamped our image upon the demand for less and better government nearer home. By so doing we might have pre-empted the growth of the S.N.P. and Plaid Cymru. Yet it was during this period that the Liberal Party acquired its maximum number of M.P.s since the war.

THE RESULT OF THE 1964 General Election was a blow to me. It put paid for the time being to any realignment on the Left. (The phrase was Mark Bonham Carter's, adopted by me. I am reminded of Belloc's footnote referring to a line in one of his poems—'A phrase I stole with subtle daring from Wing Commander Maurice Baring'. Maurice Baring thought that he was my wife's godfather; under this happy delusion the only time I met him he gave her £50.) Their victory gave a new lease of life or at least prospect of office to panting Labour Members desperate lest they should never taste the spoils of government. This victory was too the beginning of the end for the social democrats or Gaitskellites upon whom rested the main hope of Liberals for a realignment. I did not realise then what a blow Gaitskell's death had dealt to the Social Democrats. Looking back I wonder whether there was ever much in the high-sounding vessel of British social democracy. In after years it proved hollow. They personally hardly lived up to their battle cry that socialism in their eyes was about equality.

A further blow was the size of the Labour majority, so small that it meant another loathsome General Election within a year or two. But small as the majority was, it was, nevertheless, an over-all majority. The Liberal Party had very little, if any, bargaining strength. A government in the position Labour held in 1964 is wise to make as much splash as it can before going to the country again as soon as possible. This is what Labour did in 1964–66 and 1974. They made no effort to gain more support in the House of Commons by compromise with other parties. In each case they proved electorally right.

However, there was one issue on which Liberals might play an important part. That was the nationalisation of steel. Woodrow Wyatt and Desmond

Donnelly, both Labour M.P.s, were opposed to it. If they voted with the Opposition the Government could not carry the measure. Woodrow had a scheme which would have allowed some government control of the industry without public ownership. I had several conversations with him and Desmond. In the end we achieved the postponement but not the abandonment of steel nationalisation. Woodrow, who had been a Labour Minister, and Desmond showed considerable courage. Looking back, I now feel on this as on other issues I did not press the Liberal luck hard enough. Just possibly we could have widened the issue until it became a wedge which might have led to co-operation on other matters. Some Labour members were growing restive with the trend of their party.

In 1965 David Steel won Roxburgh, Selkirk and Peebles. It was a triumph and a well-deserved one. For all our centralisation, for all the grip of the major parties on certain classes there are curious persistent variations on the political map of Britain. Why for so long should Norwich return Labour Members and Preston, Tories? Why is Greenock a Liberal stronghold in local politics while in other Clyde towns you could hardly find a Liberal with a magnifying glass? The Borders are a distinct region, peppered with Dukes and Fox Hunts but with a strong radical tradition. In the woollen towns the workers are Liberal rather than Socialist. So must be many of the farmers and farm servants. Since the fifties Roxburgh and Selkirk had returned a Tory. But the tinder was there. David ignited it. He was a charismatic candidate, young, good-looking, confident, articulate. What more could you want? Only organisation—that too was provided. Liberals flock to the standard when they smell victory. The Borderers are a gregarious lot. Apart from a few places in the North of England, it is the only constituency in which Liberal Clubs flourish. No nonsense about temperance. Rugby football and common ridings go with beer—and indeed with whisky. Clubs are an excellent foundation for the vote. Nor at that time—I do not know what has happened since—had the Borderers lost their appetite for public meetings. On the eve of poll the platforms and the bodies of the halls were packed.

The Liberal Party since the war has to a large extent depended for its successes on local personalities. This can be seen in the Borders and in Liverpool and in the influence of Provost William Riddell in Greenock. As a believer that communities must fashion their own growth and that political power should be decentralised and flow upwards from the public I find this encouraging.

The 1964 Parliament was notable for the Declaration of Intent and the attempt to set up a new ministry to take over some of the Treasury's functions. Neither was successful: but one possible way to cope with inflation may be to establish some agreement on what over-all production may be achieved within, say, the two or three years to follow and then to allow wage and salary bargaining within that total: though I do not myself at present see how this could settle wages or salaries to the general satisfaction, yet we shall soon have to consider all possible devices, among them those canvassed in 1964–65.

I went into the 1966 Election without high hopes. It seemed certain that Labour would win but would not make much of their victory. The moral content had dripped out of Socialism. My criticism of the Labour Party was not so much that they were Socialists, though I did not believe that Socialist planning could take over from the market, but that they were not true Socialists. Socialism should practise the golden rule. Socialists should not be ambitious for power and material perks. But state Socialists were as greedy, as selfish and as hungry for power as any capitalist. The organisations they dominated became more and more materialist and less mindful of their neighbours.

The public does not yet realise that modern Socialism in Britain, of which corporatism is a child, will make it impossible to build a welfare society. For a welfare society can only exist when organisations, whether big corporations, Trades Unions or groups of workers, just as much as individuals, have regard to the needs of others, particularly the poor. By blackmail and disruption these organisations are cutting away the root of the very society in which they claim to believe. It is contemptible to use corporate coercion to seize more for yourself, while demanding more social services and higher pensions. This was to become more apparent in the next fifteen years. Socialism was repeating the mistakes which had brought capitalism into disrepute.

It was during the 1966 General Election that my eldest son, Andrew, died. His death came as an unforgettable personal tragedy to Laura and myself, a sad blow to our family which fell just when he seemed to be settling down in Edinburgh.

During the Autumn of 1966 I went to Eastern Europe and then to Russia to write some articles for the *Guardian*. The first glimpse of memory reveals the appalling British Embassy in Warsaw, a bleak, ugly and impractical building. It had recently been completed and only eleven bugging devices had been removed. There were certainly more, a tiny monument to the barbarism of Communist methods. The only safe place was the middle of the garden. Rain poured down. The Ambassador and I stood under umbrellas in the middle of the Embassy lawn while he explained, with lucidity, the state of affairs in Poland.

The middle of Warsaw, rebuilt on the old model, was a great improvement on the centre of most Western cities. The architects had not been too proud to rebuild in the old styles. As in all Eastern European capitals, however, one building stood out by its hideosity—the Headquarters of the Community Party—a gift from the Russians.

We went to see the minister in charge of planning. He was exhausted, as well he might be. Talking to him I learnt firsthand the human impossibility of the Communist system. No one can plan a country. To do so you would have to be seer, boy scout, computer and power station. Nor could the job be done by a million planners—or a million machines, or a mixture of both. The multiplication of bureaucrats, figures, graphs, only make confusion worse. The modern Tower of Babel is not a welter of languages but an anarchy of statistics and regulations.

In Hungary I went to see the Prime Minister in the Parliament building. This is a neo-Gothic pile on the Danube. The Prime Minister struck me as both over-worked and frightened. The building was deserted and unused. No sign of wear on the carpet: not a smudge on the walls, not a sound behind any door. It could not have been a more telling witness to the non-existence of Hungarian democracy. I had been to Budapest before the war when even under the rule of Horthy it had been full of life. Communism is like the plague, it leaves silence behind it. The people strolling about on the banks of the Danube and at a Dalmation resort where we went one Sunday seemed unnaturally quiet. Bucharest by comparison had some sparkle. And so did Mr. Ceaucescu—a tough dictator but possible to talk with. I asked him how the Rumanians could get rid of him. He replied that it would be difficult, as it has proved. Again, offensive and ludicrous spying everywhere. To have a private talk in the Chancellery, the Ambassador and I were locked into a gigantic safe.

Our man in Bucharest, Mr. Glass, now Sir Leslie Glass, had come originally from the Indian Civil Service—an unusual provenance for an Ambassador. Like his colleagues in Warsaw and Budapest he was well-informed about the local dictatorship. He had also undergone some curious experiences. Perhaps he has written down the following tale himself and, if he has, probably with greater accuracy but, in case he has not, it is worth preserving if only to show the hazards of diplomatic life. Soon after arriving in Rumania to take up his first ambassadorial post he received a summons to the President's diplomatic shoot. Though not given much to shooting, for the honour of Britain he dare not refuse. So he presented himself according to instructions at the railway station and boarded a sumptuous train in which each sleeper was stacked with drink and other comforts. Off they rolled to the Carpathians. Jeeps and other contrivances took them into the forest where every gun was provided with a metal plaque bearing his number. Soon the air was thick with pheasants, most of which escaped. A couple or so of beaters were, however, bagged and a member of the *diplomatique* found to be shooting with a rifle had to be disarmed. The star performer was the President himself who did bourgeois execution with a pair of Purdeys. Lunch was a delicious barbecue and the night was spent in a splendid château. The shooting continued the next day and in the evening a banquet was provided. It was broken to our Ambassador that with the port, so to speak, a few old Rumanian customs were kept up. The first of these was that, as a newcomer, he would be expected to drink a toast. What was not explained was that on the terrace outside the windows of the banqueting hall a phalanx of keepers had been drawn up. As Mr. Glass raised the glass to his lips, the keepers fired a volley just behind him causing him to leap into the air and souse himself in liquor. This went down well with the company: the honour of Britain stood high. The next old Rumanian custom had indeed a rather British tang about it, though not the kind of tradition much kept up outside the public schools—certainly not in the Indian Civil Service. He was told that on these occasions there was a ceremonial beating of those who were at the shoot for the first time. He bent over and received one or two taps on the bottom from the President. He was then presented with the cane—or rather stick—which he showed me, a rather crude affair. However, it could apparently be effective, for when the Foreign Minister bent over the President fairly laid into him to the general delight of the audience who rolled about with laughter.

After this unnerving evening our Ambassador was relieved to get back to his sleeper. Kicking off his shoes and no doubt loosening his tie he lay down on the bed with a stiff whisky. But the night's events were not over. The door opened, round it appeared the visage of the Bulgarian Ambassador who uttered the single word 'Bridge'—perhaps the only English he knew—so the night passed, not in sleep but in playing bridge with three Iron Curtain diplomats in a variety of Rumanian. Who can say that the Diplomatic Service is overpaid?

Outside the Ambassador's house was a sentry. He proved a valuable source of information—no doubt to the secret police but certainly to the Ambassador's family. He kept the children informed of the doings of their parents and the parents of the coming and going of their children. Though the Poles struck me as the most sympathetic of the three nations I visited, the Rumanians had a veneer of gaiety—we visited an enjoyable night club, for instance. But it was a veneer with an unpleasant undercoating—even apart from the general impression of the regime. A child of British parents had been very well looked after during some illness by a local woman doctor. They had therefore sent her a small present. From that moment she was persecuted by the secret police. I received a letter from an old member of the Social Democratic party. He asked if I would help him to leave the country. He had a most honourable record of resistance to the Nazis. He had been a distinguished Left politician. I enquired what I should do. I was advised by our Embassy officials to do nothing. My correspondent had apparently written before to a British delegation visiting Rumania. They had agreed to see him. After he had seen them he had been picked up by the police who kicked his legs until they had broken his ankles. They then left him. Of course this incident is nothing compared to the massacres in Communist countries, their invasions of their neighbours, the torture of dissidents. But it illustrates the nature of Communism. To describe it as bestial is to malign animals. No animals would behave in this way. How repulsive is the admiration for Communist countries shown by cosy intellectuals of the West who thrive in free societies.

From Rumania I went to Russia itself. I was surprised and moved by Russia—moved to tears rather than admiration. The surprise came from a feeling of being moved back two steps in time. My guide Karolina Yaganova, reminded me of the liberal girls of my youth. After Norman Crossland, a journalist on the *Guardian* who had accompanied me, had returned to Germany, the only person to whom I could talk was Karolina. She was excellent company. Although her manners were irreproachable she was somewhat crochety and her irritation lent an agreeable tartness to her society. She was also often tired. I was struck again how exhausting socialism is. To buy a packet of sweets you had to trail backwards and forwards choosing your sweets, getting a coupon, exchanging the coupon, paying. For the native the simplest business of living is drab and laborious. Again, like many girls of my youth, she was usually late and a compulsive telephoner. I was told that this was because she was always reporting to the secret police. I don't believe it. I know telephone addicts when I meet one, my mother-in-law, and several of my Liberal colleagues in the House of Commons all showed the same symptoms. I would have added my wife to this notable list but, if I do, she insists on adding a footnote which will be controversial and expansive. Russians have the most attractive English accents which made it a pleasure to get Karolina to talk. She was a very bad Marxist and easily got into difficulties, e.g. over Stalin whose erasure from history she defended on the ground that he had 'wrong thoughts'. If he had confined himself to thoughts many millions of lives would have been saved. I once asked her, rather stupidly, if she had ever protested against the crimes of Stalinism. 'No,' she replied, 'I was rather young and anyway would certainly have been shot.'

I was lodged in the National Hotel, reminiscent of a railway station hotel before British Rail imposed the same decoration on all of them and swamped the individuality of railway stations under plastic Travel Centres. I was given a rococo suite. In the sitting room, so I am told,

MacLean and Burgess were first produced to the press after their defection. It was encrusted with caryatids like a wedding cake and dominated by a large chandelier. My bed was decorated by sphinxes and boars' heads (small). British journalists told me that every swag and cornice was bugged. I found this, if true, had possibilities. After seeing one peculiarly repellent minister I recounted to Crossland who was still with me how pro-British I had found him and how critical he had been of his colleagues in the Kremlin.

My first visit was to the official receiver of foreign guests with whom I had an interesting conversation about the Russian form of 'democracy'. When I came out I asked Karolina if we were late. 'Yes,' she said, 'very late.' 'Why didn't you tell me?' I asked. 'How do I stop you talking?' she replied. When we were in the courtyard she asked 'Do you mind to run?' I said I did not mind to run but would we not be shot? 'You will not be shot—you may be photographed.'

The further step back in time was to the days of the Prince Consort. The view from the hotel across the Red Square particularly the Cathedral of St Basil, reminded me of South Kensington. The troops of children in pinafores, thick stockings and boots, were strangely Victorian. So was the air of culture. In a gallery of Victorian pictures I admired a portrait of a rosy-cheeked, middle-aged man with an open-necked shirt and fluffy unbrushed hair—it reminded me of Clive Bell. I could see that Karolina disapproved of it. 'Not serious' was her comment. Although I resolutely refused to inspect coal mines, schools and the other sights which were thought suitable for politicians, I had to visit one factory. It had a crèche in which rows of small children were taking their afternoon nap under mounds of blankets but with all the windows open. The nanny in charge not only looked like an old-fashioned British nanny but obviously shared their belief in fresh air.

One evening I set off on my own to see the Indian Ambassador whom I had known in London. He had only just arrived. We sat in the middle of his drawing room discussing Russia in whispers. He and the Canadian Ambassador I found the most fruitful sources of information—as I had found the Australian Ambassador in Washington. The British Embassy was unforthcoming. By the time we had finished talking it was nearly seven o'clock, pitch dark and foggy. The Indian Ambassador offered to send me to my next appointment in his car. However, he then discovered that his chauffeur and indeed the whole Embassy staff had gone. As neither of us could speak a word of Russian, getting a taxi was difficult, to explain to the driver where I wanted to go, impossible. It looked as though I should have to spend the night in the Embassy when out of the murk a tiny Indian boy appeared. The Ambassador threw himself upon

With Andrew.

The Old Manse at harvest time.

Sir Maurice Bonham Carter, my father-in-law, with Grizelda.

Lady Violet Bonham Carter.

Self, Laura and Magnus at the Old Manse.

him with relief. As the child was at a Russian school he was able to give the huge taxi driver a flow of orders and directions at which he nodded like a well-trained bear and I bumped off into the night.

Leningrad was the only place I visited outside Moscow. Karolina picked me up on the way to the station, accompanied by an Intourist youth with whom she was already exasperated. On the way to the station they had a row, partly I think because he would talk Russian which she considered rude in front of me. At the station, having got rid of him, she turned to me and remarked, 'Just an angry young man'. How she got hold of the phrase I do not know. We then had one of our little set-tos. I picked up her suitcase, after a short struggle she wrested it back from me. I presumed this was about women's libbery or because it held sinister documents. In fact, it was out of good-will to the porters who, being badly paid, rely on the small sum they get for every piece of baggage they carry. The attribution of motives as I found in UNRRA is very risky.

The Moscow–Leningrad train is notorious for its comfort. In those days at least it owed nothing to the jet age. On the contrary, it too was Victorian in its cleanliness, its antimacassars and its opulent decoration. In Leningrad the rain fell steadily. Two incidents stick in my mind. The main galleries of the Hermitage were packed with conducted tours of Russians endlessly reflected in the glass of the great classical pictures, quiet, solemn, heavy. But at the top of the building was a collection of French Impressionists where the visitors were few.

I was struck by two men who darted among the pictures with loud expressions of delight. On approaching them I found that they were French. In the interval at the ballet the audience walked round and round a strip of carpet in the foyer. Then two girls broke ranks and stepped off the carpet. Nothing happened to them. Others followed. Soon the usual theatre melée was in full swing.

I am glad to have been to Russia. I do not want to go back. Apart from its unforgettable crimes, the murders, torture and suppression which her rulers have imposed at home and exported abroad, there are the nasty features of everyday life. The Ritz may be open to all only if they are rich enough—in Russia it is the powerful and the foreigners who get special treatment. I went to the ballet whenever I wanted, eight times in all. In the National Hotel there was a dining room with every luxury set aside for those who can pay in foreign currency. Russia is a tragedy—a tragedy which strikes the heart, but it is also corrupt and grubby with depravity unequalled by the worst of capitalism. The officials seemed wrapt in anxiety and the people stunned as though they had suffered a calamity— which they have. One lights up at the Frenchmen and the French pictures in the Hermitage. I longed for a café and gaiety but when you came back

225

to the West you are struck by the triviality of the press, the aimless extravagance, most of all, the extravagance of the public authorities. It was only later that I came to rebel against the constant clamour for 'more' by every organisation but I remember even in 1968 being struck by the advertising forever stimulating appetites.

Going abroad in the years after the war always reminded me of the gulf which the thirties and early forties had fixed between my generation in Britain and our counterpart on the continent. Our European contemporaries seem to have sloughed off the poison and violence of those years; on their minds it seemed to have left no bruise, indeed some of those who suffered worse seemed the most serene. But it was a divide nevertheless.

On and off for some twenty years I attended the annual 'Konigswinter' conferences. These conferences were meetings of German and British politicians, businessmen, academics and journalists, usually held at Konigswinter on the Rhine but occasionally in Britain. Frau Milchsack was the originator, inspirer and with her husband, the paymaster of these conferences. They were and are a memorial to a memorable woman. Herr Milchsack who owned some barges on the Rhine had, with courage, dissented from the ovation given to Hitler by the Ruhr industrialists. After the war his wife had been Mayor of a suburb of Düsseldorf. The Milchsacks were seminal figures in that collaboration between some British and some Germans which strengthened German democracy and education after the war—on the British side Robert Birley played a leading part. Annual get-togethers such as Konigswinter seldom retain their vitality. That Konigswinter has done so is due to the meticulous care Lilo Milchsack has bestowed on it.

As will be readily understood, talk over beer and Rhine wine in the cafés of Konigswinter were sometimes as enlightening as the official sessions. British politicians of one party could eavesdrop on members of another party talking about each other. And over café tables all sorts of subjects other than politics were discussed. New surroundings loosened reticence. It is indeed true, as Arthur Bryant pointed out to me years later, that our attitude to death has undergone a deep change over the last two or three hundred years. Death personified in Elizabethan or Baroque poetry ('Death be not proud') as sombre or grotesque is now reduced to biological disintegration. The awe and mystery surrounding death have receded, leaving cold fear. Having lost much of our faith in religion and replaced it with no compensating faith in humanity we do not know what to make of suicide. I remember a discussion on suicide led by Peter Fleming, for instance.

In Britain we have not been confronted with the choices offered to those under the heel of Hitler or other dictators. Many men and women in

Germany and the occupied countries had to choose probable death, not in battle but by a fiendish parody of law, or suicide, or they had to trim their behaviour to patterns which revolted them. It was not only the traumatic experience of war and concentration camps which the continent endured but the knife of suspicion driven between friends, even between members of the same family.

I have mentioned earlier the anguish of Adam von Trott. Two other Germans who, like Adam, had strong British ties were often at the conference. One was Heinz (now Sir Heinz) Koeppler who, like Adam, had been at Oxford. He too was troubled by the rise of Hitler but he had perhaps a more decisive mind: Adam's mind for all its capacity often seemed to me like a tangled skein of fine wool of which it was difficult to find the end. Heinz had remained in Britain where he founded Wilton Park, which can best be described as a training centre for the indoctrination of foreigners. This, when I knew it, was ensconced in a house in Sussex (hence the name). Here Heinz lectured, cajoled and on occasions slightly bullied (in the nicest way) his compatriots into understanding the ways of British democracy. I can think of no Briton who would have been capable of doing such a job in Germany had the histories of our two countries been reversed.

The third German was Axel von den Busche. He had fought gallantly in the German Army but being nauseated by Hitler had volunteered to assassinate him, a deed which none of his senior officers among his fellow conspirators would attempt. The method chosen was that Axel, who had been selected to show off a new Army overcoat to Hitler, having concealed grenades in the pockets, was to rush forward, embrace his victim and with him die in the explosion. I can imagine few more soul-searing torments than waiting to end one's life blown to eternity with the remains of Hitler. In the end the store containing the overcoats was bombed by the British and the climax was never achieved. I would have thought, however, that in addition to the physical wounds which Axel suffered in the war, the agony of waiting would have left an indelible scar. But it certainly never corroded his behaviour to his friends.

Axel had fought in the Russian campaign. One day we were discussing travel in the Soviet Union when someone asked Axel if he had ever been to Moscow. 'Nearly,' he replied. 'Oh, and how did you get there?' 'I walked.'

Whatever the horrors many people of many nations suffered in the war, to live in a miasma of conspiracy, never knowing whom to trust or when the secret police would carry one off is something few British have experienced, one being Christabel Bielenberg whose book is most illuminating about life in a police state. From another book in a different vein, Wolfgang

Leonhardt's 'Child of the Revolution' we can take hope for Communist countries for it shows how endemic is the longing for freedom and how persistent the urge to win it.

By 1967 I had now been Leader of the Liberal Party for ten years. The Tory and Labour parties go in and out of office. Few members of these parties keep the same job for more than seven years at a stretch. No doubt to be a prominent member of these parties is more wearing, but change breaks the monotony. For the Liberal Leader there is no such relief. I found myself staring at the same grey boards in the same town halls. At General Elections when politicians must repeat the same speeches over and over again, by the end of the campaign I would listen to myself in a detached way, silently commenting that we were about to have this passage or that. I now caught myself indulging in the same trick even between elections. I found myself constantly 'striving' to obtain something or other. It was time to be gone. Also, I had never been a free backbencher. I had been made Whip during my first week in Parliament and gone straight from Whip to being Leader. I was getting tired of being constantly on call, attending House of Commons Questions at least twice a week, constantly making speeches on the Address and so forth. These last type of speeches are a particular difficulty for Liberals. Often called third when the main spokesmen on the main issues have had their hour and a half or so he must come as an anti-climax when the House is emptying. The only speech which it would be either interesting to make or tolerable to hear would be to take some points from the opening speeches and debate them. I might have been wiser to do this more often—or not to speak at all. But to buck up his followers and for the sake of a little publicity in those newspapers which report Parliament at all fully, the Liberal Leader is expected to outline his party's policies on the matter in hand. It is usually a soul-destroying business for him and everyone else, though my successors were much better at it than I was. I was not aware of any particular pressure that I should go but by Christmas 1966 I made up my mind to retire. The Parliamentary Party elected Jeremy Thorpe to succeed me, with my whole-hearted encouragement. Jeremy had been of great assistance to me ever since the days of the Carmarthen by-election and before. He is a good speaker on any occasion, clear, with an attractive delivery, an amusing turn of phrase, well briefed and capable of adjusting his style from the House of Commons or village meetings of twenty to the huge audiences which pack the Pannier Market at Barnstaple to hear him. I have never heard him make a bad speech. As Leader he was to push the Liberal vote to over six millions, a figure not approached since the twenties.

At the 1970 General Election the Liberal Party fared poorly as it often does when the Tories are on the upsurge. I held Orkney and Shetland but with a reduced majority. In this General Election Laura herself stood for West Aberdeenshire. She succeeded a popular and able Liberal, James Davidson, who lived and farmed in Aberdeenshire. Yet he had only won the seat from the Tories in 1964. So she would in any event have had a stiff fight. But she would have won had she not had the bad luck to be opposed to Col. Colin Mitchell. Col. Mitchell had been publicised for his handling of the Argyll & Sutherland Highlanders in Aden. He received constant adulation from the press during the Election. After he had won the seat he found he had no aptitude for politics and did not stand again. The incident shows the power of publicity in such constituencies where local as well as national papers are read from cover to cover. It always shows how unthinking are the ways of the press. That Col. Mitchell, though an able soldier and a nice man, was not a politician caused them no concern. To the press a name is a name, however it is made, whatever the views the holder of it professes.

We missed Laura badly in Orkney and Shetland though my other supporters did valiant work and Grizelda came up for the last few days— a great help. I was uneasy that few new active Liberals were recruited. Orkney and Shetland, like the rest of Britain, was living on inherited capital, intellectual and moral as well as physical. But we still had a store of liberal good-will. The devotion of the older Liberals was as staunch as ever, and as always the Liberal women toiled at Election chores (they worked so hard as to qualify for the description given to a stone-mason by an Orkney acquaintance of whom I had enquired if he could recommend him for hard work—'Work! he works like a fool'). Among the women there were some new recruits such as Ruth Williamson the grand-daughter of Helen Taylor who from time to time ran our Orkney home.

I have heard it suggested that Orkney and Shetland is a freak constituency segregated from the main highways of British political thought. This is not so. My supporters were Liberals in the classic mould. They came from many walks of life but prominent among them were teachers, farmers and men who ran their own businesses. Orkney schoolmasters such as Mr. Kent, Mr. Kirkness, David Partner and David Eunson, cousins of Edwin Eunson, Jim Troup and their counterparts in Shetland such as Mr. Pearson of Walls, were steeped in Liberalism. They understood the presuppositions of a free, democratic society, how it must be nourished on tolerance, mutual respect and regard for the common welfare, presuppositions Britain now neglects. The very designations of the farmers who carried Liberalism to victory, Scotts of Redland, Frasers of Cottiscarth, Woods of Berriedale, Harveys of Wattle, Marwicks of Whitemire, Chalmers of the 'Bu (and scores more) tell of their roots in the soil of their fathers. They were independent men and women who owned their land, discharged their public duties, drew their income from no remote boss, nor their opinions from passing fashions.

Much as I disliked the 1970 General Election, as I do all Elections, it was a pleasure to move around among the sanguine faces of my constituents so different from the pale, puzzled and defensive visages met on the London Underground.

As it was a summer election the days were long and the meetings late. The heckling was less brisk than it had been twenty years before, but after a suitable pause for thought I would be questioned—'speired' in Orkney parlance—about matters of moment. And there were still memorable evenings, sailing in Davie Johnson's motor boat from Fetlar with the new moon—like a sliver of finger-nail, as Johnny described it—in the indigo sky of a Shetland summer night, or being driven by Isaac Moar, post-master and 'Provost' of Hoy, an island of which he knew every corner just as he knew every twist of the history of every family. No official can take the place of the Moars of this world—a world that is I fear, passing.

Orkney and Shetland life too was always being enhanced by newcomers, such as Vivian Owers who married into the well-known family of Sandison in Unst and brought new talent to their family business of merchants. Sheriff Keith, our artist judge, was succeeded by Alistair MacDonald, an Advocate who had he remained in Edinburgh or gone to London would have had a notable career in law or politics. In Orkney we even had a rare migrant from America, Miss Bacon, who fitted admirably into local life. That such men and women should come North to occupations which in general esteem were unglamorous was a welcome sign, a budding of the reaction against material values. Even in the South similar fresh shoots of non-conformity could be detected pushing up almost miraculously through the concrete of big industry, big housing estates, big organisations, mass opinions. But could they win? It was easy enough looking round Orkney and Shetland to see the blessings that small industries and independent people enjoyed. But what was to be done with the conveyor belts of Dagenham or Coventry, the steel towns, the housing estates of Glasgow or Liverpool? Could Liberalism, with a big or small 'l' cope with these? Could it expect to flourish in such inhospitable soil?

At this General Election Johnny also stood. But he was not so lucky as I. The Liberal Party had allowed his constituency, North Angus and Mearns, to run down. He had neither the time nor organisation to build it up. In Alick Buchanan-Smith too he struck an entrenched sitting Member from another Scottish family, the Smiths, Buchanan-Smith or Adam

Smith, which like the Playfairs and the Keiths was always throwing up men and women of distinction.

Meanwhile in Scotland the S.N.P. was waxing. I believed that Liberals should appeal direct to the Scottish people to band together behind a semi-federal policy of home rule within the United Kingdom. Later in 1976 I set out my views as to the sort of constitutional change I recommended in 'A Roar for the Lion'. The Scots have only won a single major battle against the English—Bannockburn. They have been frustrated again and again by dissensions or desertion of commanding positions. I was frightened it would happen again—not that I believed the English at all were hostile to Home Rule. But my views were not accepted. When the delightful Donald Stewart took the leadership of the S.N.P. we might have done a deal. Though by then it was getting late.

After the General Election I found myself in that dubious reach of the political river where ex-Leaders either fade into a backwater or splash around to the dismay of their parties. I started two small experiments. About the Shetland experiment and its genesis I shall have something to say later. Its twin was in Greenock. Here, with money from the Rowntree Social Service Trust and the energy and public spirit of Ronald Young, a Greenock Councillor, we set up a small committee with a community worker to help the tenants of a housing estate to make a better job of running their own affairs. Patently, the Welfare Services had failed. The drab, ill-kept tenements bore witness to that. In spite of all the money spent by remote paternalists, nearly all the tenants wanted to leave. Their homes were not old; if they had been looked after they would, in some parts of London, have fetched high prices. They were one of the many monuments to the ghastly outcome of post-war official thinking, the thought that all services must be handed down in uniform helpings on standard plates by officials who know best. The Greenock scheme goes on. We were never under any delusion that it would transform the town. But it has contrived to give some people new interests and it has made some people pause and take another glance at the conventional teachings on the social services.

The Labour Governments of 1964 and 1966 were in many ways appendages of their Tory predecessors. Trouble was side-stepped. Ministers deluded themselves by making speeches (it was partly out of exasperation with endless speech making that I had launched the Greenock and Northmavine in Shetland experiments). Speeches themselves become more vapid and soporific as they are bound to do when divorced from any action, they are incantations to a never-never world over the rainbow. Every pamphlet and manifesto bore a title like an old-fashioned boy's serial 'Forward by Right' (or Left), 'Face the Future'. The Prime Minister

231

throve on Walter Mittyish dreams. He was rapturous over meetings with President Johnson who might, one would have thought by reading the accounts, have picked him up by the ears as he did his favourite dog.

Mr. Heath, as is apparent from Robert Rhodes James' book *British Politicians, Ambitions and Realities 1964–76* was determined to strike a different line. But this ended up in a large increase in government expenditure and borrowing.

Leading politicians of the 1964–74 decade were able enough. But no one was trying to re-cast the structure of British politics, industry and life: palliatives were prescribed, bandages wound round untreated sores. Meanwhile, we were moving from a liberal society to a society of competing interests and avaricious feudatories. The new Tory Government of 1970 soon began making the mistakes from which we are still suffering. They completed a reform of local government which not only led to gargantuan staffs in the new offices but set the course for the general increases in bureaucracy and local expenditure which followed. They indulged in heavy government borrowing to finance inflationary public spending. The first strokes of the increasingly depressing picture of the seventies were painted by this Government. Once again with the Tories coming under fire from non-Socialists for doing a botched job, the Liberals did well at by-elections. Among the victors was Clement Freud of the pyscho-analyst's family, a clever man as you might suspect but also a well-organised one and a staunch colleague. A horse no doubt only suitable for certain courses but on those a strong performer of whom the party hardly made adequate use.

The Heath Government came to grief on the rock of the coal miners pay (never take on the miners or the Brigade of Guards someone once said) and for the first time since the war a Government once elected was not given a second lease of life.

The first 1974 General Election was Jeremy's triumph. Once again, however, the balance just failed to tip over. We did not win quite enough votes to pass the crucial point at which we should have come back to Parliament with some fifty seats. Nor did we even gain enough seats to hold by ourselves the balance of power. Even had we accepted Heath's offer to join the government the Tories and ourselves would still have been in a minority so unless the S.N.P. had decided to support a coalition it would have been strangled at birth. As my 'count' did not take place until the evening of the day after the poll I did not reach London until the negotiations between Jeremy and Heath were virtually concluded and took no part in them. The Liberal Party at that time were hostile to any arrangement with the Tories but in any event, as I have said, it could not have got over the first hurdle of a vote of confidence unless extra support could have been drummed up from the minority parties. This, I understand, Heath showed no signs of being able to mobilise.

In Orkney and Shetland Liberal fortunes had improved. Edwin Eunson's wife, Margaret, made an energetic agent. Yet more farmers took time off from their hard-worked lives to help in the General Election. John Bremner of Bendigo became Chairman of the Orkney Liberals and Jack Scott of Skaill flew me round the North Isles of Orkney in his aeroplane. Most farmers and fishermen are men of many talents: but few can have stretched as far as Mr. Scott: Island Councillor, farmer, builder and sailor of boats, airman and active churchman, yet he never seemed in a hurry.

IN 1963 I WAS APPOINTED a Chubb Fellow of the great and good University of Yale. When Professor Tom Bergin came to ask me if I would accept the fellowship I asked if I should give a lecture. 'Not unless you insist' he replied. Johnny and I spent a delightful week at Yale. Professor Bergin was an Italian scholar and a Democrat but not a Kennedy democrat. It is apt to be overlooked in Britain that there was always a strain in the Democratic Party which was more than suspicious of the smartness of the Kennedys. The Populists were sickened by the slickness of the Kennedy band-wagon propelled by Kennedy money. For them the President was too much of a cardboard construction dressed up in Harvard clothes but unscrupulously manipulated by the old boss system. It was not a view I, nor indeed Professor Bergin shared in its more extreme form, but history will I expect knock some of the gloss off the Kennedy era. After Yale Johnny and I did a short tour. We stayed with Professor Sam Beer at Harvard, who was at Balliol when I was there. He is an authority on British politics but I remember him for two other incidents: one a religious meeting at Oxford where love was much praised. Sam enquired whether it would not be more prudent to pay heed to hate. Alas, since then hate and envy have indeed proved more potent in public affairs than has love. The other arose from his sudden addiction to parachute jumping in his late fifties. He asked me one Sunday if I would like to go with him to the parachute grounds. To get there he hired an aeroplane as one can rent a self-drive car. After we had mounted the unfamiliar vehicle Sam put on his spectacles and read the driving instructions. I was left to navigate with the aid of a road map. I was almost as perturbed as when during a General Election the Liberal Party arranged that I should make a tour by helicopter under the pilotage of Howard Fry, a Liberal candidate and a practised aviator. What I did not realise was that his high reputation had been obtained on the Trans-Atlantic route. On our first stop we narrowly missed a horse trough and during one stage I had to hold the door shut—a considerable strain on the arm. Such are the trials of electioneering even outside Orkney and Shetland. On each occasion all ended well, though Sam on arrival at the jumping ground decided that a drink in the shade was more attractive than a voyage through space on a parachute.

After Harvard we went on to stay with Max and Joanna Freedman in Washington. Max was a friend of President Kennedy. He took me to see him. What struck me about the President was his belief, which I mention elsewhere, that all difficulties could be surmounted within the Democratic system. Even then, in Britain, if you asked a Minister what he was going to do about something, you were subjected to a lecture about the difficulties of doing anything. When I asked the President what he was going to do about the Negroes he replied 'We're going to get them to vote.' That was that. The question was answered. Max, as Joanna constantly complained, was an incorrigible buyer, hoarder and lender of books. He had established a useful reputation for never writing or replying to letters but books were his addiction. When I left The White House the President asked me if I would mind taking ten books back which he had borrowed from Max—rather a creditable borrowing for a President, especially if he had read them.

Max was one of the company of Central or Eastern European Jews whose families had emigrated to the West and which included Felix Frankfurter. If the flow should dry up liberalism will be parched. If there is such a thing as a masculine brain, they have it. They are, however, receptive, subtle and without the thirst for status which pervades the male world. For liberalism they are essential. For liberalism is not at bottom about the vote, it is about how human beings should behave to one another. In probing human behaviour and searching for new philosophies the Jews have long been in the van.

The Liberal Party has been a microcosm of Britain in the diversity of its members. I do not claim that in this it is unique. It is true of all parties and not only in Britain. But it is certainly a feature of their party which Liberals should cherish. Even now the House of Commons is largely manned by the middle classes: to a greater extent than it was thirty years ago—and of course the male middle class at that. While we should never lose sight of its fundamental duty to represent communities, yet politics should engage a wide diversity of outlook and occupation. There are too few, not too many, Jews and immigrants in British political life. There are valuable minorities hardly represented at all—though some such as the

Scots and Welsh are *over* represented on a purely statistical basis in the House of Commons compared to the population generally or more particularly when compared to the long-suffering English.

In the 1964 General Election the Liberals captured four seats in the Highlands and Islands. One of these was won by Alastair Mackenzie, one of the more noteworthy men with whom I served in the House of Commons. He had been a shepherd, spoke Gaelic and was, I suspect, the first crofter ever to be elected. He won Ross and Cromarty on his own personality without the benefit of much organised support such as that which ensured the return of early representatives of the urban weekly wage earners. Through serving on the Crofters Commission and other bodies he had come by a wide knowledge of the Highlands and Islands. Once when travelling through Shetland with him I was astonished at his ability to tell me not only who lived in many crofts but who the crofters had married. Alastair behaved in the House of Commons exactly as he did at home; in the lobbies he greeted everyone who came his way and exchanged comments on the weather and other topics just as he would in Dingwall market. Ministers hurrying about their business were at first rather surprised but he became a most popular Member. Alas he was defeated in 1974 but has found a worthy successor, though a Tory, in Hamish Troy.

Politicians, some say, must be tarted up and smoothed down now that television is their main form. But I am not so sure. A few warts are rather re-assuring. Nor do the electorate particularly like their politicians to be spruce and glib. A Gaelic-speaking friend of Alastair's asked me how he was getting on in the House of Commons. I replied 'Very well; sometimes he is a little slow with his questions but I suppose that is because he is a natural Gaelic speaker.' 'Oh, indeed,' his friend replied, 'he is very slow in Gaelic, we always thought he was a natural English speaker.' Alastair would have been unwise to have smartened up his mellifluous and precise English. I have enjoyed belonging to a group of M.P.s which contained such diverse characters as Alastair, Clement Freud and that merry Cornishman, David Penhaligon.

But all too many Liberals have never reached Westminster. Just as democracy is more than casting a vote, so politics must embrace more activities than being a member of the House of Commons.

There would be much to be said for a second chamber if it could recruit men and women who by their opinions and inclination were unlikely to reach Parliament by election, being averse both to party allegiance and constituency chores or like some I have mentioned being allergic to the House of Commons. Life Peerages have been awarded, however, too often to ex-M.P.s ripe to be put out to grass. I am not much enamoured of the proposal that the second chamber should be a repository for bosses from management and the Trades Unions. That would be to put the final seal of approval on the corporate state. I follow the argument of those who claim that a Fascist chamber would correspond to the reality of the British state. It might be a good thing for Trade Union leaders to stand up and account for their actions. But neither tycoons nor Union barons have contributed much to politics—as witness their performance in the House of Commons. I am against giving a coating of respectability to Fascism.

I guess that the Trades Unions will find their world changing in the next ten years. Vicious picketing, strikes which show callousness, e.g. for hospital patients, wage increases for inefficient industries, these manifestations which seem too often to be the badge of Trades Unionism, hardly endear it to the public. It is sinking in too that the endless clamour for more money is a prime cause not only of inflation but unemployment. The Unions are casting themselves not as the successful champions of the poor but their scourge. If we are to widen democracy then we must contrive curbs on Trades Union power. If, as many of the Trades Union leaders want, we are further regimented this will end up in a Left wing dictatorship. But no Left wing autocrat will tolerate their privileges once he can dispense with their support. So do not let us contort the constitution to chime in with what may be a passing phase. Trades Unions have plenty to do without running the government. They have a big enough task without trying to boss the country. If they are thrust further and further into politics then indeed they must be brought into the arena but this might wreck both them and us. As for the CBI it is hardly a pool of political wisdom. The spokesman for management cut sorry figures when put up against Trades Unionists who appear to know exactly what they want and are well-trained to get it. Would that such dedication was used to improve the efficiency of our industry.

No, if we are to have a second chamber and the decision about that must depend on how we reform the voting system and the Commons, it should be a chamber in which not only can legislation be revised and restraint imposed, but from which the wider horizons of politics can be surveyed. Its members should speak for minorities of different kinds. They should throw into the common pool opinions drawn from a more thoughtful background than the rough and tumble of the House of Commons accommodates. I am thinking of men like Roger Fulford, the historian, whose politics have a perspective, extended in time, building on the past, looking to the future; or commentators such as Robin Day, who have become expert in weighing up political trends, John Grigg, whose knowledge of politics is extensive. If some of these and others I have in mind are Liberals that is because I know Liberals and because Liberals are notoriously under-represented. Of course there are people of all parties and of none who could kindle some new sparks in politics. What I would abhor is a second chamber filled to the brim with superannuated public figures.

To return to my constituency. With the 60s and 70s large numbers of English people have come to Orkney, particularly to the North Isles: Rousay and Egilsay seem to have been largely taken over by them and a quarter of the population of Stronsay is English. They do not *all* work in the oil industry; some farm, some live on pensions or national assistance. Though sometimes known as white settlers they are for the most part deservedly welcome. But their advent must endanger the very way of life they come to enjoy. Although many claim that they have come to get away from the brash materialism of the south, they tend to be more demanding of the public authorities than are the Orkneymen. They have not been raised in the old Orkney way of getting on with your business, helping your neighbour and keeping your head down. They are more forward in taking on public office. This may be no bad thing but it is strange to hear Cockney accents in the schools and I wonder how much longer children will know the old ways—for instance, the boundaries of the parishes and the names for their inhabitants. The inhabitants of every Orkney Parish have a name, for instance, in Harray they are crabs, in Kirkwall starlings, in Westray limpets, Firth oysters and so on.

A year or two ago I was on the pier at Kirkwall when a steamer trip from the North Isles was casting off to sail home. The children from the North Isles were calling to one another by their traditional names: many of the Kirkwall children were bewildered. The language of Orkney and Shetland poets as well as the life they describe may soon disappear. But both have put up a stout fight against pollution from the south. Each generation in every part of the world reaches its zenith and goes into eclipse; who am I a 'ferry-louper' myself to bewail the scouring of new channels in Shetland and Orkney? But I should hate that the restful, quizzical, neighbourly spirit should be snuffed out.

When not travelling abroad I spent most of the parliamentary holidays and about two out of three week-ends in Orkney and Shetland. Life at the Old Manse flowed on agreeably though by the sixties my children except for Magnus were away most of the time. But they came home for the school holidays or on visits. Orkney is a good place to visit if you can pay the fare, but that for many families is prohibitive. Once there you are quickly engulfed in local life: local life which considering the small number of Shetlanders and Orkneymen teems with variety.

When we first settled in Orkney the local chief magistrate, the Sheriff (or Sheriff-Substitute as he was then called) was Barrigal Keith. The

238

Keiths were, like the Playfairs and Boases of St Andrews, a family of distinction. One of Barrigal's cousins, Berriedale Keith, wrote a text book on constitutional law while Professor of Sanskrit at Edinburgh University. The Keiths came from Thurso across the Pentland Firth where Barrigal had a collection of modern Scottish pictures by artists such as Peploe, Leslie Hunter, Cadell and Gillies. These artists have lately come into repute for which much credit must be given to such dealers as Mr. Macaulay and Mr. Jackson of the Scottish Gallery in Edinburgh and Mr. McIntosh Patrick of the Fine Art Society. Sheriff Keith not only collected pictures but painted himself. He could be seen, looking like Sir Walter Scott, painting in Kirkwall and like many artists rather tetchy if interrupted. He and the art teachers were partly responsible for the surge in painting which has swept Orkney and to some extent Shetland since the war. Ian McInnes now the Rector of Stromness Academy, Nancy Hewison and Sylvia Wishart are only a few of the painters whose pictures give a better impression of Orkney, its landscapes, its sea-scapes and the streets of Stromness and Kirkwall than anything I can write. I say 'partly responsible' because the urge to paint, carve, work in wood is endemic in Orkney and Shetland. Many cottages have pictures of ships in which local people sailed. Orkney chairs with their high straw backs are still hand-made. In the remote island of North Ronaldsay the Scotts, particularly the sculptor, Ian Scott, have a hereditary eye for shape and atmosphere. I have two small sculptures of otters and porpoises carved from local stone by John Williamson of Lubba in Shetland which catch the grace of these animals while escaping the slickness of popular models. Both Mr. Rae in Shetland and Miss Ola Gorie in Orkney have revived traditional designs in silver jewellery while in Mr. Robert Rendall, a draper to trade, we had a poet and conchologist of more than local fame. Mr. Rendall when I knew him was almost stone deaf but whenever he came to London I would get him tickets for the gallery of the House of Commons. The faces of M.P.s fascinated him, why I was never quite sure. But the patriarch of Orkney art, though not in the least elderly either in manner or vision, was Stanley Cursiter. Stanley had been keeper of the National Gallery of Scotland and though subject to rheumatism was still painting when we came to Orkney. For shelter from the gales he had a contraption like a mobile greenhouse. At first I did not take so much to his paintings as to himself but that was because I first saw his more formal set-pieces, some of them done as the Queen's Limner. Later I grew to like his Orkney pictures very much indeed. By the late sixties he was nearly eighty, confined for most of the time to his house in Stromness which he had re-modelled and decorated. There we would visit him in the gable-end which stood with its feet in the harbour as he sat dispensing sherry, feeding his tame sea-gull and looking down Scapa Flow with the hills of Hoy on one side and the greens and yellows of Orphir on the other. The sea-gull was a combative bird which showed the scars of the fights in which as it grew older it was not always victorious. Stanley was of the stamp of Edwin Muir, reflective, enthusiastic, spry, with bright eyes below white eyebrows, devoted to Orkney and always keen to discuss her future.

He was I am sure a trial to his tailor (a phrase of his own) for he was always impeccably dressed. He was fastidious in whatever he did. His prose, like his painting, was concise, though both could have a lyrical quality. He wrote a book about himself in seventy pages and a life of Peploe from which I have gathered more knowledge and feeling about art than from anything else except Patrick Heron's talk. His *Peploe* is almost as slim as his autobiography, but both give the heart and spine of the matters in hand. Everyone who has ever tried knows how difficult it is to end a book. *Peploe* has a perfect finish. 'These pages are but a gesture—a hand waved in greeting and farewell.'

As I am myself chronically disorganised, my room loaded with pictures, papers, books, furniture, I particularly admire those who are orderly, especially when they have a touch of genius as well. High in this galère I put Stanley Cursiter, along with my father, Moira Kennedy and Jasper Ridley. Laura was inspired to get Ian Scott, the North Ronaldsay sculptor, to carve a bust of Stanley which now stands with those of Edwin Muir and Eric Linklater in the County Library commemorating three Orcadians who were friends and companions in the Arts.

John Betjeman was much taken with the north and occasionally stayed with us. He was a most heart-warming guest. On arriving at the Old Manse on one of those dreich days when the sky seems to be on the roof and every bush is shrivelled with wind, salt and rain—days known in Orkney as 'coarse'—he fell into an ecstasy over Jimmy Brown's haystacks investing them with a Monet-like beauty which up till then we had not appreciated. He also managed to convey to Laura the impression that she had personally sited them outside the window especially for his pleasure.

Long before he became our revered Poet Laureate I had received, in the thirties, a letter from Anthony Squire recounting how John's arrival for lunch had cheered up the whole Squire household, then in one of its periodical crises. 'Oh Jo, do you like the latest Betjeman rhyme he told me at lunch today? It goes:

> "D. H. Lawrence
> went to Florence
> But Compton Mackenzie
> went to Firenze."

He is a tremendous rhymster you know, our Betj; it was he who made up the now hackneyed:

> "I sometimes think
> That I should like
> To be the saddle of a bike".

A delightful fragment that. Well, the sleigh-bells ring, the coachmen stamp their feet, the dogs are champing, my mistress waits and I must onaway.'

Stanley Cursiter and John Betjeman got on like houses on fire. A largely illegible letter from John describes a visit to Stanley's Stromness house where he saw 'Two exquisite Brabazonish water-colours by him (Cursiter) of Iona and a good oil with the paint laid on thick and Peploe-esquily.'

Another link between them was the house of Melsetter near Longhope. Stanley had been trained as an architect and worked with Lethaby who had been in charge of the restoration and enlargement of Melsetter. Lethaby was a hero of John's and Melsetter was not only of the Betjeman period, late 19th-century, but retained some William Morris-ish features. It is indeed a distinctive house, rather southern in character, built round a courtyard. By coincidence the man who had bought and restored it made a fortune out of bicycle saddles. It might well bear a plaque to the memory of John and Stanley's friendship.

Stanley was not the only lover of birds in Orkney. Bird watching is almost a light industry, certainly 'a tourist attraction.' George Waterston and his friends by setting up the Observatory may have kept Fair Isle from being abandoned and certainly have contributed to the growth in population. The list of birds reported from that island is so large and varied as to verge on the improbable, varying from the nightingale to the black browed albatross. I am no bird expert but I notice some changes, bad and good. The skuas, big gulls and hoodie crows seem to have increased to such an extent that some check would be welcome. The grey seal was to be slaughtered in huge numbers with the blessing of the Seals Advisory Board and to the benefit of Norwegian commercial interests. Why no slaughter of the bigger gulls and other birds which eat more fish and do more harm? At the Old Manse the corncrake used to be for us what the cuckoo was in the South, the sound of summer days. Now I seldom hear it though I saw one in 1977 on our drying green. Small garden birds, chaffinches and hedge sparrows, for instance, seem to have decreased, perhaps due to the increase of hawks and crows but numbers of wagtails run about the lawn in the autumn while in winter to my astonishment I regularly see snipe on it. I have hardly ever until lately seen a snipe on the ground. Now on a winter's afternoon two or three can sometimes be seen feeding like blackbirds within a couple of yards of the sitting-room window. Either our lawn yields something particularly delectable or snipe have changed their habits. Not only do they drive their bills up and down in full view but if disturbed they go no further than a nearby bush.

Fishing in most Orkney lochs is free, a legacy of udal law, now some-times abused by visitors who slaughter the trout by foul means for money. Shooting is to be had, mostly of ducks. Golf for those who can stand the wind, badminton, squash, football (in summer), even bathing (but do not put too much trust in the Gulf Stream) and in Lerwick Mr. George Batty, the ice-cream seller from London, used to press-gang some 'volunteers' to play cricket. I must repeat that in Orkney and Shetland we have more than enough to do, so much so that every now and again we have to 'get away from it all' by taking a holiday in the somnolent south.

Orkney and Shetland too are a paradise for children; they rampage more or less where they like and grown-ups spoil them. Not only children but adults enjoy limitless hospitality. The Scott family of Kierfiold constantly entertained us. Pat Scott ran the distillery but his healthy colour was entirely due to sun, wind and exercise: whisky he hardly touched. Any community is lucky to have a family such as the Scotts. They were for ever ready to promote forays to outlying islands, picnics, dances, shoots—every form of amusement. One mid-winter expedition was to shoot rock pigeon on the Yesnaby cliffs. Between Yesnaby and America there is nothing but the Atlantic driven in foam out of a mud-coloured sky spewing sleet across the waves. Pat was an expert shot, he and Johnny killed a few of the pigeons as they jinked round the corners and over the heather. For me it was a humane exercise for I seldom hit any.

The Scotts were by no means the only hospitable family in Orkney. Lords Lieutenant seem to get insufficient recognition, at least if they are as busy as Col. and Mrs. Macrae who held the office in Orkney. Even if he had not been Lord Lieutenant Bobby Macrae would have filled his house with friends; as it was, not only was Grindelay always stocked with friends but with innumerable delegations descending on Orkney for all sorts of jaunts and investigations. Colonel Macrae had a remarkable career in the Army. A regular soldier he had been captured in 1939 and spent the war as a prisoner. Being a prisoner-of-war for so long incapacitated many people mentally or physically but not Bobby who went back to the army and was a successful commander in Korea. Orkney also in Brigadier Robertson had one of the very few territorial Brigadiers. Next to the Macraes' house round the north shore of Scapa Flow was the home of the Johnsons. Halcro Johnson, who is still active in his eighties, had been a civil engineer in India and was now a farmer. He is also a fervent mathe-matician. Indeed, almost before I had met him I was startled to receive from him at the time the change-over to the decimal system was in the air, a powerful plea for the duodecimal system.

Orkney before oil and its discovery by the rest of Britain was a bustling place with a taste of its own and plenty going on. A plethora of voluntary societies and charities flourished in the islands. To me it is miraculous how the women manage to run the homes, so constantly are they engaged in the raising of money by sales, suppers and coffee mornings. And there is too a widespread interest in the history of the islands and a feeling among some, particularly the older islanders, for the furniture and ornaments which used to be the everyday furnishing of the houses. Dr. T. M. Y. Manson and Tom Henderson, the curator of the Lerwick museum, have done much to preserve the records that illuminate the old life of Shetland. I only wish they had been better supported in their fight to keep some of the old buildings. In Orkney there were two remarkable men, Mr. Wood the postmaster of Rendall and Mr. Copland, a journeyman painter in Kirkwall who, long before the antique supermarkets boosted the value of what was once rated as junk, appreciated the design and workmanship in everyday objects. Mr. Wood has a great quantity of antiques still on view as a collection in Orkney. Mr. Copland who lived in a small house in Kirkwall and worked on as house painter into his eighties bought and sold at incredibly low prices. He would pick up some piece at a local sale. His neighbour, Mr. Tulloch the joiner, would repair it with loving care and if there was no room for it in Mr. Copland's house a good home would be found for it. Among those who have contributed to the Orkney tradition room should certainly be found for this trio.

Nor have Orkney and Shetland lacked men and women of public spirit willing to give their time and energy to all sorts of unpaid tasks. Malcolm Stewart, the Laird of Hoy, made over his estate to a Trust which has done a lot for the north end of the island. Laura was active at its inception. Curiously, the Islands Council, though giving money to many less worthy causes, has never subscribed to Hoy. In Shetland the 'forty fiddlers' have swelled to eighty or more. Kirkwall and the island of Westray provide a joint choir which practises in the old roofless church on Egilsay and tours Scotland; Stromness Academy supports an orchestra. There is a Society also for drama and another for opera.

Another sign of the vitality of Orkney and Shetland as a community was the composition of songs and verse. Robert Rendall and George Mackay Brown and T. A. Robertson (Vagaland) achieved renown outside the islands. But there were many other poets and musicians. I quote from two of Mr. Windwick's songs. Mr. Windwick was a printer on the *Orcadian*. The first, 'Partans in his Creel' are the meditations of a girl on her attractive but feckless young man. Here is an extract:

243

'There's a peerie croft among the heather where he says we'll bide
    taegether
While's he'll mak a living wae his boatie on the sea.
There's a wee bit hoose his faither biggit, stootly thatched and
    snugly riggit
Waiting tae be taken ower by Willie and by me.
Willie stands around and whistles: Willie's fields are fu' of thistles
Thistles never bought a body any milk an' meal.
Na! I think I'd better tarry, bide a wee afore I marry—
No' till Willie catches mair than partans in his creel.'

This poem was only written some twenty years ago—partans—
crabs—were then valueless and usually thrown back into the sea; now
they are profitably processed in both Orkney and Shetland. I quote from
another of Windwick's songs about the Orkney custom of making home
brewed ale:

'It's weary workan a' the day wi' harrow an' wi' ploo boy:
There's hens tae maet an' calves tae gae an' seun we'll hae a soo tae
    ferry.
Ach! I think it's time tae quit—so divvle tak' the soo boy
When I geung ower on Friday night for Isie's gaen tae brew!
Tae brew-ew-ew; tae brew-ew-ew; owld Isie's gaen tae brew!

A'm plaguit wae a dortan wife, aye doon about the mou' boy,
An, girnan ower the storms o' life dour an' cauld in every weather.
Late yistreen I telt her strite tae sleep aside the coo boy,
When I geung ower on Friday night, for Isie's gaen tae brew!
Tae brew-ew-ew, tae brew-ew-ew; owld Isie's gaen tae brew!'

At a supper in the Orkney island of Rousay Mr. Corrigal from Harray
sang a song he had composed in which all the Rousay characters were
mentioned. Rousay is in fact not one of the richer Orkney islands. Some
extracts:

'Weel, here we are foregathered in a vast and happy throng
And here am I to do my best to cheer you with a song.
We're here to have a jolly time and cast aside our cares—
The poor hard-up musicians and the Rousay Millionaires.

For music's no' the kind o' job that brings the money in
And we a' come frae the Mainland where the soil is poor and thin.
But Rousay is a wealthy place, ye'll see it in a glance,
It's known throughout the county as a nest of high finance.

And the Dickey man of Langskaill is a hero, that's the truth;
He even flitted North when ither folks were flitting South,
He thinks the Rousay folks the wisest folks he's ever seen,
Since them that hadna' muckle sense cleared oot tae Aberdeen.

And a song aboot the Rousay folk wad never never do
Unless I made some mention of the famous wife o' Tou
The worthy Anna Bella we love so tenderly—
In all your joys and sorrows what a tower of strength was she.

And Johnny Sinclair is the fellow that commands the Rousay Navy
He seems tae be the man that brings the mails across fae Evie,
He has a muckle pocket book that's always getting fatter;
He says deep litter's paying even better than deep water.'

Weddings, Harvest Homes, Suppers on this excuse or that with songs
and recitations ending in a dance still fill the halls of Orkney and Shetland.

After an evening beside the shores of Stromness loch trying to shoot
duck against the few patches of waning pallor in the winter sky it was
pleasant to return to the Old Manse. We would then turn on the television. Now I seldom look at television except to look at old films of
Ginger Rogers and Fred Astaire or when reminded of some viewable
programme by Grizelda. It seems that the streak of genius which gave
birth to 'That Was the Week, that Was', 'Dr. Finlay's Casebook', 'Till
Death us do Part', and 'Dad's Army' is drying up. I wonder if it is another
casualty of the inflationary disease? Is the B.B.C. suffering as much from
dropsy as the rest of the economy? It seems to take them months to do
the simplest film. Is £2¼ million on 'The Sound of Music' well spent?
They also seem unduly concerned with their rating. The justification for
financing them through licence fees is that they should not be subjected
to commercial pressure. Yet they seem frantic to show they are as popular
as the commercial companies. I should have thought that they would have
rejoiced at being relieved of any obligation to cover all football, for
instance. They could then put the money saved to other uses.

In some ways the old life still goes on in Orkney and Shetland. But even
before the impact of oil it was changing. There was more money about.
Tractors had replaced horses and ponies. Houses were being enlarged,
refurnished and equipped with washing machines and television. Change
was accelerating. Modern fashions, the change in local government and
eventually oil changed the landscape as well as the attitude of some of the
local people. Our own village of Finstown was at night drained of all
character by sodium lighting. Looking west we now might be looking at a
mining village of the south, the sunset is killed by the garish reflection

from below. Even the Merrie Dancers which now and then illuminate the night with their ghostly greenish light hanging like hair high in the heavens could be obliterated. Mid-summer nights in the far north lap one around with their radiance, a blue-green-black sheen like the plover which cry on the marshes, like the white breast of a plover too is the horizon when the silver light of dusk and dawn intermingle. The old Orkney County Council never built a house. So long as everyone knew they never would do so people in the countryside provided their own houses. The burghs had always built houses but now some appalling groups of Council houses have been put up in the countryside. At Dounby in Orkney a group of boxes face directly into a public lavatory. Of course we were subjected to 'adventure playgrounds' and more kerbs on the roads. Meanwhile, social workers—admirable many of them—are employed to do what Orkney and Shetland people did for each other. The deadening blight of centralised education and centralised planning is spreading. With it spread a more insidious canker. There has been much talk of the Shetland and Orkney way of life. This was essentially a way of life which depended on personal decisions, co-operation and consideration for your neighbours. But now we are surrendering to corporate direction.

However, there is hope. Modern trends have been mitigated. The 'Do It Yourself' movement is catching on. There has been an uprising against the despoiling of the earth. The South of Scotland Electricity Board would like to prospect in Orkney for uranium. It has for the moment been routed. We feel that we have done our bit by accepting oil. I hope the ecologists will broaden their counter-attack. The enemy is subtle and has many allies. There are the persistent public authorities for ever extending the pall of uniformity. There are the insidious claims by business and government that they must give the public what they like which often means what the authorities think they ought to want. When after the war cars were covered by tatty, so-called embellishments of chrome, I was told, 'Ah, but they would not sell without it'. On the contrary, it was public demand which eventually banished the tawdry stuff. There is the cry that we must emulate the southern Joneses. Most curious of all is the confusion about preserving old buildings: some rot, some are demolished to make way for cars, others are embalmed by the Ministry of Works, others still become holiday cottages or tourist attractions—I am becoming very suspicious of tourism now sold as a commercial undertaking and garnished with spurious attractions.

The eye of some Orkneymen and Shetlanders is as responsive as ever to their islands, indeed so is their ear. The fiddlers of Shetland are more numerous than ever. This must be a good omen for the future. A new generation will regret the clumsy buildings by which our islands are being defaced. Already some stout councillors speak up against the more ludicrous of the planning laws which forbid the building of houses on sites which local people fancy. We are still being flattened by concrete. Agricultural land is nibbled away, road widening and graceless housing with its urban colours affront us. I shiver at some of the 'improvements' in Kirkwall. But all is not lost. And Orkney at least has suffered less than some other places.

The St Andrews shops of my youth have lost their character to plastic mass-produced shop-fittings—luckily so shoddily made that they can easily be destroyed. Almost alone, Aikman and Terras, those worthy grocers, retain their old front. But in Orkney to this day the floor of Edwin Eunson's emporium of ironmongery is laid with flagstones and just down the street in Kirkwall long counters of solid wood, polished by the palms of generations of Orkney hands, stretch into the back of James Flett and Sons, the General Merchants in Kirkwall, backed by wooden shelves with a wooden gallery above. Tankerness House in Kirkwall has been restored and is a pleasure to look at, the Cathedral of Kirkwall still presides over the town clustered at its feet, its dignity unimpaired and after a fierce struggle against the official vandals the 18th century house of Papdale has been saved from destruction, largely through the efforts of my wife.

15

BETWEEN THE AUTUMN General Elections of 1974 and 1979 I shuttled up and down leading the life of an M.P. increasingly immersed in the consequences to Shetland and Orkney of the discovery of oil in the North Sea.

Six, according to some counts eight, parties now sat in Parliament. The exact number depended upon how you reckoned the kaleidoscopic representation from Northern Ireland. The Government had only some 38% of the votes cast at the second General Election of 1974 and represented less than 30% of the electorate. Whatever you might think about the various dogmas of the 'Mandate' the Government's support was too small to give it any semblance of democratic right to carry out drastic changes. These two factors, the multiplication of parties and a government which was so poorly endowed with popular credentials were of course closely related. The result was a new turn in Parliamentary affairs, to which little or no heed was being paid inside Westminster.

In the summer of 1976 Jeremy resigned and I was urged by the two leading contenders for the leadership to resume it myself—at least until the General Election. Indeed most of the Parliamentary Party with two or three exceptions thought this the best that could be made of a bad upset. I refused. Party Leaders, like heavyweight boxers, seldom stage come-backs. 'Give a lead' some exhorted. I wince whenever I hear the periodic cries that we need leadership—and worst of all, leadership from the old folk. The British either avert their eyes when offered a lead or dig in their toes like the most obstinate of mules. It took a world war before they would have Churchill. Nothing short of a nuclear bomb could catapult Grimond into leadership—and it wouldn't be worth it. If I were ever to go back to the treadmill of Party Leader—which has its bright spots—I would want to stay for some time, as I said, unwisely, on radio. My colleagues would not have liked that: and rightly. Both David Steel and John Pardoe were fitted for the job. Too well fitted perhaps, making it hard to choose between them but the choice would have to be made sometime. By keeping them champing on the side lines it was not likely to be made easier nor their tempers sweetened. One colleague, David Penhaligon, said I was too old. That was true and I was deaf forbye. Mr. Callaghan, is slightly older than I am— but capping a ministerial career by becoming Prime Minister is a different ploy from being harnessed again for the long haul to the next Liberal revival.

However, I took the job until the election of a new Leader could be held. I had been turning over where Liberals should go in the circumstances of the 1970s. I explain such conclusions as I reached in the next chapters. My brief return to the leadership, agreeable as it was, convinced me that I was right to have politely put aside the flattering cup of a second two to five year stint. Though we could probably have thrashed our differences out, I had differences with the majority of the Parliamentary Party who in my view were too indulgent to the Labour Government and too oblivious to the need for a restatement of liberalism. So David Steel was elected Leader. If the Liberal Party in Parliament is something of a teacup by comparison with the two big parties in Parliament, no teacup has ever been rocked by such storms as greeted the new Leader. The handling of the Thorpe affair would have been enough. But to this was added the decision which led to the Lib-Lab pact.

In the spring of 1977 the Tories put down a straight vote of censure. It simply read 'This House has no confidence in Her Majesty's Government'.

David Steel telephoned to me (as he did to all other Liberal M.P.s) to find out what I felt about our vote. He himself at the weekend was inclined to vote against the government and so was I. He asked me what he should do if the Prime Minister asked to see him. I said he should go. An M.P., let alone the Leader of a Party, must have a strong reason indeed if he is going to refuse even to discuss a matter with the Prime Minister at his invitation. Also, I thought we should see what Callaghan had to offer. I went down to London from Orkney on Monday. On Tuesday there was a party meeting at which it was agreed that David Steel should negotiate with Callaghan. After various comings and goings a document was drawn up giving the heads of the agreement. To this every M.P., except myself, agreed—though some, particularly David Penhaligon, expressed misgivings. I was, however, the only formal dissentient. David Steel was right therefore in claiming that the Parliamentary Party endorsed the decision—indeed most were keen on it—and as far as the majority was concerned were just as responsible for it as David was himself

After his final visit to Callaghan we were to meet at 2.00 p.m. in David's room on the Wednesday. I was a few minutes late to find my colleagues so enthusiastic on the pact that by five minutes past two they, having endorsed Callaghan's acceptance of the terms, had dispersed. However, I insisted that the announcement could not say that we were unanimous.

In my view we could not retrospectively approve of the actions of the Labour Government which over three years had done so much harm. Though they might temporarily show contrition the Labour Party's policies remained the same. As soon as they were relieved of the fear of defeat they would revert to these policies. Fifteen or twenty years previously it had been reasonable to believe that the social democrats might gain the upper hand in the party. If that had happened there could have been a changed Labour Party or a realignment. For me it was impossible to believe in any such change by the spring of 1977. The Liberal Party must therefore obtain something from the pact which would, in the medium term at least, strengthen the hand of the non-socialist but progressive element in our politics. The only immediate way to achieve this was by electoral reform. That was therefore the prize, the only prize, which could have justified the pact. My colleagues were influenced by pessimism about the chances of the party in a General Election. Many people considered that the pact was agreed simply to save our bacon at the polls. I did not think so badly of our chances. Our showing in the opinion polls was poor but no worse than it had often been before. The Party always picks up during General Election campaigns. David Steel would have made a good impression on television. Further, under the present system, the standing of a party through the country does not determine the number of seats it wins. This is particularly true of the Liberal Party. I thought that we should probably lose some seats but come back with perhaps nine or ten, in much more favourable circumstances. I believed the circumstances would be more favourable not only because Liberals usually do better with a Tory government but because there was a chance that the Labour Party would fare so badly that the internal argument about its future would break out with violence sufficient to split off sizeable pieces of the party. A General Election seemed to me to offer not disaster to the Liberals but the chance of the century: a chance that there would be a shake-up on the Left from which they could gain lasting advantage. Therefore we were, so far from being weak, in a strong position. Either Callaghan delivered Electoral Reform or electoral disaster might split the Labour Party. Either would suit the Liberal Party.

I had other misgivings about the pact. Pacts have not proved advantageous to the junior partner. Further, there was a constitutional objection.

I was one of the critics who had argued longest about certain features of our politics. I had been suggesting for twenty-five years at least that it needed reform. I had often warned the Liberal Party that if they were successful they must face the inevitability of coalitions, especially if they won proportional representation. I could not be accused, therefore, of blindness to the defects of the system. But the system still existed. It has too, one feature which I believe should be preserved. That feature is the existence of opposition members, at arm's length from the government, sent up to air the grievances of their constituencies in the House of Commons and to keep a critical eye on those in power. In these days, when liberal values are threatened by the growth of government, Liberal Members have a special obligation to discharge this role. From the point of view of Parliament and in the interests of open government it is also desirable that there should be a clear understanding of the obligations of the opposition and a clear distinction between opposition and government. Of course Ministers should, and do, consult with members of the opposition. I have never known a Ministry refuse to see me on any matter about which I wanted to approach them. But this is quite different from consultation by the government under a formal pact with another party. These consultations are secret. The rest of the opposition is excluded from them. It is not clear how far the second party to these discussions is responsible for the outcome. In fact, the actual working of the pact turned out better than I expected. But it certainly seemed to me then, and still seems to me now, a dubious arrangement. A full coalition, though I would have opposed it, might have got over some of these difficulties. But that was not suggested by anyone and would not have been supported by Liberals.

Could we have got better terms? Could the Liberal negotiations have got a firm commitment to Proportional Representation, at least for the European Elections? David Steel thought not. He made a point of his refusal to ask Callaghan for concessions which he could not have delivered. He accepted Callaghan's assertion that the Labour Party would have rejected any such commitment. Some of them would, it was asserted, have rebelled even against a three line whip. I myself was surprised that the Cabinet, by a majority, accepted even the terms agreed upon. But Christopher Mayhew, who has long experience of Labour politicians believes that had the Liberals insisted upon electoral reform in the European Elections as a condition for their support they would have got a firm commitment. He maintains that the left wing of the Labour Party would not, in the face of certain and heavy defeat for the government at the polls, have incurred the blame for making a pact impossible. We shall never know if he would have turned out to be right. The only concession the Liberal Party got was that the Cabinet would recommend a variant of the list system in the Bill for European Elections, there would however be no whipping, a free vote would be allowed. It was highly likely that the proposal would be rejected and rejected it was by a majority of 98.

In the summer of 1977 the Liberals could claim some successes. They were, for instance, crucial in the defeat of the Chancellor's proposal to increase the petrol tax. The Government in my view carried out the pact not only to the letter but in its spirit. Consultation was copious. I was put in charge of energy. The minister, Tony Benn, was punctilious in asking me to give my views on the Electricity Bill which he was drafting. I found this an interesting and amiable experience but it impressed me with the difficulties of such consultations. I was met by the ministers concerned, all supported by their civil servants. I could not compete with their detailed attention to the various aspects of the proposed Bill. Nor did I try to enter into such competition. I made some general criticisms. For instance, it seemed to me that Benn's proposals would lead to greater centralisation and an increase in government patronage. I was against both.

As the summer of 1977 drew on the Liberal Parliamentary Party had to make up its mind whether it wanted to prolong the pact or whether it would end it with the session. I remained in favour of ending it. Obviously the Queen's Speech was vital. A majority of the Parliamentary Party felt that if they could not only prevent further measures of nationalisation but get some Liberal policy written into the speech they should continue the pact. Inflation was falling and the outlook seemed to be improving. The pact was not popular with the voters but my colleagues felt that the Saffron Walden by-election, where we retained second place, might be the turn of the tide. The voters, they suggested, had not yet had time to take in the new departure in politics. The bad results in other by-elections were due to people still thinking in the old grooves. The electorate had not yet appreciated either the need for co-operation between parties, nor the advantages which it offered. This was now the main argument of Liberals in favour of the pact. We should abandon party warfare. The endless recriminations between the parties followed by constant changes in legislation were damaging the economy and destroying any hope of a common effort. Liberals might have cited the benefits which the Free Democrats had bestowed on Germany by acting as a fly-wheel or, to change the metaphor, a brake on violent swings of policy as the big parties took or left office. It was an argument of some force. Liberals could point to the fall in the Stock Exchange prices when an election seemed imminent and its subsequent rise when the pact was signed. Apart from the economic uplift in the latter half of 1977 many people who were not socialists believed that Callaghan would do a better job than Mrs. Thatcher. Labour seemed to be more capable of handling the Trades Unions. Several people said to me that they did not want a General Election. So from the point of view of the country's economic well-being in the short run there were strong arguments for the pact—and I never pretended otherwise. Indeed, I thought it was a rational, though on balance, mistaken venture. In the longer run I believed that the country would lose from it.

But I was not impressed by the Saffron Walden result. We had an excellent candidate. We were second to the Tories in 1974. We might have expected therefore some switch of Labour votes to the Liberals. If the pact was to benefit us at all it must be by a tactical switch of Labour votes in constituencies of this sort. Further, if we were to run the dangers with which the pact threatened us, we must do better than merely holding most of our vote in such seats.

The Liberal Party in the seventies swayed between two criticisms of its opponents. Sometimes, it said that they were too close together. 'Which twin is the Toni' was a Liberal slogan based upon a well-known advertisement which showed a picture of two girls with indistinguishable permanently waved hair, 'Toni' being a do-it-yourself outfit which it was claimed gave you as good a result as expensive professional perms. But now when defending the pact Liberal propaganda stressed the polarisation allegedly taking place in politics. They sometimes justified their changed attitude by claiming that under Mrs. Thatcher the Tories had moved to the Right. But it was not an entirely comfortable change in the angle of our attack.

While the pact ran, the Liberal Party could hardly campaign against Labour policies, especially as Callaghan and Steel got on well together. Yet the Party sometimes voted against the Government, for instance when with the Tories we carried an early amendment to the Scotland Bill.

The pact was renewed in July 1977. The Liberal Assembly in September endorsed its renewal by a large majority. Though still opposed I had always thought that it was going to prove difficult to find the right moment to end the arrangement.

When the List system for European elections was rejected in the Commons, it came as no surprise to me. I did not see that it altered our situation. A meeting of the Parliamentary Party was called on the evening of the defeat for the next morning. As I already had an engagement that morning and did not see that anything unexpected, or indeed damaging, had occurred, I did not attend. I was only told of it late the night before. That afternoon I was astonished to hear that with the Party in a mood of near panic Steel had gone to see Callaghan apparently to protest against a

253

breach of the spirit of their agreement. Callaghan had honoured his undertaking and said so. Nevertheless, a special assembly was called. By the time it met, however, cooler winds prevailed and a resolution which envisaged an end to the pact in 1978 but no immediate repudiation, was passed. Nevertheless, some damage was done. It would have been wiser to have claimed immediately after the division on the European elections that the size of the vote for electoral reform was a triumph. It was certainly a bigger vote than had previously been achieved. We had now exhibited a volatility in our support for the pact which must damage any confidence in it. And we had chosen a bad issue. The public were not likely to be impressed by a party which claimed to have conferred great benefits on the country but which then announced that it would throw all this to the winds because we could not get the List system in European elections. The public was not deeply interested in these. The List system, though better than first past the post for such elections, is a bad system. In any case, whatever system was chosen would have to be re-considered for subsequent European elections. As I wrote at the time of my own position 'It is one thing to advise a man not to take a lease of a house, quite another to advise him, having taken the house, to burn it down'. All our hopes were now pinned on getting some Liberal measures on the statute book and on a popular budget for which we could claim credit. It would have been folly to have cast these hopes away.

Meanwhile, Richard Wainwright had won attention to the plight of small businesses and Geraint Howells had obtained some concessions for farmers. We did badly in by-elections in spite of the publicity. But by the time the General Election comes we may be doing better. At any rate, the party cannot complain that the press and broadcasting have ignored it or its policies. It has had far fuller coverage than at any time in my memory. At this short perspective I have no ready explanation for the degree of our failure in the immediate past. Though always against the pact I did not expect it to be as electorally unpopular as it has so far proved. The electors no doubt feel that for the moment at least the Liberal Party is an appendage of Labour. This would account for some falling off. Many Liberals or Liberal sympathisers are against socialism more than they are against conservatism. That we do better when a Tory government is in office indicates that to some extent we are a haven for loosely attached Tories, disappointed in their government.

Nevertheless, there might have been factors to counterbalance this loss of anti-socialists. Liberals had an answer to those who ask what is the point of voting Liberal however good their policies? What will happen? What effect will a Liberal vote have? The answer now was that the party had affected the policies of a government. They could do so again as with anything between six and eleven parties in the House of Commons (according as to how you define a party) a hung parliament might well result from any General Election. Hung parliaments are growing in popularity compared with unhung. So while I was afraid of some fall in the Liberal vote the size of the fall surprised me. In the volatile state of politics when party allegiance was loosening I thought the party might have picked up from among the loosely attached almost as many as it lost. Between the two 1974 Elections the party was supposed to have lost two and a quarter million votes and acquired some two million.

The waywardness of many Liberal voters makes it imperative that the leaders should jockey and nudge their potential followers into throwing their weight behind the Party. They must make the most of what talent is to hand. Of late the Party has muffed some of its chances. Apart from a failure to garner the new thinking outside the party in the last few years, it has hardly cashed in on its available credit. Meanwhile the Conservatives, though they did not generate much newly-minted thought—what party or politician does?—were putting together the teachings of the market economists and monetarists in a packet which could be presented as the policy of change and as a challenge to the conventional socialist/capitalist mixed economy bureaucratic thinking of the Establishment. The speeches of Sir Keith Joseph were clear and his thinking coherent. But the Tories were inhibited by disagreement within the party and a natural reluctance to commit themselves to detailed and radical promises which they might not be able to fulfil. They were torn between the inclination of some of their leaders to follow the old Tory policy of giving with the tides of change while preserving the essential institutions of the country—thus attempting to dominate the middle ground of politics—and the new realisation that an acceptance of Socialist advances might end in a wholly Socialist country. This dilemma was obvious in their attitude to the Trades Unions. Should they announce that they were willing to work with the moderates in the Trade Union leadership or should they denounce the power of the Unions as a danger to the country? At the week-end of 6th May 1978, for instance, Mrs. Thatcher made a speech criticizing the Closed Shop and the attempt by some Unions to force membership of a Union (and sometimes a particular Union) on everyone at work. At the same time the Tories welcomed the election of a moderate, Mr. Duffy, to the secretaryship of the Amalgamated Union of Engineering Workers. As yet, no concrete proposals were forthcoming from the party for dealing with the Unions. This aroused doubts about their confidence in themselves. Over race relations too there seemed some indecision. The Scotland Bill and the Wales Bill had been skilfully handled by Francis Pym aided by Leon Brittan from the defensible standpoint of belief in devolution coupled to effective criticisms of the particular Bills. But their Scottish spokesmen, one after changing his views several times, were against any devolution while on the back benches sat a former shadow Secretary of State for Scotland who was in favour of the Bill itself. In financial matters the Tory front bench was driven to suggest some unconvincing cuts in public expenditure after being taunted with promising lower taxes, but giving no details as to how they were to be reconciled with a reduction in borrowing. They had recanted from the galloping days of 1972 when the monetary spree got out of hand but their harder line had some flannel at the edges. I do not blame them. All Oppositions smudge their promises a little: Britain is not yet ready for any leader who puts the wheel over too abruptly.

While this parliamentary manoeuvring went on there was in the country some anger against bureaucratic attitudes and the growth of the corporate state. Civil servants, despite the strong position the Civil Service had won for itself, its indexed pay, pensions and the jobs for its senior old boys, were unhappy. The public accounts committee exposed errors in the administration of the public sector. Some civil servants were troubled by the loss of esteem for the service. Appointments to boards and commissions, e.g. British Steel, were not inspiring. Measured by the possession of motor cars, washing machines, coloured television, etc. the country was prosperous. But expectations were not being realised. The returns from extensions of the Welfare State were rapidly diminishing. The Grunwick affair had shown that there was a revolt against some pretensions of the Unions. It also showed that the Unions were ready to bully the general public for their own ends; though on this occasion they were successfully resisted. Unemployment remained high and the conviction grew that orthodox measures such as inflation or job creation could not cope with it. How far the failure of bureaucratic Socialism contributed to social violence is debatable but the housing estates and tall blocks of flats which were the legacy of Socialist planning certainly played a part.

These breaks in the weather which had seemed set for an indefinite spell of state Socialism provided an opportunity for believers in freedom and the individual. But neither the Liberal nor the Tory Party were ready to exploit it. The ravages of psephology had debilitated politics, leaving neo-Marxism as the only political philosophy in which there was much interest. Liberals should rally and take the offensive. They must demonstrate that Liberalism planted securely in freedom and ethics can spread before everyone, not merely the clever, lucky or those endowed with astute parents, the prospect of personal fulfilment in a community of which they can be proud. The general assumption was that it had led to an unfair society. It was taken for granted that the state had been com-

Magnus and two friends, Miss Mary Ratter and Mrs Peterson, who are carrying the traditional Shetland 'Kishes'.

Being carried ashore at Papa Westray.

At Lerwick harbour.

pelled to intervene to cure its defects and that in particular the welfare services and redistributive taxation were essential to make it even partially tolerable. Liberals had accepted social engineering. Social engineering and the repudiation of ideology in the works of Popper, Jewkes, Graham Hutton and others could have been a valuable antidote to the fashionable doctrine of state socialism. If the positive side of Hayek and other liberal political economists had been followed up and married to a defence of the common interests which must inspire any democratic society, then we should have had an alternative liberal political programme. But, unfortunately, the prevailing fashion was against these writers when they were at their zenith. It dismissed them as 'right wing', then a damning indictment. This meant the repudiation of a philosophy of individual freedom and acquiescence in ever-extending interference by the state. Liberals, not merely members of the Liberal Party, had accepted the mixed economy without giving sufficient thought as to the nature of the mix. After the era of the commanding 'heights' when Socialists such as Gaitskell envisaged nationalisation being confined to industries such as railways, mines and steel—still considered by a curiously 19th century form of reasoning to be the most important of 'basic' industries—nationalisation had crept forward either by the random acquisition of firms in difficulties or as a means to maintain employment. Socialists could justify this process because in their eyes any extension of state control was welcome. But Liberals, if they were to accept the 'mixed economy' should have given much more thought to the principles according to which the state should nationalise and should have produced some boundaries between the free and the nationalised sectors. The Nationalised Industries were not in fact a series of commanding heights, but at best a range of dying volcanoes. They were distinguished, not by their current economic importance, but by their historical fame and by the numbers they employed. The very idea that the economy should be directed through state ownership of a few industries was nonsensical and should have been firmly rejected by liberals. What has made the economy so difficult to manage is the incompetence of the nationalised industries coupled with their insatiable demands for capital and subsidies. So far from being commanding heights they have proved to be quagmires for successive governments. But what activities then are suitable for public control? To my mind, not only those which purvey what are called 'public goods' but many activities should be outside the market for which the profit motive is not necessary and for which the reward is an opportunity to pursue personal pleasures and satisfactions.

To 19th century Liberals the conflict between freedom and order seemed likely to arise because individuals claimed too much freedom. J. S. Mill's statement that:

'The only purpose for which power can be rightfully exercised over any members of a civilized community against his will is to prevent harm to others.'

implied that the freedom of individuals would have to be curbed: though only at the point at which they impinged on each other. But today the danger is not always that the individual will claim too much freedom but that he or she may claim too little. We have grown accustomed to our cages. There is little need to clip our wings, we are forgetting how to use them as we surrender our destinies to our managers. Liberals, too, have given the impression that most freedoms are 'private' goods. In fact many freedoms which may seem at first sight to be 'private' goods on a longer view are 'public'. For instance, in the long run it is the nation as a whole which stands to gain from liberty to choose how its children are educated and in many other areas which safeguard choice and variety. An excess of private freedom may come about in the use of drugs and some manifestations of the permissive society. It is paradoxical that this type of private freedom is often encouraged by socialists who object to the freedoms which an individual may practise for the general good. The increase in violence which has taken place recently might be cited against my view that we suffer from too little, not too much, freedom. But burglary and mugging are not what J. S. Mill had in mind when he spoke of freedom. By telling people that they must leave decisions to officials the exponents of the bureaucratic outlook have contributed to crime. For a corollary of freedom, just as important as order, is responsibility. Freedom entails the acceptance of responsibility. Responsibility is meaningless without freedom. Again and again criminals excuse themselves by repudiating responsibility—child beaters, for instance, speak of 'black outs'. Anything which diminishes freedom and enables the criminal to offer the excuse of irresponsibility encourages lawlessness.

16

THOUGH THIS BOOK is not a treatise on politics, yet as my life has been suffused by politics it may be excusable for me to indicate from time to time where I stood on matters which absorbed so much of my attention. If I do so rather baldly that is because too detailed dissertations would become books in themselves. It is only worth going into politics if you have some belief about values and how to attain them. We may absolve ourselves from taking any part in politics: we may spew upon Caesar and all his works: we may aver, alas, all too plausibly, that man cannot improve his lot by political action. But if you choose to be implicated in politics, bound by even the most tenuous threads to political action, then you cannot wash your hands of some commitment to some values. Politicians should not stumble on as though their chosen calling was of no moment, a tale told by an idiot to the gullible as we all fare on our long fool's errand to the grave.

To say this is not to encourage meddling. The ideal Government minister may well be someone who has no itch to run other people's lives (I think I am free from this vice myself). But 'hands off' needs for many people an effort of will and a determination to keep other people's hands off as well as your own: such an effort in turn needs a motive, and the motive must be the furtherance of a certain sort of country. The world has suffered grievously from political fanatics, maniacs, masquerading as prophets, ideological monsters of various hues—red, black or nowadays, Muslim. We would, I hope all prefer to be ruled by Lord Melbourne than by Lenin. But Lord Melbourne had a view of what life should be, a life in which government pretensions were suspect. If we have no such view, a vacuum opens up into which the seven devils of autocracy or bureaucratic empire-building rapidly settle.

Value on earth it seems to me must appertain to individual conscious-ness and the voluntary use of individual faculties. We can claim no value for acts forced upon us or benefits bestowed on us. Wealth is not in itself valuable, though it may be a means to a valuable end, that is to valuable states of mind or deeds, as I shall argue property often may be. The worst impoverishment is not a low income but the impoverishment of oppor-tunity, the impoverishment which comes from cramping the use of a person's faculties. Things done for us may impoverish us by curtailing our opportunities. By most religions riches are denounced as a stumbling block in the path of righteousness. As for domineering your neighbour, it is a millstone round the neck, a temptation to be shunned as Christ on the mountain top put world dominion behind him. But human faculties cannot be exercised in vacuum, only hermits blessed with exceptional grace can spend their lives in contemplation living on locusts and wild honey. Human beings require a community. Politics are about running a community in which we can create, play, express ourselves.

Thirty years ago, as I have written, in the aftermath of war, I had rosier visions of what might be achieved by governments on behalf of com-munities, though even then I never pinned my hopes on state socialism or the nationalised industries, particularly after bucketing about in UNRRA. By the middle seventies having watched idealism seep away to leave even the Welfare Services in danger of becoming just another interest I was increasingly sceptical not of common effort but of bureaucratic effort. I believed that governments had a tough but circumscribed role, com-munities should work out more of their own salvation, and that there were many activities to which the market was as inappropriate as the profit or high salary motive. I saw the mixed economy as the muddled economy. We groped in a jungle of boards, commissions and regulations, thrust down our throats from above through which no guiding light penetrated and in which the strongest organised bullied the weak. We were forgetting that only voluntary action had virtue and that such action must be informed by personal responsibility and the Golden Rule. Now if the Good Samaritan gave way to his altruistic impulses he might produce a strike of Health Service workers. Today the Pharisee would be com-mended for wisdom and restraint.

The Socialist movement in the 70s steered by no star. It had veered towards the rocks when it embraced salvation through bureaucracy. (The rudder was originally put on this course by the Fabians.) The country was and is far from ungovernable. But no one was trying to govern it. Nor was the Labour Party as the political wing of the TUC in any position to do so. If every interest extorts higher and higher wages each Union leap-frogging over each other, jostling for a bigger share from the trough of public resources, scornful of exhortations to make their business more efficient, then wages will be inflated beyond what industry can support. Inflation generates unemployment. The cry goes up for more taxes and subsidies, more jobs unjustified by results, until Liberal Democracy may collapse.

The moment was ripe, not for a defensive action on the liberal front, but for an offensive reasserting liberal values and deducing from the nature of these values the pillars on which a liberal country should rest. We should give up trying to palliate state Socialism and its bed fellow corporatism and instead reassert more fertile traditions, the free market plus co-operation plus community development. On these three pillars a self-respecting modern community could be built. With them should be linked a new appreciation of the virtues of private property. In the 19th century lumber room from which Labour Party leaders draw many of their ideas lurks a hatred of personal property. Yet they fight for property rights, rights to pensions, jobs and large salaries, which carry no responsibilities and much access to exploitation. Private property is not essential to saints. But to me some private property is not only a stockade behind which men and women can shelter from the slings of would-be dictators and the arrows of outrageous fortune, it can be an extension of personality and means by which our capabilities can be stretched. You can abuse private property but usually today to the detriment of yourself alone. No one likes misers nor to see people glutted by too much property. But you can be a glutton for food yet no one proposes to make eating illegal. Nearly all free communities (the Jesuit settlements in South America and Kibbutzim are exceptions) have encouraged the spread of property. Nearly everyone enjoys it and makes better use of it than the state. I remember my mother-in-law retorting to Low the cartoonist who was, in his engaging way, dismissing the need for it, that she doubted if he would share a toothbrush with her. (My mother-in-law's strength as a controversialist was that she had no male inhibitions against pressing her attacks in disconcerting spots. In this she possibly shared a fellow feeling with Lloyd George of whom Margot Asquith remarked 'he cannot see a belt without hitting below it'.)

I have expounded my views on the alternate strategy for Liberals in *The Common Welfare* and do not want to go over them again. I believe that official doctrines of the Labour Party today are perversions of the generous and humane instincts which should animate the Left. As Walter Kendall himself a Socialist, has said 'If all that is required of Socialism is production according to plan, for use and not for profit, under the supervision of an authoritarian command structure then the prison workshop is the proper prototype of a Socialist community'. (Quoted by Robert Oakeshott in *The Case for Workers' Co-ops*—a book which all Liberals should read.)

261

As politics by the seventies were topsy-turvy, with the Labour Party turned conservative, having usurped the throne of the Top People, it was natural that liberal ideas should be echoed by conservatives. As the social democrats had for the most deserted the political field of battle, many for the flesh-pots of the capitalist-socialist establishment, the main divide in politics was coming to be between those who would fight for a free society, (i.e. Liberals and Conservatives of various shades) and those who still supported the Labour Party now thirled to corporatism. This divide has grown more visible in recent years.

As usual co-operation between political groups with the same attitude to many issues was made impossible by the distorting pressures of Parliament. The parties not only continued their historical quarrels but within the parties bickering sputtered away. Had Liberal politicians in the 70's unfolded a more emphatic picture of the sort of country they wanted, explained more vividly the ideals of a Liberal society, differences would have shrunk. Against such a perspective the rift between, say, Peter Walker and Sir Keith Joseph would have been much less daunting. Within the Liberal camp a dialectic might have been pursued which could lead to a synthesis pulling us back from the collectivist limbo to which we are slipping. For we are not at a crisis. We are not on the edge of a crevasse on the other side of which, if only we can cross it, we can amble on through green fields for ever. We are more like men in a boat at sea who face a long and arduous voyage but have so far not even decided which port to head for.

I am not talking about a coalition, though as Lord Blake has pointed out in his illuminating essays on British Prime Ministers, coalitions have ruled us rather often and with no less acceptability than single party governments. Nowadays the cry for a coalition often degenerates into the plaintive whine of those too supine to steel themselves for the sort of decisions which need to be taken. They ape Melbourne—'It doesn't matter what we say so long as we all say the same thing.' 'Let someone who can't do anything—the Sovereign, for instance—or an octogenarian or a general mish-mash of politicians take over'—they murmur 'and then we can doze off again.' But now we should not smudge the divide between those who believe in the inevitable beneficence of the ever-growing state and those who believe that values lie in the individual and are threatened by collectivism. When the tentacles attempt to tighten their grip liberals should enter the fray together—though we may respect our opponents do not let us pretend we are all political brothers under the skin.

We need not look far to find thinkers to contribute to a new liberalism, nor authors to expound it. The *Economist* carries an annual jeu d'ésprit by Norman Macrae. This casting of bread on the waters is more than a firework display. His suggestions for flexing our muscle-bound industrial dinosaurs by articulating them into smaller units working by contract with each other, the co-operative ideas of Robert Oakeshott, the Jays (Martin and Peter) and Roger Sawtell, the constitutional suggestions for a reformed second chamber, the realization that democracy must mean more than a vote (usually ineffectual) every few years, proposals (by William Rees-Mogg for instance) for loosening the grasp of governments on the currency, these and many more ideas show that the liberal tradition is still vibrant. Sir Ian Gilmour has written two political books of distinction and wit. Nigel Lawson, like him an M.P. and ex-editor of the *Spectator*, is a publicist of ability. Arthur Seldon and Ralph Harris seem at last to be coming into their own. But when it comes to political action they, and the many vigorous young M.P.s of several parties who subscribe to the ideals of a free society, have not so far been welded together. As a result, illiberal minorities have been able to use parliamentary government for purposes disliked by the majority in the country and inimical to the common interest.

LORD KILBRANDON, who was chairman of the Royal Commission when they reported on the Constitution told me that as someone who himself lived on an island he was intrigued to discover what Orkney and Shetland might think about Scottish Devolution. When his commission split into sub-commissions to sound out the views of various parts of Scotland he therefore chose to visit Shetland. He suspected that the Shetlanders might have a viewpoint different from that of the Scottish Mainland. Rather to his surprise he found that this was not so.

He has told me that he could discover no anxieties, no demand for special treatment. In the election of the autumn of 1974 all four candidates in Orkney and Shetland were in favour of devolution. I won, having advocated Scottish self-government (though not on the lines of the subsequent Bills) ever since I had been a candidate. The S.N.P. came second. The Tory and Labour candidates also supported it. No protest was made. Few questions were asked about it.

In the autumn of 1976 I wrote to most of the organisations in the constituency, the Farmers' Unions, the Fishermen's Associations, the Trades Unions, the Chambers of Commerce, the Community Councils, etc. and a fair number of individuals—over two hundred letters in all—asking their views. The replies showed that only three or four wanted an independent Scotland. Several of those who had supported the S.N.P. candidate did not want this, the heart of the S.N.P. case. No one wanted Orkney or Shetland to cut loose from Britain. A minority wanted, or were prepared to accept devolution. A substantial majority wanted to stay as they were. The main reasons for this were not ideological. They were mainly influenced by a mistrust of government, a failure to see what anyone would gain from devolution, or suspicion of the central belt of Scotland.

Their answers showed up the failure of government. Even those who were attracted by the idea of more power nearer home to settle their own affairs were appalled by the result of the so-called reforms which had ended up in providing more and worse government, such was the lack of skill in British politics and the British bureaucracy. As for fear of the central belt, it was well summed up by one correspondent 'I can imagine nothing worse than being ruled by Glasgow Trade Unionists and Edinburgh lawyers'. When did this fear crystallize? The people of Orkney and Shetland had long complained of remote control from London.

As I have mentioned, Home Rule for Scotland was cheered in the 1950 General Election. Since then government had fallen into disrepute. Even when it attempted popular reforms they were so clumsily executed that all its fingers seemed to have turned into thumbs. Orkney and Shetland had too often found themselves at the mercy of remote forces and clobbered by disputes in which they had no interest.

In January 1977 I had got a grant from the Joseph Rowntree Social Service Trust to pay for a visit to Shetland and Orkney of Mr. Kermeen from the Isle of Man and Mr. Olafsson from Copenhagen. I had long been attracted by the idea of running our own affairs to a greater extent. I believed that political reform was starting from the wrong end. The conventional view seemed to be that political power naturally resided in Westminster so that any change involved its dispersal to Scotland or local government. I believe the opposite. If it was useful to speculate about where political power resided the conclusion must be that it came from the people who lent it to local and then to central authorities. I held that the reform of local government in Scotland before a Scottish Parliament was set up was topsy-turvy. I maintained that the setting up of a Scottish Parliament should be the occasion of a general constitutional review. I did not accept that after creating a new tier at Edinburgh on the Westminster model we should call it a day. In addition to these general views Orkney and Shetland had special claims to greater autonomy even than the other parts of Scotland. But no very great public interest was shown in these visits. The meetings were large compared with ordinary political meetings but amounted to perhaps sixty in Shetland and seventy-five or so in Orkney.

The Shetland Islands Council had been much impressed by its success over the Shetland Bill. The Bill had indeed shown what could be achieved. Its success owed a good deal to favourable circumstances (both the government and shadow government were broadly in its favour). Shetland was lucky in the committee set up to examine it under Sir John Gilmour, an old friend of mine who knew about Shetland. It is unkind to say so perhaps but they were lucky too in that the one member of the committee who had serious misgivings was defeated at the General Election in the spring of 1974. The Council were anxious to preserve what they had won. They felt that this might be impaired by a Scottish Assembly, dominated by the central belt and anxious to get its hands on the oil revenues. At one time they even suggested that the Private Bill procedure, which of course had applied to the Shetland Bill, could be used to allow them to remain under Westminster. I advised them that in my view it could not, and in this I was supported by advice from the officers of the House.

When the Scotland and Wales Bill was in committee Mr. Tulloch, as convener, and myself, along with some officials of the Shetland Islands Council had a meeting with the Ministers chiefly concerned with Scotland and the Bill. The Ministers pointed out that oil, ports, and the related matters, as well as fishing and agriculture would remain under Westminster and were not to be devolved to Edinburgh. They held therefore that Shetland's fears were groundless, the Bill needed no amendment. They left, however, some doubts. Local government reform was devolved. The powers of the S.I.C. could be reduced, indeed it might be put under the Highland Region. While most of the activities at Sullom would remain under Westminster, certain services at Sullom would not. Mr. Tulloch was also afraid that the terminal might be nationalised.

The only amendment passed to the Scotland and Wales Bill was an amendment of my own providing for separate representation for Orkney and for Shetland. As originally proposed in the Bill they would, like other Scottish constituencies have shared two members. So the matter rested when defeat over the guillotine resulted in the abandonment of that Bill.

During the interval between the Scotland and Wales Bill and the Scottish Bill the Shetland Islands Council decided to put their case to various M.P.s whom they invited to visit Shetland. I had further dealings directly and indirectly with the government over our case. I was not at that time consulted by the S.I.C. either about what their strategy should be or whom they should invite. The official mind is often obtuse—it hardly apprehends how the world works. Naturally many of the M.P.s who responded were against the Bill. They saw in the S.I.C. a possible weapon for its destruction. They egged on those councillors who wanted to contract out of devolution entirely. I had never believed this possible. Shetland depended upon Scotland for most of its administration and trade. Crofting, Scottish law and Scottish education could hardly either be administered from England or be abandoned for English equivalents. Safeguards and a special relationship I believed were what we should demand. Further, while in time I believed Shetland and Orkney should ask for a position more nearly that of the Isle of Man, I saw no evidence that the majority of Shetlanders were yet ready for such a step which would require careful consideration, a willingness to take on further responsibilities such as the raising of taxation and the waiving of some rights to British benefits. The S.I.C. also proposed to hold a referendum. I did not wholly support this proposal for though it might indicate how Shetlanders felt, the drafting of the question on such a matter with several possible options and no clear knowledge of how the Scottish Bill would turn out would be difficult and the answers of doubtful value. However, our differences were sunk and the Island authorities and I co-operated amicably for what we were agreed was the good of the Islands.

I put down an amendment drawing attention to the special interests of Orkney and Shetland, specifying particular areas for which safeguards were needed and laying it down that alterations in the matters specified could not be made without the assent of the Secretary of State. As there was still some doubt as to Shetland and Orkney opinion and as there was still disagreement between the Government and the S.I.C. about possible effects of the Bill, I put down another amendment to the effect that if Shetland or Orkney voted 'No' in the referendum a commission was to be set up to examine their future government. While I did not believe that either island group could contract out entirely and independently, it seemed to me that it would be possible for interim arrangements to be made while the commission sat. I did not see why it should take very long. Such a commission was usual before constitutional changes were made. Shetland and Orkney organisations and individuals other than the Islands Councils would have a chance to give their views. I made the setting up of the islanders showed that they were content with the Scotland Bill. because it would have been strange to demand a commission if a majority of the islanders showed that they were content with the Scotland Act. If the long-term status of the islands was to be examined, as I hoped would eventually happen, then a commission might be set up regardless of what happened to the Scotland Bill: but that would require a separate Act.

The S.I.C. sent their Vice-Convener, another member and an official to spend considerable periods of lobbying in London. They met with a good response especially from those opposed to the Bill but not only from them. Mr. Tulloch and the Vice-Convener proved persuasive advocates. Owing to the guillotine the first set of amendments mentioned above were never reached. The amendment asking for a commission was reached with two minutes to go. I had time to read out the amendment. My speech contained one sentence—'That was a damn close-run thing' (a misquotation). It was carried by a majority of 114 against the government. Some government Whips and an S.N.P. Member (the S.N.P. were solidly opposed to these amendments) tried to play out time by lingering in the lobby. Sir Myer Galpern was in the Chair, a man difficult to put upon. He sent the

Serjeant at Arms into the lobby (something I had never seen done before), the lingerers were evicted and the vote taken.

The government's behaviour was peculiar. They were opposed to the amendments, still holding them to be unnecessary (perhaps they also feared like demands from other regions). They had not, however, during the committee stage sought any further discussions with me, nor put forward any suggestions of their own. But they could almost certainly have prolonged discussion on amendments previous to mine so preventing it being passed. After it had passed they allowed two or three months to go by before the Secretary of State for Scotland gave his views in detail. These were that the amendment which had been passed would leave Shetland and Orkney 'in limbo' while the Commission sat. The Commission would require a decision of Parliament to set it up and would require at least a year to collect evidence and report. The Scottish Assembly would have to be consulted and new legislation passed. Instead he suggested an extension of the Secretary of State's over-riding powers to safeguard the islands. He said that he felt bound to put his proposals to the new Councils which were elected in May, 1978. No doubt the decision had to be theirs. But he could have made the proposals known to the old Councils. In fact he did not visit the islands for some three weeks after the local elections and gave the councils very little notice. His proposals were at first refused—as I advised. But the government had come a long way since 1976. They were not very far away from my first set of amendments. After further exchanges I negotiated with John Smith, Minister of State at the Privy Council Office (the Secretary of State had gone to the World Cup in Argentine) amendments which gave us all we set out to get. We were promised a commission whether the majority in the islands voted 'yes' or 'no' and the Secretary of State could intervene if our needs or interests or the status of the Islands Councils were threatened by the Scottish executive or Assembly. I advised acceptance. The Councils agreed that with these safeguards we should come under the Assembly.

In the course of the negotiations I had stressed the neglect of the islands by governments. We were, for instance, badly treated over transport compared with the Western Isles. While they were getting an annual Exchequer subsidy of over £3 million to keep down freight charges, we received a few tens of thousands. We got more for capital works but not nearly enough to make up the difference. I urged that we should use the sympathy we had won at Westminster to get help on these matters. The remit of the Commission would allow it to consider our case.

Thus the Shetland campaign over the Scotland Bill attained its objective.

I have told the story of Shetland, Orkney and the Scotland Bill to illustrate some aspects of politics. Parliament still counts. Resolute campaigning can still win and not only over quibbles. But the ground from which governments may be tackled is constricted. Luck is as useful as reason. Vested interests must not be antagonised. Such are the restrictions on democracy and they are tighter than should be tolerated.

A representative of a community, which is what an M.P. should be, has an interesting job in trying to find out what the community wants and in deciding what would be best for it. In the matters I have discussed party political allegiance played little part. Only the S.N.P. were as a party opposed to Shetland's demands.

The local authorities played parts which they probably would not have undertaken had they not been encouraged by their successes over the Shetland and Orkney Acts which gave them such wide powers in respect of oil development. I am not sure that Shetland Islands Council ever appreciated what went on behind the scenes in connection with these Acts. They were not elected to deal with national issues. Indeed it was on local issues that the Vice-Convener who had conducted much of the successful lobby was defeated at the May, 1978 council elections in Shetland.

So the lobby on the Shetland Bill was successful. This was due to a number of factors at Westminster where I spent much time jockeying for position and explaining our anxieties. The government were hesitant. Public opinion was largely on our side. Had concessions been made at the outset by Ministers much time and trouble would have been saved.

Our experience shows how much can be achieved by small communities or determined lobbies. It also shows that parties are not so rigid nor party whipping so compulsive as is sometimes made out. We received great assistance from members of other parties. I am not writing a monograph on the whole matter but suggesting that vast, faceless and monolithic as government may sometimes appear, it is still at the mercy of chance. It can also be influenced by pressure even from small communities and by people outside the two big parties and the bureaucracy if they try hard enough.

There are also lessons to be learnt from the story of the Shetland and Orkney private bills. Though I am sure the Private Bill procedure cannot and should not be used to make major constitutional changes, it should be studied to see how far it can be improved and used to make useful adjustments in our government. When the House of Commons timetable is so crowded and its procedure so unsuitable for the examination of particular needs the Private Bill procedure with its hearings by committees may have a role in allowing communities to play a greater part in reaching the best standards of which they are capable.

In Shetland as elsewhere the public authorities may soon be swamped. In spite of a ten- or twenty-fold increase in the number of officials their staffs are said to be overworked. Indeed, I can well believe they are. As bureaucracies everywhere get bigger the cry is echoed up and down the land. The solution is not yet more officials who must spend more time in dealing with each other and become more bogged down in tasks they cannot discharge. Already I notice how it takes ever longer and longer to get replies from the public service and the replies when they come are less clear. The answer is to halt the haphazard proliferation of government, define its proper sphere at all levels and allow individuals, firms, local associations, to make their own decisions. As in Poland so in Shetland, ordinary people can make more of their own lives than officials. A cataract of orders, directives, demands for information merely swamps efficiency and exhausts us all.

Oil has already divided the economy of Shetland, and to a lesser extent that of Orkney, into two parts. In Orkney the oil comes ashore on the island of Flotta in Scapa Flow. Most of the oil workers live in a camp on the island. Flotta has, of course, been scarified and loaded with oil tanks. Oil has been flowing to Flotta since 1976 but so far the rest of Orkney has been less affected by oil than has Shetland (which no oil had yet reached by the autumn of 1978) where the terminal will be much bigger and is on the mainland. Nevertheless, Orkney and perhaps particularly the North Isles of Orkney, have felt the pull of high wages and allowances on Flotta

In Shetland you can drive or sail far and wide in the west and the north without seeing any sign of oil; here by the Voes the old economy of fishing and crofting and knitting goes on. But the impact of the terminal is heavy. It is being built some twenty miles north of Lerwick on Sullom Voe at a headland called Calback Ness, where it will cover some hundreds of acres. To it oil will flow by two pipes from the platforms in the North Sea. All the major oil companies, thirty-four in all, have joined with the Shetland Islands Council to construct and manage the terminal. It is during the construction period that a great number of workers is needed. How long that period may be cannot be foretold because new oil fields may be discovered East or West of Shetland; but it will probably reach a peak about 1980 and then tail off. By 1978 however four thousand were employed, over three thousand of whom were incomers living in completely self-contained camps replete with shops, bars, entertainment and indoor sports. The inmates of these camps might be on separate islands for all they see of Shetland. Their lives in their well-heated and padded huts are very different from that of the wartime troops who composed 'Bloody Orkney'. The workers were earning £150 a week by 1976 and their wages have risen since then, they need not spend 5p unless they drink, brush their teeth, smoke or buy a newspaper; everything is free including travel South and back for a week's holiday once in five weeks.

Shetlanders employed at Sullom Voe do not enjoy all the perks and allowances available to those from the South, but a girl who had been earning £40 a week in a shop in 1977 found herself a job at £90 making beds, with free transport and meals thrown in. Two or more years ago I was visiting a friend when his son of seventeen came in having completed the first week's work he had ever done. He put eight £10 notes on the table and said 'Dad, that's what they gave me—is that all right?'

The Sullom Voe terminal will by 1981 be capable of handling one million four hundred thousand barrels of oil per day or about half of the British oil production and equal to two-thirds of her consumption. Shetland and Orkney between them will handle oil equal in bulk to the total consumption of Britain. Sullom will be the largest oil terminal in Europe. This oil having been stabilised and relieved of its gasses is to be shipped off in tankers of up to 300,000 tons.

The population of Shetland outside the camps reached 21,000 in 1978, having been under 18,000 a few years before. This huge cuckoo of oil which has settled in Shetland cannot fail to disturb the native birds, the traditional way of life and industries.

Though Sullom is the area where the paraphernalia of oil is seen most dramatically, Lerwick Harbour is full of strange vessels such as ocean-going tugs and oil platform supply vessels with their high bridges fore and their low platforms astern. Sometimes when you look across the harbour from Lerwick a tall rig illuminated at night like a Christmas tree lies, an exotic monster, between you and the island of Bressay. Lerwick harbour now extends some two miles from its old confines, occupying once again the herring stations. At the Southern tip of Shetland Sumburgh airport, which when I first arrived there was a single hut, now hums all day with aeroplanes and helicopters.

People and local authorities have to grapple with all this. It may be that the Shetland Islands Council by the Bill giving it such wide powers to take a share in the development of oil, has bitten off more than it can chew. It might have been wiser to be content with the levy exacted on every barrel of oil. But then again Shetland wanted a say in the decisions which so vitally affected her. The danger of pollution alone is something from which Shetlanders could not stand aside.

The local councillors of Shetland and Orkney have taken the strain which all this has imposed with a resilience which must increase our admiration for democracy. But the sea may be even rougher for them in the years to come. The two men now in charge, Mr. Tulloch and Mr. Eunson, were among my first adherents in the Islands. They have deserved well of their neighbours. But the running down of oil may bring in its wake problems even more difficult than its advent has posed. Housman wrote 'Get you the sons your fathers got and God will save the Queen'. The sons and daughters of the present generation of islanders will have to be at least as tough and public-spirited as their fathers. We must hope that the public of their day will be served by political institutions less adrift in the face of new demands and more pliant to the wishes of the electorate.

In Orkney and to an even greater extent in Shetland the Islands Councils is branching out into national, and even international, affairs. Whether this is a result of the loss of interest in the old national politics and the old parties or whether it is a fortuitous corollary, I am not sure.

In Shetland, the 'Shetland Movement' has drawn up a manifesto which ranges over a variety of subjects which thirty years ago would have been placed in different political categories. Most of these subjects too would have been classified as outside the scope of councillors elected on local issues. The Shetland Movement embraces the future structure of government in the Islands which is a constitutional matter and fishing policy which is a matter for Westminster and Brussels.

In Shetland and Orkney the local councils have large commitments at Sullom and Flotta in connection with oil. They run oil ports. Shetland I.C. are partners, even if largely sleeping partners, in industrial enterprises. They are being drawn further and further into industry. From being shareholders in various undertakings of large size and new to the islands, Shetlanders are now talking of taking over small indigenous businesses. If this trend goes on they will soon be trying to run fishing boats and fried fish shops. We should be considering the implications of such an extension of the traditional activities of Councils. If we do not pause and take stock soon, we may lapse into the error Britain has made over public control of industry. It is doubtful if the granting of special powers to deal with the handling by a local authority of matters connected with the discovery of oil were intended to extend so far. If they are extended the code of conduct for local councillors may need to be amended. But, above all, local councillors are neither elected to exercise these new functions nor have they the means to do so. They are very much part-time, unpaid, busy people.

I am not writing a hand-book on local government. I mention this new departure because it may deeply affect the future of Orkney and Shetland. It is also symptomatic of the new outlook. The schoolmasters and merchants who were active in politics twenty-five years ago, the hecklers at the back of the Lerwick town hall, the writers and readers of the local newspapers, were concerned about large political issues: they resolutely held to Liberal, Labour or Conservative principles; they read or argued about politics and wrestled with general questions affecting mankind. Now politics are more like the running of a faceless conglomerate: the local directors leave many decisions to their officials and few people are much interested in what aims the parent company should pursue so long as it pays off.

That the party system needs revision has long been my view. But I adhere to my belief that political principles should set our course. We should not shrug our shoulders over the eternal controversies of politics. However, as someone who feels that we must revive communities I look with a modicum of benevolence at the turn which Shetland politics are taking. My optimism is indeed cautious. I am uncertain how far the Shetlanders will go in taking more responsibility on their own shoulders. They could be about to surrender even more abjectly to bureaucratic interests intent on pushing out their empire. Local councillors are already heavily laden. The burden on local councillors is in few places more onerous than in Orkney and Shetland. Nevertheless, in this, Orkney and Shetland may be blazing a trail others must tread. We should expose and examine this adventure into new fields. The public should be alerted to what is happening. The public knows too little. Lippman long ago likened the public as it looks at public affairs to a deaf man in the back row of the stalls. The deaf man is more bemused today than he was in the twenties when Lippman wrote, for the number of actors on the stage of public affairs has multiplied with authorities and boards of every kind: while sub-plots hatch out daily and dressers and stage hands are legion. The bewilderment of the deaf and remote man will not, as I have already said, be dispelled by simply providing more information. The play must be simplified. The plot must be clarified. The audience must have standards by which they can judge the moment to applaud or boo. But above all, as I have mentioned, the public still requires an impartial body of representatives not engaged in huckstering, not a dedicated set, much less a private interest on their own, and it is difficult for a local authority which is entangled in commercial undertakings to fulfil this requirement.

Meanwhile, alongside the oil economy the old economy of the islands runs on. But for the old economy of crofting, fishing and knitwear the clouds which had been long discernible were getting larger and blacker. People still want Shetland jerseys but here too the future may be precarious. Said to be pure Shetland wool is difficult to spin, being short and often dirty. In spite of many efforts to promote one there is no spinning mill in Shetland. There are few pure Shetland sheep on the islands now. But the crossbreeds still retain some of the agility and hardiness of their forebears. As elsewhere, the towns have grown at the expense of the country. Standardisation and centralisation of thought as well as conduct and an expanding bureaucracy were changing Orkney and Shetland before oil was discovered. There is some revolt but new habits are strong. More money, so much needed and so welcome, nevertheless brings with it the abandonment of much that was typical and in its way enjoyable. Shetlanders who worked their own crofts or boats are becoming 'hands' to be hired, checked in, put on a weekly wage and regimented. This expensive economy is draining men and women from the traditional way of life. It teaches no skills. When the oil boom is over, indeed when the construction boom associated with oil is over, we may be left with a generation accustomed to a high standard of life but with no means of earning it. The crofter finds prices forever rising while his income does not keep pace.

The effect of modern trends upon the political economy of Shetland worried me. I had, as I have said, started a small scheme in conjunction with the local doctor, Dr. Dowle, in Northmavine, the northerly district of the mainland of Shetland, to encourage all-round development. The thought which led to this scheme and a parallel project in Greenock was that the conventional type of personal social services had been pushed as far as they could go. These services also suffered from defects. I believed we should put far more effort into giving everyone a better chance in life rather than trying to ameliorate failure. This meant bringing every community up to the best standard of which it was capable. Each community had different possibilities. The social services with their poor law background aimed too low. Every community should have the greatest possible control over its own future. The existing social services were handed down—again a poor law legacy—and increasingly handed down from the centre. Welfare should not be confined to monetary payments for the relief of poverty. It should include all kinds of opportunity for self-expression and employment, transport, health, housing, etc. All these affected the community and its welfare. We were too departmentalised. In Shetland crofting and fishing and the industries which went with them were vital to welfare. I procured money from the Joseph Rowntree Social Service Trust to finance these experiments. We had just appointed Miss Sampson to be the community's civil servant in Northmavine when oil-related construction started. She proved a great success. But more and more young people in Northmavine got jobs at Sullom Voe, just to the South. They became commuters; and very tired commuters at that, too tired when they got home to do much more about crofting or amusement. For this last they looked to their week off when they usually left Shetland altogether.

The crofter or fisherman and their wives were people of many skills. They tilled the croft and usually had another job, fishing, knitwear, road work, etc. They were handy with tools. They worked at home so that amusement and work were to some extent intermingled as in Abbotsford Crescent kitchen or the Orkney farmyard. All that went. The local show Miss Sampson was organising had to be cancelled. Dr. Dowle kept in operation the small fish processing factory which he had started but it was not easily done. All over Shetland knitwear manufacturers found their knitters tempted by the oil-related work. Shops lost their assistants and there was a grave fear that fishermen would go off to supply vessels and the stand-by boats at the rigs and platforms. It was splendid to have this new employment at high wages but it was temporary, and it taught no skills. There was little or no 'spin off' from oil. Traditional industries which had been expanding and on which we should have to rely in the future were suffering. I was afraid that the aftermath of oil might be as disastrous as the death of coal mining for some mining villages.

By 1977 these fears were aggravated by the cloudy future for fishing. Shetland fishermen did very well in the middle seventies. But the closure of distant waters drove more and more English and Scotch trawlers into Shetland waters. Boats had acquired immense catching power. Meanwhile, the Europeans claimed these waters as European and there was no agreement on a common fisheries policy. The results of this could be most serious. To take an extreme example, suppose the attractions of oil, allied to a failure of the fishing (*all* herring fishing was banned in 1977/78), drove out of business the three fishing boats which maintained the population of Skerries in Shetland, the islands would have to be evacuated. They had no hinterland: no possibility of other means of livelihood. Fishing was the one occupation which had maintained the population. Though fishing was the industry most seriously threatened, knitters and shop assistants too went off to work at Sullom. Their employers could not compete with the wages offered by the oil construction firms. The Islands Councils were getting considerable sums from oil with the prospect of more. But that alone would not rebuild fishing or knitwear once they and the way of life which went with them were disrupted. The Councils found also that they were involved in heavy expenditure. Rates and rateable values rose dramatically. So did the price of food, drink and hotel rooms. Taxis proliferated. Certainly houses were improved and equipped with new carpets and curtains, refrigerators, washing machines and deep freezes. The size and number of cars increased (Orkney has always had a lot of cars but many are old, rusted though trusted, rather than new and shining). But local productive investment did not gain at anything like the same rate.

We must offer training for the era which will succeed the oil con-

275

struction boom. But what sort of training? Too often training escalates into highly sophisticated, fashionable but sometimes slightly out of date technology, or boils down to packages of expensive equipment such as decorates the 'domestic science' departments of too many schools. 'Structure plans' and such like dog the responses which changing moods and opportunities demand. When employment in oil-related industries runs down the service occupations may be the expanding market. We must adapt our training to meet each new scene. We must trim quickly to new turns of demand, unfettered by rigid presuppositions.

18

SHORTLY AFTER I HAD resigned as Leader of the Liberal Party Laurence Scott asked me to become a Trustee and Director of the *Guardian*. I had not been in the *Guardian* building in Cross Street since I visited it with David Astor and Adam von Trott before the war. Thirty-five years or more had passed since I had been in the *Guardian* lift but I found it just the same, still stumbling and creaking up and down, packed with printers, journalists and office boys. Indeed, much of the building had not changed since C. P. Scott's day; it has now been pulled down, but the panelling and the table round which we met are preserved among the hallowed riches of Manchester; friendly Manchester where it is a pleasure to buy a gallon of petrol or chat to the bus conductors.

Laurence Scott, his brother Charles and their cousin, Richard, the Chairman of the Trust, were as noteworthy as many better-known dynasties, whether of the press or the aristocracy. They carried into the last half of the 20th century much of the ability and outlook of C. P. Scott. Those who think of the age of Liberalism as a time of greed should consider the history of such families as the Scotts and the Rowntrees. Those Marxists who believe that all motives are material might also do so. Had the Scott family sold the *Manchester Guardian* and kept the *Manchester Evening News* they could have been rolling about the Mediterranean in steam yachts. They showed no regret nor envy. The Scott Trust was devoted to the well-being of the newspapers, particularly the *Guardian*, the Scott family were content to serve it. All the ordinary shares in the *Guardian* and the *Manchester Evening News* were held by the Scott Trust. No dividends were declared, so all profits could be ploughed back into the papers. The printers and journalists who are reducing Fleet Street to anarchy would benefit from following the example of the Scotts. They may call themselves Socialists but some of them show little concern either for the general well-being nor for the welfare of their papers.

The advantages of Trust ownership were obvious. We did not have to worry about shareholders. But it did not mean that we could ignore profitability. On the contrary, especially in inflationary times, the prospect of replacing our machinery etc. was always a spectre at the table. Absence of shareholders helped our relations with the chapels but it did not exempt us from the difficulties of labour relations. We were not a workers' co-operative, so the workers, though they could not complain that the surplus they created went to shareholders, had not a direct stake in the business like say, the Mondragon or Scott-Bader employees. How far the staff should be associated with the management of the papers was a matter we intermittently discussed. I believe that there is no single pattern for workers' participation which can be applied uniformly throughout industry. Editors kept the chapels well informed of what was going on and we had active and retired journalists (including Richard Scott and Francis Boyd) among the trustees. But these journalists were not chosen by their colleagues but by the Trust. When Peter Preston was appointed editor we went through an elaborate process of consultation. Should we, could we have gone further? Yes, I think we could but in the circumstances we were wise to err on the side of caution.

The future of the paper was, as I have said, at one time somewhat precarious. In such circumstances some confidentiality is necessary. To have exposed all possibilities and difficulties to universal discussion could have led to panic and chaos. To have had among the trustees or on the board members whose first loyalty was elsewhere would have inhibited frank discussion. There were, too, many employees who did not want this type of open deliberation but only a well managed enterprise in which they could get on with their jobs. If workers are to take part in the running of a business they must have a stake in it and give their first loyalty to it and not to their Union—this, owing to the present structure of the press and indeed of British industry could not be achieved.

Whatever the structure, good industrial relations depend on personal relations. The *Guardian* and *Manchester EveningNews* were lucky to have Charles Scott in charge of personnel. But even so we were somewhat class-ridden, industrial class, that is. I can't believe that the segregation of management practised in British Industry is necessary or helpful. Directors' dining rooms, for instance, should be used somewhat sparingly —there may be occasions when directors want to talk in private but common canteens should surely be the normal rule.

If an undertaking is owned by a trust it can only raise new capital by loan. It cannot offer equity shares. This too can be a drawback. The Scott

278

Trust has, I believe, preserved the traditions of the *Guardian*. These have been good for Britain. But I do not think it offers a model which should be universally followed. However, it is certainly one of several ways forward. What was central to this way was that the trust owned the shares. It was in a different and much stronger position than, for instance, the trust once set up to watch over the *Times* which had not the sanction of ownership.

When I joined it the fortunes of the paper were in crisis. The *Manchester Guardian* had just moved to London, struck 'Manchester' out of its title and cast out to become a complete national daily. Financially, it was in difficulties and there had been some talk of amalgamation with *The Times*. A protagonist in the move to London and an opponent of any merger was the editor, Alastair Hetherington. I am sure we were right to cherish our independence. Anyone who wants to pursue further the possibility of *Guardian*-like trusts as a contribution to the future of the press should read David Ayerst's *Biography of a Newspaper*—and incidentally anyone who wants to learn how to write the best kind of journalism should study his prose—in the same class as those other *Guardian* giants Alistair Cook and Max Freedman.

Beside the Scott Trust the other Trust on which I served was the Joseph Rowntree Social Service Trust. Joseph Rowntree, who saw ahead of his time, set up a trust to look after the village which he founded for his cocoa factory workers at York. This is now the richest of the Rowntree Trusts as property has grown more valuable. He then set up a straightforward charitable trust, largely for Quaker purposes. Finally, he gave money for the Social Service Trust which is not strictly a trust at all but a limited company. What makes it so valuable is that since we pay tax we can do what we like with the money. We have less of it, of course, but we are almost the only body of our kind which is free from the strings of charitable law. I have found sitting on the Trust one of the most interesting jobs I have ever done.

I hope that one day a monograph may be written on the work of the Trust. Such trusts can play a useful part by financing off-beat experiments: experiments which would be thrown out by state-financed organisations or, if grudgingly accepted, would grow stale in their hands.

A full examination of the utility of the Rowntree and other trustees remains to be undertaken. Here I only want to make two points: to emphasise once again how many people there are in Britain who give up time and ability to public work and how varied they are. There are eight trustees. The Trustees or Directors of the Rowntree Social Service Trust. Ted Goodman and Roger Wilson have a common background that is liberal (with a small 'l'—Roger, I imagine, votes Labour) but they are very different from each other, both original and both deeply interested in human beings. The Rowntrees, Roger, and David Shutt have continued the Quaker tradition which, as I mention elsewhere, has much to contribute I believe to the working of Parliament. Bill Morrell, a most admirable chairman, and Richard Wainwright lead busy lives (as indeed do the other directors) one on a provincial newspaper, the other as an M.P. Trevor Smith is a whole-time lecturer: indeed he devotes more than the usual ration of time to his job. He is constantly and expertly helping those who ask his advice. Roger Wilson is still an active lecturer while, though retired from academic life, Pratap occurs in various capacities throughout these memoirs. It is a good thing, I believe, to have a bunch of such people together without too much protocol. Richard Rowntree has been commendably a little worried that we are responsible to no one but ourselves. This does not worry me.

Another lesson which we have learnt is the good that can be done by giving people of enterprise small sums, quickly. Some of our more grandiose operations have not paid off as have some which have cost a few hundred, or in these inflationary times, a few thousand pounds.

Such trusts should not compete with the affluent public research organisations but, taking a different perspective, they may indulge in speculative thinking about our condition which we are told is debarred to cabinet ministers or civil servants in the deluge of every day decisions by which they are swamped. Trusts may do something to plug the gaps in our welfare state (though they cannot do very much) and they may rescue a few of those who have fallen through the sieve of the welfare services. Pratap has proved that it is possible to run such an organisation most efficiently on a tiny staff, which never grows.

These matters added to the general issues of inflation and the troubles of the Liberal Party took up much of my time between 1974 and 1978.

In 1976 we flitted from Kew Green to the 'garden city' of Bedford Park, carrying with us Mary MacDonald and her son who had lived in part of our Kew house and now settled in the top of our new house, absolving us from much worry and discharging such irksome tasks as answering the telephone and door bell, shopping, etc.

Magnus had now moved to Stromness Academy. He refused to leave Orkney for a boarding school. Neither Laura nor I pressed him to do so. So as a parent I have had some experience of different types of secondary education. Two sons at Eton, one at Stromness Academy and a daughter as a day girl at St Paul's. All very good schools, all had advantages. For pure teaching with a view to examinations I would put St Paul's first. Eton taught well and to some extent at least still offered those other advantages it had when I was there. As I have said, the level of schoolmasters in Orkney was high. At Finstown school, Mr. Tulloch had a worthy successor in Mr. Kent. When Grizelda and Johnny were there his influence both in the school and parish was profound.

The way of life in my constituency was changing but it continued. Shetland and Orkney had been through upheavals and invasions before. The old Norn language lingered on in the 'Du' and 'Da' ('you' and 'the') of Shetland and in the local words for anything connected with the sea, such as the names for sea birds and parts of a boat and for different areas of the sea itself showing how strong a link it had been. Dr. Ernest Marwick, journalist and broadcaster, like Mr. Mackay, the Sanday schoolmaster, largely self-taught, recorded much Shetland and Orkney lore. Steeped as he was in the history of the islands, attuned to their ways and widely read in European literature no one could have done it better. He followed in the footsteps of his namesake, Dr. Hugh Marwick, Director of Education in Orkney when I first went there, a man of learning as well as an administrator who wrote a definitive work on Orkney place names and provided the most delicious cress sandwiches (until I wrote this book I did not realise how full my memories are of food). We had plenty of researchers and television teams but they flocked down the same paths too often and missed much that was worth recording.

For instance, there lived at this time in the island of Westray an old farmer, Mr. Drever of Broch. I have mentioned that in some ways he was in the tradition of my cousins at Oakbank. If you wanted to get a taste of what Scotch farms may have been like at the time of Scott you could get it at Broch, a gaunt farm house with little modernisation. Mr. Drever was devoted to cart-horses. It is said that in his agricultural return soon after the war he entered 34, or it may have been 36, cart-horses. When the officials questioned this he replied that they were quite right, he now had two extra foals. I remember sitting in his kitchen one night, ceremoniously drinking whisky at the table where he sat on such occasions, his cap upon his head, in front of the huge black cooking range while a woman was patiently feeding a sick lamb from a bottle. Suddenly the lamb died. It was unceremoniously kicked aside. Life went on. In old age Mr. Drever got rid of his horses. I was therefore surprised when a few years later I saw five outside his house. He had bought a fresh lot. He could not live without them. One night when I was chatting with him I told him I had been touring the North Isles. 'You needn't have bothered' he said, ticking off the islands on his fingers, 'there's nothing in Sanday but pride, poverty and drink. There's no poverty in Stronsay, just pride and drink.' 'What about your own island of Westray?' I asked. 'Hypocrisy and preaching' he replied.

Then there was Tom Sinclair, the boatman on the island of Rousay. I once met him and his wife, hay rakes over their shoulders, coming along one of the clover lined roads of Rousay. It was the sort of weather the Romans must have met in the Pentland Firth when they thought the water was land, it was so calm. I enquired after a mutual acquaintance who had suffered a stroke. 'He's been struck aside' Tom answered in his deep bass voice. 'They say he's very cheerful. He was a big strong man and they say he's very cheerful. I would rather be dead.' Don't we all fear the day when our friends say 'He's wonderful for his age'.

The kitchens of Orkney and Shetland continue to be pleasant places with peat fires, the hanging clocks brought presumably from some pedlar, all made in New England, often decorated with pictures of American opera houses and public buildings painted on glass. Tea is always ready, often accompanied by bere bannocks.

Meanwhile in 1945 my brother-in-law, Billy, became Chief Scout, a job which he did conspicuously well though I always found his attachment to youth selective and I would not have had complete faith in his ability to discharge all the humbler chores of scouting: for instance, I am not sure whether he would have unfailingly got a fire to light even if supplied with fire-lighters and petrol. After retiring as Chief Scout Billy was made Governor of Tasmania in 1959.

In these and his many other public activities my sister, Gwyn, loyally supported her husband. Though she never shirked it, she was not cut out for public life. I seem to remember that she gracefully resigned from the Girl Guides owing to difficulty in refraining from laughing on parade. She never seemed comfortable in smart clothes, retaining to the end of her days the look of a little girl who, having been told not to climb trees in her best stockings, had composed her face into a suitable solemnity which she knows she will find difficulty in supporting for long. However, she worked for many good causes though not always perhaps quite as they expected. I once arrived at Rowallan to find her preparing to regale a committee of the R.S.P.C.A. with a delicious snack of freshly boiled lobsters.

When my sister and brother-in-law were away, Fiona, the only daughter, presided over the house. Bobby was active in providing luxuries and adornments of all sorts and supervised the gardens. Billy and Gwyn had never lived a Spartan life but neither were they continuously or acutely aware of their surroundings. Billy had filled the house with pictures by McBey. Now Bobby unearthed all kinds of long-put-away Victorian knick-knacks and curious old photographs—such as the opening of Glasgow sewage works in the last century. If the large Rowallan greenhouses could not supply enough flowers they arrived from London —so did champagne—although my brother-in-law was a leading teetotaller. However, Malvern Water was supplied in the bedrooms. When Bobby was away my sister filled the bottles up from the bath taps. Unlike one strain of Grimond–Corbett blood which remains pale, even in Orkney and Italy, as evinced by Johnny, Bobby developed a complexion suitable to a Master of Foxhounds which he became. What an odd selection of my friends were keen hunters, Bobby, my sisters, my brother-in-law's sister, Elsie, my brother-in-law, Willie, a judge in Texas, Hugh Boileau, Reggie Paget and Raymond Carr, the Master of St Anthony's College. I myself have never pinned much faith in the sagacity or good-will of riding horses, those 'perilous imbeciles' as Renoir described them: glue would not keep me in a saddle nor am I brave enough to laugh it off when catapulted out of it.

Having myself been unintelligible when young and deaf when old I sympathise with Bobby over his conversational difficulties. Even those with hearing like a weasel have found him on occasion difficult to follow. It is said that he worked for a season with Jardine Matheson but this has never been proved. However, he gave up a great deal of time to seeing that people enjoyed themselves. Margot Asquith would have approved of Bobby's way of life and 'heart'. My sisters adored him and Gwyn readily handed over to him tasks which she only spasmodically attempted.

The next eldest son, Joey, also had 'heart'. Considering that my brother-in-law approved of a strict upbringing for children, was a teetotaller, Chief Scout and in theory a disciplinarian, the out-turn, as the Chancellor of the Exchequer might say, of his children though on the whole satis-factory was unexpected. Joey farmed but, as far as I ever saw, largely through the windows of a comfortable house, from which he also directed successful operations on the Stock Exchange. He was an excellent host or guest and thoroughly deserved his wife Catherine, one of the large family of Actons whom he had picked up in Rhodesia. She contributed a very valuable element to Rowallan and indeed to other places. She found the climate cold and had no athletic ambitions. So just when one badly needed a rest and some beautiful object on which to rest the eye, there she was looking elegant in the drawing room and always ready for gossip.

The second son, Attie, having left Eton prematurely was sent to Gordonstoun. He then became a national hunt rider and later a trainer. From early youth he had been devoted to animals. He seldom stayed long at Rowallan owing to the calls of his horses at Newmarket. Unlike Joey, Catherine and the Grimonds who normally put in the best part of a week at Christmas, he would arrive on Christmas eve, grin round rather enigmatically and leave after lunch on Christmas Day taking, alas, Peggy Petre with him. Nancie and her younger son, Mark, would motor over from Teasses and her elder son Tim and his wife sometimes came from

London. But Rowallan had plenty of room. Fiona was a marvellously capable and self-possessed hostess when my sister was away. In many houses a sigh of relief goes up when even one's nearest and dearest tear themselves away, simply because it relieves congestion. Rowallan never felt congested; it was a house in which guests lived rather than stayed, as I suppose they did in the 18th century when visits of at least a month were the fashion. Of my sister's other children, the eldest lived in Spain and the third son had been killed in the war. When Billy and Gwyn died Rowallan was inherited by their grandson, Johnny. Fiona married Garry Paterson and bought a house near Newbury. They are, however, I am glad to say, readily available in London.

Johnny had stifled his yearning to work in Africa. In May 1973 he married Kate Fleming and settled down on the *Economist* for which he has worked for some years. The Flemings, like the Grimonds, had originally come from the neighbourhood of Dundee. Indeed, there was a story, apocryphal I am told, that Robert Fleming, Kate's great grand-father, had, when employed by those cousins of ours, the Gilroys, made them a great deal of money by investing in American Railways. He felt entitled to ask for a rise in salary. He was summoned before the Gilroys, seated round their great mahogany board room table to be congratulated on his good advice. 'We see', they told him 'that you are paid £50 a year, we are prepared to make it guineas.' So he left to make a fortune in London. I am now told that he was never employed by the Gilroys but at any rate had he not made off south we should never have had Kate in the family which would have been a tragedy, for her parents Peter and Celia lived at Merrimoles near Henley and though the Flemings still owned the Black Mount in Argyllshire it is a long way from Orkney. I have always looked forward to daughters-in-law and have not been disappointed. They have a more difficult time these days for they must still run a house and family, but now they in some degree are expected to do a multitude of other things as well not least to entertain their relations in law.

One of the most agreeable of jaunts in the '60s and '70s was going to stay at Busento with my brother and sister-in-law, Mark and Leslie Bonham Carter. The villa had been built by Leslie's mother, another Leslie, to her own design. She ought to be made President of the R.I.B.A. or at least employed to re-design British Embassies. The nub of the house was a terrace above the Bussento river which by some dispensation of a water works or the Almighty never went dry. Across the river lay a carpet of trees concealing allotments where grew the exotic vegetables of southern Italy; from this green sea rose like rocks from sea-weed the roof and towers of Policastro, an ancient town, hardly more than a village but the seat of a Bishop. All around stood mountainous ramparts, here and there their towers capped by villages, their ribs clothed in scrub and above them the honey-golden atmosphere of the Mediterranean. What pleasure to lie in the river while the grey water tugged at the banks and tried to pluck you off the stones into its tingling embrace or to be on one's back in the milky, placid Mediterranean, so different from the savage winter seas which churned and crashed around Orkney, gazing at the deserted cliffs where the spare ruins of an anti-Saracen tower looked out from a promontory.

Those who live much in the north yearn for the sun and expand under its beneficence. How nice for a week or two to be sun-lapped in a warmth which makes it possible to mingle indoors and outdoors. How often do glittering days in Orkney prove bitterly deceptive when you step outside the front door.

I have long believed that women should play a much bigger part in our affairs. Indeed, I sometimes think that without such a change the human race may be doomed. Already the cupidity of the male for both prestige and resources, the vice of the Barbarian, is endangering civilisation. One day male aggression may explode in the nuclear bomb. But the most flagrant view of male-dominated governments is shown in our failure to use women in the endless web of public offices. Laura, Leslie, Cressida, Grizelda, Kate and the Sinclair daughters, scores of women I know, are admirably equipped to serve on public bodies. They would bring to them in addition to brains much more lively than the worn apparatus of the typical male board member, talents which are very varied embracing diplomacy, organisation and human relations of every kind.

Apart from Busento I have, alas, been to the Mediterranean all too little since the war. A long week-end is all I have ever spent in Venice. For most of our stay that subject of so much fine writing refused to play up for us. No veils of shimmering light, no sparkle on the ripples: the towers and domes sprang not from pearly mists but drenching rain. It was as cold as Shetland. The crumbling palaces, with their flunkeys long departed dabbled their worn steps in the choppy waters of the Grand Canal. The rain dripped from the eaves and splashed in the puddles until by lighting a candle for the Virgin I procured an afternoon of blazing sun and sun-shot cloud like the Assumption of the Virgin in the Frari. That week-end, however, was redeemed not only by the excitement of Venice, which not even rain can obscure, but by the Kee family, most sympathetic of travelling companions. Another trip of happy memory was to stay with Nicko (Sir Nicholas) and Mary Henderson in Spain. Nicko, then our Minister in Madrid, arranged a short tour to the walled cities of the interior. The architecture of Spain seems to me almost more breathtaking and less tourist-ridden than the wonders of Italy: some of it has a dignity and curious brindled colour I have seen nowhere else. I owe the Hendersons many pleasant memories but, above all, I am grateful for the Spanish expedition. Incidentally, Cynthia Kee and Mary Henderson should be added to the list of under- or wrongly-used women: God knows they have been busy enough. Mary has now presided over three Embassies. I cannot understand how the Ambassadresses survive on an endless treadmill of cocktail parties. As for Cynthia, she teaches all day and entertains all evening. Blessed with a capacity of associating ideas almost as unexpected as Jasper Ridley's I often wonder what she makes of the schoolchildren or they of her—but they are exceedingly lucky to have her. I fear that in another ten years unless we carry the counter-revolution against bureaucracy teachers like Cynthia will no longer be found in our schools. They will be dismissed as 'unstructured' or 'unqualified'.

Are the male walls of Jericho about to collapse? In the last thirty years we have seen campaigns which seemed when launched to have little hope of success pushed by a few resolute protagonists to victory: the right to surrender a peerage, the abolition of the death penalty, students on the courts and councils of universities—none of these causes had anything approaching the justification or support of the cause of women. Only ten years ago it would have been unthinkable that the Tory party should be led by a woman. Yet progress is slow. Women have been emancipated since the First World War. My brother-in-law Billy's sister with her friend Miss Dillon went one further than the V.A.D.s and women workers in that war by driving an ambulance in the Balkans during the Serbian retreat. The reason for this delay for their full recognition as the equals of men could be that women are still trying to break into a man's world. The triumph will be when the customs of the world are changed to make it a mixed male/female world. Home life and public life, the ordering of work (look around the House of Commons itself) are still tailored for men. How justified was Barbara Castle's cry 'If only I had a wife'. But just as on a mountain false summits continually disappoint the climber, so perhaps quite soon the landscape may change and for women it will be down-hill all the way.

Meanwhile all our children had left school and Grizelda and Johnny had daughters of their own. They will grow up in a different world from pre-war St Andrews or indeed the London and country houses of my own and my wife's youth. But they seem to behave so far in much the same way as their parents. Jessie, the daughter of Kate and Johnny, even makes the same noises as her father did at her age. Katharine, Grizelda's daughter, commutes about the world visiting Tony Richardson in France and America. I think as a child I should have found it disturbing, but then I was used to the first 'Jessie' in my life, the long, slow, years in a nursery where nothing changed, not even the linoleum which I had crawled on. But Katharine, my granddaughter, seems to take it all as it comes. Aeroplanes are as familiar to her as cabs were to me. I see now that battening on their children is a hereditary trait of the Grimonds, like shopping, just as my parents spent months at Rowallan, so I am constantly to be found in their houses. Indeed, both Laura and I see a good deal of our families. Even apart from Bussento I am often at Mark and Leslie's house in London where friends of all ages from Leslie's mother to the three Carter daughters are constantly entertained. Laura's brother, Raymond, has become a merchant banker in the house of Warburg and lives with his wife Elena not too far away in Hampstead. The Corbetts and Tim Black are to be found for at least long periods in London and I drop in on my sister in Fife from time to time. Even Cressida, now an eminent Greek archaeologist—an occupation particularly suited to her as it combines the need for the highest intellectual activity with, I imagine, considerable physical strength, lives in Wiltshire and is becoming more accessible. Meanwhile her extremely intelligent son has become Mrs. Thatcher's speech-writer—an event which must cause his father, when he looks down, a good deal of humming and hair-twisting. Magnus alone after a brief trial of 'abroad' shows a steady determination not to leave Orkney.

I mention all this which may not seem very exciting because I find the ripples of family life interesting. It is extraordinary how quickly families expand and vanish, cousins disappear into limbo, a spreading generation leaves hardly a soul behind. Of the descendants of my wife's eleven uncles we see hardly any. Friends too change. From Dalnawillan days we still occasionally see Elizabeth and Michael Lyle, the Lyle daughters and Catherine, Robin and Margaret Sinclair. From Mockbeggars, Natalie and Humphrey Brooke: John Gilmour I see almost every day in the House of Commons and Lionel and Christian Brett appear from time to time but of my surviving contemporaries male or female from the pre-war world I see very few. I do not think this particularly matters though I rather enjoy coming across old friends or even acquaintances every now and then, a little gossip, for instance, with Frank Wilson who is still my family's solicitor though ostensibly retired. But families, I believe, though subject to rending earthquakes of disruption, have certain advantages to give to their members. In a troublesome world it is worth clinging to some family ties. As I mentioned, I count it as a blessing that my parents never demanded demonstrations of affection. That does not mean that we were not affectionate. I adored my father but it would perhaps selfishly never have occurred to me either that I had to reassure him about this or that he did not return it. One of the great reliefs to my mind of being intimately related is that special behaviour is not demanded nor moral nor intellectual judgements. I take the family as the green of the grass or the warmth of the fire. I do not censor the grass for not being green enough: if the fire burns brightly so much the better but, if not, it is not a matter for blame. I am not sure that I have always felt like this or that for all children it is the right prescription. But to me it is a great relief. I have not, at least for years, considered how I should behave to my sisters or had a moment's tremor that they might not be glad to see me. Neither liked my politics—neither mentioned the matter. What orphans suffer from may not only be lack of affection but the absence of a haven sheltered against the tides and storms of personal, particularly sexual, relationships and worry about success.

I like watching the currents of family life as they surface in curious places, the odd similarities which bob up among relations. I notice that Johnny has the same fingernails as my father: nails as familiar to me as his watch-chain from clambering over his knees. My great-grandfather was at one time known as 'flowery Grimond' from the button-holes he always wore plucked from the indoor plants in his houses: Gelda's and Johnny's houses are also full of plants thriving under their care—not at all the subject of that excellent column 'The revolting Garden', one of *Private Eye*'s best features. I hope it has saved many plants from the torture of bad gardeners. The Grimond liking for America may also be hereditary. My grandfather was christened 'George Washington' because his mother was American. Of course, as they get older children get more like their parents but also sometimes unexpectedly like their aunts or uncles. The Grimond-Richardsons lacked professionalism: the Bonham Carter-Asquiths have perhaps an overdose of the critical faculties, perhaps both lack the opportunity to do things with their hands. As Juliet Henley, most percipient of the Liberal girls, once said to me she doubted if Violet had ever baked a cake. Perhaps Kate will put this right as well as bringing new and excellent looks to the family.

One of the casualties of inflation is personal entertainment. At business lunches, conferences, receptions, banquets, official meets official, manager hob-nobs with manager, Ministers of the Crown are tethered next to those who lobby or flatter them, or both. Apart from the waste entailed, for food and drink must be sumptuous even at lunch time, it cannot make up for the decline in private entertaining. Apart from the enjoyment, dropping in to private houses relaxes politicians, gets them out of the Westminster greenhouse and makes them listen to people who have no axe to grind. Mr. Asquith had no government car. How good for him to see the meter ticking up and perhaps even endure the cabbies' opinions.

Now ministers and top officials are wafted from their offices to their clubs, quilted by secretaries, assistants and chauffeurs against the blasts of the ordinary world.

Those like Mrs. Ann Fleming, Leslie and Mark, and indeed Kate and Johnny who still open their houses for what used to be known as browsing and sluicing, confer, in the economist's language, a 'public' as well as a 'private' good. As for travelling, it may not broaden the mind about other countries but it certainly sheds new light on one's own. I have, as I say, twinges of regret that I have not travelled more in Europe, particularly around the Mediterranean. I have never been to Greece. But at least I have seen something of France, Italy and Spain, caught a glimpse of Egypt and strolled around some of the most beautiful cities in the world, in my own time, with my own companions, free to drop into any café at any moment. In twenty years we may not be so lucky. Already we have been indoctrinated to accept restrictions on our money: soon it may be on ourselves. Only on tours so rightly called 'packaged', shall we be able to spend a few niggardly but hectic days in a tourist camp.

My spasmodic harping upon the benefits of chat, entertaining, social life, may seem obsessive, perhaps even flippant. I touch on it in connection with 'the season', Universities, travelling and visiting, it is to be enjoyed in pubs and even in tea shops. Long may it flourish, loud should be the fulmination against those who would kill all private enjoyments by making their cost prohibitive. Such intercourse is, above all, highly instructive, it spreads news, it sifts views. Without it education curls up at the edges like a dry leaf: without it life would degenerate into mere existence—indeed we should never learn to live.

It was Lord Reith who said in a television interview 'I never learnt to live'. To explain himself he went on, 'I doubt if I've ever been young'. After a brief acquaintance with him I think I know what Lord Reith meant. In his case perhaps it didn't matter, perhaps in a queer way he was always young in that he was brash with the dour but endearing doggedness of some young Scots. He was to me like a large combative dog which at one moment rears up straining at the leash and barking at other dogs only to turn round with its tongue hanging out asking to be stroked. Two incidents make me think of him in this way. I was once with him at a luncheon party when sycophantic and silky compliments were being showered on a member of the cabinet. Lord Reith looked up from frowning at his cheese: 'Who are you talking about?' On being told, 'I despise that man' was all he growled and went back to brooding over his plate. However, after lunch when I drove back to Westminster with him he was almost benign. I was once sitting in our garden in Orkney when to my astonishment his large and craggy face rose over the hedge like the sun at dawn. That he was holidaying in Orkney and in a most amiable mood did not dampen his belligerency. On our way to a picnic in a neighbouring island he discovered on the boat a man with whom he had enjoyed a flaming row some years before. He sat glaring at the far end of the boat and the two had to be disembarked at separate piers. Yet after the incident he could not have been more engaging. Disappointed in life he may have been but neither soured nor vindictive, a Victorian grandee out of his time.

However that is a detour from what I wanted to say about his remarks about learning to live. All too many children today without the great personal mine of ambition, ability, honesty and faith on which Reith could draw, never realise that their lives are for living by them and no one else but that to live them well needs some attention. They are packed off at the age of three to have even their play organised, they are patted and rolled and kneaded into the bureaucratic mould. They become afraid of freedom like caged birds and either descend drearily into the blank cages of the organisation-man, starting that descent even at the university, or turn beserk.

The old-fashioned 'bringing out' of girls was partly to show off their faces in the marriage market. But it was also in a snobbish and fumbling method of teaching them to live, to escape from 'the tunnel' of eleven to sixteen through which so many boys and girls, as in Reith's case, make such a heart-rending and lonely passage. Nowadays, as I have said, boys perhaps need bringing out even more than girls. But both often fail to get from their parents that introduction to life which every badger gives to its cubs. When I visited a famous and cheerful girls' school recently I asked if the girls read much. Not much, I was told, and chiefly storeis of violence and the Second World War. They were much absorbed by death. That doesn't surprise me, adolescents often are. But a diet of war stories, that is surprising. I am stumped to guess what it means but something surely must be missing from their youth.

A THEME CAN BE DISCOVERED between the disjointed snapshots which make up this book, however rambling the text may seem. My career has been in the House of Commons. But, as I have remarked, the House of Commons is not only concerned with party manoeuvres and voting: politics, like art, are at the heart of life. Politics are many sided, one side is certainly anchored in the community in which we live. So a politician can surely write about his constituency and what it has meant to him. If he pretends, as he should, to found his politics on what he has learnt and felt, then upbringing, friends and family must be germane to his theme.

Further, the political odyssey falteringly travelled in the preceding pages might be summed up as starting from the starry-eyed hope that all would be well if only the Liberal Party could return to the forefront of our affairs; passing through a phase when it seemed that the reform of the general political system would be enough to put things to rights ending up with the recognition that we must look at the wider currents in our lives. One such current is our relationship one with another our standards of judgement, how far and for what purposes we accept a common way of life and to what sort of government we entrust our liberties.

Ever since some order has been clamped on mankind, violence has been kept in check by force. That force, in countries which have had even fleeting claims to liberty and democracy, has been backed up by some ethic held in broad agreement by an influential element in the community. Of course such an ethic has been constantly derided and jettisoned. But whether it has been the Catholic church, an aristocracy of birth, an educated class, or a series of institutions which look to something other than their own advancement, some such body of opinion has in all civilisations

—as against barbaric tyrannies—set some standard and ultimately after even rebellion or revolution has given some legitimacy to the acts of democratic government.

Some people doubt whether an egalitarian classless society can either breed such a body of opinion or respond to it. Perhaps that remains to be seen. I certainly would agree that a proletariat in which individuals are only to be valued for the role they play and in which they only come together to push the material interests of the groups into which they are corralled cannot do so. But though there are too many people around rubbing their hands at the prospect of proletarianising us all, I do not think they need win.

Had my parents and the other citizens of the St Andrews of my youth foreseen another world war, all Eastern Europe groaning under the iron heel of Russia, freedom snuffed out over most of the world, Communism applauded even after the horrors of Russia and South-East Asia, political murders every week in Northern Ireland and the pound worth one pre-war shilling, they would have concluded that we were about to pass the boundary from which no democracy could return. We have indeed swallowed a lot of ruin.

As I have said, even in the fifties, let alone all in the twenties of this century, no one anticipated the acceleration which we have suffered in our social and economic troubles.

Though we have been caught in storms which shook the world, originating far outside our control, Britain herself must take the blame for a record of affairs grossly mishandled in the last fifty years. In foreign affairs we look back on a long roll of ineptitude—or worse. Abyssinia, appeasement, our dealings with Russia, Cyprus (read Lawrence Durrell's *Bitter Lemons*), the E.E.C., Suez, the Middle East, Central Africa—it is a sorry tale. The policy-makers in the Foreign Office were oblivious to common sense, obstinate when they should have been yielding and then like putty when some obstinacy might have been in order. Nor were the Whitehall ostriches kept short of warnings. They were often too haughty or too blinkered to take any notice. As for home affairs, we have tolerated, indeed fawned upon, the forces which have caused inflation and unemployment. We have shown little foresight in preparing for the future and less dexterity in dealing with the present.

Though like the prophets of Baal wailing to the god that failed, we bleat for more and more to be done for us by the state and its acolytes, yet those acolytes have an exasperating capacity for obstruction. My wife has some notes made by her grandfather, Mr. Asquith, for his speeches. Today when anyone suggests that a piece of expensive mismanagement might be corrected, a battery of difficulties are wheeled up to beat back any solution. Perhaps this is just as well as the execution of any reform today, however well intentioned, is usually botched. But it is surely a symptom of decay, a fungus which is creeping through Britain contributing to the disillusion of the electorate and the wobbly allegiance it affords to the political parties. If all other objections fail we are assured by modern bureaucrats that any suggestion of change will be 'administratively impossible', no matter how absurd, indeed 'administratively impossible' the existing debacle may be. For instance, despite the evidence from each hemisphere that federations can tax locally and federally, loud were the cries of 'impossible' when it was mooted that the Scottish Assembly should levy taxes. In relation to the proposed Irish constitution Mr. Asquith wrote:

'This brings me to explain what are the processes of taxation which under the new state of things will be exercisable in Ireland:

(1) The Imperial Parliament will continue to tax the whole United Kingdom.
(2) The Irish Parliament will have the power
    (a) to reduce or discontinue for Ireland any Imperial tax with the result that the "transferred sum" (the "block grant" in modern terminology) will be correspondingly reduced;
    (b) to impose Irish taxes of their own whether by way of addition to Imperial taxes or otherwise, with the result that the "transferred sum" will be correspondingly increased.'

This seems simple, workable, intelligible—fatal objections in the eyes of modern draughtsmen. Mr. Asquith's language is indeed a refreshing brook when compared with the turgid mud of latter-day political jargon. Of the farm workers (then paid 18/- a week) he wrote: 'Finally, as regards the labourer he should be secured not only a living wage and decent home but what I may call outlet and outlook.' Mr. Asquith then goes on to give his proposals as to how farm servants might become small-holders.

Looking around London it is uglier, dirtier, more expensively and incompetently run than it was ten years ago. Many of the people in the Underground railway look like refugees from a prison camp. The standard of life may statistically be rising but it is difficult to discern greater well-being in either the homes or faces of most people. A certain mulish worry seems a prevalent expression. Yet their avowed inability, in spite of the vast armoury of tools now at their disposal, to conduct affairs economically or competently does not prevent our governors from essaying constant interference in our lives when it suits them. While sane and simple change particularly if it decreases the size of bureaucracy and the waste of resources is vetoed as administratively impossible unwanted upheavals in local government and the tax system are inflicted upon us.

Looking at the blemishes on our public affairs and reflecting how liberalism with a small 'l' has been castrated, its clothes filched and its champions thrown on the defensive, the fears of the pessimists might seem well justified. Perhaps it is only a matter of time before maelstroms at home or attack from abroad sink the Western world in a welter of doubt and recrimination. But it does not strike me as certain. Nor need we drown in our own contradictions.

Let us clear these last out of the way. It is ironic that an age which has incomparably more resources than any before it is so given to wringing its hands about inadequate means. We have resources unimagined by our ancestors. 'Ah', I shall be told, 'but there are now so many of us that even marvels of modern science cannot cope.' Indeed the forecasts of population are terrifying and not to be ignored. But it is some comfort to reflect that had the computer been invented in the last century it would have been predicted that as the rise in population must require more horses we should all by now have been up to our knees in horse dung. Our children will profit from new inventions. It may be that the proliferation of the human race will change its character. The Druses say, I have been told, that just because we choose to breed innumerable children we should not assume that Allah will furnish them all with souls. As all over the world women are emancipated birth-rates will fall. In any case growth in numbers cannot account for the plight of the British. Of course, if no one will do anything for themselves and if everyone must be paid for doing anything—sometimes it seems to me that no one will read Jane Austen or play the piano without a grant—then money will be short. What many clamant beggars—even universities, the Arts Council and the B.B.C.—should practise is more discrimination. The Greeks did not disdain economy; on the contrary, they respected it and treated it as an ally. Their artists worked with their own hands and brains on the hardest of materials. Economy is the hall-mark of art. Baroque exuberance may erupt in fancies and colours, figures and sways of rioting imagination but, if it degenerates into sugary plaster concoctions, it soon palls. Musicians do not clamour for more strings on the violin. It is too much fat, too many cooks cluttering up the kitchen which causes the trouble. We have succumbed to the worship of the great idol of 'more'. Technical and economic determinism, blind to human values, now decides where we must go. Science and machinery, we are told, under the bureaucracies will conjure up more and more of everything. Our role is to sit up and beg, being content with whatever was thrown us. The Christian and Greek teachings which though seldom followed at least pointed the right way are now derided. The Greeks taught the delights of self-expression, play, creation, art. They treated human communities as heirs of past triumphs and guardians of the future. They and their Christian successors hoped that we might by adding to its heritage leave the world a better place. Both the Greeks and Christians rejected the atrocious ambition that we must squander our patrimony, drain the earth of its vitality and deck ourselves out with finery for the sake of prestige. These were the aberrations of the Barbarians. We see now a cult of barbarism—in airlines tricked out with the most expensive planes available, in gigantic buildings, in the burning up of energy, in the scramble for new gadgets and the trampling down of non-conformity. Human beings are discounted.

I am not rattled by apocalyptic nightmares that human beings are spawning machines they cannot control. 'Woe' has been cried at each new invention. We need not go to the other extreme and welcome every new invention as a boon, we should discriminate between inventions and their possible uses. The silicon chip is at present being cast as devil ex-machina. Like gunpowder it may do good or harm. The inventors of gun-powder did not announce that everything must be blown up at once. If they will help to get us what we want, then make or buy inventions. If not, then let others have them. I am unmoved by talk about Britain becoming a scientifically backward country. I do not long to live in a scientifically forward country—whatever that may be. It is not the wonders of its science I like about America. I am not so gullible as to be impressed by the mere possession by a nation of expensive objects—be they machinery or decoration. When I see the aeroplanes of the national air line of some poverty-stricken state I think what rogues its rulers must be, and when I read that some British gallery has spent a million pounds on Italian pictures or French furniture 'to save our heritage' I think what fools its trustees must be. In both cases I pity the taxpayers who must put up the money.

New products and new techniques may upset people's lives. We should certainly shield them from such upsets as far as we can, but that is a different matter. Do not let us lose our heads. It is for us to decide, through the free market I hope, whether we will pay the price for them and there is no shame in buying them from other countries. The apparent contradiction between the might with which science endows us and our chronic bankruptcy is due to our own mismanagement.

Whenever I hear the words 'status' or 'prestige' I reach for my gun. I once attended a banquet at which Mr. Attlee, after he had ceased to be Prime Minister, was present in full fig. During dinner having dropped something he slid dexterously off his chair under the table. The search proved troublesome so one of the flunkeys came to his aid. Their rumps could be seen bobbing about above the table like the sterns of two terriers down a rabbit hole. In due course Mr. Attlee surfaced breathless but triumphant. About half past ten he left to catch the Green Line bus to Cherry Cottage. Seldom can a man have been less concerned about 'face'. I awarded him a round of heartfelt, if silent, applause.

The seeds of the present discontents were sown when we deposed the individual for the sake of organisation and our institutions in favour of interest groups. Let me give an example to illustrate what I have in mind. On the day after my eldest son died during the 1966 General Election my wife was returning from the North Isles of Orkney. A posse of journalists had gathered on Kirkwall pier to pester her. No newspaper proprietor, editor or journalist would of their own volition do such a thing among their own friends. But journalists, like many others, excuse themselves by throwing the responsibility on their profession. On this occasion it came on to rain. The Kirkwall dockers ordered the journalists and everyone else to shelter in a warehouse. The dockers then locked the warehouse and Laura escaped home. I have always been grateful to those dockers for a spontaneous act of decency, much in accord with Orkney behaviour. Now, however, dockers themselves are infected with the general rot. They invoke Union solidarity when exploiting their monopolies, they often show scant consideration for the trade which is the blood of Britain, or for the welfare of passengers who are their fellow citizens.

Unbridled aggression is more and more of a threat. At one time male aggression may have had its uses in defence of the nest. But the male human animal carries aggression far beyond what can be justified. Now that human beings are more and more regimented, the danger is multiplied while the weapons of aggression could annihilate us all. Associations must accept that the golden rule applies to them, as well as to individuals, or rather it applies to the individuals as members of an association. But such an acceptance of canons of behaviour which are the least that can ensure survival, let alone happiness, are not only obscured, they are rejected. The governments of so-called sovereign states debauch their economies, impose the most ruthless tyrannies and resort to wars which may well become nuclear—and they do so in the name of their sacred obligations. Officials of Trades Unions consider it their job to be aggressive. Socialist Governments in the free world employ arms salesmen, indeed they make the sale of arms an important part of government policy.

We must assert some morality to govern the conduct of associations. And this must be codified in law. Law has come to mean whatever those who are temporarily in charge of government may enact, however selfish, oppressive and intolerant it may be and no matter how small the number who support it. But this type of 'law' is a diseased bastard from the true stock. The true conception of law is a code of rules handed down, derived from morality and enforced upon us all, including governments. Of course, particular laws can be changed to meet changing circumstances, but not at the whim of those temporarily in power, and not to feather their nests. 'The rule of law' is the rule of general law. And with the rule of law goes acceptance of a constitution, extended in time, mindful of minorities. Britain has had no need for a written constitution because up to now her statesmen have acted constitutionally—look at the deliberation with which Mr. Asquith moved over to the House of Lords. But now all this is being cast aside; hence the need to contemplate some Bill of Rights.

Much of the dispute about how inflation is to be stopped is beside the point. It may very well be, for instance, that a tighter rein on the supply of money, a sharp cut in government expenditure and a balancing of such expenditure against taxation would stop inflation (certainly some such measures are needed). But when the advocates of this policy tell us that therefore the pressure for higher wages and salaries does not matter, they are blind to the obvious tactic of self-interested corporations who will do their best to block any monetarist move.

If Government has lost its skill, if the party system is withering, and individuals are being dragooned into bureaucracies which themselves less and less obey morality or a general law, what hope is there? I believe there is hope in several directions. Rebels are in the field.

In planning and architecture there are signs that those in charge are changing their tune. There is a striking contrast between architecture and medicine. The latter can claim some of the few unquestioned successes of the last hundred and fifty years. You may well question what good politicians, lawyers, philosophers or publicists have conferred on mankind. But that two in three children do not die and that pain has been rendered less excruciating and that tuberculosis has been almost eradicated are unquestionable blessings. Architecture and planning, on the other hand, have recently been a potent cause of misery. Why this contrast? I suggest because medicine has had to keep in close touch with individuals, its use has been pressed into their hopes, troubles and fears. Architecture has drifted off into abstractions.

But now architects are examining their dogmas. Friends of mine are in the forefront of this re-examination. Lionel Brett (now Lord Esher) has saved York from the desecration wrought in too many cities, his brother-in-law, Sir Martyn Beckett, builds houses both handsome to look at and easy to live in. I recently met an architect who is begging an Arab state not to build a university irrelevant to the poverty of the country and which even at its best will always trail one step behind American and European technology. The Friends of the Earth dispute the lore which teaches that we must tear up and destroy more and more of our real heritage—the countryside and its harvests. Lone prophets, such as Mr. Tyme, the scourge of motorway maniacs, are no longer without honour. In books such as *Charge* by Arthur Seldon a new path to a more satisfactory country has been blazed. These harbingers of a new and imaginative eye are as yet in a minority. The destruction of cities goes on, universities and other mastodons are still at their labours of barbarism but at least there is more protest than ten years ago. These revolts may be sporadic, certainly the armies which they attack are entrenched still in the citadels of government but the enemy is not as confident as he was. But there is another source of optimism. John Stuart Mill wrote 'The emancipation of women and co-operative production are, I fully believe, the two great changes which will regenerate society.' I hope and believe he may be right. I am now Chairman of Job Ownership Limited which has been founded by Robert Oakeshott to nudge existing businesses towards becoming co-operatives and to assist at the birth of new co-operatives. Liberalism and Socialism might get a new breath of life by a partnership between co-operative membership and the free market. There is surely a better way of conducting business than by drilling management and men into opposing armies.

As for women, could they not supply that body of opinion which I have suggested is essential to a free society? Much has gone wrong in the professions for lack of critical clients. Architects are stimulated by patrons, planning cannot be executed in a void, it must be guided by an informed audience. Women are not yet so regimented as men, they stand to gain or lose more by decisions for the longer term.

But it is not only the prospect of co-operation and more feminine influence which cheers me. We have not succumbed to dictatorship, wars, stresses and inflation. We have had no revolution—and revolutions always leave horrors in their wake. We have escaped these disasters because there is still a humane, critical and unselfish public though it may have been thrown on the defensive. We have made grave mistakes in education, mistakes which are the off-spring of the attitudes I have already pilloried. But many schools still turn out well-balanced pupils, capable of making up their own minds. Since this is a personal record I quote an example from my own family. Some years ago, Magnus when at Stromness Academy offered me a programme for Orkney:

1. Renovate old buildings—offer them at a non-profitmaking price to council house tenants on condition that they redecorate them.
2. Bring small industries to the country areas.
3. Collect waste-paper, old cars etc. for re-cycling.
4. Investigate new ways of generating electricity e.g. tidal power, gas, wind.

5. Bring back village policemen and beat patrols.
6. Council work force should be used as a special task force in areas where there is a shortage. (Keynes 'The important thing for government is not to do things which individuals are doing already ... but to do those things which are not done at all.')
7. Make planning more flexible ... cut unnecessary council buildings and staff ... inspect what is happening, make council officials, councillors, etc. get out and about and see how and if their measures are working.

This wisdom if not from babes and sucklings comes from the innocent eye. Only recently those in authority despised it, now it is gaining popularity.

The pleas of educational writers such as Mr. Colin MacLean, the ex-editor of the *Times Scottish Educational Supplement*, Robert Innes at Stirling University and Lord Young for more diversity in schools are biting on many minds. At Oxford, too, the home not only of lost but of noble and victorious causes, the counter-attack against the bureaucratic intellect and bleak corporatism seems to be gaining ground. Lord Blake and ex-Warden Sparrow of All Souls have shown that Masters of Colleges need not sacrifice scholarship to committee-minding. Vice-Chancellors should take heart.

If you look only on the public mask which Britain wears you see her beset by illusions, timidity, lassitude, her standards drooping, some of her once magnificent institutions corroded by fear or greed, her cities decaying or wrecked by motorways and monster blocks. Yet in spite of crime and inflation private life in Britain is often exhilarating, unselfish and wears a smiling face despite broken homes, the boredom of routine work and debilitating draughts of state syrup. As more and more mothers go out to work and fathers find their amusement from outside their home and friends, the family may seem to hover on the edge of dissolution, uncertain of its future, in recoil from its old assertiveness. The bright hopes of Lord Beveridge that the state, the family and the individual would climb together to a new plateau of prosperity have been deflated. The aspirations of the post-war Liberals may seem 'pie in the sky' though scornful cynics may say they 'have flopped to earth unnoticed'.

But such judgement would be unduly harsh. In material ways most people are better off than they were thirty years ago and if we have seemed sometimes to forget that there are many other varieties of poverty besides material impoverishment, this myopic view is now questioned. Some years ago we were all swept along in the rush of the Gaderene swine, now as well as the grunts of 'faster, faster,' some other accents can be heard, questioning the headlong career towards 'more' and 'bigger' and asking whether there may not be a precipice before us.

Grizelda, Kate and Johnny too seem to lead lives they like. I have suggested that by dropping the guard of conventions we have not made growing up easier for all children but at least children are relieved of the worry that they will trip over some unforeseen hazard drawing down reprobation on their bewildered heads.

I detect too that a consensus may be growing amongst the young about the sort of world they want—and if achieved it will be a world much more congenial to my ideas. Political debate which seemed in danger of being banished from education and the press is once more rearing its welcome head. Novel ideas for the better ordering of our disordered political economy are coming from many sources. Mr. Norman Macrae, for instance, has expounded in the *Economist* his scheme for new patterns of industrial development including the hiving off from overblown conglomerates of the services for which they are ill-fitted.

I have bewailed the ebb of political involvement in Orkney and Shetland, yet the third Arthur Irvine with whom I have been intimately connected in politics gives much of his time to the Liberal cause in Shetland and Mr. Crossan, a busy hotel manager, forfeits his leisure to keep a Liberal nucleus in being which may erupt into new political life.

The depths of good-will in this country are as fathomless among individuals as the depths of ill-will sometimes seem when men and women are herded together. We should certainly heed the terrible destruction in Cyprus and Lebanon, wrought by bands of malevolent bigots. But we should also remember the countless good deeds done every day among friends. It is for us to devise new public machinery which will prompt goodwill rather than ill.

I finish on an ambivalent note. I suspect that in the next ten years external threats may be more lethal than internal. I fear the avarice, in stability and imperialism of dictatorships such as Russia. The shadow of nuclear destruction lies over us. But the nuclear menace from abroad may shake us out of our self-pity for our self-inflicted wounds. It might make us jerk up our heads from our obsession with our navels. Each age nurses the seed which comes to the surface in its successor. I do not think the immediate past has been Britain's finest hour, but there is some vigorous seed germinating which could blossom into a harvest of brighter and above all more variegated flowers than we have seen in the last decade.

Index

ABERDEEN University, 179–80, 182
Adam, Robert, 37
Adam, Tom, 66
Alchin, Gordon, 66
Alexander, J., 28
Alington, Hester Margaret, 43
Alice (housemaid), *see also* Kidd, 23
Allaway, Deborah, 214
Alliance Trust Company (Dundee),
    78–9
Alsop, Andy, 160
Amery, Julian, 158
Anderson, Arthur, 117
Anderson, Jessie, 22–3, 39, 286
Appleton, Sir Edward V., 179
Arabs, 175–6
Asquith, Herbert Henry, 1st Earl of
    Oxford & Asquith, 70, 73–4,
    85, 149, 182, 202, 288, 292–3,
    297
Asquith, Margot, 28, 72–4, 179,
    261, 283
Astor, David, 88, 178, 277
Astor, John Jacob, 178
Astor, Michael, 178
Attlee, Clement, 1st Earl, 132, 295
Auchterlonie, Willie, 21
Australia, 173–4
Ayerst, David, 279

BACON, M. A., 230
Baikie, Andrew, 158

Baldwin, Stanley, 1st Earl, 82–3
Balfour, Miss (of Shapinsay,
    Orkney), 131
Balfour, Arthur James, 1st Earl of,
    28
Balliol College, Oxford, 54–7
Banda, Dr Hastings Kamusu, 101–2
Bareau, Paul, 201
Baring, Maurice, 218
Barnicott, John, 183
Batty, George, 242
Beckett, Sir Martyn, 297
Bedford Park, 280
Beer, Professor Sam, 234–5
Bell, Clive, 224
Benckendorff, Count Constantine,
    89, 96
Benckendorff, Connie, 96
Benn, Anthony Wedgwood, 252
Bergin, Professor Tom, 234
Betjeman, Sir John, 240–41
Beveridge, William Henry, 1st
    Baron, 64, 132, 153, 199, 299
Bevin, Ernest, 95, 132, 155, 158,
    193–4
Bielenberg, Christabel, 227
Birkenhead, F. E. Smith, 1st Earl
    of, 85
Birley, Sir Robert, 43–4, 226
Birmingham University, 181–2
Black, Kay, 60
Black, Mark, 60, 283

Campbell-Bannerman, Sir Henry, 73
Cant, Ronald, 57, 59
capital punishment, 67–8
Carr, Raymond, 283
Casson, Sir Hugh, 185
Castle, Barbara, 286
Ceauçescu, Nicolae, 221
Chamberlain, Joseph, 181, 197
Chamberlain, Neville, 83, 194
Chambers, Sir Paul, 183
Charteris, Martin (*later* Baron), 77
Charteris, Gay, Lady, 77
Cheape family, 27
Checkland, Sydney George, 15
Chesterton, G. K., 26
Chew, Kenneth, 180
Chile, 196
Chitnis, Pratap, Lord, 138, 201, 203, 214–15, 280
Christie, Brigadier, 93
Churchill, Sir Winston, and General Strike, 32; on 'canine virtues', 74; at house-party, 83; views of, 83; and Violet Bonham Carter, 83, 85–6; in war, 95, 99; and 1945 election, 130, 132; on Attlee, 132; and 1950 election, 143; in parliament, 155, 193; on Russia, 157
Cocks, T. G. B., 173
Cohen, Max, 137
Cohen, Rex, 101
Cole, G. D. H., 85
Collingwood ,George Ernest, 48–9
Collingwood, Robin George, 58
Collins, Billy, 40
Collins, Ian, 40
Confederation of British Industry (C.B.I.), 45, 237
Conservative Party, and 1945 election, 130, 132; and 1950 election, 142–3, 154; and Party boundaries, 151; nature of members, 151, 154; leadership process, 189; and

working class, 194; and Liberal Party, 197–8, 206, 254; policies, 208–10; and 1964 election, 216–17; 1970 government, 232; and free society, 262
Cook, Alistair, 279
Cooper, Lady Diana, 90
Cooper, Duff (*later* 1st Viscount Norwich), 130
Copland (Orkney painter), 243
Corbett, Archie *see* Rowallan, Archibald Cameron Corbett, 1st Baron
Corbett, Alice Mary *see* Rowallan, Alice Mary, Baroness
Corbett, Attie, 283
Corbett, Billy (i.e. Thomas Godfrey Polson Corbett; *later* 2nd Baron Rowallan), marriage, 18–19; in St Andrews, 22; at Rowallan, 36–7; as chief scout, 60, 282; character, 60; as Governor of Tasmania, 282; complexion, 283; family, 282–3; death, 284
Corbett, Catherine (*née* Acton), 283
Corbett, Fiona *see* Paterson, Fiona
Corbett, Gwyn (JG's sister; *later* Baroness Rowallan), in JG's childhood, 17; marriage, 18–19, 31; character and behaviour, 40–41, 60, 282–3; death, 284
Corbett, Joey, 283
Corbett, John Polson Cameron, 284
Corbett, Robert, 282–3
Cormack, Elspeth, 113
Corrigal, Mr (of N. Bigging, Orkney), 114
Corrigal, Mr (poet, of Harray), 244
Cowie, Harry, 201, 208, 215
Cox's (jute firm), 24–5
Cramer, Red, 137
Cranmer, Norfolk (house), 77

197; and coalitions, 197–8, 203–4, 212, 232, 251; fortunes, 198–206, 212–13, 217, 236, 252–5; policies, 205–12, 216; organisation and finance, 213–16; and formal parliamentary speeches, 228; Thorpe becomes leader, 228; in 1970 election, 228–9; composition of membership, 235; in 1964 election, 236; and petrol tax, 252; and state power, 256–8
Liberal Unionists, 197
Linklater, Eric, 103, 111, 113, 131, 240
Linskill, W. T., 21
Lippman, Walter, 157, 204, 273
Lloyd George, David, 147, 149–50, 197–8, 261
Lloyd George, Gwilym, 149
Lloyd George, Lady Megan, 74, 147–50, 188
Locheim, Katie, 189
Lorimer, Sir Robert, 37–8
Low, David, 261
Lubbock, Eric (4th Baron Avebury), 202–3, 214
Lyle, Michael and Elizabeth, 287

MACAULAY (of Scottish Gallery), 239
MacCarthy, Desmond, 71–2, 85
MacDonald, Alistair, 230
MacDonald, Mary, 280
MacEwen, Sir Alexander, 103
MacEwen, Robin, 103
MacFadyean, Sir Andrew, 215
McFie, A. F., 18
McInnes, Ian, 239
M'Intosh, Professor William Carmichael, 20
McIntyre, Fergus, 91
McIntyre, Louis, 24
McVey, Duncan, 39
Mackay, Mr (Sanday schoolmaster),

145, 169, 281
Mackenzie, Alastair, 236
MacLachlan, Donald, 191–3
MacLean, Colin, 299
MacLean, Sir Fitzroy, 177
MacLeod, Capt. J. (Jacko), 129
McNeil, Pamela (*formerly* Paton), 56
McNeile, Robert, 56
McNicol (Sinclair ghillie), 70
Macrae, Norman, 262, 300
Macrae, Col. Robert, 242
Maeshowe (Orkney), 108–9
Maggie (St Andrews cook), 23, 26
Magnus, Saint, 111
Malawi, 101–2
Malindine, Edwin, 202
Man, Isle of, 266
Manchester Evening News, 277–8
Manson, T. M. Y., 243
Manstein, Field-Marshal Erich von, 178
Margaret, Princess of Denmark, 112
Markiewicz, Constance Georgina, Countess, 47–8
Marten, Henry, 43–4, 53
Martin, Mr (R. & A. caddy), 28
Marwick, Ernest, 146, 281
Marwick, Hugh, 110, 281
Mathews, Ryan & Partners (architects) 31
Mathieson, Miss (JG's governess), 23
Maxton, James, 194
Mayhew, Christopher, 251
Melbourne, William Lamb, 2nd Viscount, 259, 262
Melville, Arthur, 109
Menzies, Sir Robert, 174
Meyer, Gerry, 105, 145
Middle East, 175–6
Milchsack, Lilo, 226
Mill, John Stuart, 257–8, 298
Mitchell, Colonel Colin, 229
Moar, Isaac, 230
Moar, Ronnie, 158
Moira *see* Ogilvie-Niven

263; *see also* House of
  Commons
Partner, David, 229
Paterson, Fiona (*née* Corbett), 282,
  284
Paterson, Garry, 284
Paton, Jimmie, 115
Paton, Dr Jock, 30
Paton, John, 29–30, 56
Paton, Margaret, 29
Paton, Neil, 30
Paton, Pamela *see* McNeil,
  Pamela
Patrick, A. McIntosh, 239
Patton, Gen. George S., 99
Peacock, Alan, 201, 211
Peake, Osbert, 150
Pearson, Mr (Shetland dentist), 124,
  229
Penhaligon, David, 236, 249
Peploe, Samuel John, 239–40
Peterson, Jack, 201
Peterson, Willie, 125
Petre, Peggy, Lady, 283
Philipson, Sir Robin, 185
Picts, 110–11
Pilkington, Mark, 56, 69
Piper, John, 183
Playfair, Elliott, 29
Playfair, Nigel, 29
Poland, 220–22
Pollock, Sir Donald, 179
Popper, Karl, 257
Porter, Dr T. C., 43
Powell, Anthony D., 93–4
Powell, Violet, Lady, 94
Preston, Peter, 278
Preston, Phyllis, 214–15
Prestonpans, 140–41
Prince, Frank, 81
Prior, R. E., 43–4
Price, Morgan Phillips, 152
Pym, Francis, 255

Quakers, 279–80
Quant, Mary, 184

Rae, Mr (silversmith), 124, 239
Randall (Shetland crofter), 115
Rees-Mogg, William, 263
referendums, 172
Reith, John Charles, Walsham,
  Baron, 289–90
Rendall, Robert, 239, 243
Rhodes, James Robert, 232
Richardson, Foster (JG's uncle),
  17–18
Richardson, Jo (JG's aunt), 18
Richardson, May, 17
Richardson, Tony, 286
Riddell, William, 219
Ridgway, Jack, 160
Ridley, Adam, 79, 287
Ridley, Cressida (*née* Bonham
  Carter), 70–71, 78; character,
  72, 74–5, 79; and husband's
  death, 98; as archaeologist, 287
Ridley, Sir Jasper, 55, 79
Ridley, Lady (*née* Benckendorff),
  55, 79
Ridley, Jasper, friendship with JG,
  49, 55–6, 78–80; and Sinclair,
  69; marriage, 70; shooting, 76;
  killed, 98; orderliness, 240;
  character, 286
Ridley, Nicholas, 79
Robert II of Scotland, 36
Robertson, Jackie, 130, 146
Robertson, Brigadier, S., 242
Robertson, T. A., 243
Rognvald, Saint, 111
Ronald, Miss (of Aberdeen), 66
Roosevelt, Franklin Delano, 153
Rosebery, Archibald Philip
  Primrose, 5th Earl of, 179
Ross, Sir Frederick Leith, 134
Ross, Maj-Gen. R. K., 100–101
Rowallan (house), 36–41, 282–4, 287
Rowallan, Archibald Cameron
  Corbett, 1st Baron, 36, 39
Rowallan, Alice Mary Corbett,
  Lady, 36, 39
Rowallan, Thomas Godfrey Polson